HUMANITARIAN FICTIONS

Humanitarian Fictions

AFRICA, ALTRUISM, AND THE NARRATIVE IMAGINATION

Megan Cole Paustian

FORDHAM UNIVERSITY PRESS   NEW YORK 2024

Cover image: *Muse Morning*, by Femi J. Johnson

Visit us online at www.fordhampress.com.

Library of Congress Cataloging-in-Publication Data available online at
https://catalog.loc.gov.

Printed in the United States of America

26 25 24   5 4 3 2 1

First edition

For my father, J. Andrew Cole (1953–2004), who laid the foundation for this book in so many ways.

Contents

HUMANITARIAN FICTIONS

Introduction
The White Savior Narrative and the Third Sector Novel

Narratives . . . are always immersed in history and never innocent.
Whether we can unmake development and perhaps even bid farewell
to the Third World will equally depend on the social invention of new
narratives, new ways of thinking and doing.

— ARTURO ESCOBAR

Narrative, then, in its relation to history in the present African context
represents an imaginative mode of reconstruction: of consciousness, of
spirit, and, ultimately, of vision.

— ABIOLA IRELE

Humanitarianism has a narrative problem. This is especially evident in relation to Africa. Stories of aid to Africa follow a set of conventions including
plot trajectory, setting, character types, and themes, all of which are affected
by the core principle of salvation by Western means. Boiled down to its most
fundamental elements, the narrative includes a heroic white protagonist,
British or American, who—in defiance of mainstream apathy—embarks on
a quest to save suffering Africans. In terms of setting, the West is a place of
familiarity and stability, which one must sacrifice for a higher purpose. Africa,
in contrast, is a place of violence, poverty, and seemingly bottomless need; it
is also a source of adventure and enchantment—mysterious and magnetic
but vaguely defined. Often, African characters blend into that landscape as
representatives of the need that drives the Western altruist to respond. This
familiar story voices a challenge to global inequity, but it does so in a language
that reinscribes that inequity. With its enticing style and wide circulation,

1

the tale of African sufferers and Western saviors has shaped the vocabulary of international altruism with consequences for humanitarian ethics and action.

This narrative problem hit a high-water mark of public visibility when *Kony 2012* became a viral internet sensation in March of that year. Produced by Invisible Children, a U.S.-based humanitarian advocacy organization, this thirty-minute video aimed to raise awareness and funds to stop the atrocities of Ugandan warlord Joseph Kony and to support "lifesaving programs" such as rebuilding schools and creating jobs.[1] Within a week of its release, the video had generated over 100 million views and a groundswell of altruistic enthusiasm. Its message had struck a chord. It also left much to unpack: the relationship between social media and social activism, the connections between humanitarianism and military intervention, the entanglement of nonprofit organizations with market-driven money-making strategies, and of course the question of basic effectiveness. My interest, however, is in *Kony 2012* as a narrative phenomenon. Emblematic of humanitarian storytelling about Africa, the video illustrates a number of common tropes. It features an American protagonist, Jason Russell, cofounder of the organization, who provides the point of view and throughline. Upon meeting Jacob Acaye, a Ugandan boy mourning the loss of his brother to Kony's troops, Russell promises that "we're going to stop them" (7:49). From there, he guides viewers through his nearly decade-long mission to make good on that bold promise. He draws "hundreds of thousands of people" into the movement, including his young son, who is excited about "stop[ping] bad guys" (17:45, 9:34). In sum, *Kony 2012* tells a slick new version of a familiar tale of good guys, bad guys, and deceptively simple solutions, assuring viewers, "Now we know what to do. Here it is" (21:40). White people with empathy and enthusiasm can solve, it seems, Africa's most vexing problems.

For many, this message didn't sit well. Critiques were swift and severe. They addressed the video's misleading and incomplete history, an organizational strategy invested more heavily in marketing than in work on the ground, and particularly the organization's call for increased militarization, including the mobilization of U.S. troops. Many focused on the story itself, which touched a nerve, particularly among African viewers for whom such a tale was instantly recognizable. These critics argued that *Kony 2012* misdirects our attention, produces the wrong goals, glorifies white heroes, and flattens African victims.[2] Most powerful was the response from Nigerian American novelist Teju Cole, who coined the term "White Savior Industrial Complex" to capture the sensation. The problem for Cole was not only this instance of narrative but its general prevalence: "One song we hear too often," he writes, "is the one in which Africa serves as a backdrop for white fantasies of conquest and heroism. . . . A nobody from America or Europe can go to Africa and become a godlike savior or, at the very least, have his or her emotional needs satisfied."[3] Since gaining currency around *Kony 2012*, "white savior" has become a fixture of internet parlance. In 2017, the term got its own Wikipedia page. To accuse a story, movie, advertisement, or social media post of white saviorism is essentially to say the following: it centers on a white hero and marginalizes black victims; it glorifies Western intervention and depicts Africa as a place of darkness and helplessness; it implies that moral authority and technical expertise are properties of whiteness, while powerlessness and incompetence lie with blackness.[4]

While the *Kony 2012* backlash, and particularly Cole's article, brought the white savior critique into popular discourse, this line of thought already had a long history in postcolonial theory, based not on humanitarianism directly but on the civilizing mission of the colonial state. For example, Gayatri Spivak has famously used the formulation "white men are saving brown women from brown men" to show how colonial power deployed a narrative of salvation in a project of self-justification.[5] The civilizing mission is embodied by Kipling's phrase "The White Man's Burden," which disguises colonialism as a moral obligation.[6] Achille Mbembe describes how this "burden" functioned as a paternalistic mask for violence: according to the discourse of civilization, "it was Europe's duty to help and protect [Africans]. This made the colonial enterprise a fundamentally 'civilizing' and 'humanitarian' enterprise. The violence that was its corollary could only ever be moral."[7] To civilize and to save went hand in hand, putting the Western traveler in the position of savior, a position defined not by compassion but by power. While, as Mbembe shows us, colonialism coopted the language of "'humanitarian' enterprise," this doesn't tell us much about humanitarianism minus the scare quotes.

Among scholars of humanitarianism itself, the critique of the white savior narrative is also familiar, long preceding *Kony 2012*. The viral video made it infamous, but the problem status of humanitarian storytelling was already well established. To confront it, critics from various fields have ventured into the language of the literary. They ask about humanitarianism's "scripts and narratives of involvement" and about "the kinds of obligations we feel as a consequence of those stories."[8] Some critique humanitarian narrative as a delusional "fairy tale," a "moral fable," or a "false morality play."[9] Others emphasize tone and vocabulary, questioning the effects of the particular terms we use to address suffering, the voices that narrate it, and the affective response those voices solicit.[10] These critiques demonstrate that stories matter. Often, they imply that a better story would give us a better humanitarianism, but this remains an unfinished gesture.

What is missing from this conversation about humanitarian narrative is the actual study of narrative. While labeling white savior narratives has become a fairly common gesture, it doesn't tell us much about the story *as* story. *Humanitarian Fictions* argues that literary analysis conducted through a postcolonial lens can fill in that gap. My focus is not on the narrative as articulated directly in humanitarian marketing materials, journalistic accounts of suffering, celebrity appeals to provide aid, or popular movies that channel this narrative but on novels that embed and interrogate those forms.[11] Novelists are interpreters of narrative and producers of narrative. Teju Cole gestures at this dynamic in framing the White Savior Industrial Complex. Locating himself within the conversation as both an African and an American, he adds, "I also write all this as a novelist and story-writer: I am sensitive to the power of narratives."[12] It is no coincidence that this preeminent critique of white saviorism came from a novelist, and it is this sensitivity to narrative that *Humanitarian Fictions* will trace. By examining how novelists have responded to the white savior narrative, this project brings literary criticism to bear on an already vigorous interdisciplinary conversation about humanitarianism and its discontents. Novels about international aid register humanitarian discourse as a dominant force in shaping both Western consciousness of Africa and African encounters with the West. While critiques of the white savior narrative come in various forms, the novel — that extended, complicated, multivocal form of narrative — is best positioned to tease out its methods and meanings.

Humanitarian Fictions will advance three primary arguments. The first is essentially the premise for this study: humanitarianism has a narrative problem, and analysis of the novel — with its critical sensitivity to narrative — can help us assess the implications. As postcolonial theory has made clear from its inception, stories are both a tool of imperial domination and a channel for resistance. Through stories, European colonial states defined their projects abroad, building up what V. Y. Mudimbe calls the "colonial library."[13] That library was soon tampered with, leading Gaurav Desai to "reimagine the colonial library as a space of contestation" characterized by "a complex series of interactions between colonizers and the colonized rather than a unidirectional process" by which Europe "invents" Africa.[14] We might think similarly of the *humanitarian library* as a space of power and contestation that, along with its Western texts, integrates "African resistance, collaboration, and accommodation in all their forms."[15] To explore the space of humanitarian contestation, I will insert literature into a broader, multidisciplinary conversation on humanitarianism and its history with the aim of understanding how literature speaks beyond its specialized field of study. Historians, political scientists, and development anthropologists tell us that the white savior narrative is damaging. By reappropriating narrative elements like character and setting, plot and point of view, novelists can offer a fuller assessment of how the narrative operates in the world and what effects it has on humanitarian ethics and action.

My second claim is that the origin of humanitarianism's narrative problem lies in colonial-era Christian missions, which developed and popularized a language of African salvation by Western means. The roots of the contemporary white savior narrative are religious, and therefore, examining literature about missions enables us to excavate a longer, more nuanced tradition of response. Accounts of anglophone African literature's history typically revolve around the nation, with the target of critique shifting from the colonial state to the disappointments of the postcolony, but humanitarianism makes its promises in terms of the *non*state. Therefore, examining modes of engagement with religious missions—which were themselves humanitarian institutions, establishing schools and clinics—can help us understand African encounters with humanitarianism today. This analytical approach disentangles nonstate forms of both care and control from the colonial story.

My third claim is that literature, in addition to challenging the dominant humanitarian discourse, can play a valuable role in imagining and articulating alternatives. The novels I assemble undermine altruistic enthusiasm and make us rethink the taken-for-granted concepts of the white savior narrative—such as altruism, progress, and universal humanity—giving pause in all the places where the savior narrative does not. Part of the literary response to humanitarianism is about dismantling the rhetoric of salvation, but there is more to it than critique, particularly for African authors. African writing isn't merely a reaction to the West; it operates not only in the mode of opposition but in the mode of creation. The West has no ownership of humanitarian concepts, and African writers offer up their own versions. To respond more meaningfully to global inequity, humanitarianism needs new terms, including vocabulary and terms of encounter—who makes decisions and holds authority, who is benevolent and who is indebted, who sacrifices and who merely survives. *Humanitarian Fictions* explores the lies and limitations embedded in humanitarianism's existing concepts and analyzes how literature revises and reimagines them.

Humanitarianism calls for a transnational, transcontinental frame that does not take the state as its starting place. Each of the following chapters will link writers from different points on the humanitarian map including Britain, the United States, and African countries spanning the continent: Nigeria, Kenya, Somalia, Zimbabwe, Botswana, and South Africa. To illuminate the historical unfolding of nonstate projects of African improvement, the book follows a roughly chronological arc from religious missions to secular humanitarianism. The aim is not to sketch a complete literary history but to establish an origin story for contemporary humanitarian fictions and to reveal the residual religious presence that lingers today. To lay the groundwork, I begin from missionary narratives of the nineteenth century and relate them to a set of canonical writers — Joseph Conrad, Chinua Achebe, and Ngũgĩ wa Thiong'o — not typically read in this frame. From there, I constellate a group of late twentieth- and early twenty-first-century writers — including Bessie Head, Tsitsi Dangarembga, Nuruddin Farah, Zakes Mda, Philip Caputo, and Chimamanda Ngozi Adichie — who build a complex case that is at once for and against humanitarian values and practices.

Through the lens of this body of literature, *Humanitarian Fictions* asks: When aid is offered across boundaries of nation, race, culture, and social status, how is the story told? How does that narrative define humanitarianism's goals and key players, its sense of progress and how it should be achieved? What kind of ethical orientation toward the world does such a narrative produce, and what does it mean for the actual enactment of social change? Ultimately, how do novelists alter that narrative and to what end? Literature provides a robust critique of the white savior narrative *as* narrative while also revealing points of attraction and ambivalence. Additionally, it models alternative ways of narrating change, representing what Abiola Irele calls "an imaginative mode of reconstruction."[16] *Humanitarian Fictions* reveals how literature has been shaped by the dominance of humanitarian discourse and how literature in turn reinvents that discourse, building a narrative framework better suited to humanitarianism's unfulfilled aims to alleviate suffering and create a more equitable world.

Narrating African Improvement through the Nonstate

The most common way to critique humanitarianism is to connect it to the civilizing mission of the colonial state. The very premise of the white savior narrative is that benevolent Westerners possess the expertise, the ability, and the right to enter foreign lands and save those who cannot save themselves. The imperialist echoes are undeniable. In his memoir of humanitarian disillusionment, *The Road to Hell*, Michael Maren explains:

> When colonials came ashore, they didn't say, "We're here to steal your land and take your resources and employ your people to clean our toilets and guard our big houses." They said, "We're here to help you." And then they went and took their land and resources and hired their people to clean their toilets. And now here come the aid workers,

who move into the big colonial houses and ride in high cars above the squalor, all the while insisting they've come to help.[17]

Novelists from Bessie Head to Philip Caputo draw similar parallels, depicting the arrogance of aid workers who segregate themselves from local populations and bask in the authority that they would not possess at home. Many critics, including David Rieff, claim that humanitarians are "too close to the old colonial norms," updating them for the contemporary world and "functioning as an adjunct to imperial domination."[18] This suggests that the "non" in nongovernmental organization (NGO) is illusory. Through official aid, which transfers funds from one government to another, states take on the role of donor.[19] They also claim to act as humanitarians themselves, using the language of care as a banner for military intervention.[20] In Noam Chomsky's words, "virtually every resort to force is justified by rhetoric about noble humanitarian intentions."[21] According to this line of thought, humanitarian action allows nations of the Global North, most notably the United States, to impose their will throughout the world while also easing their conscience.

The critique of humanitarianism as the new empire has offered a much-needed counterdiscourse that resists the dominant narrative of white saviors liberating black subjects, but it is only part of the story. It doesn't account for the fact that humanitarians have aimed consistently (though not always successfully) to transcend the state in the service of some higher calling, siding with the disempowered and dispossessed. The white savior impulse is in part about *not* relying on the state, not waiting for government intervention, in the face of inhumane circumstances. This impulse responds to African states' failure to protect and provide for their citizens; it also channels Western humanitarians' impatience with their own governments' inaction. In the Kony narrative, Russell and his organization call on the U.S. government to intervene but do not wait for a response. NGOs essentially say, "If governments don't do it, we will." In this moral framework, humanity overrides national sovereignty, positioning humanitarian organizations not as an arm of the state but as an alternative, even an opponent. Despite those efforts, such organizations are entangled with and compromised by state power, and governments themselves adopt the mantle of humanitarian care. Nonetheless, the distinction between imperial power and nonstate assistance is a significant one that is not lost on humanitarianism's so-called beneficiaries.[22] The critique of humanitarianism as a mask for imperial power is not wrong, but the predominance of that story obscures the remarkably complex history of African interactions with such institutions and deflects the urgency of the questions confronted by humanitarians today, albeit in dreadfully insufficient ways.

To say that humanitarianism, with its concentration in the nongovernmental sector, is distinct from the civilizing mission of imperial states is not to say it is innocent. In fact, its claim to apolitical moral purity is part of its danger. Such a position can lend authority to underlying racist assumptions and grant immunity to ineffective humanitarian practices. Take, for example, Chinua Achebe's comparison between Belgium's King Leopold and the missionary-humanitarian doctor Albert Schweitzer: "Paradoxically," Achebe writes, "a saint like Schweitzer can give one a lot more trouble than a King Leopold II, villain of unmitigated guilt, because along with doing good and saving African lives Schweitzer also managed to announce that the African was indeed his brother, but only his *junior* brother."[23] Leopold represented state violence and greed; in contrast, Schweitzer spoke with the backing of moral authority. Humanitarianism claims disinterest in a way states never can, and this stance gives it persuasive power. It is articulated not in the language of good governance but in terms of moral goodness. The independent moral framework can make its calls for universal inclusion especially compelling; this framework can also make the inequalities it reinscribes—like affixing "junior" to the front of "brother"—especially pernicious. It is important to distinguish between a state-driven "civilizing mission" and the nonstate approach to aid because they manifest in unique ways and garner unique modes of response. Collapsing humanitarianism into empire causes us to overlook its ambiguous appeal as well as its particular mode of power and the ethical problems that ensue under the aegis of a moral cause.

To hold this distinction between state empire and nonstate humanitarianism in view, I frame my argument in terms of the third sector. Named "third" to mark its separation from the public sector (government-owned agencies and services) and the private sector (for-profit enterprise, not controlled by the state), the term refers to the body of organizations that are nongovernmental and nonprofit. Also known as the voluntary sector, it includes international NGOs, charities, and civic organizations such as the International Committee for the Red Cross, Oxfam, and Save the Children, which raise funds from donors.[24] Within third sector humanitarianism, there are two major branches, and both are relevant to this study. The first is emergency aid, which addresses immediate needs in times of crisis; it aims to save lives by providing food, medical care, and shelter. The second is development aid, which targets ongoing needs and generally aims to get at the roots of endemic problems by improving systems of nutrition, education, sanitation, and the like. Both branches are driven by "compassion across boundaries"[25] and by the belief that everyone—regardless of nationality, race, religion, and so on—deserves to have their basic needs met. The United Nations is also a part of this realm;

while it is an intergovernmental organization, several of its offshoots—particularly UNICEF (United Nations Children's Fund), UNHCR (United Nations High Commissioner for Refugees), the World Food Programme, and the World Health Organization—work in coordination with NGOs to address emergencies as well as ongoing needs like healthcare and education. In its focus on life-saving services, humanitarianism operates in some degree of conflict with government and corporate interests, while at times aligning with those interests (strategically or unwittingly). *Humanitarian Fictions* thus posits that the third sector distinction is essential but also unstable. Because these lines blur in life, they will at times blur within this book through analysis of Peace Corps volunteers, for example, who operate as humanitarians while also explicitly representing U.S. national interests. Overall, this book will focus on the nonstate actors at the core of the humanitarian idea because doing so enables us to see the complex interactions between anti-imperial and humanitarian sensibilities, which conflict *and* coincide.

Humanitarian History and the Missionary Sensibility

The importance of the nonstate for interpreting humanitarianism and its narratives is partly a question of history. In recounting humanitarianism's past, scholars often look to the founding of the International Committee of the Red Cross (ICRC). This origin story places humanitarianism's spark in 1859 when Henry Dunant observed the suffering caused by the Battle of Solferino in Italy. Disturbed by the toll of war, he went on to found the ICRC a few years later. By this account, humanitarianism begins from a relatively small circle within Europe and gradually expands outward to include other populations. This story privileges the humanitarian response to war and foregrounds the ICRC's core principles—independence from political parties and states, neutrality in conflicts, and impartiality in distributing aid to people in need.[26] The Red Cross's apolitical framework has indeed permeated the spirit of humanitarianism more broadly. But this origin story does not account for Africa's outsize place within the humanitarian imagination; nor does it explain the emergence of white saviorism as a dominant mode of humanitarian relating. Beginning from the contemporary white savior complex and moving backward takes us to a different starting point: Christian missions in the context of colonial Africa. This also foregrounds a different set of principles, most notably salvation.

Several historical accounts of humanitarianism suggest that the business of saving lives is inextricable from the history of saving souls. Peter Stamatov, for example, situates the origin of "long-distance advocacy . . . between the sixteenth and eighteenth centuries," explaining that "religious actors engaged in the first sustained activities to defend and represent the interests of geographically and culturally distant populations. . . . [They] systematized a set of advocacy practices that were to become the standard tools" of humanitarian institutions.[27] This suggests that humanitarianism's roots are longer and its geography wider than the secular framework posits. Michael Barnett ties the religious influence specifically to evangelicalism with its emphasis on salvation: "Evangelicalism transformed religion into reform. . . . The missionary impulse demanded urgent action because of the fear that 'men were going to hell around them: they *had* to make every effort to save as many as they could.'"[28] Barnett calls the period from 1800 to 1945 the era of Imperial Humanitarianism. Viewed in this light, it becomes clear that humanitarianism was always about Westerners relating to global "others." In Barnett's words, "The centerpiece of Christian mission is to cross frontiers, geographical, cultural, economic, social, and political, in the service of Christ and his Kingdom. The period of classical missionary activity . . . represented the only sustained humanitarian activity during the period of European expansion and colonialism."[29] The political dynamics around missionaries, whose project intersected with but was also distinct from the project of empire, foretell the uneasy relationship to the state that NGOs have today. I will unpack missionaries' relation to colonialism in chapters 1 and 2 and the meaning of the NGO in chapter 5, but for now, suffice it to say that religious conviction was the driving force behind humanitarian practices of care across global boundaries.

Even as this movement became increasingly secular over the course of the twentieth century, the religious did not drop out. Faith-based organizations maintain a large presence on the humanitarian scene, and the distinction between missionary and aid worker is often fuzzy.[30] More significant for my purpose is the point that even thoroughly secular organizations that provide "saving" services in food relief, healthcare, or clean water have grown out of a missionary mode of relating to Africa. That pattern shows up in the literature, with secular humanitarian characters who are reminiscent of nineteenth-century missionaries and missionary characters who maintain a presence into the twenty-first century.

The continuity between religious missions and secular humanitarianism is a matter not only of institutional history but of sensibility. They address many of the same problems and deploy many of the same concepts to do so. The vocabulary and narrative structure of humanitarianism today have grown directly out of Christian missions. This applies to humanitarianism's moral discourse and sense of higher calling; it applies to its nongovernmental, non-profit structure and to its universalism that includes all of humanity and supersedes the boundaries of the state; it applies to the language of emancipatory salvation stemming from the biblical theme of setting captives free; and it applies to the structure of altruistic giving. The humanitarian narrative is driven by a righteous demand that transcends all other interests. According to Andrea Paras and Janice Gross Stein, secular organizations like MSF (Médecins Sans Frontières or Doctors Without Borders) situate "their activity beyond the profane and the political" and in doing so claim "moral authority for action"; they "locate their authority in the language of the sacred."[31] Christian universalism's particular significance to humanitarian history lies in providing a way of thinking about humanity in sacred terms—everyone deserved to be saved. This conviction drove missionaries across continents and colonial lines and continues to drive secular humanitarianism today. Although mainstream humanitarian discourse no longer depends on divine authority, the notion of sacred *humanity* now has pride of place. The seemingly areligious discourse of humanity is infused with traces of Christian religiosity. Humanitarianism, in other words, is a form of mission.[32]

Linking the missionary to the NGO, this book's examination of humanitarian fictions will demonstrate how religious vocabularies and concepts continue to inflect humanitarian thought, even in its most secular-appearing forms. Bono has replaced David Livingstone as celebrity spokesman, the project of saving lives has usurped that of saving souls, and the ontological discourse of savage and civilized has become the mere underside of a materialist discourse of the powerful and powerless. Still, the narrative framework of missions has remained much the same, a continuity to which literature has been particularly attuned. Contemporary humanitarian fictions are post-missionary; often, they are postsecular as well. By tracing the evolution of humanitarian fiction through the historical lens of missions, this project reveals the influence of religious thought on third sector institutions and the narratives they generate. This also draws attention to a collective, spiritualist streak within the discourse of humanity and reveals its vexed affinities with both empire and anti-imperial resistance.

The Grand Narrative of African Salvation

The history of the white savior narrative is a missionary history. Colonial-era missionaries produced a vast archive of narratives about the journey into Africa to save the "heathen." The salvation story ultimately exceeded missionary texts themselves to generate a widespread cultural script. The white savior narrative can be understood as a subcategory of Jean-François Lyotard's concept of master narrative—particularly the grand narrative of emancipation. Master narratives are vast, even universal in their reach, providing an explanation for history and the workings of the world through the trajectory of progress, modernization, or emancipation. They serve to legitimate the way things are and the way their disseminators want things to be; they can justify the status quo as well as projects of transformation. "The important thing," Lyotard tells us, "is not, or not only, to legitimate denotative utterances pertaining to truth, such as 'The earth revolves around the sun,' but rather to legitimate prescriptive utterances pertaining to justice, such as 'Carthage must be destroyed' or 'The minimum wage must be set at x dollars.'"[33] Or, we might add, "Africa must be saved by the West." This linguistic and conceptual scaffolding first emerges in narratives by and about missionaries themselves. Missionary societies and supporters built up a grand narrative of African salvation by Western means, and their work is the root of white saviorism today. Chapter 1 will sketch out that history. For now, I aim to outline the key features of this missionary story that has rippled far beyond missionaries themselves.

As a subcategory of the grand narrative of emancipation, the white savior narrative shares with it a faith in the inevitable force of progress and a tendency to force-fit the world into its own image. This story, too, is defined by "its great hero, its great dangers, its great voyages, its great goal"[34]—specifically the Western humanitarian, the African wilderness, the journey into the "heart of darkness," and the goal of saving the "benighted" African. Drawing on and extending Lyotard's definition of the grand narrative of emancipation, we can break the white savior narrative down into five key components. First, the missionary, or some secular version of him (for it is a gendered category), serves as the narrative's great hero; he is noble, self-sacrificing, even holy, often taking on the role of a kind of god. Second is the great and dangerous voyage, essential to the mission plot; these are adventure stories about the journey into Africa and about the risks of residing in remote and mysterious corners of the earth. Third, the great goal is to save that dangerous place and its ever-benighted people. While that has often taken the more specific form of religious conversion, I will be thinking of the concept of mission and the goal of salvation more flexibly. One might argue that any humanitarian practice that aims for transformative change is also a practice of conversion. According to the grand salvation narrative, that transformation is necessary, inevitable, and successful. Mission heroes aim to improve African people in diverse ways and save them from diverse threats, and they rightly anticipate their good intentions being carried out. Thus, the plot essentially matches the goal—the narrative is one of inevitable progress, and glorious ends can justify all means. That brings us to the fourth component: the certainty associated with such an optimistic trajectory. A sense of heavenly ordination prompts an unquestioned and unquestioning confidence. The narrative builds a vocabulary that matches its content. Its tone is authoritative and unwavering in its commitment to the great goal. Its rhetoric is powerful and soaring, and its optimistic imagination expounds on the potential of "unbounded good."[35] Finally, its rhetoric is founded on a structure of contrasts—light and dark, high and low, white and black, visible and invisible, powerful and powerless—and it seeks always to redeem the latter, bringing it into the enlightened glow of the former. The distinction between good and evil is self-evident, and the path of the altruist is thus clear.

When humanitarian organizations mobilize grand narratives effectively, they can succeed at remarkable levels, showing the power of the narrative form as well as its problems. The opportunity for Americans to take on the role of savior has led to the mass popularity of some humanitarian campaigns like Invisible Children's *Kony 2012* as well as Save Darfur, which also had a deep lineup of celebrity endorsers and mass public support.[36] While many humanitarian crises in Africa have roused little American interest, the story built up around a crisis can be transformative. In his aptly titled book, *Saviors and Survivors*, Mahmood Mamdani contrasts the public outcry over violence in Darfur with the minimal public response to the wars in other parts of the continent where death rates and human rights violations have been no less staggering:

> Congo, like Angola, is the norm. Darfur is the exception. With Darfur,
> media reports on Africa entered the arena of *grand narratives*. What
> used to be seen as meaningless anarchy—in which men, sometimes
> women, and increasingly, children, fight without aim or memory;
> in which wars can go on endlessly, even for decades; in which there
> are no clear stakes and no discernible outcomes; and in which it is
> difficult even to distinguish among *protagonists*—has now become in-
> vested with an *epic* significance. Why the contrast between the relative
> silence that greets most African wars and the global publicity boom
> around the carnage in Darfur?[37]

In an argument about global politics, Mamdani uses the language of literature. He suggests it is the power of the grand narrative—of heroic protagonists and epic goals—that mobilized so much interest around Darfur. It seems that Save Darfur seized on precisely the kind of story Westerners love to tell about themselves and love to tell about Africa. The same can be said for *Kony 2012*. To channel this narrative is to tap into a deep well of emotional energy and response. Humanitarian organizations often draw from this well to articulate their aims and raise funds. It is unsettling but not surprising that they would defer to elements of grand narrative because they are, by necessity, operating on a marketing logic (since they need to sell their cause) and balancing it with a moral logic.

Marketing logic and moral logic don't reconcile easily, and the downsides are significant. Movements that aim to transform unequal positions of power can ultimately reinforce them by channeling that aim into the structure of the white savior narrative. It is an issue not merely of attitude but of efficacy—affects and effects. Therefore, popular success cannot be equated with practical success. The white savior narrative produces a dangerous mix of compassion and heroic confidence; its sense of inherent moral rightness can be blinding. Such a narrative limits the humanitarian capacity to anticipate and confront messier moral realities, and it circumvents the need to consult the people receiving assistance. *Knowing* what is right means not having to ask. The results can range from basic ineffectiveness (say, a donated water pump that falls into disrepair) to irreversible damage (say, perpetuating violence rather than eliminating it).[38]

Literary renderings of white saviorism throw its fundamental tropes and assumptions into question. They also break down the binary between benevolent care and imperialist corruption. The authors studied here are both interpreters of the savior narrative and adversaries who offer new narratives to unseat it. There is an illustrative scene in Graham Greene's *The Heart of the Matter* (1948) in which the savior narrative is read, but read against the grain, capturing a key move within humanitarian fictions. The reader, Henry Scobie, takes a book from the stuffy shelves of a missionary woman who insists that she is "not teaching the children here [in colonial West Africa] to read in order that they shall read—well, novels."[39] (A character who distrusts novels is typically, in the hands of a novelist, not one to be trusted.) Despite the slim pickings, Scobie selects a volume in hopes of entertaining an ailing child. The boy quickly voices his desire for a murder story and asks the title of this one. Scobie sets about the task of introducing the pious book at hand:

Scobie said dubiously, "A *Bishop Among the Bantus*."
"What does that mean?"
Scobie drew a long breath. "Well, you see, Bishop is the name of the hero."
"But you said *a* Bishop."
"Yes. His name was Arthur."

"It's a soppy name."

"Yes, but he's a soppy hero. . . . The real heroes are the Bantus."

(111–12)

Scobie begins to improvise and opens up a new reading of the bishop through a recasting of missionary heroism. He goes on to describe the way Arthur Bishop (transforming "a bishop" from generic noun to proper name) pursues these Bantu pirates as a secret agent of the British government, discovering all their secrets "so that he can betray them when the time is right." "He sounds a bit of a swine," the boy concludes, and Scobie agrees (112). Moving to the first page of the book, he makes a quick decision about how to approach it: "Scobie found his eyes fixed on an opening paragraph which stated, *I shall never forget my first glimpse of the continent where I was to labour for thirty of the best years of my life.*" In spite of the words on the page, he instead says "slowly, 'From the moment that they left Bermuda the low lean rakehelly craft had followed in their wake'" (112–13).

In this scene of generous improvisation, Scobie misreads the white savior narrative, giving it a new and unsanctioned form, a form of which the missionary who lent him the book would surely disapprove. In this autobiographical narrative, as it is written on the page, the bishop is the great hero; the first line alone foretells a story of hard work and reward, but Scobie recasts the character as a nefarious double agent, working on behalf of a devious British power. This missionary, he instructs, is a "soppy hero" at best, and actually the story's real heroism lies with the African characters. He imparts this new version of a mission story to a young British boy, representative of an upcoming generation of Europeans arriving in Africa. This scene itself is a brief narrative of benevolence, of helping a person in need, and the success of Scobie's altruistic act is contingent on a narrative transformation. With it, the boy is greatly cheered. This scene of creative reading suggests that the white savior narrative is worn out and wrong, and a new story is required.

I recount this anecdote for the questions it raises. The careful misreading Scobie offers leads us to ask, What are the implications of telling the story of missions differently? What if the heroes, perspectives, and outcomes were switched, and what might be revealed by seeing a missionary bishop as a duplicitous character and really "a bit of a swine"? What is at stake in this kind of revision and what ethical possibilities might it contain? These are the kinds of questions *Humanitarian Fictions* takes up. The texts I gather under the rubric of third sector literature work through exposure and sabotage, revealing the troubling ways in which the white savior narrative functions, undermining its great heroes and grand plans, and endorsing new vocabularies of care and assistance.

Africa and the Humanitarian Atlantic

Within the humanitarian imagination, Africa is the epicenter of suffering. As Susan Sontag explains, "postcolonial Africa exists in the consciousness of the general public in the rich world . . . mainly as a succession of unforgettable photographs of large-eyed victims."[40] White saviorism certainly applies to other locations and operates on different scales, but Africa is the ultimate target of the Western humanitarian imagination — no place needs saving like Africa needs saving. The white savior narrative is part of the cultural unconscious that shapes the way the continent is understood at an individual level and the way policy is determined at an international level. To adapt the words of Edward Said, Africa is "not a free subject of thought or action."[41] Part of this problem lies in the tendency to speak of "Africa" as a singular whole, and that is one of the risks of framing this project in continental terms. As Achille Mbembe reminds us, "To a great degree, what is called *Africa* is first and foremost a geographical accident" containing a vast range of diversity which is belied by that singular designation.[42] At the same time, Mbembe distinguishes between the "sphere of geography" and the "sphere of representation" in which "this accident [of geography] is subsequently invested with a multitude of significations, diverse imaginary contents, or even fantasies, which, by force of repetition, end up becoming authoritative narratives."[43] The white savior narrative lies within this "sphere of representation" and is one such fantasy by which Westerners relate to Africa. *Humanitarian Fictions* explores how the place of Africa within the Western imagination has been molded by the story of the benevolent mission and how writers, both African and Western, have responded. The continent does indeed face compounded crises of poverty, inadequate infrastructure, corruption, and violence, but what does it mean when crisis becomes the dominant framework by which a continent is understood and when the international response is so consistently articulated in terms of salvation?

Traversing three continents, this book configures a triangle I call *the humanitarian Atlantic*.[44] The humanitarian model of care transcends the boundaries of the state, and its networks touch much of the globe. It is about a relationship of rescue as people in one place attempt to alleviate the suffering of distant others; it assumes loyalty should be based not merely on local ties or shared citizenship but shared humanity that links Africa to the world. As I will explain in chapter 3, the concept of shared humanity cannot be taken at face value since it has been used to obscure meaningful differences and to justify acts of control in the name of inclusive care. Still, it is the logic undergirding the humanitarian map. *Humanitarian Fictions* thus redraws the boundaries of literary classification based on a shared problem space rather than a shared national space. This demonstrates the value of transnational literary study for problems that are, by definition, transnational. Although African writers dominate this study, it does not focus exclusively on African texts. Instead, this problem-based literary history brings together British, U.S., and African writers typically read within separate traditions. I assemble a set of novelists who address forms of international assistance that are nongovernmental and not-for-profit, led by missionaries in the colonial era and by aid workers and volunteers after decolonization. References to Western writers lean British in the earlier years and American in the later years as the locus of global power shifts to the United States as the postcolonial mission nation.

Written from various moments in history and from various points on the humanitarian network, the texts I gather here all think about problems of African need in a global context of care. Humanitarian discourse conditions contemporary relationships between Africa and the West and cultivates an imagined community that links people across nations and continents. By crafting an archive on the basis of that network, *Humanitarian Fictions* reveals how experiences of the "global" are generated by more circumscribed narratives that link particular places on the globe. This lies in contrast to studies of literature and human rights that are more narrowly tied to nation—focused on U.S. writers with global subject matter, for example—or more thoroughly global—connecting writers from Africa, Asia, Europe, and the Americas.[45] By triangulating British, U.S., and African writers from across the continent, I demarcate a humanitarian Atlantic of literary production that forms a constrained network of globality. This is an Afrocentric globality.

The novels I interpret are set in a number of African nations: Botswana, Kenya, Nigeria, Somalia, South Africa, Sudan, Zimbabwe, and the Democratic Republic of the Congo. This kind of coverage precludes a deep dive into any one national context or literary tradition. Framing my archive in this way may risk falling into what Mūkoma wa Ngũgĩ calls "Africa-Is-a-Country literary criticism" that reads African literature "as representative of a single country, culture, and language—coming from a singular body politic."[46] My point, however, is that the texts included in this project, coming from multiple national and local contexts, respond to a shared global context that is defined by humanitarian action and its attendant narratives which do, indeed, think in continental terms. Addressing the problematic flattening of Africa in the context of anthropology, James Ferguson writes that, despite legitimate criticism of studying "Africa" in general, "the world is (perhaps now more than ever) full of talk, not of specific African nations, societies, or localities, but of 'Africa' itself."[47] He goes on to caution that "refusing the very category of 'Africa' as empirically problematic, anthropologists and other scholars devoted to particularity have thus allowed themselves to remain bystanders in the wider arena of discussions about 'Africa.'"[48] With *Humanitarian Fictions*, my goal is to see how literature speaks to that "wider arena," and so I will join the talk of "Africa."

Also relevant is the canonical status of the African novelists I have selected for analysis. *Humanitarian Fictions* hardly strays from the usual suspects. I am mindful of Neil Lazarus's critique of the tendency in postcolonial literary studies "to write with reference to a woefully restricted and attenuated corpus of works."[49] Indeed, this is a limitation of my archive, and much work remains to be done to draw a more diverse network of writers into this conversation. My purpose, though, is to explore what happens when widely read and extensively analyzed authors are positioned in the new framework of the humanitarian Atlantic. The standard timeline of anglophone African literature is built around the changing nation with a first generation of authors writing against the colonial state, looking toward a horizon of independence, and a second generation expressing disillusionment with the postcolonial state. This book repositions canonical texts in relation to humanitarian narratives and nonstate networks of solidarity.

All of the writers in this study are thoroughly transnational themselves, and their lives map onto the network of the humanitarian Atlantic in various ways. Western writers including Joseph Conrad, Barbara Kingsolver, Norman Rush, and Paul Theroux have spent extended periods in Africa. The African authors I address—including Chinua Achebe, Ngũgĩ wa Thiong'o, Bessie Head, Nuruddin Farah, and Zakes Mda—have written about their homelands from exile. Their life paths are definitively cosmopolitan, positioning them as members of an international community reaching well beyond the nations of their birth. As Eleni Coundouriotis notes, the projects of contemporary writers like Nuruddin Farah and Chimamanda Ngozi Adichie are influenced "by their location outside Africa" and "by their exposure not only to the production of humanitarian discourse about Africa but also its reception."[50] They experience the vectors of the humanitarian Atlantic differently than people who have spent their lives on just one of its shores.

Across the board, their cosmopolitan position is a matter not only of biography but of stature. Their texts are part of an international marketplace that, like humanitarian narratives themselves, represents Africa to the world. They can even satisfy some of the same tastes as the likes of *Kony 2012*. The contemporary white Western writers—Barbara Kingsolver, John le Carré, Philip Caputo—are known less for prestige among literary critics than for mass popularity. Their novels are akin to a genre Elizabeth Anker calls the "human rights bestseller."[51] The African writers in my archive are among the best known in the world, and their names grace the pages of the *London Review of Books* and the *New York Times*, not only as subjects of discussion but as contributors. These writers have access to and influence on a Western audience sympathetic to humanitarian causes. They test out what Rita Barnard calls "the text's potential hailing of a cosmopolitan audience."[52] This is not to say they write with the West in mind as the primary audience. For instance, Kwame Anthony Appiah notes in the foreword to *Nervous Conditions* that "Tsitsi Dangarembga's novel lacks the telltale marks of an author addressing an Other from Elsewhere."[53] For another example, Ngũgĩ, following his "farewell to English," writes first in Gikuyu, prioritizing a relatively small audience in relation to the global English market for whom he then translates.[54] My point about audience, then, is not about intent but about reach.

Through wide circulation of their work, the African authors studied here participate directly in the global discourse on African problems and humanitarian projects. As members of a global literary elite, they speak from a position of cosmopolitan privilege, although they didn't start off that way and, in Bessie Head's case, such fulsome recognition did not arrive in her lifetime. Exceptions aside, they often write about African lives quite different from their own. Tejumola Olaniyan's argument linking literary institutions to NGOs applies:

> In both their genres and languages of expression, both the literature and the criticism [by African writers] are implicated in the systemic extraverted mentality that I have described as structurally and historically constitutive of what NGOs are. . . . Even the ruling self-identity of African literature and African literary criticism—that is their dominant liberationist temper and rhetoric—is only a little or no different from what I have described as the missionary mentality characteristic of the NGOs. . . . The Westernized African elite is an NGO elite.[55]

While I would take the critical edge off the term "missionary mentality" in its application to the writers included in this book, they do share elements of the NGO position as they represent African pain and poverty to the world and ask readers to pay attention. As Appiah puts it, African literature "is grounded in an appeal to an ethical universal; indeed it is based . . . in an appeal to a certain simple respect for human suffering."[56] This is a fundamentally humanitarian sentiment, reminding us that ethical universals and the discourse of human suffering are not the exclusive domain of the West. As much as African literature and humanitarian discourse conflict, they also share a key point of resonance in their commitment to the disempowered, the marginalized, and the dispossessed. Both insist, in their very different ways, that lives which have been pushed to the periphery are worth thinking about. *Humanitarian Fictions* cultivates this rich—but underthought—alliance.

The Third Sector Novel

While the subfield of literature and human rights has seen expansive growth over the past two decades, the particularities of *humanitarian* literature have received little comment.[57] This book aims to change that. Although human rights and humanitarianism often go undistinguished, they are unique phenomena in need of teasing out. Overlapping but distinct from human rights, humanitarianism is a mode of response to human rights standards that have been violated or simply ignored. In contrast to the human rights narrative, which generally centers on the rights-bearing individual, the humanitarian narrative is inherently about a *relationship* of assistance. It centers on altruism as a way of fulfilling those rights, including basic needs like food, water, and healthcare. It focuses less on rights than on needs, less on legal frameworks than moral ones, less on the problem than on the solution (and the one who will find it). As we have seen in studies of the bildungsroman and the sentimental novel by scholars including Joseph Slaughter, Lynn Festa, and Lynn Hunt, a narrative form produces a particular orientation toward the world, a way of being-in-the-world and taking on its problems. This scholarship has shown the importance of "literary modes of thinking" beyond the realm of literature itself.[58] The stakes are significant. As James Dawes puts it, "Whether or not the human rights movement continues to inspire our devotion and efforts, whether or not we turn to alternative vocabularies, institutions, and tactics to realize visions of social justice—all of this will depend quite literally upon a competition among stories."[59] *Humanitarian Fictions* will trace the "competition among stories" in the context of humanitarianism in Africa, drawing out elements of the underexplored third sector: relationships of giving and receiving, postsecular visions of humanity, communal practices of care, and African agency within a global frame.

Literatures of the third sector think about questions of suffering and need in relation to nonstate, nonprofit modes of assistance. They feature international travelers who are at least nominally external to governmental and for-profit sectors and who are working to "save" Africa in some way, although the space given to those travelers varies widely. Critical humanitarian fictions gesture to the elements of the white savior narrative outlined above and transform them, sometimes to undermine the grand narrative and sometimes to ameliorate its damages with less grand alternatives. In many rewritings, the great mission hero becomes a pathetic failure, a violent outlaw, or both. In other cases, the missionary-humanitarian is marginal to the story overall. At the very least, this Western figure—maybe a protagonist, maybe a side character—is brought down from heroic stature. Often, the more ethical humanitarian characters in these novels are African, and many are women. The exotic adventure plot of the grand narrative sometimes resurfaces within these novels, particularly in the Western versions by Conrad, Kingsolver, and Caputo; in these cases, Africa remains a space of adventure, catastrophe, and difference. In texts by African writers, however, the setting is never a vague backdrop, but a specific, multidimensional place, sometimes dangerous, often ordinary. In this literature, the third element of the grand narrative, the great goal of African salvation, is no longer glorious, inevitable, or even necessary. Promises of salvation give way to practices of destruction. In many cases, the valued aim is sufficiency, not salvation. Rather than projecting the certainty of white saviorism, these novels cultivate doubt and shift the source of knowledge away from the West and into African communities. Finally, they deconstruct the binaries that structure the white savior narrative—light-dark, benefactor-beneficiary, politics-ethics, powerful-powerless, sacred-profane. In so doing, they operate as, in Kenneth Burke's words, "a disintegrating art, which converts each simplicity into a complexity, which ruins the possibility of ready hierarchies" and "can at best serve to make action more labored," challenging the dangerous confidence and simplicity of white saviorism.[60] Consistently, these texts explore the relationship between the worldly and otherworldly, the compelling yet problematic notion of development through altruism, the entanglement of altruism and power, and the risks and possibilities of (secular and religious) faith, its displacement, and loss. Much of their work, then, lies in unsettling things.

This book is also a project of proliferation. Assembling a body of texts into a field of third sector literature reminds us that the dominant story isn't the only story. In contrast to savior narratives that center on a single protagonist, novels with paired protagonists or large casts of characters demonstrate how missions and humanitarianism are constantly experienced in multiple ways. Novels with African focalizers instead of Western ones open new windows on the humanitarian encounter, showing it to include text and subtext. Interactions between foreign humanitarians and African people come to be characterized by overt tension and debate or by what Homi Bhabha calls (drawing on a missionary sermon) sly civility. Like colonial power, humanitarian power has "a desire for 'authorization'" that is troubled by "the native refusal to satisfy the colonizer's [or the aid worker's] narrative demand."[61] Much more is happening under the radar and around the margins than either celebrations or critiques of Western humanitarianism would suggest. The point, then, is not only to change the dominant story but to unearth the other stories that are already present as part of a dynamic narrative field in which the supposed beneficiaries of humanitarian aid are in fact active participants. The notion that humane care for Africa is of Western provenance begins to appear ridiculous once we consider the agency—both overt and covert—of Africans themselves in such projects. The literature of the third sector repositions supposedly powerless people within the humanitarian encounter and expands the narrative world of humanitarianism. By sketching that world, *Humanitarian Fictions* argues for a reexamination of the relationship between global altruism and African agency.

Even as they dismantle the white savior narrative, third sector novels are often invested in preserving some aspect of the mission impulse—that impulse to assist across differences of culture and color, power and privilege—while holding on to the radical critique of its imperialist complicity. This both-and perspective is especially prevalent among the African writers who are committed to addressing the very real problems of the African present and who are also attuned to the limited choices available in far-from-ideal contexts. They tend to be even more ambivalent toward humanitarianism than their British and American counterparts. Their responses are at least more subtle as authors wrestle with the challenge of being caught in an impossible situation, following African characters as they navigate the third sector, negotiating between potential benefits and compromises involved in accepting aid. For characters in these humanitarian fictions, assistance—be it in the form of mission education or material resources—comes at a time of poverty and dispossession produced by the colonial and neocolonial orders. In this context, strategic alliances with missions offer a way of surviving and even subverting imperial violence.

Not reducible to an easy equation with empire, religious and humanitarian missions have therefore been a vexed site of contestation not only between Africans and supposedly altruistic foreigners but among Africans themselves. Confronting missions has meant grappling with their oppressive, imperialist elements alongside their promises of social transformation. *Humanitarian Fictions* foregrounds the material context in which choices about missions have

been made, never in a vacuum of idealism but in the flux of the nonideal realities of African life in a colonial and neocolonial world. They narrate missions
at the impasse, at the breaking point between desired ideals and constraining realities, facing a mix of attraction and repulsion, both ideological and
material. The novel, with its dialogic form that sets multiple discourses and
ideologies in conversation, enables authors to explore these tensions within
individual characters, between contrasting characters, and in the narrative
voice itself.

A scene from NoViolet Bulawayo's 2013 novel, *We Need New Names*, illustrates many of the dynamics I associate with third sector literature. The narrative follows a group of children in Zimbabwe as they confront the challenges
that define the humanitarian problem space—poverty and hunger, a lack of
adequate shelter and healthcare. NGOs pop in and out of the narrative, occasionally through physical appearances but more often as a subject of conversation. They are important to the story in terms of characters' consciousness
but peripheral in terms of action. When the representatives of an unnamed
NGO arrive to distribute aid, it is a rare but welcome appearance (Bulawayo,
53). Through their cameras, the NGO workers immediately latch onto the
children who "are embarrassed by [their] dirt and torn clothing" (54). These
kids fit the image of humanitarian subjects on the surface, but readers do not
perceive them through the camera lens. We see them instead through the
eyes of the young narrator, Darling. She and her friends demonstrate a savvy
awareness of geopolitics as they play the "country game," in which players
each represent a country; in setting up the game, all fight to "be the U.S.A.,
which is a country-country" (51). In contrast, Darling wonders rhetorically
about the position of countries similar to her own: "who wants to be a terrible
place of hunger and things falling apart?" (51). This children's game reveals
a painful understanding of global hierarchy and resource distribution that
distinguishes "country-countries" from "rags of countries" (51). To interpret
the magnetism of the United States for Darling and her friends, we can apply
James Ferguson's theory of African "yearnings for cultural convergence" with
the West, which "can mark not simply mental colonization or capitulation
to cultural imperialism, but an aspiration to overcome categorical subordination."[62] While their words may be derisive to their own country, the young
characters in *We Need New Names* are on some level resisting their conditions, marking those conditions as a form of injustice. In these circumstances,
the characters desire humanitarian assistance but are realistic in their understanding that the NGOs will not, in fact, transform their positions or the
uneven status of nations.

The power dynamics between Zimbabweans and foreign humanitarians are immediately evident. The gaze of the NGO workers through sunglasses is foreboding and impenetrable. As Darling observes, "Eyes look at us that we cannot really see because they are hidden behind a wall of black glass" (54). The children know that they are not the equals of these visitors: "We are careful not to touch the NGO people, though, because we can see that even though they are giving us things, they do not want to touch us or for us to touch them" (54). Although their authority seems intimidating, the children are unfazed. In fact, Darling explains, "One of the ladies tries to greet us in our language and stammers badly so we laugh and laugh until she just says it in English" (54). Even as they embarrass the people they come to help, "the NGO people" are themselves subject to mockery and the attendant embarrassment. Their gaze may be illegible, but locals are also illegible to them. The white foreigners depend fully on their local representative, Sis Betty, who translates and manages behavior and expectations on both sides: "It's Sis Betty who finally gets us to stop by screaming at us, but she does it in our language, maybe so that the NGO people do not understand" (56). Betty instructs the children to not "act like baboons" in front of "expensive white people," then "turns to the NGO people and smiles her gap-toothed smile. They smile back, pleased. Maybe they think she just told us good things about them" (56, 57). There is a strong undercurrent of activity to which the foreigners remain oblivious.

The people in Darling's community react in a variety of ways to the distribution of "gifts" (57). Sometimes they respond with insecurity, like the children's parents who "stand in their own line, trying to look like they don't really care, like they have better things to do than be here" (57). Sometimes they assert their dignity, like MotherLove, who, in the face of "grinning" white women, "turns and strides away, head held high, the bangles on her arms jingling, the stars on her dress shining, her scent of lemon staying in the air even after she is gone" (58). For the kids, whom the narrative tracks most closely, the emotions are multiple. They can hardly wait for the NGO truck to arrive: "It's the gifts that we know are inside that make it hard to wait and watch the lorry crawl" (53). Once it appears, they explode with energy, "singing and screaming like [they] are proper mad" (53).The energy seems impossible to contain, and though they try to act polite, they are overcome: "At first we try and line up nicely, as if we are ants going to a wedding, but when they open the back of the lorry, we turn into dizzied dung flies. We push and we shove and we yell and we scream. We lurch forward with hands outstretched" (56). They are reduced, in some ways, to the status of insects, orderly ants turned unmanageable flies, but even such a description remains playful, not pitiful, and once the kids have received their gifts, the tone again changes: "When the NGO lorry finally leaves, we take off and run after it; we have got what we wanted and don't care how they want us to do" (58). Still, after receiving "a toy gun, some sweets, and something to wear," their circumstances remain unchanged (57). As the scene comes to an end, they decide to "go and play war": "we take off and run and kill each other with our brand-new guns from America" (59). Are they mimicking American children with toy guns or echoing the proxy wars the United States fought in many African nations, including Zimbabwe during the Cold War? Is this a deluded, self-destructive form of empowerment or a subtle but meaningful threat, leaving the power of givers and receivers uncertain? What does it mean that NGOs deliver too little food for sustenance but enough toy guns for each child to have one? As is evident in this ambiguous moment, humanitarianism is a site of imperial authority and potential violence, but it is also a site of on-the-ground resistance, of what Bhabha calls sly civility and camouflage.[63] Through the multiplicity of African characters, it is also clear that there is no singular African response.

Third sector novels write back against humanitarianism, but they also write with it. Even intensely critical accounts do not categorically oppose humanitarianism or call for its dissolution. As Bulawayo shows, humanitarians take seriously the urgent questions of food, clothing, and safety, responsibilities the government in the novel has not only neglected but actively and violently rejected. The NGO idea is compelling to people in need, and it is also clearly inadequate. My intent is not to set up a binary between the bad and the good, the savior narrative and the antisavior narrative, the popular and the literary, the *Kony 2012* types and their critics. Rather, my aim is to map out a more mixed and motile narrative field that circulates around the node of white saviorism.

This project uncovers a transnational vein of storytelling about Africa that I call, collectively, *humanitarian fictions*. I will describe them as celebratory and critical, Afrocentric and Western-centric, colonialist and anticolonialist, racist and antiracist—and some, like *Kony 2012* itself, an uneasy combination. Humanitarianism is a new colonialism; it is also a new anticolonialism. For that reason, a strictly oppositional framework—humanitarian and antihumanitarian to parallel colonial and anticolonial—isn't adequate to the task of capturing the nuanced field of third sector literature. In contrast to anticolonial literature that posits a fundamentally different world than the one colonialism imposes, this literature envisions a world that actually shares many fundamental features with the humanitarian paradigm. This shared paradigm is ethically oriented and uses the language of morality to critique material inequity. It confronts questions of what to do in the face of human suffering and explores responses that lie outside of government and private enterprise. It is open to religious modes of thought as well as to transcendent, universalist notions of humanity. It demands global responsibility as characters reach beyond the local and call upon "the world" for help. It focuses on the injustice of suffering and is invested in, for lack of a better phrase, "making a difference." But ethics, here, is always also politics. Notions of the right and the good, this suggests, cannot be separated from an analysis of power.

The confluence of ethics, politics, and progress has long been part of the anglophone African literary tradition. Writers are often explicitly committed to improving the continent through storytelling. Achebe explains "that behind it all is a desire to make our experience in the world better, to make our passage through life easier. Once you talk about making things better, you're talking about politics."[64] He suggests that this is a moral imperative for writers: "I do think that decency and civilization would insist that the writer take sides with the powerless. Clearly there is no moral obligation to write in any particular way. But there is a moral obligation, I think, not to ally oneself with power against the powerless."[65] Through words like beneficence, decency, civilization, moral obligation, and advocacy, Achebe links this literary discussion to the vocabulary of humanitarianism, which defines its own loyalties in much the same way. As Didier Fassin puts it, "The humanitarian politics of life is based on an entrenched standpoint in favor of the 'side of the victims.' The world order, it supposes, is made up of the powerful and the weak. Humanitarian action takes place in the space between the two, being deployed among the weak as it denounces the powerful."[66] For Achebe—likely the most influential voice in African literature—the best fiction performs a kind of humanitarian work.

Chapter Overview

Moving from religious missions to secular humanitarianism, the following chapters each take up a central and problematic concept within popular humanitarian narratives: the moral cause, the emancipated African, the universal human, the benevolent gift, and the nongovernmental organization. Chapter 1, "The Moral Cause," begins in the nineteenth century, a high time for Christian missions, which produced popular tales of adventure, sacrifice, and African salvation. The chapter first traces the emergence of the white savior and accompanying tropes within narratives by and about missionaries. This origin story lays the groundwork for the study of literature that turns the celebratory tide. Joseph Conrad's *Heart of Darkness* (1899) is the anchor text for this chapter. While readers of Conrad have typically focused on colonial pillage through both the state and the private sector, *Humanitarian Fictions* adds a new layer to the discussion, resituating the text within the framework of third sector missions. *Heart of Darkness* mimics and challenges the virtuous fervor that characterized popular missionary biographies of the era, revealing that when benevolence gets channeled across differences of culture, race, and status, the results can range from unintended damage to murderous destruction. Conrad deflates the missionary narrative's unwavering confidence through thematic and formal transformations of its standard elements, recommending and aesthetically cultivating an ethics of doubt. To convey the scope of the Western literary challenge to missionary narratives, I then read Barbara Kingsolver's *The Poisonwood Bible* (1998). In echoing Conrad a century later, this novel illuminates the power and persistence of the white savior narrative in shaping American thinking about Africa. It also models the capacity of the novel's dialogic form to dispute missionary monologue. To close, a brief reading of Paul Theroux's *Girls at Play* (1969) demonstrates the limits of Western literary interventions.

To get a better assessment of what Western missions mean for African communities, it is of course necessary to hear from African writers themselves. If Conrad's voice has been the most influential within Western humanitarian fictions, Chinua Achebe and Ngũgĩ wa Thiong'o take the foundational role within the anglophone African tradition. Chapter 2 explores how they respond not only to the missionary vision of "The Emancipated African" but to Conrad's mode of critique. While they, too, upend the enthusiasm of missionary sentiment, they also suggest that missions, as put to work by African subjects, enabled new practices of freedom and new political collectivities, making Christianity an ambiguous ally of anticolonialism itself. Drawing on their early novels and recently published childhood memoirs, this chapter demonstrates that, although missions played a role in the story of colonial imposition, they have also been central to African writers' own narratives of anticolonial improvement through their use of education and literacy. African narratives of mission education exemplify a form of critical engagement with third sector assistance that gets picked up in texts of the contemporary humanitarian era, revealing this literary history's relevance in the postcolonial present when missionaries have lost their position in the popular imagination only to be replaced by transnational, nonstate agents of a different kind.

With the religious groundwork laid, the book moves to secular humanitarian missions. Chapter 3, "The Universal Human," asks how we might imagine an ethical form of community that extends beyond the state and beyond the rhetoric of salvation. The concept of universal humanity—the idea that human beings are, in some ways, all the same, and that we can therefore know and act upon others' needs—underpins the white savior narrative and produces its imperialist tendencies. Yet it is a point of cautious attraction within this body of literature. This chapter works through that ambivalence with readings of Zakes Mda and Bessie Head, both exiles from South Africa who think about apartheid's organization of humanity from a remove. Writing from the United States and Botswana respectively, Mda and Head are themselves participants in an international network of concern. In this chapter, I address the hollowness of the existing international community and demonstrate how fiction reimagines it as a legitimately inclusive foundation from which to confront global inequity. Mda's *The Heart of Redness* (2000) sets the stage for the problem of thinking in terms of the everyone, depicting the challenges and risks of identification across difference alongside the pull of universal standards for equality. In *When Rain Clouds Gather* (1968) and *A Question of Power* (1974), Bessie Head combines a thoroughgoing critique of universal humanism with an insistence on its necessity in a critical, decentered form. An effective international response to African poverty, this chapter suggests, will depend on replacing the rhetoric of salvation with an ethics of sufficiency. Head's theorization of postcolonial, critical humanism re-orients the ethical compass of humanitarians as well as their critics.

The fourth chapter, "The Benevolent Gift," shifts from the theoretical question of international community to a more pragmatic one: How does literature represent the relationship between the idea of international community and actual systems of material distribution? Put differently, what does the internationalization of concern actually mean for social welfare globally and for the literature that represents it? This chapter begins from a reading of Tsitsi Dangarembga's *Nervous Conditions* (1988), which reveals how the humanitarian gift structure emerged at the Christian mission station as African people coped with the material erosion wrought by colonization. I then bring together novelists from Somalia and the United States, Nuruddin Farah and Philip Caputo, whose novels—*Gifts* (1992) and *Acts of Faith* (2005)—wrestle with the insufficient and often destructive ways in which humanitarian aid has addressed and represented the problems of poverty and hunger, teasing out the knotty relationships between giving and receiving, dependency and self-sufficiency, domination and emancipation. In response to the dramatic shortcomings of existing humanitarianism, their work reimagines the aid relationship and freshly theorizes inequity and resource redistribution. Through narrative techniques including focalization shifting and genre mixing, they multiply the meaning of the gift. These novels model a more honest, theoretically and historically informed discourse around donors and recipients. By overestimating Western giving—as a form of either benevolence or dominance—we often underestimate the agency of African people in the recipient position.

The fifth and final chapter, "The Nongovernmental Organization," responds to a growing body of African fiction that, rather than confronting foreign aid directly, seeks smaller-scale alternatives centered on African agency, sidelining the foreign altruist. Within these novels, Western aid is peripheral at best. Through Chimamanda Ngozi Adichie's *Half of a Yellow Sun* (2006) and Ngũgĩ wa Thiong'o's *Wizard of the Crow* (2006), as well as a brief reading of NoViolet Bulawayo's *We Need New Names* (2013), I explore the on-the-ground narratives of third sector care that get left out when humanitarianism is defined, as it generally is, by Western intervention. Although these novels do not focus on humanitarianism in a conventional sense, they follow local characters as they organize around health, hunger, and poverty, supporting their communities through volunteer work; they, too, struggle with the tensions that pervade the NGO. My analysis reveals not only how Africa has entered global consciousness through the discourse of the NGO but how that discourse has affected African consciousness of the globe. By sketching a network of third sector care that lies outside the purview of its major international networks, these novels reconceptualize the NGO as a grassroots effort rather than a foreign intervention. In situating humanitarian fictions outside the typical aid-centric frame, Adichie and Ngũgĩ complicate the third sector approach and repoliticize the nominally apolitical humanitarian space.

A brief epilogue, "Rearticulating the Humanitarian Atlantic," returns to the framing concepts for each chapter—morality, emancipation, humanism, giving, and nongovernmental aid—to assemble this literature's combined lexicon of humanitarian ethics. I also expand on the key elements of the grand savior narrative as outlined above—"its great hero, its great dangers, its great voyages, its great goal"[67]—to synthesize the alternative building blocks of humanitarian storytelling that third sector novels collectively offer.

The Plurality of Humanitarian Fictions

I mean *fictions* in a couple of senses. The term should signal both the false and the literary. The former casts doubt on popular humanitarian modes of storytelling about Africa; the latter draws attention to their use of fictional techniques as well as to the literature that represents humanitarianism. As I have already suggested, literary narrative (say, a novel that is critical of humanitarianism) and popular narrative (say, a fundraising video that celebrates humanitarian work) do not lie in strict opposition. Both operate in the realm of fiction, both appeal to international audiences, and both draw on the white savior narrative, though they have different aims and results. As the *Kony 2012* campaign illustrates, organizations use the techniques and tropes of fiction (such as adventurous plot structures and heroic protagonists) and do so deliberately, albeit not necessarily with those terms front of mind.

In sum, humanitarian fictions can be literary narratives that speak truth through the medium of fiction, they can be false or distorted narratives that claim to be true, and they can be nonfiction narratives that apply literary techniques as a deliberate form of persuasion. For the sake of evaluation, we might bear in mind Achebe's explanation that "there are fictions that help and fictions that hinder . . . beneficent and malignant fictions."[68] While literature is an especially rich source of beneficent fictions, this should not imply that mass-circulating popular narratives like *Kony 2012* are uniformly bad or unavoidably malignant, nor do I mean to suggest that humanitarian organizations are intentionally deceptive, although that is sometimes the case. My point is that they, too, are storytellers in need of a fiction workshop.

Because NGOs are constantly engaged in a struggle over how to tell their story in a way that will captivate donors, their work depends on literary practices. Humanitarian organizations and journalists often know they are mobilizing the techniques of fiction in order to persuade their audiences to act, and many are aware this involves compromises. Take, for instance, the debate between Teju Cole and *New York Times* columnist Nicholas Kristof, who writes extensively about global suffering and Western projects that confront it. His stories feature what he calls "bridge characters" to connect American readers to African issues:

> The problem that I face—my challenge as a writer—in trying to get readers to care about something like Eastern Congo, is that frankly, the moment the reader sees that I'm writing about Central Africa, for an awful lot of them, that's the moment to turn the page. It's very hard to get people to care about distant crises like that. One way of getting people to read at least a few [paragraphs] in is to have some kind of foreign protagonist, some American who they can identify with as a bridge character. And so if this is a way I can get people to care about foreign countries, to read about them, ideally, to get a little bit more involved, then I plead guilty.[69]

Kristof exemplifies the use of fictional techniques in nonfiction humanitarian writing and shows it to be more purposeful than we might assume. For journalists and NGOs, engaging an apathetic audience is a primary goal, and protagonists are indeed powerful. Herein lies a conflict between ethos and ethics—the bridge character offers a voice that readers find persuasive, but their tastes are partly conditioned by racism and ethnocentrism that value some voices over others. Cole responds that the term "bridge character" is merely "Kristof's euphemism of white saviors in Third World narratives who make the story more palatable to American viewers."[70] Kristof chooses efficacy in the name of ethics. Cole chooses ethics. In my view, Kristof isn't wrong, exactly—the narrative challenge he describes is real—but Cole is more right. *Humanitarian Fictions* will show the advantages of the novelist's profound sensitivity to narrative. Fiction can be more true than texts that claim to tell the truth.

Through readings of the third sector novel, this book will critique humanitarianism for the unequal relationships it cultivates—racially and economically, internationally and interpersonally—while also reorienting its terms in order to envision a more ethical form of global responsibility, motivated by sufficiency rather than salvation and based on mutual obligation rather than sacrifice and dependency. The texts I study here compete with the white-centric, West-centric stories that dominate reporting and fundraising, offering strategies that people of "ignorant goodwill"[71] can learn from. They offer a reeducation in the face of what Martin Luther King Jr. called "sincere ignorance and conscientious stupidity,"[72] the affective hallmarks of white saviorism. Therefore, reenvisioning humanitarianism through the lens of literature is relevant not only to critics but to aid workers and organizers. Storytelling is, after all, a fundamental part of the humanitarian act.

Drawing on literary models of critical commitment, I argue for the role of the novelist as an interlocutor for humanitarians themselves. These groups share an interest in imagining new kinds of global coalitions—apart from government and capitalism—that affirm the value of humanity and confront the unjust systems that give some lives more value than others. This, too, was part of the *Kony 2012* story. Alongside the power it conferred on Americans to "change the course of human history" (8:30), it sought an ethical version of cosmopolitan commitment: "We built a community around the idea that where you live shouldn't determine whether you live" (15:30). Operating in the humanitarian spirit of volunteerism, it led people in the West—predominantly white and predominantly American—to denaturalize their inherited privilege and power: "All this was funded by an army of young people who put their money toward their belief in the value of all human life" (16:27). Of course, in this gesture to metaphorical militarization, we can see how both challenging power and seizing it can happen in the same action, even in the same breath. *Humanitarian Fictions* turns to literature for rhetorical strategies and visionary resources that can reinvigorate a humanitarian discourse that continues to imagine Africa and its improvement in religiously inflected, imperialist ways.

1
The Moral Cause

We can view contemporary humanitarianism as a kind of palimpsest; if we look closely enough, we find traces of the religious past everywhere. Observing disasters in faraway places, which we do more quickly and more frequently than ever before, invokes the immemorial question: What does morality require? We must *do something*, we announce. Often, we don't know what, and so we turn this imperative into the passive voice: Something must be done. Bumbling as it may be, this moral impulse is the seed of humanitarianism, and it is, at its base, a missionary impulse. Today's humanitarians are seen as the new "moral crusaders," and NGOs (nongovernmental organizations) are "largely driven by spiritual moral imperatives."[1] This religious resonance is the legacy of missionaries who set the precedent for international projects of altruism. Evangelicalism, with its emphasis on salvation granted by God and the duty of Christians to save others, was particularly influential.[2] Missionary organizations were the first humanitarian organizations, and their publications addressed the body as well as the soul, often soliciting donations and asking readers to support the moral cause by proxy if not in person.[3] While humanitarian discourse would become increasingly secular during the twentieth century, the religious foundation has continued to exert influence. Arguments that situate humanitarianism securely in the secular domain thus overlook some of its most fundamental and persistent dynamics. This goes for its literary history as well. While my aim is ultimately to move beyond the confines of religious missions, contemporary humanitarian fictions can be better understood through an analysis grounded in the missionary tradition from which they emerged.

The Christian mission supplied humanitarianism with a language and a story. Problems in today's white savior narrative — the centralization of the white hero, the negative representation of Africa, the marginalization of African people, the colonialist imposition of Western plans, and overconfidence in good intentions — can be traced back to the mission impulse, which drove Europeans into the continent and beyond the bounds of the colonial map. At the heart of religious and secular projects of African improvement is the notion of the moral cause — the imperative that demands benevolent action on behalf of strangers. This chapter asks: How does this moral sensibility shape Western storytelling about Africa, and what effects does such a narrative produce? To embark on a mission is an act of faith — faith in some higher purpose, be it God or humanity or, as is often the case, some combination of the two. Even the secular mission to save and assist is a project of transcendence, operating within "the inviolable sphere of ethical action" and "situat[ing] its activity beyond the profane and the political."[4] The narrative aims to instill faith on multiple levels — in declared ideals, in mission leaders and the path they have set out, in the relationship between good intentions and good outcomes, and in the altruistic traveler's capacity to understand and improve the world. Faith and its corollaries remain central to the humanitarian project.

    This chapter will explore the history of the mission impulse and its appearance in British and American literature about Africa, demarcating a problem space I have called the humanitarian Atlantic. These narratives follow the path of the virtuous traveler who aims to assist others across the boundaries of race, culture, and continent, all in pursuit of a (nominally) moral cause. Beginning from its uptake in nineteenth-century biographical and fictional missionary writing, I will chart the shifting place of the white savior narrative in Anglo-American literary history, exploring how it has been expressed and contested, reversed and revised.[5] This account revolves around Joseph Conrad's *Heart of Darkness* (1899), which represents a watershed moment in the literary history of white saviorism, providing the foundation on which a critical tradition was built, aimed at the formal and thematic dismantling of the savior narrative. Scholars have typically positioned *Heart of Darkness* within discussions of modernism and imperialism, and logically so.[6] While some have praised its early anti-imperial stance, others — most famously Chinua Achebe in "An Image of Africa" — have critiqued its racism, focusing on how it perpetuates images of Africans as savages, almost but not quite human. While much has been said about Conrad as travel writer, modernist writer, imperial writer, anti-imperial writer, Polish-born English writer, and so forth, his position as a mission writer within a religious textual tradition has escaped comment.

    My argument builds upon the existing framework but tilts it to read *Heart of Darkness* as a direct response to the literature of nineteenth-century missionary heroism. *Heart of Darkness* incorporates the primary features of the religious white savior narrative and takes them to new ends: the great hero in the form of Kurtz with his godlike plans to remake his subjects; the perilous journey into a mysterious land; the discourse of darkness and light, civilized and savage, enlightened and benighted; even the celebratory ending, in which the late traveler is remembered and mourned as a martyr. Conrad thus participates in that religious narrative tradition in a way that would have been recognizable to his contemporaries. The "noble cause" is here submitted to modernist style and sensibility, opening it up to irony, complication, and critique.[7] By embedding the elements of the heroic missionary tradition, Conrad simultaneously withers its power and reveals the secular expansion of its terrain.

Heart of Darkness set a new precedent for Western literature about Africa. Across the twentieth century and into the twenty-first, writers would return to Conrad's iconic novella in order to extend it, to challenge it, to echo it, to test new versions of its characters, and to confront new forms of "darkness" alongside new "emissar[ies] of light" (14). To unpack this post-Conradian tradition, I will focus on Barbara Kingsolver's *The Poisonwood Bible* (1998), which, published almost exactly a century after *Heart of Darkness*, was written deliberately in its wake.[8] *The Poisonwood Bible*, like *Heart of Darkness*, is a story of travel into the dense Congolese forest to an outlying village at a river's edge, this time following a family of American missionaries—a Kurtz-like preacher, his wife, and four daughters—who become subject to horrors of their own making. Also like Kurtz, the mad preacher never makes it out of Africa. Conradian tropes and language are woven throughout the story, and in fact, Kingsolver cites *Heart of Darkness* in her bibliography. I use *The Poisonwood Bible* to illustrate what is actually a broader phenomenon; *Heart of Darkness* became an anchor text for numerous authors including Graham Greene, Saul Bellow, Paul Theroux, and Philip Caputo, launching a critique of the white savior narrative which transformed the way white Western writers narrated the journey to Africa.[9]

Heart of Darkness and *The Poisonwood Bible* dismantle the triumphalist expectations of the salvation narrative, showing how Western models of African improvement have ranged from ineffective to intolerably destructive. The higher calling to save another generates a deep investment in the faithful self. It also defines a place and a people that need saving. Confidence, certainty, and resoluteness characterize the tone of the white savior narrative and the valued qualities of the mission hero. Doubt, in this schema, becomes a kind of enemy. In place of the romantic narrative, Conrad and Kingsolver write tragic tales of missionary intervention. Rather than representing the best of humanity, missionaries and their ilk come to embody the very worst; altruism becomes complicated by impulses toward greed and violence; tragic endings replace triumphant ones. In effect, *Heart of Darkness* and *The Poisonwood Bible* undermine the white savior narrative's inflated confidence and recommend an ethics of doubt. These texts provide resources for interrogating transnational altruism, even in its most secular-seeming manifestations, and help us understand the historical evolution of the white savior.

Missionary Heroism of the Nineteenth Century

The white savior impulse originates in Christian missions. The missionary's moral cause grew and flourished at the crux of abolitionism, evangelicalism, and imperial expansion. In the latter half of the eighteenth century, religious revival, coincident with the rise of the British abolition movement, led to a shift in the tone of imperial rhetoric that replaced blatant mercenary aims with missionary claims; those claims did not preclude the realities of mercenary motivation, but the tone of this expansionist rhetoric was indeed distinct. Patrick Brantlinger argues that when the British abolished the slave trade at the beginning of the nineteenth century, they "began to see themselves less and less as perpetrators of the slave trade and more and more as the potential saviors of the African."[10] Through this transition, the white savior complex was born. This sentiment grew over the course of the nineteenth century, culminating in the Berlin Conference and Scramble for Africa in its final years. By this time, the view of Africa as a global apex of evil that the British had the "duty to exorcise" had become dominant.[11] In *Heart of Darkness*, this transition figures in the map of Africa as it evolves within the European imagination: Africa "had ceased to be a blank space of delightful mystery—a white patch for a boy to dream gloriously over. It had become a place of darkness" (9). As "emissary[ies] of light" (14), missionaries were just the right types to traverse this darkened map, which they helped to draw within the European imagination.

Christian missionaries were prime purveyors of enthusiastic narratives of African improvement, serving as the benevolent voice of European expansion. In the nineteenth century, the influence of this literature was pervasive and its reading public, massive, extending far beyond those directly involved in missions. No travel writer was more famous than the missionary-explorer and autobiographer, David Livingstone. Livingstone's *Missionary Travels and Researches in South Africa* was a runaway success, selling more than 70,000 copies just within the first few months of its release. Over the course of his career, this Scottish missionary of humble origins came to occupy the position of British national hero and saint. Imperial Britain had developed a great taste for stories of goodwilled adventure, of forging out through the unknown world in order to improve it, and while Livingstone was the most widely celebrated and known of such adventurers, he was one among many textual heroes. Publishing extensively for recruitment and fundraising, mission societies became the central disseminators of this new, magisterial story of travel to Africa.

Missionaries were prolific writers of diaries, letters, reports, histories, memoirs, ethnographies, novels, and children's books, filling vast archives with tales of the world abroad.[12] The mission societies controlled considerable wealth, enabling the frequent publication of magazines and books that painted a romantic picture of missionaries and their work. Titles like *Pioneer Days in Darkest Africa* and *A Hero of the Dark Continent* are in themselves suggestive of the tone and message of these narratives. *The Romance of Missionary Heroism: True Stories of the Intrepid Bravery, and Stirring Adventures of Missionaries with Uncivilized Man, Wild Beasts, and the Forces of Nature in All Parts of the World* (yes, that's all one title) is especially capacious. As the author of the latter text, John Chisholm Lambert, explains in the introduction, he hopes that "some of those into whose hands this book may come will be induced by what they read to make fuller acquaintance with the lives and aims of our missionary heroes, and so will catch something of that spirit which led them to face innumerable dangers, toils, and trials among heathen and often savage peoples."[13] The stories contained therein are as adventurous as the title promises, and it seems they were indeed effective for stirring up interest in missionaries.

The purpose of such narratives was not only to inform but to inspire, and this goal had implications in terms of plot, character, setting, and style. In other words, narrative technique was harnessed to perform moral work. Humanitarian fundraising campaigns echo this approach today, hoping their audiences "catch something of that spirit," too. In a study of missionaries' accounts of their "call" to the mission field, Ruth Rouse finds that the Bible was hardly ever mentioned but that literary and biographical tales of missionary heroes were frequently cited as pivotal influences.[14] As Anna Johnston has shown in the British imperial context, the aims of missionary publications were to raise support and engage new potential missionaries, so they tended to conform closely to a set of conventions built for that purpose. Missionary writing consistently emphasized the positive, while many of the failures and disappointments that were the reality of the experience went unrecorded. "Backsliding missionaries" who lost their faith or "formed attachments to local women or communities" fell out of historical documentation, and the heroes of these narratives did not experience doubt, compromise, or straightforward failure.[15] Nor did their writers: "By its nature, missionary literature is hardly ever self-critical. Even today, it is still as self-serving as a trade journal or a school magazine. Quite unashamedly, its intention is to raise morale, money and manpower."[16] J. D. Y. Peel explains, "Mission was intended to be governed by a script, ultimately derived from Scripture, but it also had to respond to practical contingencies that could not be controlled. The reassertion of discursive control in the narratives served to restore faith in mission itself."[17] Therefore, in order to account for failure and hardship, missionary journals "sought to redeem them through narratives of being tested by suffering, of errors corrected, of the precedents for hope and perseverance and so forth."[18] Romantic images of piety, nobility, and rousing success glossed over the difficult and disappointing realities of mission life, producing an inspiring but incomplete narrative.[19]

The story of Alexander Mackay, "The Hero of Uganda," a chapter in Lambert's *Romance of Missionary Heroism*, is exemplary. Published in 1907, this global collection of missionary stories follows in the footsteps of its Victorian predecessors. The bulk of Mackay's tale documents feats of skill, bravery, and unwavering faith, ranging from the "demonstration of the white man's mechanical power" to his defiance of a local king who massacres thousands of people in random acts of blood lust.[20] Events that could be construed in terms of failure are instead framed as

> a time of fiery trial for the mission. Mackay and his companions
> were daily threatened with death, and death was made the penalty of
> listening to their teaching or even of reading the Bible in secret. Many
> of Mackay's pupils and converts were tortured and burnt to death; but
> in Uganda as elsewhere the old saying came true that "the blood of the
> martyrs is the seed of the Church."[21]

Africa, by this representation, is a setting primed for adventure, a place of terror and depravity where missionaries and their converts must constantly face violence by shadowy, unnamed sources. Like a foil character, the setting allows the protagonist to shine in a way he would not against a softer background. To represent violence, Lambert couches it in readymade narrative tropes ("the fiery trial") and truisms ("the blood of the martyrs") that redirect readers from what would be a terrifying climax (torture and death by burning) and toward the abstract realm of Christian discourse. There is no internal focalizer to give readers access to the scene; the "wisdom" of an old saying takes over the narrative voice, overriding the perspectives of any witnesses. This move away from direct narration enables Lambert to draw readers' inter-

pretation away from devastation and toward success, which is ultimately the
place of emphasis:

> Inquirers became far more numerous than ever; men stole into the
> houses of missionaries by night and begged to be baptized; and there
> were cases when bolder ones went openly to the court and proclaimed
> that they were Christians, though they knew that their confession
> would immediately be followed by a cruel death. . . . Certain it is that
> it was by the tearful sowing of Mackay and his companions in those
> gloomy days that there was brought about that time of plentiful and
> joyful reaping which came in Uganda by and by.[22]

Again, we see narration through abstraction. The perspective is totally removed from the physical world in which the story unfolds. The narrator takes
a God's-eye-view with both the time to wait and the vantage point from which
to see what good is reaped long after "tearful sowing." This point of view
exists beyond the constraints of human experience. The "gloomy days" are
neatly packed into a sentence that begins with certainty and ends with joy.
Mackay's own death to malarial fever is similarly abstracted within a vision of
glory. After his death, thousands of Ugandans gather to worship, overflowing
the church building and, by their very presence, attesting to the missionary's
heroic success. Wrangling a happy ending out of a death story allows it to serve
its purpose to inspire the audience and rally them around the moral cause.

While the popularity of such narratives crystallized around biographical and
autobiographical missionary accounts, these romantic images of the Christian
mission found their place in novels as well. The dramatic characters of missionary autobiography were ripe for adaptation to heroic fiction. Brantlinger's
survey of nineteenth-century novels featuring missionaries reveals a strong
tendency toward hero worship.[23] His examples range from the historical romance of Sydney Owenson's *The Missionary* to the youthful adventure fiction
of Robert Ballantyne in *The Coral Island*, *The Gorilla Hunters*, and *Jarwin and
Cuffy*. In Charlotte Yonge's bestseller *The Daisy Chain* (1856), "Ethel calls
becoming a missionary 'the most glorious thing a man can do!' (517), and
many Victorians agreed."[24] In *The Coral Island*, Ballantyne affirms that sentiment. The youthful castaways witness incredible transformations wrought
by Christian missions, a "convincing proof that Christianity is of God!"[25]
They (and the pirates with whom they sail) determine landing spots based
on patterns of Christianization; they seek areas with high conversion rates
to avoid being "captured by the ill-disposed tribes" and potentially "roasted
alive and eaten."[26] The African setting becomes a patchwork of relative safety

and relative danger based on mission influence. They are captured nonetheless, but a British missionary arrives just in time to save them physically and the idolatrous villagers spiritually. The suspense of the narrative is driven by concern for the fate of European characters, not African ones. In this period, the missionary had a proud place at the forefront of both the popular and the literary imagination as a hero in a hostile land.

While many of these texts are unfamiliar today, the glorified literary missionary has also taken more enduring forms. Perhaps the most memorable example comes from Charlotte Brontë's *Jane Eyre* (1847). As narrator, Jane gives her final word to the missionary St. John Rivers. Although she has rejected his proposal to become a missionary's wife and the novel exposes his imperial cast of mind, she ultimately treats him with great respect. Her closing description offers a glowing assessment of his character:

> As to St. John Rivers, he left England: he went to India. He entered on the path he had marked for himself; he pursues it still. A more resolute, indefatigable pioneer never wrought amidst rocks and dangers. Firm, faithful, and devoted; full of energy, and zeal, and truth, he labours for his race: he clears their painful way to improvement; he hews down like a giant the prejudices of creed and caste that encumber it. He may be stern; he may be exacting; he may be ambitious yet; but his is the sternness of the warrior Greatheart, who guards his pilgrim-convoy from the onslaught of Apollyon. His is the exaction of the apostle, who speaks but for Christ, when he says—"Whosoever will come after me, let him deny himself, and take up his cross and follow me."[27]

Although *Jane Eyre* is not a missionary novel per se, St. John enters the scene with the key characteristics of the white savior narrative attached to him. He is a character of allegorical proportions, as is a convention of missionary literature. In this scene, the missionary is superhuman, comparable to Greatheart, the heroic protector of *The Pilgrim's Progress* who ensures the advance of the Christian travelers. The missionary is thus the supposed vehicle of progress and its prime defender against the pagan forces that hinder it. Although St. John's strand of the narrative never actually follows him to India, it doesn't need to. The grand missionary narrative is less about the land to which one travels than about the "indefatigable pioneer," the mythic figure, the faithful apostle forging ahead on the "painful way to improvement"—or, in other words, the white savior.

In Jane's description of St. John, we see all the core tropes of the white savior narrative: the missionary hero sacrificing his all "amidst rocks and dangers," the high-minded goal of improvement and the triumphant tale of its quest, the confidence of being on God's side, and the elevated language of lofty pursuits. To deliver this message, the unique voice of the generally opinionated Jane drops away. The abstraction we see here mirrors the narrative strategy of Lambert's missionary narratives. In this passage, Jane's narratorial voice becomes mythic and removed from interiority that characterizes most of the novel. This extracts St. John from Jane's critical tendencies and elevates him to the realm of humanitarian neutrality. Yet even through the triumphant rhetoric, we begin to see the risks of such unwavering zeal. St. John's work is more about clearing away, hewing down, and defending against than it is about giving or caring or building anything up. And for all his self-denying, he is quite a dominating self. As the final line suggests, following Christ becomes contingent on following the human leader who speaks on his behalf, and this commitment to improvement contains a destructive edge.

My larger point here—which applies both to the specific history of missionaries and to the argument of *Humanitarian Fictions* as a whole—is that the Western consciousness of Africa has been profoundly shaped by missionary narratives and their nonstate project of African improvement. They cast a transnational vision of progress, related to but also distinct from the state-sponsored civilizing mission, articulated in terms of a moral calling that transcends the earthly realm of governance. Their tales of romantic adventure brought the missionary hero who saves and civilizes into literary prominence along with a heroic narrative trajectory that instills faith in the ultimate triumph of the mission, even as the hero endures awful trials in "the dark places of the earth."[28] This narrative form and cluster of tropes did not die out with the end of the Victorian era. They continued to appear in missionary publications, political discourse, and popular culture.[29] In the second half of the twentieth century, they would appear more prominently in secular (or semisecular) iterations—Western altruists venturing into inhospitable lands to save Africans' lives though not necessarily their souls.

Thinking through and beyond the Missionary

With *Heart of Darkness*, Conrad undercuts the white savior narrative by appropriating its expectations, characters, and high-flown rhetoric. From a boat on the Thames, the main narrator, Charles Marlow, recounts his journey up the Congo River to find the illustrious (and infamous) Mr. Kurtz at an inner ivory station. Like popular missionary narratives of the nineteenth century, *Heart of Darkness* tells of the white man's adventure in the "dark places of the earth" unreached by "civilization" (5). At the center of the action, Kurtz is a captivating mission figure. In life, he bravely pursues his cause, and in death he is commemorated (by the underinformed) as a martyr, a model of "goodness shown in every act" (95). Like the missionary hero destined to save Africa, Kurtz is a man of unwavering faith who also inspires the "faith" and "devotion" of others (94, 69). As a journalist explains to Marlow, "He had faith—don't you see?—he had the faith. He could get himself to believe anything—anything" (90). Kurtz's faith is not conventionally religious; it isn't exactly in God but in himself. He insists, even as he is taken away from his ivory station in the end, "I'll carry my ideas out yet—I will return. I'll show you what can be done" (77). In *Heart of Darkness*, the moral cause is not centered on religious salvation but more vaguely on "ideas." In setting up the story for his listeners, Marlow also puts it in these terms: "What redeems [conquest] is the idea only. An idea at the back of it; not a sentimental pretence but an idea; and an unselfish belief in the idea—something you can set up, and bow down before, and offer a sacrifice to" (8). The idea, in other words, is a kind of god.

With Kurtz and Marlow, both members of "the new gang—the gang of virtue" (30), we witness the dispersion of the white savior narrative beyond the religious missionary. On the one hand, the new "gang of virtue" marks a contrast to the gang of vice, drawing attention to altruistic motivations, or at least rationale, for travel (with the altruism immediately undercut by the name "gang"). But this "new gang" also marks a transition in the history of the virtuous traveler, anticipating the humanitarian developer's outgrowth from the role of the religious missionary. Colonial humanitarianism was the task of missionaries, but around the turn of the century, when Conrad was writing, the explicitly religious discourse was expanding into a secular humanist discourse; what would then distinguish the "new global institutions of care in the twentieth century" was "the apparent willingness of individuals to cite humanity and not God as their reason for caring for the welfare of others."[30] We can better understand Kurtz and Marlow and the discourse surrounding them by situating them within this transitional moment. They are not actual missionaries, yet they exist within a missionary-saturated framework. They are understood within British imperial culture through Christian terminology and imagery, much like that ascribed to Brontë's St. John.

We are introduced to this religiously infused rhetoric by Marlow's aunt, who, through her connections, has secured him a position with the generically named Company. When Marlow goes to say goodbye to her before his departure, he finds her "triumphant": "It appeared," according to her description, "that I was also one of the Workers, with a capital—you know. Something like an emissary of light, something like a lower sort of apostle. . . . She talked about 'weaning those ignorant millions from their horrid ways,' till, upon my word, she made me quite uncomfortable" (14). The savior narrative appears to have taken firm hold beyond its religious provenance; through the structure of this narrative, Marlow's aunt understands him as a missionary hero—as one of God's "Workers" with a capital W, carrying light into the darkness. This is a dominant discourse, which echoes the abstract narrative voice of preceding missionary texts. The savior narrative is powerful enough to trigger an automatic assumption that a white person going to Africa must be on some kind of altruistic mission, even when he declares otherwise. In contrast to the celebratory missionary accounts described previously, this one is filtered through the unbelieving voice of a narrator who does not accept its terms. Marlow introduces the critique of his aunt's triumphant attitude, pointing out that "there had been a lot of such rot let loose in print and talk just about that time, and the excellent woman, living right in the rush of all that humbug, got carried off her feet. . . . I ventured to hint that the Company was run for profit" (14). While he will attribute her misconception to "how out of touch with truth women are," he nonetheless shows it to be a much deeper cultural phenomenon. The heroic missionary narrative circulates through a proliferation of "print and talk" and infiltrates the way that travel to Africa is understood, regardless of actual motives.

This Christian-derived language is spoken not only on the home front but by the travelers who define their own roles in relation to Africa. Kurtz takes this discourse to the Congo and more firmly into the terrain of transnational development. The secularized savior narrative receives its fullest articulation in his report for the International Society for the Suppression of Savage Customs, which Marlow describes as "a beautiful piece of writing":

> He began with the argument that we whites, from the point of development we had arrived at, "must necessarily appear to them [savages] in the nature of supernatural beings—we approach them with the might as of a deity," and so on, and so on. "By the simple exercise of our will we can exert a power for good practically unbounded," etc., etc. From that point he soared and took me with him. The peroration was magnificent, though difficult to remember, you know. It gave me the notion of an exotic Immensity ruled by an august Benevolence. It made me tingle with enthusiasm. This was the unbounded power of eloquence—of words—of burning noble words. (61–62, brackets in original)

Marlow emphasizes the emotional effects of Kurtz's text. To "tingle with enthusiasm" is to experience the affective dimension of the white savior narrative according to which, in Teju Cole's satiric words, "The world is nothing but

a problem to be solved by enthusiasm."[31] Even for a skeptic like Marlow, the
narrative is irresistible when articulated so eloquently. Part of the appeal of
white saviorism is its grandeur. The potential for good is "unbounded"; the
path to progress involves a "simple exercise" of will; "Benevolence" merits a
capital B. Kurtz's rhetoric of African improvement, like Marlow's aunt's, is
punctuated with Christian references. His report, as summarized by Marlow,
weds the languages of development and religion, infusing the former with
spiritual authority. For Kurtz, development is next to godliness. This creates
an ontological gulf between white Europeans and black Africans, the former
becoming superhuman ("supernatural") and the latter, subhuman ("savages").
The onus is thus on "we whites" to bring "them" up to scratch. This description also reveals the entanglement of race, religion, and authority, putting
the "white" in Cole's White Savior Industrial Complex. As was the case with
Charlotte Brontë's St. John, following the deity and following the white man
become one and the same. The white man in this structure is God's emissary;
the West, accordingly, is not only a political authority but a spiritual one. If
development is next to godliness, then whiteness and Westernness are right
there with it. In other words, the power of the white West gets deified. This
history clarifies the racist resonance in contemporary humanitarian discourse
that never explicitly mentions race.

While the link between whiteness and divinity can be applied to colonialism and its justificatory civilizing mission, Conrad also illuminates a narrower
phenomenon — a set of Europeans, exemplified by the figure of the missionary, who are in Africa not in the name of country or commerce, but in the
name of virtue itself. *Heart of Darkness* asks us to think about the sham of
colonial benevolence generally but also more specifically about those who,
like Kurtz, travel to Africa "equipped with moral ideas," a group that gets
separated in name (though not necessarily in action) from those who aim
merely to "tear treasure out of the bowels of the land . . . with no more moral
purpose at the back of it than there is in a burglar's breaking into a safe" (37,
36). Although the outcomes for mercenary and missionary types become indistinguishable in *Heart of Darkness*, they emerge from different frameworks.
Therefore, it is beneficial to situate Kurtz specifically within this category of
"special" whites (30), nonstate travelers with "moral purpose" irrespective of
moral practice. Kurtz is set apart from colonialists and capitalists not merely
by his own rhetoric but by that of other Europeans in the Congo. His success
within the Company is suggestive of the popular rise of the virtuous discourse;
he has personally profited from speaking it well, gaining a position as chief
of the best ivory station. The envious manager of a lower station describes
him as an "emissary of pity, and science, and progress, and devil knows what

else" (30). The fact that Kurtz has become a kind of "special being" in the Company (30), rewarded over the straightforward materialists, points to the growing power of missionary discourse in defining international development after the Scramble for Africa. It is his status as a traveler with "moral purpose" that makes Kurtz particularly dangerous.[32]

Linking the religious language of the missionary narrative to more secular claims about development, *Heart of Darkness* prefigures the emergence of a third-sector humanitarian impulse within a profit-oriented, quasi-governmental setting, growing out of the framework of Christian missions. *Heart of Darkness* takes up the missionary figure, extending beyond his strictly religious manifestation, to look at international actors whose roles are external to the state—enabled by it, absolutely, but external nonetheless. Kurtz and Marlow are partially political outsiders—Brits in the Belgian Congo. Their relation to the for-profit sector also consists of a mixed insider-outsider status. Marlow travels as part of a for-profit company, while Kurtz, an employee of the same company, defines himself as more of a volunteer. Regardless of their divergent self-definitions, the other employees tend to place Kurtz and Marlow together in a camp separate from their own. The language of virtue comes from another Company employee who positions Marlow, like his aunt does, as a kind of missionary: "You are of the new gang—the gang of virtue."[33] Although Conrad breaks down the distinction between virtue and vice, revealing the bankruptcy of the moral cause, this "new gang" represents an emergent impulse toward international projects of improvement following a third path, the path of the missionary, as a deliberate, if not entirely accurate, contrast to the paths of the colonialist and the trader. Reading Kurtz not only as imperialist or profiteer but as missionary opens up new frameworks for situating Conrad and the writers who follow him. The literature of the third sector explores global expansion that occurs beyond the aegis of government or profit, all the while showing the ways this third sector is indeed entangled with both. As Conrad's gossipy side characters show, different narratives get attached to those who are independent of government and profit, even if only in name.

The Moral Cause and the Ethics of Doubt

By distinguishing the "gang of virtue" from materialist interests, *Heart of Darkness* subjects the "burning noble" discourse of the third sector to a more precise critique (30, 62). Against missionary confidence, this cultivates an ethics of doubt. Foundationally, this occurs at the level of style. Through techniques like multiple narrative frames, meandering syntax, and lack of referents, the book destabilizes meaning. While the narrative revolves around Kurtz, readers access him only through layers of narration: Marlow tells his story, which an unnamed frame narrator then relays. Much of what Marlow himself learns about Kurtz comes from the mouths of others. For example, his early impression of the man is based on secondhand gossip. He overhears a company manager mimicking Kurtz, saying, "'Each station should be like a beacon on the road toward better things, a centre for trade of course, but also for humanizing, improving, instructing.' Conceive you—that ass!" (40). Marlow is straining to hear a conversation he is not a part of while pulling himself out of a doze, relaying to readers "bits of absurd sentences" and stringing them together as he comes to consciousness (38); not until the end of a convoluted paragraph does he even provide the context that "They had been talking about Kurtz." This creates a sense of perceptual murkiness, forcing readers into an experience of doubt, of having to question their comprehension and circle back to follow along.[34] My point here is that Conrad's famously ambiguous style responds specifically to the religious savior narrative and the missionary texts that disseminate it, formally refuting its stylistic certainty. Progressing through this kind of text is a nonlinear experience. One must grope carefully through Conrad's Congo; his style makes it impossible to march through with the confident cadence of the white savior. This is mirrored thematically as the sailors on the river squint unseeingly through the thick vegetation of the shore. The text constantly produces a sense of knowing that one does not know Africa, let alone how to save it.

The novel form in general lends itself to this kind of uncertainty because of the way it handles voice and character, putting multiple discourses into debate. Mikhail Bakhtin argues that the novel's protagonist exists in a unique narratological world: "The crucial distinction between him and the epic hero is to be found in the fact that the hero of a novel not only acts but talks, too, and his action has no shared meaning for the community, is not uncontested and takes place not in an uncontested epic world where all meanings are shared."[35] In this case, while Marlow is the protagonist and main focalizer whose movements the novella follows, Kurtz is the primary figure of interest, echoing the fascination of the missionary hero. He is the voice of the moral cause, and in fact Marlow pictures him in those terms: "I had never imagined him as doing, you know, but as discoursing. . . . The man presented himself as a voice" (58). Kurtz speaks and is spoken about, leaving his perspective "always open to contest."[36] In this way, the discourse of African salvation comes under question. As Bakhtin explains, "The idea of testing the hero, of testing his discourse, may very well be the most fundamental organizing idea in the novel. . . . In the epic world, an atmosphere of doubt surrounding the hero's heroism is unthinkable."[37] Conrad takes this "atmosphere of doubt" to an extreme. In contrast to the nominally nonfiction narratives that enshrined missionaries like Mackay as epic heroes, the form of the novel complicates their position (as was the case even in *Jane Eyre*). The first time readers encounter the voice of Kurtz, not only is it coming through three layers of narration, but it is immediately followed by the manager's epithet for him, "that ass!" (40). This follows the accountant's description of Kurtz, the first Marlow receives, as "a very remarkable person" (22). Each of these speakers has his own agenda, and no perspective is beyond dispute.

Within this contested world, missionary characters and their discourses take on new meanings. The heroic missionary becomes a pitiful failure. This trope is captured by a British teacher in Paul Theroux's *Girls at Play* who asks, "Who wants to live in Africa, what white people? Only cranks, fools, failures."[38] Her phrase nicely articulates the stock of characters from which Conrad and Kingsolver draw, throwing into relief the indefatigable pioneer, devout laborer, and ambitious warrior we saw in *Jane Eyre*. Characters of the celebratory missionary narrative go to Africa in a grand gesture of faith, forgoing good circumstances at home to do God's work abroad. Mackay of "The Hero of Uganda," for example, is highly educated and highly skilled: "So marked were his constructive talents that one of his employers offered him a partnership in a large engineering concern; but what would have seemed a tempting opportunity to most men was no temptation to him. Already his heart was in the mission field."[39] James Hannington, "The Lion-Hearted Bishop" of the same collection, has left a good life in England where he was "happily settled" with a role in the church and "a wife and young children to whom he was passionately attached. But the call he heard was one to which he could give no denial. For Christ and for Africa he felt that he must be willing to suffer the loss of all things."[40] These figures sacrifice good lives at home for an undisputed higher purpose abroad. In contrast, Kurtz goes to Africa because there isn't much else for him; he seeks to fill the holes in his own life by claiming to improve others'. In England, he is confined by his class status, and he hopes that in Africa he can supersede it. Marlow recalls, "He had given me some reason to infer that it was his impatience of comparative poverty that drove him out there" (94). This affects Kurtz's pride as well as his marriage prospects. His engagement "had been disapproved by [his Intended's] people. He wasn't rich enough or something" (93). Going to the Congo is an opportunity to secure his "ascendency," to write his own story with himself as the hero (72). Through inference, Marlow puts together the subtext that underlies Kurtz's grand tale. Declared intentions for the good of others are layered with selfish aspirations.

Around this less-than-respectable character, Conrad weaves a plot that fails the expectations of the savior narrative — which has inspired Kurtz's own expectations — turning its trajectory, romance, and triumphalism upside down. If Kurtz's beginning is humble, his ending is far worse. Heroes paired with grand outcomes in the white savior narrative are replaced by failures with catastrophic ends. In Kurtz, we see a particularly dangerous relationship between declared goodwill and good results. His grand missionary narrative assumes a happy ending and demands very little of the beginning and the middle: the "*simple* exercise of our will" is supposedly enough to produce "good practically unbounded" (61). This is the problematic underpinning of the moral cause, which implies not only that white people can improve Africa but that it will be a straightforward task. This oversimplification, *Heart of Darkness* suggests, is one of the key pitfalls for humanitarian fictions of the white savior variety. By pairing dazzling expectations with a dismal outcome, Conrad highlights the white savior narrative's problematic faith in the equation of good intentions and good results. Instead of saving anyone from "savage customs" as he intends to do, Kurtz turns savage himself, adorning the pathway to his house with heads on stakes. "Power for good practically unbounded" becomes unbounded power. The mission hero self-destructs, and anticipated glory becomes actual horror. In contrast to the missionary narrative tradition, there is no "time of plentiful and joyful reaping [to come] by and by."

This isn't simply a matter of good intentions gone wrong. The moral cause is more deeply compromised than the logic of unintended consequences would suggest. As an ivory trader, Kurtz is in the Congo primarily for material reasons, no matter how insistently he claims the contrary. In Kurtz, then, we have two character types rolled into one — the missionary and the mercenary. Typically, the white savior depends on the presence of minor white characters who are colonialists, capitalists, or both because the contrast defines his singular goodness. *Heart of Darkness* obliterates that contrast. In this tale of devastation, written against preceding narratives of glory, the "emissary of light" becomes a priest of darkness. Kurtz's dying words — "The horror! The horror!" — serve as a summing up of his dark reign on earth, showing how those who travel for glory can turn out to be hypocritical, dictatorial, and often violent (86). In *Heart of Darkness*, the language of "heavenly mission" has a racist vision of extermination appended to it (8). To his final report for the International Society for the Suppression of Savage Customs, that "beautiful piece of writing" about "august Benevolence," he adds a postscript: "at the end of that moving appeal to every altruistic sentiment it blazed at you, luminous and terrifying, like a flash of lightning in a serene sky: Exterminate all the brutes!" (62). "Altruistic sentiment" and violent rage coexist in the same person and even in the same declaration of values. In the words of J. Hillis Miller, "The benign project of civilizing the dark places of the world becomes the conscious desire to annihilate everything which opposes man's absolute will."[41] Kurtz embodies the crux between altruism and annihilation. Through this uncomfortable mingling of two types within a single character, Conrad asks readers to think through the relationship between benevolent goals and brutal realities, between "good practically unbounded" and "exterminate all the brutes." He chips away at the easy acceptance with which good intentions are so often met and chastens the expectation of positive ends. *Heart of Darkness* and the novels that follow in its footsteps point to the entanglement of altruism, profit-seeking, and violence, anticipating arguments that foreign aid does more damage than good and ultimately inflicts its own kind of violence.

The remote setting that brings missionaries and mercenaries together also contributes to their murderous potentialities, less available in spaces with greater accountability. These isolated places, beyond the paths of almost all other white people, serve as a release from the bounds of civility. An Englishman in a colony not his own, Kurtz lives far beyond communities familiar to him, and the detachment this creates is not amended by genuine connection in his destination. This detachment also appears in Marlow's language when he describes African people as "bundles of acute angles" sitting under trees and as "a whirl of black limbs, a mass of hands clapping, of feet stamping, of bodies swaying, of eyes rolling" (20, 43). Black bodies are treated as landscape. Neighbors considered less human to any degree are surely not arbiters of accountability. In such isolation, the traveler lives with "no external checks" (26), facing what John A. McClure calls "the archetypal temptation of the colonial wilderness";[42] this enables a character like Kurtz to unleash the most violent impulses, and his presence in Africa is thus not only unhelpful, but outrageously destructive. Instead of the enlightened minds he promised, we find, on the path to Kurtz's house, heads on stakes.

Good intentions in *Heart of Darkness* and related white-people-in-Africa novels give way to accidental destruction at best and murderous rage at worst. These critical humanitarian fictions ask if the impulse to "exterminate the brutes" is always the sordid underside of projects of good intentions. Is it the predictable result of plans that will meet the inevitable resistance in environments unfamiliar to their creators? Emerging from this discussion are two concentrated nodes of ambivalence in the missionary mentality in both its religious and its secular humanitarian forms. The first is the tension between self-sacrifice and self-serving. The second has to do with the relationship between benevolent care and violence. Since transforming people is the goal, the missionary mentality risks hatred toward those people, especially when they resist transformation. V. Y. Mudimbe's description of the terms of African conversion clarifies that this risk of violence is inherent in the totalizing faith that the white savior narrative espouses: "a person whose ideas and mission come from and are sustained by God is rightly entitled to the use of all possible means, even violence, to achieve his objectives."[43] On the one hand, missionary types have been in positions to interact with local people on a more intimate level than colonialists and traders. But, on the other, threaded through this interaction is a vein of tension between human sympathy and explosive racism, between a desire to help and a desire to kill, whether it manifests itself in actual violence as is the case with Kurtz or violence in more symbolic forms. Conversion, whether it means souls to Christianity, minds to enlightenment, or African lands to European property, wipes away or (to use Brontë's phrase) "hews down" the previous order. A narrative of improvement dependent on conversion implies a basis of destruction. In other words, these humanitarian fictions reveal how narratives of salvation are also narratives of annihilation. Through its fundamental dialogism, the novel form is apt to display both.

Transforming the destructive potential of the moral cause would depend on a practice of doubt. With doubt, an altruistic goal can be held within the context of a different narrative, accompanied by a different way of thinking about oneself in relation to that goal and to the people one aims to assist. Through altering the white savior narrative, Conrad effects a dramatic dwindling of confidence. The problem with confidence is a problem of perception defined by certainty of one's view of the world and in one's capacity to fully grasp it. Confidence in the mission allows one to carry on in the face of numerous signs not to. A better alternative, if it exists at all, would replace absolute confidence with the self-conscious practice of doubt. Kurtz's only moment which even approaches "moral victory," in Marlow's estimation, is in the ultimate declaration of self-doubt in his final words, "The horror! The horror!" (86).

This critique of missionary confidence gestures toward a better alternative only by implication. One image stands out as a crystallization of this idea. Before meeting Kurtz, Marlow discovers one of his paintings, emblematic of his character: "a small sketch in oils, on a panel, representing a woman, draped and blindfolded, carrying a lighted torch. The background was somber—almost black. The movement of the woman was stately, and the effect of the torch-light on the face was sinister" (29–30). As a torchbearer in darkness, she mirrors the position of the "emissary of light," but in this image, self-delusion like Kurtz's is literalized: this emissary of light is blind. Notwithstanding the inability to see, she moves ahead with dignified confidence, as if unaware of her own blindness. It is an act of faith. Despite her stately pose, the over-all tone of the image is sinister, so her comfortable confidence seems mis-placed. The precarious nature of this movement—simultaneously confident and unseeing—characterizes the "emissary of light" more generally. It is also significant that she is blindfolded, not actually sightless; her blinders can po-tentially be removed. *Heart of Darkness* calls for a much closer examination of the mission discourse and the jump that is made from declared intentions to an easy sense of triumph. The first step toward more vision, however, is in fact less, seeing the fact that one does not fully see.[44] Travelers who are aware of their limited vision will tread more carefully. Transnational altruism would be less glamorous but also less dangerous if it were to replace its inflated march with a humble, tentative step.

With its own sense of "moral ownership"[45] of suffering, contemporary humanitarianism too often positions itself "beyond criticism"[46]—the gang of virtue in contrast to the gang of vice. Often, humanitarians practice a faith worryingly close to Kurtz's. As Michael Barnett explains, they act on "a be-lief that God is on their side; that they represent the best of humanity; that they have the expertise because of their experience and education; and that a victim's lack of resources or education indicates that he might not know what is in his best interests."[47] The white savior narrative, as a sanctification of international action on the basis of moral purpose (as opposed to power or profit) reinforces that insularity. Its self-perpetuating quality justifies the mis-sion's existence and enables its ongoing presence, often in spite of its effects. This also taps into questions of motives. What actually underlies humanitar-ians' noble cause? Critics suggest that "the conventional, widely popularized humanitarian position of moral high ground and mastery can actually be a fiction on many levels."[48] For example, Liisa H. Malkki finds that humanitar-ian interest is less about selflessness than about "self-escape, self-loss, dehu-manization, self-humanization, self-transformation, the care of the self, the relation of self to others, and the relation of the self to the world," all of which she finds to be common driving factors.[49] This is not to say that aid workers are latter-day Kurtzes, but that he does encapsulate ethical risks faced by hu-manitarians today.

White Savior Pathology in *The Poisonwood Bible*

The Poisonwood Bible takes the white-people-go-to-Africa story into the era of decolonization. Through the expanded role of Kingsolver's Kurtz figure, Na-than Price, we gain a fuller view of white saviorism as pathology. While *Heart of Darkness* is set in the early years of Belgian colonization of the Congo,

Kingsolver's missionaries enter the country in 1959, the year before independence, and the narrative follows them nearly to the end of the century, a period in which the language of mission became concentrated in the United States as the postcolonial mission nation. When the Price family arrives from Georgia, they view the place through a lens like Marlow's. Orleanna Price, self-described as "the conqueror's wife" and "a conquest herself," explains that she, her husband Nathan, and four daughters "stepped down there on a place we believed unformed, where only darkness moved on the face of the waters."[50] This perspective situates not only the Congo but the whole continent at the origin of the Judeo-Christian timeline, just before God says, "Let there be light." The dark, unformed, watery place also recalls Marlow's journey "up that river [which] was like travelling back to the earliest beginnings of the world, when vegetation rioted on the earth and the big trees were kings" (Conrad, 41). The youngest daughter, Ruth May, has been warned by another American child in Sunday school that her family "better not go to the Congo on account of the cannibal natives would boil [them] in a pot and eat [them] up" (Kingsolver, 21). This echoes sensationalist missionary narratives as well as *Heart of Darkness*, in which Marlow calls the local crew members "cannibals" and is relieved that they eat hippo meat rather than eating him. When Nathan, the preacher and patriarch in *The Poisonwood Bible*, first arrives in the village of Kilanga, he responds to local people who have come to welcome his family with a message that parallels Kurtz's: "Get ye *out* from this place of *darkness*! *Arise* and come forward into a *brighter land*!" (28). Whereas Kurtz communicates more through his reputation than his presence within the narrative, *The Poisonwood Bible* offers a more extended encounter with the self-appointed "emissary of light."

That sense of African darkness is an important part of the journey, since risk and sacrifice are key elements of the white savior narrative. Nathan's most fawning daughter, Leah, explains that their family constitutes "God's special delegation to Kilanga. [Father] says we're being brave and righteous. Bravery and righteousness—those are two things that cannot go unrewarded in the sight of the Lord. Father never doubts it, and I can see for him that it's true" (244). Again, in parallel with Kurtz, Nathan situates himself in the category of special whites who go into Africa driven not by profit but by moral purpose. Materially speaking, the Price family gives up a great deal for the sake of the mission. The daughters narrate their departure from the United States in a section called "The Things We Carried," which documents, almost as an inventory, the possessions they leave behind and those they smuggle under their clothing, the trappings of a middle-class American life. The great cost is an essential part of Nathan's performance. He puts it this way: "God created a world of work and rewards . . . on a big balanced scale. . . . Small works of goodness over here . . . small rewards over here. . . . Great sacrifice, great rewards!" (37). Nathan follows a narrative logic; a story that begins with sacrifice ends with a proportionate reward. This form of sacrifice is transactional and ultimately self-serving, thus flipping the supposed positions of benefactor and beneficiary, but Nathan isn't aware of the irony.

The nature of that transaction depends on the personal needs of the "savior." The unwavering strength of Nathan's commitment to his moral cause belies deep-seated psychological vulnerabilities. Fashioning himself as a mission hero, he displays "frightful confidence in himself" and remains impervious to change or critical reflection (94). He never speaks of his past, only of present labor and future reward. But in a brief backstory, his wife Orleanna describes damages he sustained as a soldier in World War II. As the only surviving member of his company, he had returned "home with a crescent-shaped scar on his temple, seriously weakened vision in his left eye, and a suspicion of his own cowardice from which he would never recover" (197). The psychic wound is the most serious. He cleaves to the white savior narrative for psychological self-protection, demonstrating its function as a compensatory tool. For Kurtz, it was insecurity about class. For Nathan, it cuts more deeply. Kurtz is a rising figure in his company; Nathan, however, fails to convince churchgoers in the United States that he would even be an adequate missionary, but he seems compelled to prove his bravery to himself at the very least. He thus forces himself upon the Congo "without the entire blessing of the Mission League, and bullie[s] or finagle[s] his way into [a] lesser stipend" in order to gain their tentative support (197, 69). They concede to letting him go only because "no one else volunteered" (39). Eventually, the Mission League cuts off even his minimal compensation, and the local community votes to reject Christianity. Unwelcome but unperturbed, Nathan stays on. His mission is driven by a crisis of ego and of masculinity. In addition to occupying Kilanga, he dominates his family. Orleanna feels "swallowed by Nathan's mission, body and soul. Occupied as if by a foreign power" (198). It is no longer implied that missionary figures are the West's finest stock. Characters like Nathan and Kurtz go to Africa hoping to achieve levels of success and glory which are out of their grasp at home, jumping on board with the white savior narrative to do so. They aim to become the heroes they have read about. For Nathan, it is also about internal stability; it is as if he couldn't live with himself otherwise. This demonstrates the performative function of the white savior narrative. It provides a ready-made script, which enables the actor to take on the moral cause not only as a goal but as an identity. It is a project of self-definition and self-glorification.

In *The Poisonwood Bible*, the pathological nature of the white savior complex is internally rooted and externally damaging. Missions and madness seem to go hand in hand. This is foreshadowed when another missionary couple "insist[s] that [the Price family's] mission last no more than one year—not enough time for going plumb crazy but only partway" (39). The assumption here is that Africa somehow breeds madness; instead, the novel shows the white savior complex to be the source. Nathan's preexisting psychological need for self-glorification finds dramatic opportunity in the Congo where it couldn't back home. Take, for example, his attempt to replicate the miracle of the loaves and fish. The over-the-top grandeur of the project ensures its doom: "To Kilanga's hungry people Our Father promised at summer's end the bounty of the Lord, more fish than they had ever seen in their lives. . . . So determined he is to win or force or drag them over to the Way of the Cross. Feed the belly first, he announced at dinner one night, seized with his brilliant plan. Feed the belly and the soul will come" (70). This "brilliant plan" involves buying dynamite from a mercenary pilot and throwing it into the river to stun the fish to death. This plan represents a deranged extension of a more common strand within the missionary's moral cause. Heather D. Curtis describes the "devotional discipline of imitating 'that Saviour who fed the hungry multitudes on the slopes of the Galilean shore,'" a practice by which "American evangelicals served as agents of divine blessing to the afflicted."[51] Christ himself becomes a character role to enact. Nathan's loud, violent entanglement of mission and masculine performance is dreadfully shortsighted, but he seems strangely oblivious to the damage. Following the dynamite's explosion, the fish

> came rolling to the surface with mouths opened wide by that shocking boom. . . . The whole village feasted all day, ate, ate till we felt bug-eyed and belly-up ourselves. . . . Slogging up and down the riverbank in trousers wet to the knees, his Bible in one hand and another stickful of fire-blackened fish in the other, he waved his bounty in a threatening manner. Thousands more fish jerked in the sun and went bad along the riverbanks. Our village was blessed for weeks with the smell of putrefaction. Instead of abundance it was a holiday of waste. (70)

Evident in this scene and throughout the novel, the line between altruism and violence dissolves. The missionary who attempts to insert himself into a redeeming narrative privileges drama over long-term results. Furthermore, Nathan's "devotion to all mankind" exists alongside a blatant disregard for life (8). This applies to the fish wastefully killed and, more importantly, to the people who depend on the river for food and who will face the consequences of its instantaneous overfishing. This disregard for life also applies to people more directly. Nathan will continue to insist on river baptism, even after finding out that the river is infested with crocodiles that have killed children, and thus baptism becomes a kind of terrorism (214). The transcendence of his moral cause untethers Nathan from the reality around him.

In these novels, would-be heroes of good intentions produce personal and public destruction. The mission impulse proves—sometimes literally—explosive. As a result, the movement "straight from [a] divinely inspired beginning to [a] terrible end" replaces the white savior narrative's triumphant plot (9). After his youngest daughter dies from a venomous snakebite, Nathan's unwavering dedication to the mission effectively dismantles his family. Her death is not an accident of nature, but a consequence of his own uncompromising will: the snake is planted by the local *nganga*—whom Nathan calls "witch doctor"—after Nathan refuses to heed numerous warnings to leave (131). By the end, the preacher turns into a mad wanderer. His family, having left Kilanga, receives word that he is "bearded, wild-haired, and struggling badly with malnutrition and parasites. Our house had burned. . . . Father ran off to a hut in the woods he was calling the New Church of Eternal Life" (417). Shortly thereafter, he leaves Kilanga and "vanishe[s] into the forest" (435). Through it all, he never gives up the mission. Years after the family's separation, Leah explains to her sister, "The people in that village [where he was loitering] had asked him to leave a hundred times, go someplace else, but he'd always sneak back. He said he wasn't going to go away till he'd taken every child in the village down to the river and dunked them under. Which just scared everybody to death" (486). He exhibits a troubled dependency on the village. When they eventually chase him away, he climbs up a colonial watchtower, which the villagers then set on fire, and he is killed by burning or by the animals that drag him off after he falls. The self-assuredness that characters like Nathan and Kurtz display is tied to their sense of a firm, unambiguous plot trajectory from sacrifice to reward. That narrative depends on glorious ends to justify any means, and those ends have been lost. Reversing the message of the white savior narrative, these men serve as warning, not as inspiration.

From Missionary Monologue to Dialogue and Doubt

As much as Kingsolver draws on *Heart of Darkness* as a precursor to her own novel, she also writes in the wake of African authors who challenged Conrad. By integrating the voices of writers and anticolonial leaders such as Chinua Achebe and Patrice Lumumba, Kingsolver expands her novel's intertextual world.[52] In the Author's Note, she includes *Things Fall Apart* on the short list of texts most crucial to her own writing and research. Achebe's novel resonates throughout Kingsolver's in the form of allusive echoes — in the efforts of chief Tata Ndu to defend his village from missionary encroachment, in the broader community conflict around the growth of the church, in the contrast between the absolutist and the accommodationist missionary, and in the congregation of outcasts (those who have birthed twins who had to be abandoned according to custom and those who, like Okonkwo of *Things Fall Apart*, have accidentally killed a clansman or child). In addition to such allusions, *The Poisonwood Bible* is shaped by Achebe on a philosophical level in its attitude toward missionaries, toward African history and tradition, and toward the claims of independence and the voices of its advocates. This is in itself a formal refutation of the white savior narrative as Western monologue.

Subscribing to the grand savior narrative produces a certain mode of inhabiting the world. One's place within the narrative determines how one situates oneself in relation to others, particularly those one has come to assist. It determines who speaks and who listens, who accepts help and who offers it. It determines who has a voice in decision making, whose vote counts and how much. V. Y. Mudimbe has argued that resistance to dialogue is definitive of missionary discourse. Coming from the "authority of truth," from a "speech that is always predetermined, pre-regulated, let us say *colonized*, . . . the missionary does not enter into dialogue with pagans and 'savages' but must impose the law of God that he incarnates."[53] Nathan's uncompromising narrative enables him to believe God is always firmly on his side and that any real conversation with local people would compromise his mission. Like Kurtz, Nathan is an orator and not a listener; their preacherly speech is defined by its "resistance to interruption."[54] The novel's title is derived from this resistance. Each Sunday, Nathan gives a sermon that requires translation. But, "mistrusting his interpreters," he repeatedly proclaims in his rudimentary Kikongo, "Tata Jesus is Bängala." He intends to say that Jesus is holy but instead compares him to poisonwood. This mistranslation isn't dependent on knowledge in a technical sense — he can spell the word correctly — but on an ability to manage the subtleties of the language. A change in tone transforms the word entirely, but understanding that would require careful, self-conscious listening, and Nathan distrusts any assertion that is not his own.

Arrogance, anger, and fear coalesce around his "resistance to interruption." When Nathan attempts to plant an American-style Kentucky Wonder Bean garden — an act of cultivation emblematic of his imposing vision — Mama Tataba, a local woman who helps around his house, tries to correct his technique. She points to his "flat-as-Kansas" beds and instructs him to mound the dirt into hills (63, 40). He dismisses the Congolese method and after she reshapes the dirt on her own, he goes back to flatten it. A kind of battle is underway. Of course, she turns out to be right. The torrential rain washes the seeds away, and Nathan finds himself back in the garden again "revising the earth": "Our father had been influenced by Africa," his daughter notes: "He was out there pushing his garden up into rectangular, flood-proof embank-ments" (63). This is exactly that kind of influence—the interruption in his own narrative—which he will soon steel himself against:

> Nathan would accept no more compromises. God was testing him like Job, he declared, and the point of that particular parable was that Job had done no wrong to begin with. Nathan felt it had been a mistake to bend his will, in any way, to Africa. To reshape his garden into mounds; to submit to Tata Ndu on the subject of river baptism; to listen at all to Tata Ndu or even the rantings of Mama Tataba. . . . He would not fail again. (97)

This moment is a reaffirmation of absolute faith. Nathan is in the Congo spe-cifically to reshape Congolese people, to make them submit, to make them listen, not the reverse. He seeks to sculpt a new Africa without making a dent to his own person. Nathan's resolute statement comes at the beginning of the novel's second book, "The Revelation," essentially the beginning of the end. The local community will ask him to compromise and will even democrati-cally vote him out of the church, but he will continually struggle to force an unruly reality into the strictures of his own narrative. In Nathan's eyes, failure is any violation of the savior narrative's singular trajectory. Conversion, in a broad sense, is here intended to be a heavily policed, one-way street. Mission is monologue.

By contrast, Kingsolver plays up the novel's fundamentally dialogic form. This dialogism is embodied in the character of Brother Fowles. As with Kurtz and Marlow, the doubling of the mission figure—one extremist and one skep-tic—sets their respective discourses in competition. Also an American mission-ary, Brother Fowles ran the Kilanga mission before Nathan until the mission-ary society removed him on the basis of his "unconventional alliances with the local people," most notably his marriage to a Congolese woman (38). He illus-trates a more ethical mission impulse dependent on doubt. That is not to say he is a nonbeliever. Kingsolver leaves room for the religious by showing that Fowles isn't theologically tepid; he displays vast biblical knowledge and pulls up passages by memory at least as easily as Nathan. Yet in contrast, he gives most attention to the places he has "always been a little perplexed by" (251).

Nathan quickly jumps at the opportunity to prove himself an authority over what he sees as the weakness of confusion, and his daughter Rachel recounts the exchange:

> "The American Translation might clear that up for you. It says, 'washed their wounds.'" Father sounded like the know-it-all kid in the class you just want to strangulate.
>
> "It does, yes," replied Brother Fowles, slowly. "And yet I wonder, who translated this? During my years here in the Congo I've heard so many errors of translation, even quite comical ones. So you'll forgive me if I'm skeptical, Brother Price." (251)

Nathan is incapable of dealing with such subtlety or the kind of questioning Brother Fowles represents. We would never hear Nathan saying an open-ended "And yet I wonder . . . ." It is a language foreign to his character, as his reaction shows: "Sir, I offer you my condolences. Personally I've never been troubled by any such difficulties with interpreting God's word." "Indeed, I see that," Brother Fowles responds, "but I assure you it is no trouble to me. It can be quite a grand way to pass an afternoon, really" (251). Through Brother Fowles, *The Poisonwood Bible* endorses a style of being which lives comfortably within the uncertain space of knowing what one does not know. For him, even the Bible, that final word on morality, is unsettled.

The Poisonwood Bible goes beyond *Heart of Darkness* in modeling what ethical uncertainty can look like; it is not just about doubt itself but about combining doubt with dialogue. Brother Fowles is as much a rewriting of Kurtz as Nathan is, but what we have with Fowles is a revised model of "going native."[55] He yields to the village environment (which is not defined by darkness in his view) and subsequently becomes a more ethical version of foreign presence. He, too, is a sincere believer, but through the influence and internalization of local voices, he becomes far more genuinely altruistic than Nathan, who replaces him at the Kilanga mission; his own "conversion" to local tastes and practices makes for a different model of altruism altogether, based on mutual affection and kindness rather than one-sided benevolence. He is a dialogic missionary, as opposed to Nathan's monologic one. He, too, disagrees with the practice of polygamy, for example, but his approach takes the form of spending "many afternoons with a calabash of palm wine between [himself and Tata Ndu], debating the merits of treating a wife kindly" (257). This isn't merely a strategy for effective proselytizing; shocking to Nathan's sensibilities, Fowles actually likes Congolese people. His relationship with the Mission League (which places and funds missionaries) frayed as his relationships with local people grew. In Nathan's appraisal, Fowles has "gone plumb crazy, consorting with the inhabitants of the land" (38). For Kingsolver, he is a better man by being a bad missionary. Against the singularity of the missionary mentality, Brother Fowles recommends that Nathan actually go to Tata Ndu for help — in other words, that he reveal his vulnerability, his uncertainty, his dependence on locals: "*We* are the branch that's grafted on here, sharing in the richness of these African roots," Fowles explains. The concept of grafting counters the "hewing down" we saw earlier. A graft depends on the life of the root. It is tentative and can be rejected. Sensitive to his own dependence, Fowles sees himself less as a benefactor than as a beneficiary of the Congolese, and unlike Nathan, he survives the era of independence. Ethical travel, for these authors, only begins to become possible when the savior narrative — along with its "frightful confidence" — is suspended. For Conrad, it is an issue of doing less damage, but this doesn't leave any positive space for missions. Kingsolver, on the other hand, recuperates the possibility of doing some good through her version of a bad missionary.

The Poisonwood Bible also infuses dialogue and doubt through its poly-vocal narrative form. Kingsolver establishes distance from Nathan's domi-neering voice through chapters that rotate among multiple narrators. Never conveying his story directly, Nathan loses narrative control. The Price family's story is instead told through the voices of his wife and daughters, who offer semi-external positions as women and children who are in the Congo not by their own choice but through the cooptation of Nathan's grand plan. This technique breaks the singularity of the white savior narrative, the sense that the story is an absolute truth that can be told — and is worth telling — in only one way. It also slows the narrative down and thickens it with repetitions, ambiguities, and contradictions. Additionally, the point of view is multiplied through time; the daughters narrate events as they unfold over the span of three decades, their voices shifting as they grow through childhood and into adulthood (for the three who survive). They are open to change. For example, Leah, initially her father's most loyal daughter, comes to see Brother Fowles as a better role model. The novel's polyvocality, then, is not only synchronic (delivered through multiple narrators) but diachronic (staggered across time); individual narrators have multiple voices of their own as their perspectives evolve over the course of many years.

Through its competing discourses and evolving voices, the novel's sense of the moral cause gravitates away from the spiritual realm and toward the material world. Whiteness is marked not by religious superiority but by un-just wealth. Most people in Kilanga aren't interested in the Prices' spiritual message. They are, however, interested — not greedily but pragmatically — in the *things* the Americans bring. Brother Fowles and his wife, Celine, are insufficiently religious by Nathan's standard, but their efforts are well received when they distribute powdered milk, food, vitamins, and preventative malaria medication to communities along the river. Their work combines the theological and the material. In spite of the Price family's otherworldly focus, confronting material inequity is unavoidable. When they arrive at the airport, children quickly gather around them. As Leah explains, "The minute they saw our white skin they'd rush at us, begging in French: '*Cadeau, cadeau?*' I held up my two hands to illustrate the complete lack of gifts I had brought for the African children" (17). The local children are reading the foreign children in a way that identifies patterns of global inequity. By this reading, to be white in Africa is not to be morally superior but to be materially advantaged. Years later, Leah reflects back on this problem of the gift when hungry children appear in her dreams: "[They] begged me for a handful of powdered milk, my clothes, whatever I had. *But I've brought nothing to give you,* I told them, and my heart took me down like a lead weight, for no matter whether these words were true or false, they were terrible and wrong" (394). This is a question of moral cause, but the morality has shifted from the spiritual realm to the material. This is also evident when, after her youngest daughter dies, Orleanna empties the house of her possessions and passes them on to local women:

> Once I'd moved our table outside, with my baby laid out upon it, I could see no sense in anything but to bring out the rest. Such a bewildering excess of things we had for one single family, and how useless it all seemed now. . . . This stuff cluttered my way. What relief, to place it in the hands of women who could carry off my burden. Their industrious need made me feel light-headed. . . . My household would pass through the great digestive tract of Kilanga and turn into signs unseen. It was a miracle to witness my own simple motion, amplified. As I gave it all up, the trees unrolled their tongues of flame and blazed in approval. (382)

What the novel seems to call for is a material reckoning, not a religious one. And while this feels like a conversion moment for Orleanna, it doesn't make a savior out of her. No one else is saved by her action; they simply have more of their needs met as material goods disperse into a slightly fairer distribution.

The question of material relief is relevant at not only an individual level but an international one, and this point also emerges from the novel's dialogue. By representing conversations between Leah and Anatole, the local translator whom she eventually marries, Kingsolver introduces debate over American aid and its relationship to African recipients. Here, too, cross-cultural dialogue replaces American monologue. In Nathan's view, aid is the next horizon of U.S.-based salvation. He uses this language explicitly: "The Belgians and American business brought civilization to the Congo! American aid will be the Congo's salvation!" (121). Anatole provides an alternative. When Leah complains of the apparent contradiction between black hostility to white colonials and the notion that "they want America to give them money," Anatole clears it up by removing the framework of altruistic sacrifice (281). What Congolese people want, he suggests, is something far less heroic:

> "When someone has much more than he can use, it's very reasonable to expect he will not keep it all himself."
>
> "But Tata Boanda [the village leader] *has* to give it away, because fish won't keep. If you don't get rid of it, it's just going to rot and stink to high heaven," [Leah replies.]
>
> Anatole smiled and pointed his finger at [her] nose. "That is just how a Congolese person thinks about money." (281)

While this is an overgeneralization, it is also a useful idea. The framework of sacrifice and reward produced the domineering and ultimately deranged Nathan. Through Anatole, the novel asks us to think beyond the language of sacrifice, and his discourse beats out Nathan's in the end. A different starting place is necessary for a different outcome and for a more ethical form of transnational care.

Leah, who comes to reject her father's mission, moves toward Anatole's view and reflects the evolution of missions from the explicitly religious to the humanitarian. She moves to Angola with Anatole, and civil war breaks out soon after. She becomes a humanitarian, though independent of a sponsoring organization:

> I teach classes in nutrition, sanitation, and soybeans, to women who respectfully call me Mama Ngemba and ignore nine-tenths of what I tell them. Our hardest task is teaching people to count on the future: to plant citrus trees, and compost their wastes for fertilizer. This confused me at first. Why should anyone resist something so obvious as planting a fruit tree or improving the soil? But for those who've lived as refugees longer than memory, learning to believe in the nutrient cycle requires something close to a religious conversion. (523–24)

She echoes her father's efforts in the garden in her own effort to improve the soil. She, too, seeks converts of a sort. Her methods of improvement require people to transform their thinking in order to alter their material conditions. Leah is a secularized missionary. She has been chastened by the "sins of [her] father" and asks "to be converted" (525). She listens and learns to understand that which initially confuses her. Still, the echoes of her father's missionary discourse reveal the resonance between the religious missionary and the secular humanitarian. Humanitarianism represents both a rupture and a continuity. *The Poisonwood Bible* redirects the moral cause to the material world and leaves its more conscientious characters wrestling with problems of inequity rather than with any ontological limitations of African people that Nathan projected onto them.

African Adventure and the Temptation of the Tragic

While the white savior narrative is dramatically transformed in *Heart of Darkness* and *The Poisonwood Bible*, we must still note the limits of that transformation. The elements of risk and adventure are a point of continuity with the celebratory white savior narrative, and their shared tendency toward popularity is not unrelated. These novels continue to satisfy some of the same desires catered to by the savior narrative. Stories of white altruists in Africa by contemporary writers such as Philip Caputo, John Le Carré, and Paul Theroux, as well as Barbara Kingsolver, often achieve bestseller status, and their success likely has something to do with the Western taste for African adventure, even when it deviates from the expectations of white saviorism. Again and again, these authors have returned to *Heart of Darkness* as a framework for exploring what it means for white people in Africa to act on the basis of conviction and belief, showing the ideas upon which these characters act to be enticing—as is Kurtz for Marlow—and enormously dangerous. The American protagonist of Saul Bellow's *Henderson the Rain King*, for example, is struck by an overwhelming compulsion to make improvements while in Africa, but his solution to a plague of frogs in a water cistern creates an explosion that blows the whole cistern to bits. In Philip Caputo's *Acts of Faith*, a pilot who risks his life flying aid into Sudan to help those displaced and dispossessed by war becomes an "aid entrepreneur" and ultimately a gunrunner and war profiteer.[56] Even the missionary of Tim Jeal's *For God and Glory*—the most positive mission figure from any of these texts—sparks conflict and civil war, leading to his own death as well as that of his most prized convert.[57] In these novels, faith in one's cause, in oneself, in one's grand idea is thrown into question as a mode of being in the world and a sensibility for guiding international action, but this does little to transform the image of Africa itself.

By way of illustration, I will turn briefly to one final example. Set at a rural girl's boarding school, Paul Theroux's *Girls at Play* features American Peace Corps volunteer B.J. Lebow. Upon her arrival in Kenya, B.J. proclaims that "Africa's the sexiest place in the world," consistently referring to the continent, not the country in which she stays.[58] What she discovers is that Africa is not that "sexy"; in fact its dullness is the greatest shock to her expectations. Part of what novels like *Girls at Play* and *The Poisonwood Bible* document is boredom—the domestic banality of everyday life in Africa. Africa is, in this sense, normal—but then we must also recognize that ultimately, in these novels, it isn't. In San Diego, B.J. wouldn't have been "sucked breathlessly" to her end in a muddy, "black swamp" (333). In Bethlehem, Georgia, Ruth May of *The Poisonwood Bible* wouldn't have died from the bite of a snake, planted by a neighbor. In London, Kurtz wouldn't have decorated his home with heads on stakes. These literary critiques of the white savior narrative turn romance into tragedy, and tragedy on African soil is just as enchanting. What Africa provides the Western imagination shifts from the romantic adventure of progress to the tragic adventure of regression, destruction, and violence. That is Africa's new "sexiness," cultivated in part by *Heart of Darkness*'s legacy.

In *Girls at Play*, B.J. derives her romantic, exoticized expectation of Africa partly from Conrad himself, based not on a direct analysis but on *Heart of Darkness* as a cultural signifier. The book gets enmeshed in her Hollywood education on Africa, repositioned within an uncritical mission discourse. This demonstrates how narrative expectations shape life trajectories as characters choose their destinations based on preexisting white-people-go-to-Africa plots. When B.J. decides to go home, it is because Kenya, as it turns out, holds none of "the exotic, the mysterious" that had filled her imagination, an imagination populated by "Mistah Kurtz, Allnut and Rose, . . . Stanley and Livingstone"; "Hollywood was a shortish drive up the freeway [from her California home] and that is where most of Africa was," she concludes.[59] As B.J. envisions her own role as a Peace Corps volunteer, she folds Conrad's Kurtz in with the heroism of Victorian missionary exploration and the glamour of Humphrey Bogart and Katharine Hepburn who play Allnut and Rose, the protagonists of *The African Queen*, a film about an unmarried British missionary finding love with an uncouth Canadian boat captain in the African jungle. Kurtz is right there in Hollywood with "most of Africa." This Africa of the American imagination embodies both the romantic and the tragic. *Heart of Darkness* in this formulation isn't a refutation of Western narratives about Africa at all. Instead, it is a vehicle of the mission imagination itself, reinforcing that quintessential image of Africa—the dark and degraded "Africa" that Westerners do not often realize is a fantasy separate from the continent itself. As Chinua Achebe suggests of *Heart of Darkness*, even the most critical literature about missions can reinforce "a particular way of looking (or, rather, not looking) at Africa."[60] With all its emphasis on seeing, it can introduce new blind spots and perpetuate old ones.

Thus, while *Heart of Darkness* is the archetypal Western critique of the white savior narrative, it must also be ambiguously situated within mission discourse. The text has become a vessel for the preservation of important parts of savior narrative rather than its undoing; the book's afterlife exceeds its contents. Its meaning in terms of how it has functioned culturally is not to be found within the text itself but in the aura around it, the echo it has left behind. As Rob Nixon explains,

> *Heart of Darkness* has exerted a centripetal pull over Western representations of Africa unequaled in this century by the way of any other text over the portrayal of any single continent. Journalists, historians, novelists, anthropologists, filmmakers, advertising hacks, and, most conspicuously, travel writers have drawn so routinely and with such license on the novella that the figure of Africa as a heart of darkness has become intelligible even to people who have never read any Conrad. The trope has accrued, in the process, a rhetorical force only distantly dependent on the context and form of its initial usage.[61]

For its difficulty and modernist style, *Heart of Darkness* might not be read as frequently as it is referenced, but it has certainly lived on in popular culture, even when unread.[62] Kurtz's degeneration into violence, illness, and a sexual relationship with an African woman violates the triumphalist expectations of the savior narrative, yet it also embodies the fears lurking around the edges of such narratives. Brantlinger argues that the "myth of the Dark Continent," which has provided the fuel for so much mission discourse, "contains the submerged fear of falling out of the light, down the long coal chute of social and moral regression."[63] Kurtz models that story, and to an adventurous character like B.J. Lebow, there is something very "sexy" about it. This body of literature thus has a dual effect—at once undermining the foundations of the white savior narrative and propping up its tropes of African adventure, which, even when tragic, are enticing. This remains a point of uneasy overlap.

The critique of Western intervention thus remains remarkably satisfying to Western tastes, partly *because* of its tragic form. This is one reason that I make no hard distinction between good and bad humanitarian fictions as a savior narrative/anti-savior narrative dualism would. The relationship between popular and literary discourse around missions is messier than that. In *No Longer at Ease*, Chinua Achebe's protagonist suggests that Graham Greene's *The Heart of the Matter* "was nearly ruined" by the suicide at the end. Suicide, he suggests, "ruins a tragedy. . . . Real tragedy is never resolved. It goes on hopelessly forever. Conventional tragedy is too easy. The hero dies and we feel a purging of the emotions."[64] The catharsis provided by tragic endings risks offering a simple resolution to the thorny problems these novels take up. Characters' individual tragedies can also detract from the far more consequential social tragedy visited upon Africa through the intervention of foreigners. Despite this literary tradition's critical consciousness about African travel, it often gets coopted into something too enjoyable and too easy. Nonetheless, critical attention to these novels can be productive for drawing out the complexities that can be quickly overrun by the simpler pleasure of catharsis. While the tragedies in these texts may become coopted by the romantic stories of missionary adventure, we need not read them in that limited way. The transformation of the characters, plot, and tone also transforms our expectations, conditioning us—if we take up their call—to read humanitarian fictions as critics rather than consumers, skeptics rather than believers.

Mobilizing a Crisis of Humanitarian Faith

Contemporary humanitarianism grows out of the mission impulse, driven by a moral purpose and a sense of a higher calling. It, too, is a practice of faith, a faith that can go too far. Critics of humanitarianism point to the way its high-minded discourse positions aid in what David Rieff describes as a realm "beyond criticism."[65] It has a remarkable capacity, Alex de Waal observes, to "absorb criticism, not reform itself, and yet emerge strengthened."[66] This comes at a cost in terms of actual outcomes. As Barnett writes, "the accepted narrative protects the virtue of humanitarianism, but at the expense of a fuller, and decidedly more complicated, picture of its lived ethics."[67] In this chapter and those that follow, I aim to flesh out that more complex picture of humanitarianism's altruistic idea by analyzing narratives that challenge the accepted one to which Barnett refers.

Heart of Darkness, *The Poisonwood Bible*, and *Girls at Play* explore perversions of moral purpose. This is a problem religious missions and secular humanitarianism share. David Kennedy explains, "Humanitarianism tempts us to hubris, to an idolatry about our intentions and routines, to the conviction that we know more than we do about what justice can be."[68] Conrad, Kingsolver, and Theroux confront such overzealous faith with an array of embarrassments. In doing so, their narratives dislodge that faith, opening it up to the more pliable (and also less breakable) ethics of doubt. In *The Dark Sides of Virtue*, Kennedy claims that this kind of chastening, or "disenchanting" as he calls it, is necessary for the renewal of humanitarian work in a time when it is confronted with an overwhelming record of unintended consequence, compromise, and failure. He proposes that we embrace "a posture or sensibility for humanitarian work" that would "recognize and engage the dark sides," which are inevitably entangled with the most noble "humanitarian yearnings."[69] One might counter that intensive self-critique and the resultant self-doubt would immobilize the impulse to help others. What I take from these texts, however, is a mobilizing crisis of faith, a crisis which is the necessary foundation for humanitarianism's radical rethinking. Barnett explains that even though "faith is required to imagine an always elusive humanity, to persevere despite the onslaught of disappointment and the cascade of evidence of humanity's failings, . . . frequently it is a *crisis* of faith that has bent the path toward realizing progress in humanitarianism and humanitarianism as progress."[70] Only from that place of crisis will humanitarian discourse be able to fundamentally transform its narratives, its expectations, its methods of looking—and not looking—at Africa.

A productive crisis of faith for humanitarian thought will necessarily unseat the hero who has so long stood at its helm, but it must also give a fuller account of African agency within the humanitarian encounter. Ngũgĩ wa Thiong'o's response to Conrad captures the limitations of many humanitarian fictions by Western authors, critical as they may be: "Conrad always made me uneasy," Ngũgĩ writes, "with his inability to see any possibility of redemption arising from the energy of the oppressed."[71] Despite the attention to African input by writers like Kingsolver, these are still stories told by Westerners primarily about Westerners primarily for Westerners. Writing about the early days of establishing an African tradition of written anglophone fiction in the mid-twentieth century, Achebe notes that "there weren't any models. Those [Western novels] that were set in Africa were not particularly inspiring. If they were not saying something that was antagonistic toward us, they weren't concerned about us."[72] The task for humanitarian fiction by the Western writer lies primarily in cultivating a critical self-consciousness of various Western missions and dissolving the easy security of good intentions. It will be necessary to hear African responses to missions in order to find a fuller, more complex perspective that adds weight to the critique along with a fuller analysis of "redemption arising from the energy of the oppressed." I turn now to those stories.

2

The Emancipated African

The white savior narrative is a grand narrative of emancipation. It promises that through Western benevolence the benighted African will be freed from spiritual depravity, cultural backwardness, physical suffering, or material poverty. In the colonial era, humanitarian intervention, as led by missionaries, "was intended to produce emancipation and liberation as defined by the civilized."[1] The irony, of course, is that liberation on foreign terms involves subjugation to foreign power. This chapter will focus on African responses that reframe Western definitions of African liberation and forecast contemporary humanitarianism's transnational, cross-cultural interactions. The writers addressed here help us think through two fundamental questions: How do African people interact with institutions of Western benevolence that promise emancipation in either spiritual or material form (or some combination of the two)? How have African writers narrated the relation between freedom, missions, and empire?

One logical place to go for this analysis would be the writings of African missionaries and ministers themselves who, like European missionaries of the nineteenth and early twentieth centuries, documented their endeavors. A handful of critics including David Attwell, Leon de Kock, and Olakunle George have undertaken this project with studies of writers such as Tiyo Soga, John Knox Bokwe, and Bishop Samuel Ajayi Crowther. According to George, these writers have been largely overlooked in literary scholarship due in part to the common impression that African literature before the mid-twentieth century is "important but immature," aligned with "Western ideology and . . . not sufficiently decolonized."[2] For the critics like George who challenge that assumption, interpreting early authors' works involves disentangling African

Christianity from colonial complicity. As Attwell argues, this early literature demonstrates "that resistance is a many-faceted thing, [which] has been with us from the beginning, though sometimes at subtextual levels that require careful excavation."[3] In some cases, this practice of excavation means uncovering the "distinctly secular sub-text [that] underpins an overtly Christian text."[4] In other cases, it means reading what George calls the "novelization effects" through which "texts dialogize hegemonic or official discourses" in a way that might, for example, draw on "classic Victorian missionary discourse as well as traditional Yoruba feudal values."[5] Through their analyses of subtext and dialogism, these critics complicate perceptions of nineteenth- and early twentieth-century mission writers, unearthing secular projects and emergent nationalism within religious discourse and clarifying that Christian enthusiasm does not merit the conclusion that such writers were the dupes of colonial power.[6]

This chapter aims for a similar complication of African writing about missions but takes a different tack. While the critics mentioned above have made important inroads through the study of Christian writers, my focus will be on writers who are explicitly secular and explicitly anticolonial, whose critiques of missions are text, not subtext. Analyzing the works of Chinua Achebe and Ngũgĩ wa Thiong'o, the two most canonical and prolific African novelists, reveals that while missions were surely implicated in colonialism — and part of the burden of anticolonial writing has been to critique them — these religious institutions have also been central to Africans' own narratives of liberation ranging from the reformist to the radical, particularly when the horizon of improvement was decolonization. Somewhat akin to Marxism in this sense, Christianity was a discourse from without, which fueled emancipatory narratives generated within Africa. Missions, I argue, have been a vital part of a dual process, foundational to two kinds of stories — those that Westerners have told about Africa and those that Africans have told about themselves and their continent. I aim to clarify why anticolonial thinkers who often distanced themselves from their Christian upbringing were also intensely attracted to certain elements of missions, revealing how they drew missions into complicity with their own anticolonial projects. In contrast to critical distance, these writers model a practice of critical proximity, wrestling with the real, yet always problematic, value of missions within struggles for African freedom.

Both Achebe and Ngũgĩ, who came of age in the years of the Nigerian and Kenyan independence struggles, have published autobiographical works in recent years that, in their emphasis on missions specifically, ask us to reopen the subject. Breaking with *Humanitarian Fictions'* general focus on novels, this chapter weaves together fiction and memoir because life and literature are so thoroughly intertwined in this area. It is worth bearing in mind that, as Apollo Amoko points out, "the 'factual' autobiography and the 'fictive' *Bildungs-roman* [contain] considerable correspondences and convergences, at least in the African context."[7] That is certainly the case here. While these authors are some of missions' most exacting critics, Achebe and Ngũgĩ suggest that the mission presence was multifaceted, a field of intense debate among African people who viewed missions with a mix of hope and disappointment, desire and disgust. Achebe's *The Education of a British-Protected Child*, a book-length compilation of autobiographical essays, was published in 2009, soon followed by Ngũgĩ's *Dreams in a Time of War: A Childhood Memoir* in 2010. Combining literary and biographical history, these texts show the entanglement of missions in the personal lives and public works of African writers. The question that emerges is not simply whether missions were good or bad for Africa; rather, they push us to ask, how have missions been used to various ends — imperialist *and* anti-imperialist, coercive *and* liberating, racist *and* antiracist, brutally violent *and* surprisingly humane? And ultimately how have African people worked to privilege the latter in each of those oppositions? This can also help us answer a question of particular salience today: If humanitarian missions continue to be implicated in contemporary forms of imperialism, how can they be turned toward more genuinely emancipatory ends?

In returning all these years later to the sites of their mission upbringing, Achebe and Ngũgĩ open a new window on the history of African literature — highlighting the centrality of missions in its formation — while also enabling us to rethink the demands of postcolonial critique. By addressing these long-standing figureheads of anglophone literature, this chapter will consider their roles both as mission students, who turned to missions out of necessity under colonialism, and as postcolonial intellectuals, who have returned to the subject for different reasons in the twenty-first century. As such, their engagement with missions offers a model of intellectual work that cultivates strategic alliances between progressive politics and religious thought in the pursuit of post-neocolonial horizons. This approach to African agency also speaks to questions of cultural imperialism and adaptation beyond the mission, to the way African subjects actively define their relations to the West and all its various gods.

Christianity and Colonialism

If missionaries promised freedom from various forms of deficiency, what did they actually deliver? One answer goes like this: "When the white man came to Africa, he had the Bible and the black man had the land. The white man said, 'let us close our eyes to pray.' And when they opened their eyes, the white man had the land, and the black man was left with the Bible."[8] I want to think through the implications of this anecdote because it models a set of arguments against missions that have become commonplace, arguments that are necessary but insufficient for understanding the history of missions in Africa and its relation to literature. First, they point to the link between cultural and political empire—the idea that colonizing culture through Christianization was part of a larger scheme to conquer African lands. The Bible was, in other words, a pawn of deceptive politics, a mask for domination. Also implicit here is the Marxist critique of religion as the opium of the masses. According to this line of argument, missions offered Africa a kind of anesthetic, facilitating not only the colonization of land or of culture, but the colonization of vision and consciousness. The Bible, then, was a tool for dulling the critical senses and distracting African people from the real problem—political disempowerment and material dispossession. Christianity, from this perspective, came with an otherworldly imperative that one should wait on the next world to the neglect of the present one.[9]

These claims have calcified into a kind of shorthand for talking about missions that is rooted in African nationalism and echoed in postcolonial theory, binding the cross to the flag, the Christian to the colonialist. Missions preceded empire, opening new paths to European travel and commerce, and with the consolidation of empire they operated on a radically uneven terrain of power. This inequity also played out in the unidirectional politics of conversion, and missions did irreversible damage to African cultures and communities. Thus, in the period leading up to decolonization, the affinity between missions and empire seemed to be a settled matter. Outlining this intellectual current, J. D. Y. Peel notes that the rise of postcolonial studies in the 1980s, with its renewal of interest in colonial power, reinvigorated this sensibility and solidified the view that "conversion is control at its most complete, and it is this which makes mission colonialist to the core."[10] The missionary has thus come to register, by V. Y. Mudimbe's account, as "the best symbol of the colonial enterprise": "With equal enthusiasm, he served as an agent of political empire, a representative of civilization, and an envoy of God. There is no essential contradiction between these roles. All of them implied the same purpose: the conversion of African minds and space."[11] With these roles so neatly aligned, missionary history could function as evidence for the analysis of colonial history without making clear distinctions between them.

In postcolonial theory, the missionary's text serves as a standard case study in the critique of colonial discourse. Mudimbe claims that "missionary speech is always predetermined, preregulated, let us say *colonized*."[12] It is, in other words, expressive of and inseparable from colonial discourse. Homi Bhabha's work also exemplifies this tendency. In *The Location of Culture*, Bhabha's primary sources come frequently from missionaries, putting Christianity at the heart of colonial enterprise, with the Bible "bearing both the standard of the cross and the standard of empire."[13] Bhabha thus uses the missionary as a key figure for understanding colonial power and conversely uses colonial power as the primary lens through which to understand the missionary. This generates a nuanced view of power that emphasizes its instability, but it takes for granted the stable relationship between missions and colonialism. Bhabha's reading of sly civility—a concept he draws from the paranoid expression of a missionary—accounts well for the agency of people who would demurely evade the Christian message.[14] However, it does not account for more direct forms of agency that colonized people exerted in response to missions, particularly for those who embraced Christianity.

Taking missionaries as the prime exemplars of colonial discourse prevents us from seeing how missions have been articulated with projects (and related narratives) of anticolonial resistance. The taken-for-granted link between the missionary and the imperialist—which appears not only in academic debates but in the popular language of cultural relativism—fails to capture what is, in reality, a remarkably mixed legacy with which colonized subjects knowingly engaged. African studies scholars have worked over several decades to draw that point out. Ogbu Kalu, an early advocate for this position, insists that "the history of christianity is not just the history of what missionaries did. The responses of Igbo people [and African people more generally] are a crucial part of the story. In the pattern of these responses lies the explanation for the rapid spread of missions."[15] This reveals how history itself is bound up with narrative choices—emphasizing some actors and storylines while marginalizing others. Lamin Sanneh makes clear the consequences: "over-emphasis on the 'colonialism paradigm' in mission history effectively silences indigenous agents and ignores how they 'translated' the gospel into their own social and spiritual realities for the fulfillment of their own goals."[16] Similarly, Olúfẹ́mi Táíwò asserts that, all too often, intellectuals do "not differentiate between what Christianity did and what colonialism wrought, and as a result give short shrift to the ideas and strivings of Africans who accepted Christianity but not colonialism."[17] By critiquing Mudimbe for "his failure to recognize native agency, much less give it its due," Táíwò redirects our attention: regardless of whether missionaries "meant to conform their actions to the lofty ideals they penned . . . once those ideas were put down and Africans had access to them, we cannot ignore what their audience, the African converts, thought or did with those ideas."[18] Scholars' repeated calls to move away from the missionary-

imperialist equation toward a more supple view of missions and their role in
African history is suggestive of the hardy persistence of that narrative.[19] According to the grand narrative of African salvation, missions were God's gift to
Africa; the dominant counternarrative redefines them as the West's imperialist
curse. When African agency takes center stage, however, the story takes a third
form, which this chapter seeks to uncover. To do so, it will focus less on how
missions oppressed African people than on how African people reinvented the
freedom that was the mission's false promise.

If mission stations of the colonial era were meant to produce "good"
Africans—"black Englishmen" who would assist in the turnover of land and
authority—they ultimately turned out a great number of very "bad" ones, for
whom the Bible, believed or not, was an insufficient consolation prize. Africa's
major anticolonial (and antiapartheid) activists and political leaders in the ini-
tial years of independence in the sixties and seventies (and in the case of South
Africa all the way into the nineties) were educated at mission schools, including Jomo Kenyatta, Kwame Nkrumah, Agostinho Neto, Léopold Senghor,
and Nelson Mandela, among numerous others. This is one of the great ironies
of missions in Africa—that these colonially enabled and colonially enabling
institutions became the training ground for Africa's most vocal, persistent, and
militant anticolonialists. Thus, historians J. F. Ade Ajayi and E. A. Ayandele
have described the mission school as an "incubator for African nationalism."[20]
This observation applies to nationalism's literary expressions as well. It is often
noted, but seldom analyzed, that African writers who grew up under colonialism were educated primarily at mission schools and that this education was
seminal in the development of various literary traditions across the continent.
African literature must be brought to bear on this debate as it speaks directly
and insightfully to the ways in which missions have resonated with both colonialist imposition and anticolonial resistance. The point is not to displace the
narrative of missions as a force of colonial domination—and certainly not to
embrace a missionary rhetoric of the emancipated African—but to consider
how Africans' own narratives of emancipation were often built upon cautious
engagements with missions.

Novels of Missionary Arrival

The critique of missions has been foundational to the anglophone literature of
decolonization. Achebe defined his task as a writer as a process of undoing the
discourse of salvation: "I would be quite satisfied if my novels (especially the
ones I set in the past) did nothing more than teach my readers that their past—
with all its imperfections—was not one long night of savagery from which

the first Europeans acting on God's behalf delivered them."[21] While this is a response to colonialism and its civilizing mission more generally, it also speaks directly to the religious institutions through which Europeans enacted God's supposed deliverance. The impulse to upend the Western narrative of Africa's salvation has generated a good deal of literary energy. Achebe and Ngũgĩ write novels of nondeliverance in which missions fail to produce the glory they promise and wreak havoc instead. They tell stories of things falling apart in the wake of mission intervention, of previously stable societies, families, and individuals fragmenting. Missionaries are catalysts of catastrophe. In Achebe's *Things Fall Apart* (1958), they forge the first paths into the African countryside, ushering in a new and destructive era of colonial domination, and in *Arrow of God* (1964), missionaries encourage converts to defile the most sacred Igbo cultural symbols; they take advantage of internal rifts and the desperation caused by a delayed harvest in order to win more converts. Similarly, in Ngũgĩ's *The River Between* (1965), missionaries stir up conflict that bitterly divides the people and leads to cultural war. Ngũgĩ's preceding novel, *Weep Not Child* (1964), is structured around a reversal of the trope of missionary-sourced enlightenment: part 1, titled "The Waning Light," is followed by the dénouement "Darkness Falls." In the era of decolonization, the anglophone literature of missions took an unambiguously critical stance.

Yet while these writers became some of missions' most exacting critics, their descriptions are shot through with counterpoints and complications. The following analysis will consider the casts of characters in Achebe's *Things Fall Apart* and Ngũgĩ's *The River Between*. In each novel, we see more than one missionary type as well as a range of African responses. Some missionaries are characterized by accommodation to local practice, others by rejection of compromise. Among African characters, some wholeheartedly reject missions, some embrace them with imperious fervor, and some are drawn to the mission in pursuit of human rights. Many attempt to forge paths between the hardening sides of converts and traditionalists and draw on mission institutions in practices of self-fashioning, blending identities in new, liberating ways — sometimes on an individual level, sometimes on a collective level. Major questions get worked out in relation to missions — questions of how to survive in a rapidly and violently changing world; how to address the problems of poverty, community development, and individual human rights; how viable it would be to accept foreign assistance and on what terms. In sum, these novels work to dismantle the grand narrative of African salvation by the West, while also exploring how the mission station of the colonial era has been a pivotal figure in Africa's own narratives of (often anticolonial) emancipation.

In terms of narrative space, the earlier of these novels, *Things Fall Apart*, is like a photonegative of the liberationist savior narrative; it represents the same scene but illuminates that which was dark and shadows that which was bright. Within part 1, which spans more than half the novel's pages, white people appear only by way of rumor as Igbo characters exchange "stor[ies] of white men who, they say, are white like [a] piece of chalk."[22] Europeans rather than Africans are shrouded in mystery. The narrative focuses on the powerful village of Umuofia, the family of its famed warrior Okonkwo, and the cultural practices of the clan. Giving so much space to local life before describing foreign intervention emphasizes the fact that African history does not suddenly come into being once white people arrive, as the savior narrative would suggest. In fact, a white character doesn't physically appear until the sixteenth of twenty-five chapters. So, for Achebe, the story of missions does not begin with missionaries. In *Things Fall Apart*, they are at once pivotal and marginal. The plot begins long before they arrive, and although their presence fundamentally and irreversibly transforms local life, the white missionaries themselves receive proportionately little narrative attention in comparison to African characters.

Narrative form answers the question, whose story is this? The answer here: not missionaries'. A key strategy in the African critique of the white savior narrative is to change the narrative proportions—the space within the telling that goes to different characters or groups. In the Anglo-American examples discussed in chapter 1—*Heart of Darkness* and *The Poisonwood Bible*—those proportions continued to privilege white characters and their journeys into Africa. In *Things Fall Apart* and *The River Between*, missionary arrival is a watershed moment based not on foreign aims but on local ramifications, and white missionaries themselves receive little direct representation. In other words, depicting missionaries' effects produces a story that hardly involves them.

Even so, the language of the white savior narrative maintains a significant presence in these novels; it arrives with the missionaries but is then filtered through the varied perspectives of villagers. In *Things Fall Apart*, when a group of missionaries shows up in Mbanta, their leader, communicating through a translator, tells the crowd, "We have been sent by this great God to ask you to leave your wicked ways and false gods and turn to Him so that you may be saved when you die" (145). Some laugh, some ask questions, and some (like Okonkwo) shrug and walk away from this strange, pale man. But this isn't an entirely white mission. In fact, of the six missionaries who come to Mbanta, only "one [is] a white man," suggesting that the face of Christianity is not necessarily white (144). Furthermore, the speech of the sole white missionary in the scene is constantly filtered through local translators, so he never delivers his message directly. The power of his speech escapes his grasp. As such, it is constantly subject to interpretation, and it signifies very differently to different characters.

Some perceive the new religion as a military infiltration. For Umofia's leaders, the prevalence of African converts is the key factor in making white rule impossible to defeat. Obierika explains:

> If we should try to drive out the white men in Umuofia we should find it easy. There are only two of them. But what of our own people who are following their way and have been given power? . . . Now [the white man] has won our brothers, and our clan can no longer act like one. He has put a knife in the things that held us together and we have fallen apart. (176)

White action supports Obierika's interpretation. Between the two foreign missionaries, there is conflict not over the importance of conversion but over the tactics by which to achieve it. The hardliner Reverend James Smith sees his work explicitly in terms of war: "He condemned openly [his predecessor] Mr. Brown's policy of compromise and accommodation. He saw things as black and white. And black was evil. He saw the world as a battlefield in which the children of light were locked in mortal conflict with the sons of darkness" (184). As part of his strategy, he recruits local people to the fight, spurring an "over-zealous convert" to extremism, which "touche[s] off the great conflict between the church and the clan in Umuofia which had been gathering since Mr. Brown left" (185). Although Brown is less offensive than Smith—and is not assigned the same level of responsibility for the conflict—theirs is more a difference of tone than of type. On the one hand, Brown emphasizes conversation in a way that at times displaces conversion: "Whenever Mr. Brown went to that village he spent long hours with Akunna in his *obi* talking through an interpreter about religion. Neither of them succeeded in converting the other but they learned more about their different beliefs" (179). On the other hand, this is ultimately a conversion strategy, also articulated in terms of war. Through those conversations, he "learned a good deal about the religion of the clan and he came to the conclusion that a frontal attack on it would not succeed. And so he built a school and a little hospital in Umuofia" (181). In lieu of a "frontal attack," Brown is playing a long game. His humanitarian offerings are a means to an end.

This is an issue not merely of religion but of governance. Missionaries' interventions in the novel disrupt local societies and aid in the implementation of colonial administration. When Okonkwo returns to Umuofia after seven years in exile, he finds that "the church had come and led many astray" (174). This goes hand in hand with the British state: "apart from the church, the white men had also brought a government" (174). When Umuofian leaders destroy the new church, Reverend James Smith reports it to the District Commissioner, who swiftly jails them, humiliates them, and demands a fine for their release. In many ways, missionaries' infiltration tactics succeed.

But the novel also represents liberationist reasons for participation in the church. By Achebe's representation, Umuofia and the surrounding villages are not places of darkness or desperation; they are rich in history and tradition, and, like all societies, they are complicated. For marginalized people within Umuofian society, the new religion's central promise is about the boundaries of human value. The first to join the church are outcasts: "None of [the missionary's] converts was a man whose word was heeded in the assembly of the people. None of them was a man of title. They were mostly the kind of people that were called *efulefu*, worthless, empty men," even derided as "the excrement of the clan" (143). They find freedom in the missionaries' claim that all are "brother[s] because they [are] all sons of God" (145). One noteworthy convert is Nneka, a mother who, in each of her four pregnancies, bore twins. Considered an "abomination" by the clan, her twins were repeatedly "thrown away" in the forest (155). For Nneka, the church promises a reprieve. Okonkwo's son, Nwoye, is drawn to the church for related reasons: "It was not the mad logic of the Trinity that captivated him. He did not understand it. It was the poetry of the new religion, something felt in the marrow. The hymn about brothers who sat in darkness and in fear seemed to answer a vague and persistent question that haunted his young soul—the question of the twins crying in the bush and the question of Ikemefuna who was killed" (147). As the novel shows, human rights violations accompany Christian crusades into Africa, but Christianity can also speak to the local human rights issues that hurt people like Nwoye and Nneka. Although Okonkwo has no sympathy for Nwoye, disowning him as "degenerate and effeminate," Achebe leads readers to sympathize with him (153). Okonkwo is the clear protagonist and the narrative revolves around him, but readers are not confined to his perspective. Nwoye, too, is a focalizing character, and by centralizing his perspective Achebe prevents readers from seeing the church solely through Okonkwo's critical eyes.

Nwoye and converts like him find a form of emancipation in the church, and in contrast to Enoch and "the overzealous converts," they are not dupes of colonial power (185). In the big picture, *Things Fall Apart* is a narrative of domination. But, on a smaller scale, individual characters find their own narratives of liberation through missions. This doesn't override the novel's larger claims about colonial ascendance, but even as the bulk of the narrative goes to Okonkwo, who rejects any association with Christianity, other characters' tentative paths of liberation through the church should not be

overlooked. Their embrace of the missionary message is not the same as capitulation to colonialism, and by representing these characters' perspectives as
well as Okonkwo's, *Things Fall Apart* speaks back to the white savior narrative
with multiple alternative tellings.

In *The River Between*, Ngũgĩ goes further in disentangling Christianity
from colonial power. The converts in *Things Fall Apart* find liberation from
the constraints of the clan that has rejected or injured them. This pattern also
appears in *The River Between*, but liberation extends to the explicitly anticolonial. Missionaries are again a forerunner of the colonial government, facilitating gradual British takeover by dividing the people. In contrast to *Things
Fall Apart*, the missionary presence is felt early and throughout the text. Yet,
as was the case in the earlier novel, the narrative focus is not on missionaries
themselves or their goals but on local responses. The mission station, Siriana,
is a frequent reference, but characters' experiences there are briefly recalled
afterward, not directly represented. On the one occasion when the perspective
of a white missionary at Siriana is depicted, it is to show his disillusionment:

> When he came to the Mission, he was full of vigour and certainly
> full of great expectations. He always looked to a time when his efforts
> would produce fruits. But as years went on he realized that he was not
> making as much progress as he expected he would. This was a disap-
> pointment to a man who had left home for a wild country, fired by a
> dream of heroism and the vision of many new souls won for Christ
> through his own efforts. His call and his mission had not met with the
> response he had once hoped for.[23]

This missionary, called Livingstone, enters Kenya with the expectations of
the heroic salvation narrative; intending progress for a "wild country," he is
initially confident that spiritual success is his promise. He finds that people
use the mission's offerings more strategically than he would wish: "True, the
school and the hospital had expanded a great deal. But these people seemed
only interested in education, while they paid lip service to salvation" (*River*,
55). The mission field is far more intricate than he had anticipated, and he
finds that people don't internalize his message as a unified, singular project,
but tease out the elements they find beneficial.

Although Livingstone is frustrated by noncompliance, the number of converts is substantial, and public debates arise over conversion versus cultural
conservation. Missionary speech enters the novel through the voices of local
converts who come into conflict with the unconverted. The language of purity
and contamination circulates on both sides of this divide, and the mission
becomes a point of intense debate within the community. Instead of settling

in the most rural areas themselves, foreign missionaries in the novel develop a network of local evangelists: "the missionaries had not as yet penetrated into the hills, though they sent a number of disciples to work there" (28). Dealing with missions doesn't necessarily mean dealing with white people directly. Much of the conflict, then, becomes internal.

Joshua, Livingstone's primary disciple, takes on the white missionary discourse with exuberant devotion. We can assume that his Christian name has replaced his Gikuyu given name, though we never learn it. His own cultural background becomes a subject of shame and erasure. He identifies himself in belief, action, and speech with the foreign missionary: "He meant to be an example to all, a bright light that would show the way, a rock on which the weak would step on their way to Christ" (31). In framing his opposition to female circumcision, he also echoes the discourse of missionary heroism: "He would journey courageously, a Christian soldier, going on to the promised land. Nobody would deflect him from his set purpose" (31). This brash discourse includes a racialized view of conversion. He prays that his people will "leave their ways and follow the ways of the white man," and his self-righteousness combines with rage: "He felt like going out with a stick, punishing these people, forcing them on to their knees" (32). This resonates with the self-righteous rage of white savior figures like Kurtz in *Heart of Darkness* and Nathan in *The Poisonwood Bible*. Conversion, here, is a cultural revolution, which demands the alignment of whiteness with goodness, blackness with corruption. For Joshua, allegiance to Christianity is indeed an alignment with whiteness, which demands not only conversion or discontinuation of particular practices but a total surrender of one's previous life. This, however, is not the only approach presented in the novel.

In *The River Between*, Ngũgĩ takes advantage of the novel's dialogic form and tests out different modes of interaction with the mission, negotiating between the radical convert and the radical conservationist. Joshua's opponents plead "to preserve the purity of our tribal customs and our way of life" and warn "against being contaminated by the ways of the white man" (65, 72). Some characters, including Joshua's daughters, seek a middle ground that blends elements of Gikuyu tradition and the new faith. Muthoni, for example, rebels against Joshua in seeking circumcision: "No one will understand. I say I am a Christian and my father and mother have followed the new faith. I have not run away from that. But I also want to be initiated into the ways of the tribe" (43). Her father disowns her, and she stays in another village with her aunt. The middle ground, in this case, is an untenable, even unlivable position. Each side, the convert and the conservationist, wants desperately "to preserve the purity" of their "way of life," and both sides become dangerously ossified, refusing to collaborate to help Muthoni (65). Following the circumcision, she contracts a deadly infection; when she finally gets to the mission hospital, brought by Waiyaki, who is a student at the time, it is too late.[24] Her death is then filtered through the novel's competing discourses, which come not only through characters' speech but through the free indirect discourse of the external narrator:

> The elders from Makuyu gathered together, made a few irrelevant remarks and then looked at one another. They understood. This new faith had contaminated the hills and Murungu was angry. . . .
>   And Joshua's followers gathered. They talked and sang praises to God. Muthoni was an evil spirit sent to try the faithful. It was now clear to all that nothing but evil could come out of adherence to tribal customs. (58)

The narrative perspective itself is unstable, pulled between conflicting views, which readers then navigate alongside the characters. In this novel, the debate over ideological positions is staged not between foreign missionaries and locals but among locals themselves who take varied positions in response to mission discourse. That discourse escapes its origin, splintering and entering into a dialogue in which white missionaries are not participants.

As a mediating figure, Waiyaki, son of the revered elder Chege who warned the people against the mission, seeks unity among the growing factions. He aims for a cultural blend but not an even one—still in opposition to, not complicit with, white rule. He adopts elements of Western culture without political surrender of Joshua's variety. The keeper of tradition who "knew, more than any other person, the ways of the land and the hidden things of the tribe," Chege sends his son to Siriana Mission Center, telling him, "Learn all the wisdom and all the secrets of the white man," but with the injunction, "Be true to your people and the ancient rights" (20). Waiyaki ends up in a more complicated position than his father had anticipated, and local leaders condemn him as a threat to their purity. Initially seen as a protector of his people, he gains fame as a leader of the independent school movement. He establishes "the first people's own school to be built since the break with Siriana" (67). In some ways, his project mirrors the Christian language of Joshua and Livingstone: "In starting self-help in education, Waiyaki had seen it as a kind of mission" (68). In contrast to Joshua, however, his mission diverges from white authority. Here, he takes a promising idea and practice—a Western model of education—and rejects Western ownership. Straying from the dis-

course of cultural purity articulated by both Christians and cultural conserva-
tionists, he chooses what Kwame Anthony Appiah has called *"contamination*
as the name for a counter-ideal."[25]

For all his independence, Waiyaki also takes on the missionary discourse
of what I called in chapter 1 the moral cause. With this higher purpose, he
rapidly gains converts:

> Schools grew up like mushrooms. Often a school was nothing more
> than a shed hurriedly thatched with grass. And there they stood,
> symbols of people's thirst for the white man's secret magic and power.
> Few wanted to live the white man's way, but all wanted this thing, this
> magic. This work of building together was a tribute to the tribe's way
> of co-operation. It was a determination to have something of their own
> making, fired by their own imagination. (68)

While this kind of education was initially white in source, it isn't white in its
development or its application. This is a far cry from Joshua's prayer that his
people would conform to "the white man's way" in its entirety. The language
around Waiyaki's mission parallels Joshua's, but his role as savior is framed not
in compliance with the white man but in opposition:

> The white man was slowly encroaching on people's land. He had
> corrupted the ways of the tribe. Things would now change. It may take
> years, but far, far into the unknown future things would become differ-
> ent. A saviour had come. He had opened the eyes of the people. He
> had awakened the sleeping lions. They would now roar, roar to victory.
> The children were getting learning. (94)

The concepts of enlightenment, awakening, and salvation continue to frame
Waiyaki's view of positive change, as does the savior narrative's spirit of adventure: "The feeling that this was in a way his mission had come to him
before the meeting that marked the height of his glory. And he had been
training himself for his mission: end the Kameno-Makuyu feud and bring
back the unity of the tribe" (100). We can hear the echoes of missionary self-
glorification here.

Yet, again in contrast to the mission of Joshua and Livingstone, Waiyaki's
mission is characterized by uncertainty. For example,

> Waiyaki often found himself trying to puzzle out the meaning of the
> old prophecy. Did Chege really think Waiyaki would be that saviour?
> Was he to drive out the white man? Was that the salvation? And what

would a saviour do with the band of men who, along with Joshua,
stuck so rigidly to the new faith? (80)

The very elements that are supposed to be most steadfast—the nature of salvation and the task of the savior—are wavering. At some points, Waiyaki presumes "his mission of enlightenment through education would prosper" (110).
At others, he worries "his mission of enlightenment through education would
come to nothing. No!" (127). He wonders, too, if this mission is even his:

> They called him a saviour. His own father had talked of a Messiah
> to come. Whom was the Messiah coming to save? From what? And
> where would He lead the people? Although Waiyaki did not stop to get
> clear answers to these questions, he increasingly saw himself as the one
> who would lead the tribe to the light. Education was the light of the
> country. (101)

The language of salvation came not only from the missionaries but from his
father and a Gikuyu prophecy. This suggests that messianic thinking and the
discourse of salvation are not exclusively Christian. Instead, Waiyaki finds a
point of resonance between the language of local tradition and that of Christian conversion. He is focused on his higher calling and simultaneously con-
flicted. His mission discourse shares the high-minded commitment to African
improvement, but it emerges from a combination of local and foreign sources
and strays from the white savior narrative in its openness to questions and
course changes.

Significant, too, is the fact that Waiyaki's mission to save the hills becomes
increasingly political. Originally, it is about education only. It becomes most
meaningful, however, when he realizes that it should not be education for
its own sake. It is education for the sake of freedom. His moral cause needs a
political dimension:

> People wanted action now. The stirrings in the hills were an awaken-
> ing to the shame and humiliation of their condition. Their isolation
> had been violated. But what action was needed? What had he to do
> now? How could he organize people into a political organization
> when they were so torn with strife and disunity? Now he knew what he
> would preach if he ever got another chance: education for unity. Unity
> for political freedom. (143)

He is a critical consumer of "the white man's secret magic" in the form of
schooling (68). *The River Between* demonstrates how the colonialist hope
that Christian education would prepare African people for submission can

backfire. Here, education is not merely a tool of advancement, a leg up on the colonially imposed social ladder. For Waiyaki, it is most valuable for its potential to incinerate that social ladder. This demands that one carefully tease out the good from the bad, a skill and sensibility Waiyaki develops over the course of the novel:

> [He] knew that not all the ways of the white man were bad. Even his religion was not essentially bad. Some good, some truth shone through it. But the religion, the faith, needed washing, cleaning away all the dirt, leaving only the eternal. And that eternal that was the truth had to be reconciled to the traditions of the people. A people's traditions could not be swept away overnight. That way lay disintegration. . . . A religion that took no count of people's way of life, a religion that did not recognize spots of beauty and truths in their way of life, was use-less. It would not satisfy. It would not be a living experience, a source of life and vitality. . . . Perhaps that was what was wrong with Joshua. He had clothed himself with a religion decorated and smeared with everything *white*. He renounced his past and cut himself away from those life-giving traditions of the tribe. (141)

Waiyaki distinguishes multiple languages and practices of a supposedly sin-gular religion, and he assembles religious, racial, and political frameworks so that the spiritual is never divorced from the social. As this moment exempli-fies, the most extended theological meditations within the novel come not from Joshua and certainly not from Livingstone but from the characters— Muthoni, Nyambura, and Waiyaki—who are critically grappling with the in-tersections of the spiritual and the social, working to integrate the "life-giving traditions of the tribe" with aspects of Western culture that can, with revision, be "a source of life and vitality." Through their hybrid position, these charac-ters illustrate Bhabha's point that "other 'denied' knowledges enter upon the dominant [Christian] discourse and estrange the basis of its authority."[26] They take ownership over the language of the church and the school and destabi-lize the colonial alliance of these institutions.

   In this rewriting of the salvation narrative, the possibility of African free-dom lies in the religion not of the missionary but of the African adapter. *The River Between* argues against thinking in terms of purity, with either African or Western cultures as contamination, partly because this cultural fixation blocks the political goal: African freedom and self-determination. At the end of the novel, Waiyaki is ostracized by the tribe for his proximity to a Christian woman, Joshua's daughter Nyambura, and his mission is incomplete, meet-ing increasing resistance. He is still envisioning the "political movement that would shake the whole country, that would tell the white man 'Go!'" (151). We are left in a place of tension with a mission that is yet untested.

Christian Missions, African Novelists, Ambiguous Allies

The tension represented in *The River Between* is very much alive within the personal histories of both Ngũgĩ and Achebe. It is often noted that African novelists of their generation were products of mission education, but analysis of the significance is limited. Achebe, the son of an early convert and evangelist, was raised in the church and educated in its schools. For primary school, he attended St. Philip's C.M.S. (Christian Mission Society) Central School. For secondary education, he went to the Government College, Umuahia, a colonial state school shaped by Christian influence with an English minister as its founding principal. Ngũgĩ did not come from a Christian family himself, but converts had a large presence in his upbringing, too, and his mother sent him to the local mission station early on, embracing the opportunity for education regardless of religious content. He started at the missionary school, Kamandũra, and transferred in grade 3 to Manguo as part of the independent school movement. While this was a breakaway movement from the missionary-run school system (connected to Waiyaki's story in *The River Between*) it maintained religious affiliation, espousing a Christianity "shorn of its Western propensities."[27] Alliance High School, Ngũgĩ's final destination in *Dreams in a Time of War: A Childhood Memoir* (and the subject of his follow-up, *In the House of the Interpreter*), was established by the Alliance of Protestant Missions. The coming-of-age stories of these writers are saturated with missionary affiliation and influence.

That influence was accompanied by substantial anxieties. As Alison Searle explains, the educational endowment of missions "threatens a consuming alienation at the very moment of empowerment."[28] African discourse around missions is constantly negotiating that doubleness, the costs and benefits of mission school, and not within literature alone. Nelson Mandela, for example, balances skepticism with an appreciation for the services missions provided and turns the discussion toward their utility for Africa. Colonial-era missions, according to this line of thought, were indeed domineering but also useful in an environment where options for Africans people were tightly constricted:

> These schools have often been criticized for being colonialist in their attitudes and practices. Yet, even with such attitudes, I believe their benefits outweighed their disadvantages. The missionaries built and ran schools when the government was unwilling or unable to do so.

The learning environment of the missionary schools, while often morally rigid, was far more open than the racist principles underlying the
government schools. Fort Hare [a missionary college] was both home
and incubator of some of the greatest African scholars the continent
has ever known.[29]

The most critical reading of these schools would say that they were straightforward institutions of social control, colonizing minds to keep bodies in
check. Missionary intent aside, something quite different than social control
was often accomplished. Surely, they didn't educate Mandela into complicity
with white rule. In this assessment, he doesn't replace the critique but supplements it with the additional dimensions of the story, and the evidence of
independent African thought emerging from mission education is striking.
In *Dreams in a Time of War*, Ngũgĩ explains that his secondary school "had
indeed produced its fair share of an essentially cooperative leadership. But
contrary to the conscious intentions of its founders, Alliance had also birthed a
radical anticolonial nationalist fever."[30] The structure of response illustrated in
both Mandela's and Ngũgĩ's descriptions is not defined by an either-or choice
but a both-and, simultaneously rejecting and embracing various aspects of
missions — a partial conversion, a partial conservation.[31]

This both-and structure, which holds together the sides of the inherited
dialectic and carves new positions in between, is not a romantic resolution or
a sign of free choice. In the face of overwhelming and unavoidable colonial
power, it is the place of survival. Africans under colonialism and apartheid
were working in an environment without ideal options. When the most pressing problem was white rule, missions were evaluated for their tenuous balance
of costs and benefits within that political context and often judged to be an
ambiguous ally of African independence movements. In *The Education of a
British-Protected Child*, Achebe is constantly qualifying his position in relation
to missions, negotiating between their potential advantages and dangers in the
context of his dialectical inheritance. He writes, "I am a prime beneficiary
of the education which the missionaries had made a major component of
their enterprise. My father had a lot of praise for the missionaries and their
message, and so have I. But I have also learned a little more skepticism about
them than my father had any need for."[32] In his childhood memoir, Ngũgĩ
makes a remarkably similar statement: "From Lord Reverend Kahahu," a local
convert and mission figure, "I myself learned to revere modernity; from Baba
Mũkũrũ, the values of tradition; and from my father, a healthy skepticism
of both" (*Dreams*, 86). This stance characterizes anglophone African literature more broadly as it contains the trace of mission influence and balances

an implicit reverence for mission-based modernity with a skeptical sense of reservation.

Achebe advocates this mode of thinking that stakes itself in the middle ground. It is a value he draws from Igbo thought but seeks to apply more generally: "Why do the Igbo call the middle ground lucky? What does this place hold that makes it so desirable? Or, rather, what misfortune does it fence out? The answer is, I think, Fanaticism. The One Way, One Truth, One Life menace" (*Education*, 5). This "One Way, One Truth" language comes out of Christian doctrine, and in deploying it, Achebe pushes back against both the most triumphant and the most critical accounts of missions. He arrives at this perspective through his own dual inheritance: "Those two—my father and his uncle—formulated the dialectic which I inherited. Udoh stood fast in what he knew, but he left room also for his nephew to seek other answers. The answer my father found in the Christian faith solved many problems, but by no means all" (*Education*, 37). Missions are partially enabling though incomplete. And for Achebe, tradition doesn't provide all the answers to the problems of an invading modernity either. In his novels, purists don't survive. Ezeulu of *Arrow of God* and Okonkwo of *Things Fall Apart* lack the flexibility of his uncle Udoh; they refuse compromise and end up mad or dead. Purism is, in the extensiveness of the new dispensation, untenable. The mission station can provide a path toward new narratives of survival:

> In the new world that was emerging, of money and taxes, mining and military conscription, the syringe and the bicycle, the book and the blackboard, the white shirt and the wellington boot, this was *the way to go on*. The bravery games in the cattle villages and the lessons learned around the village fires had little to say about this world. Old solutions no longer seemed to be working; old systems no longer guaranted [*sic*] a man status and respect; old beliefs ceased to be convincing. In growing numbers Africans turned to the missions.[33]

Missions become a source for making the best out of a terrible situation, an expression of what Jean and John Comaroff have called the "will to make livable lives."[34] The question becomes, how to make good on this irreversible situation, how to move beyond the survival of colonialism toward its subversion? Africans found, in missions, resources for thinking out those problems as well.

What then, for the anticolonial project, is at stake in the middle ground? As Achebe asks, what possibility does this place hold and what misfortune does it fence out? What might it offer that has been inaccessible in the polarized debate over missions, and what resources does that grounding provide for dealing with the related debates over humanitarianism and its universalist values today? In terms of the academic discussion of missions, Achebe and Ngũgĩ shift the question from the terrain of ethical *ideals* (praising missionaries as saviors or condemning them as imperialists) to that of political *options* in a material environment. Applicable to their experience as mission students, this also has implications for their roles as postcolonial intellectuals. They demonstrate a version of committed critique that breaks the lines of orthodoxy, the sacred and the profane as separately defined by missions' apologists and critics (including themselves), viewing politics as "urgent collective action in an imperfect world (with allies and under circumstances that one might not have chosen for oneself), rather than as a radical refusal of all imperfection and, with it, of all action."[35] There is a risk in fundamentalisms of both varieties—the hardening of each discourse can become paralyzing, and thus there exists significant potential for movement within tempered modes of thought. Bruce Robbins has argued that the "moral messiness of politics" demands getting messy, lest one "condemn oneself to an indefinite wait—and, in effect, . . . withdraw from the project of political change."[36] Through their engagement with Christianity and its history in Africa, these writers confront one such form of "moral messiness," forging points of ambiguous alliance between postcolonial critique and global popular culture, including religious culture. They enlist multiple discourses of emancipation in order to find the most tenable path. To borrow the words of Olakunle George, "positive agency—in the domain of language or that of concrete politics—can emanate out of an act that is otherwise conceptually limited,"[37] and this certainly goes for the concepts African writers drew from their mission educations.

People of the Book

Viewed through the lens of African literature, missions were as much about literacy as about conversion. Indeed, it is impossible to understand the impact of missions in Africa without addressing education, as the two were so closely intertwined, with mission schools serving as the primary academic providers in the colonial era. There is a particularly close relationship between Christian missions and the flowering of African literature. Achebe and Ngũgĩ don't merely depict these stories of missions; these are their own stories, too. They are not the Okonkwos of these narratives but the Waiyakis. Simon Gikandi explains that "more than religious belief, it was the mission schools that were to prove indispensable in the emergence of an African literary tradition."[38] The skills on which the very identities of these writers *as writers* are based associate them implicitly with missions. Missions are thus woven into the very fabric of secular African writing. Missionaries had their hand in all aspects of the writing process. They developed orthographies for unwritten African languages and spread literacy through their schools. Mission presses were, in many places, the first to publish African writers and were, for many years, their only outlet for publication at all.[39] While missionaries learned indigenous languages and translated the Bible to make it locally accessible, they were also the primary source of English so that their trace is always "embedded in the textual nature of . . . African literature written in English"[40] as a language acquired through mission education.[41] African anglophone writing is, in and of itself, a complex manifestation of mission history.

Lamin Sanneh's work on missions and African vernaculars reveals that this trace of the mission lies in African-language writing as well. Although English was associated with missions and conversion, it was not a requirement for participation in the church, and biblical literacy did not require knowledge of a colonial language. The sacred, Sanneh shows, could be accessed in African tongues. He describes a bidirectional linguistic encounter in which missionaries validated the indigenous by learning African vernaculars and then translating sacred texts while also giving African students access to the global medium of English. The work of translation, with its emphasis on local legitimacy, put missions at odds with colonial rule, with its "current of foreign legitimacy ([and] the corollary of local inadequacy)."[42] This makes for an interesting reversal of Fanon's famous claim about colonial dominance through language: "To speak a language is to take on a world, a culture."[43] Sanneh suggests that missionaries, in taking on the language of the colonized, took on their world and culture in ways that did a disservice to colonial authority. While some missionaries encouraged the formation of political associations, their vernacular work alone "helped nurse the sentiments for the national cause, which mother tongues crystallized and incited."[44] In other words, the authorization of indigenous languages corresponded to the authorization of their speakers, and value for the indigenous was crucial to theorizing nationalism. One of the implications for literature is that missionaries' language activities enabled writers of both Achebe's and Ngũgĩ's varieties (after Ngũgĩ's "farewell to English") by equipping mission students for writing in *both* colonial and indigenous languages.[45] Thus Ngũgĩ's decision to write first in Gikuyu doesn't quite break with his mission heritage but puts it to use for the conservation of the local language.

Recalling debates with Ngũgĩ over the proper language of African literature, Achebe comments that Ngũgĩ, in opposing the imperial imposition of European languages, is "too good a partisan" to confront the "inconvenient" history of "imperialist agents (in the shape of Scottish missionaries) desiring to teach Kikuyu children in their mother tongue, while the patriotic Kikuyu are revolting and breaking away because they prefer English!" (*Education*, 104). Adding nuance to his earlier claims, Ngũgĩ recounts precisely this situation in *Dreams in a Time of War*. In the memoir, English is portrayed as one of the main motivations for breaking off from missionaries who were not teaching *enough* English. The independent school "was seen as having a more challenging curriculum, demanding rapid acquisition of English as we entered modern times" (114). Later, he describes the years of Emergency in the 1950s when Gikuyu became the subject of derision and the political context and demand for its use changed (177). The relationship between missionary teachings, Western control, and African demands thus qualifies the imperial imposition argument that Ngũgĩ himself has advanced.

Simon Gikandi, in reflecting on his own biography as well as that of Ngũgĩ, explains that missions and literacy were so closely linked that Gikuyu Christians were called *Athomi*—literates or "people of the book."[46] This extends beyond the anglophone context. For example, Angolan convert and pastor Jesse Chipenda recalls his father's response to how he had changed after visiting his mother's village and learning to read: "He believes in Jesus, and he has a book."[47] In other words, books and belief went hand in hand, even in language itself; in Umbundu, Chipenda's mother tongue, the verbs "to believe" (*oku tava*) and "to read" (*oku tanga*) are closely associated.[48] The founding figures of anglophone African fiction were logically book people, their histories entangled with the mixed inheritance of literacy, Christianity, and the English language.[49] George explains that, although the identity they "insist upon is emphatically no longer a Christian one," contemporary writers occupy a position closely resembling that of nineteenth-century African missionaries, partly exterior to the people they represent.[50] By entering the literate order, novelists were indeed converts of a sort. Literacy was also viewed as a form of conversion, since one did not acquire literacy alone; it came, Gikandi explains, with a whole set of associations: "To become readers, the colonized were required not only to acquire literacy but also to adopt Western values, vocations, modes of dress, and a 'European demeanor.'"[51] Therefore, "one was not merely a Christian because one believed in a certain doctrine; rather, conversion was apparent in one's ability to live a modern life, a life manifested in a new monetary economy, mode of dress, set of cultural values, and even architecture."[52] The accoutrements of mission education were in some ways welcome and in others worrisome. As Ngũgĩ puts it in *Dreams in a Time of War*, "Successful conversion was measured by how quickly, deeply, and thoroughly one divested oneself of one's culture and adopted new practices and values."[53] Novels of mission education such as *The River Between* and *Things Fall Apart* are mindful of the alienation and distance that it would build between the student's own culture and history, as are the writers' autobiographical accounts.[54]

At the same time, many Africans perceived the schools to hold emancipatory potential of a form not necessarily anticipated by missionaries themselves: "There is no doubt that the spread of literacy and knowledge of other languages both widened horizons at many different social levels and greatly enhanced the ability of ordinary people to question or subvert traditional attitudes as well as imperial and colonial assumptions."[55] A pedagogy of conversion, even as it seeks to implant a new orthodoxy by replacing an old one, renders belief and tradition questionable, thus destabilizing, to a degree, the new orthodoxy itself. Andrew Porter points to a dual destabilization of local tradition and colonial imposition. Of course, these competing traditions—both rendered questionable to a degree—meet on far-from-equal footing. Thus, the relationship between loyalty to local knowledge and the acceptance of foreign learning is never quite settled for the African writer. In his essay "Biggles, Mau Mau, and I," Ngũgĩ wrestles with the contradiction of attending a "colonial school in a colonial world," which aimed "to produce leaders who of course, had the necessary character and knowledge to faithfully but intelligently serve King and Empire," while receiving continuous encouragement to "cling to education" from his brother who was away in the forest fighting against that King and Empire.[56] The essay's title alludes to an uncomfortable triangle between the author, the figure of colonialist literature, Biggles, loyal "first and foremost to the flag,"[57] and the Mau Mau freedom fighters, most intimately his own brother, who opposed everything Biggles stood for—except, somehow, education. How Biggles and the young Ngũgĩ fit together represents an anxiety over the influence of the mission school: would reading Biggles mean a betrayal of the relationship between "Mau Mau and I"? Could all three ever really reside together as closely as they do in the title?

As Paulo Freire famously insists, there is "no such thing as a *neutral* educational process."[58] Biggles, as Ngũgĩ knows, is anything but a neutral character. Rather, he is part of an educational system backed by imperial interests. Freire goes on:

> Education either functions as an instrument which is used to facilitate
> the integration of the younger generation into the logic of the present
> system and bring about conformity to it, *or* it becomes "the practice
> of freedom," the means by which men and women deal critically and
> creatively with reality and discover how to participate in the transfor
> mation of the world.[59]

Clearly, Biggles belongs in the former category. But Freire later qualifies this either-or statement to suggest that it is possible for a critical capacity to emerge even in students under the former regime.[60] That slipperiness is a function of literacy itself. Literacy is particularly vulnerable to practices of freedom, since the capacity to "deal critically and creatively with reality" by interpreting for oneself is enabled by the capacity to read for oneself.

A large part of the anticolonial potential in mission education was found in that capacity. Much progressive thought has viewed literacy as a vital element in the process of liberation and accordingly, people in power see it as a threat.[61] In Noni Jabavu's *The Ochre People*, for example, a young anti-apartheid activist seeks "to *convert* [people] to religion if possible even though he wasn't a minister, but mainly to the idea of educating their children."[62] Like Waiyaki's mission for education, the activist's interest is in educating them out of the apartheid order, not into it. This re-inflects the idea of conversion, leading it to signify a conversion *out* of the oppressive order that is the reality of the day.[63] While mission education involved "an irreversible move away from the existing foundation of identity and community,"[64] literacy also contained the seed of rebellion. In *The Education of a British-Protected Child*, Achebe links the mission school and the rise of political consciousness in spite of the curriculum. He recalls the school library that housed adventure stories for boys: "Even stories like John Buchan's, in which heroic white men battled and worsted repulsive natives, did not trouble us unduly at first. But it all added up to a wonderful preparation for the day we would be old enough to read between the lines and ask questions . . ." (21). With the ellipsis, he gestures toward the success of that preparation. Achebe has indeed read between the lines and asked questions very unsettling of the colonialist texts he read as a boy.[65]

On Reading and Rebellion

How, then, did people of the book—so closely affiliated with colonial culture—become such committed anticolonialists? What kind of preparation could the likes of Biggles offer for the project of decolonizing the mind and the nation? If missions have been central to both colonialist and anticolonialist consciousness building, as these writers suggest, then how did African people manage to privilege the latter? Since literacy was naturally the focal point of powerful and even enchanting attraction among many of those who became writers, I want to direct that question specifically toward literacy to explore how these writers have theorized and demonstrated the components of its emancipatory potential.

I will enter this issue by way of an illustration. In *The Education of a British-Protected Child*, Achebe alludes to the story of Moses. The reference is brief but significant for the way it positions the writer, offering a window on

Achebe's theorization of the problems and potentialities of mission education. He compares himself to Moses as a way of contemplating how a concept from his indigenous culture, the luck of the middle ground, managed to penetrate the powerhouse of colonial culture: "my traditional Igbo culture, which at the hour of her defeat had ostensibly abandoned me in a basket of reeds in the waters of the Nile, . . . somehow kept anxious watch from concealment, ultimately insinuating herself into the service of Pharaoh's daughter to nurse me in the alien palace" where she "taught me a children's rhyme which celebrates the middle ground as most fortunate" (*Education*, 5). The first point is simply that this is a writer as well-versed in the art of biblical allusion as in Igbo proverbs. By inserting Moses into the Igbo world and taking that story to new ends, Achebe exemplifies a central feature of African Christianity as described by Achille Mbembe:

> While theologians of enculturation worried that conversion would involve the abolition of the self, Christianity in practice was turned upside down, undone, and then outfitted in masks and ancestral bric-a-brac, all without ever being stripped of its core concept. It appeared to Blacks as, first of all, an immense field of signs that, once decrypted, opened the way for an array of practices that moved constantly away from orthodoxy. Africans used Christianity as a mirror through which to represent their own society and history to themselves.[66]

As with English itself, Achebe takes the Christian "field of signs . . . away from orthodoxy." His identification with Moses is emblematic of the anticolonial writer more broadly and provides a cue for how to think about empire and acculturation—for how to think, in other words, about what it means to be educated in "the alien palace."

Achebe's allusion to Moses raises the question of formation under a foreign power. The baby Moses, set afloat in a world where being an Israelite is enough to get him killed under Pharaoh's paranoid, oppressive regime, ends up in the house of Pharaoh himself. There, he is raised by the Pharaoh's daughter and will be mistaken by his own people for an Egyptian. In spite of this context, Achebe describes the values of Moses's own trampled culture finding their way to him in the undercover form of his own biological mother. There is much more to the story, which Achebe does not recount here but which is built into the significance of the figure of Moses, thickening the reference. What, ultimately, does his upbringing produce, with Hebrew influence situated as a small voice in the house of the oppressor? With the parallels between the enslaved Israelites and colonized Africans, the story speaks directly to the experience of African writers educated in colonial mission schools. Even if the

aim of missions was in part to produce "good Africans," servants of the colonial
order who would betray their own culture and history, the Moses story depicts
an alternative outcome. Moses emerged to become the prime defender of the
Israelites, delivering them out of slavery under the Egyptians. The accompanying education does not guarantee loyalty but in fact comes to serve the
work of rebellion in this narrative. As it applies to Achebe and writers in his
position, anticolonial discourse and narrative have indeed emerged from the
collusion of biblical traditions and indigenous ones.

In the Exodus story, it is the outsider positioned within the house of Egypt
who overthrows it, and African fiction has often depicted mission education
in this way. Education "in the alien palace" is of strategic value. In Achebe's
Arrow of God, the priest Ezeulu, despite his intense commitment to tradition,
sends his son to the mission school "to be my eyes there" and to "learn the
ways of [white] people."[67] "A man must dance the dance prevalent in his
time," he tells his son (189). Education in the ways of the white man is seen as
a form of security so as not to be caught off guard by rapidly changing times.
In *Dreams in a Time of War*, Ngũgĩ's father's land, purchased "in goats under
the traditional system of oral agreement in the presence of witnesses," is later
resold, this time "recorded under the colonial legal system, with witnesses and
signed written documents. . . . Orality and tradition lost to literacy and modernity. A title deed no matter how it was gotten trumped oral deeds" (18–19). The
man who buys the land, the Reverend Kahahu, a figure associated with the
church and the mission school, is also Gikuyu, also subject to dispossession
under colonialism. The power and privilege he has lie in his association with
missions and the capacity he gains to participate in the now dominant literate
order. There may be an element of covert resistance in Kahahu's refusal to be
dispossessed by the colonial order—this figure who appears to be most in line
with colonial values is also well equipped to compete with colonists—yet for
Ngũgĩ it is radically insufficient; the problem is that making himself at home
in this colonial modernity means putting others out of theirs.[68] While he may
extract himself from colonial dispossession, he is complicit in the dispposses-
sion of others. Still, other models of engagement are available.

Often, participation in the literate order is seen not only as a mode of surviving colonialism but of resisting it though a kind of infiltration or poaching.
According to these narratives, the liberator, like Moses, may be an outsider
but he strikes from the inside. Recall that in *The River Between*, Chege sends
Waiyaki to the mission to "learn all the wisdom and all the secrets of the
white man. But do not follow his vices," he warns; "Be true to your people
and the ancient rites" (20). Chege's hope is to empower his son so that he will
fulfill the Gikuyu prophecy and save his people from British domination. In

this view, the mission is essentially a leak. It is a place through which people reckon with and rise against white rule by learning to take up the weapons of Western modernity; one goes to the mission (ambiguously situated *within* colonialism) to gain a foothold *against* colonialism. Take, for example, these lyrics which the children in Ngũgĩ's community sing in his memoir:

> If these were the times of our ancestors Ndemi and Mathathi
> My father, I would ask you for the feast due to initiates,
> Then I would ask you to arm me with a spear and shield,
> But today, Father, I ask you for education only[.] (*Dreams*, 123)

Education stands in place of the spears and shields that have floundered against modern guns, and the mission is the supplier. Full conservation, it seems, would be ineffective resistance. The implication is that the mission is essentially arming people, regardless of missionary intentions. Scenes that seem to register aspirations to European likeness can instead signal social and political aspirations.[69]

For African people, missions were strategically useful; they were also attractive in ways that went deeper than instrumental utility. The Bible often provided inspiration and divine sanction for rebellion. Access to that inspiration was dependent on literacy, which, in theory, opens up an unlimited world of ideas. The reality, however, is determined by material constraints and limited access to textual resources. The most widely accessible book in Africa was and is the Bible. Achebe's reference to the Moses story is itself a mark of literacy and the freedom of interpretation. The Exodus story has been one of the most powerful for the vision of emancipation it provides. Ngũgĩ's work, too, abounds with references to Moses and the emancipation of the Israelites. In *Weep Not Child*, when the young protagonist begins hearing whispers of Kenyan liberation and asks "Who is Jomo?," he is told only that he is called "the Black Moses."[70] The language of the narrative takes on the language of the Exodus: "Everyone knew that Jomo would win. God would not let His people alone. The children of Israel must win" (72). This is not the way the story of Moses is being taught at Njoroge's school. Rather it is a demonstration of literacy as a practice of freedom, the text taken into the hands of its readers. Mission education thus becomes a common trope within anticolonial narratives of emancipation as a force of communal and not merely individual uplift. Njoroge's mother tells him: "Your learning is for all of us. Father says the same thing. He is anxious that you go on, so you might bring light to our home. Education is the light of Kenya. That's what Jomo says" (38). Njoroge overestimates the power of education to overcome the constrictions of colonial life — he envisions himself as "a possible saviour of the whole of God's country" (82) — and this narrative ultimately disappoints, thus chastening this adapted salvation narrative of education as surefire liberation. The emancipatory potential is more subtle and more tenuous.

Learning of the Exodus is also pivotal for Kihika, the freedom fighter and martyr of *A Grain of Wheat*: "As soon as he learnt how to read, Kihika bought a Bible and read the story of Moses over and over again."[71] He reads with a pen in hand and, between chapters, Ngũgĩ inserts a series of "verse[s] underlined in red in Kihika's personal Bible" (31, 129, 201), beginning with Exodus 8.1:

> And the Lord spoke unto Moses,
> Go unto Pharaoh, and say unto him,
> Thus saith the Lord,
> Let my people go. (31)

Through these insertions, the novel's form reflects one of its major themes. Returning to the words of Mbembe, Ngũgĩ and his characters use "Christianity as a mirror" without having "stripped [it] of its core concept."[72] They take the Moses story to new ends with the novel itself ingesting and reproducing biblical language. Recalling the anecdote about the white man showing up with the Bible, this text suggests the black man didn't close his eyes; rather, he learned to read it and used it to take his land back, privileging interpretation over mere adaptation. The Bible, the very centerpiece of missionary intentions, was also separable from them. The mission became a significant presence in locally generated African liberation narratives.

The scene of learning to read thus becomes a powerful moment of emancipatory vision, revealing parallels with the African American literary tradition. In *Dreams in a Time of War*, Ngũgĩ's description of the "magic of learning to read" (70) echoes what Henry Louis Gates calls the "trope of the talking book" in American slave narratives. Ngũgĩ writes,

> And then one day I come across a copy of the Old Testament, it may
> have belonged to Kabae, and the moment I find that I am able to read
> it becomes my book of magic with the capacity to tell me stories even
> when I'm alone, night or day. I don't have to wait for the sessions at
> Wangarĩ's in order to hear a story. (65)

It is an enchanted experience, opening up a new world and freeing him from dependence on other tellers. In this moment, he approaches the mission's offering of literacy not with critical distance, but with the passion of a willing convert. Significantly, the newness of the reading experience is characterized not by total difference from the oral culture he knew — Wangarĩ's storytelling — but by an extension of that culture, an opportunity to have more of it. He falls in love with text when he realizes that "written words can *also* sing" (65, emphasis added). The young Ngũgĩ is attracted to the modernity of the written word for the way it resonates with the oral tradition. The Old Testament story he finds most compelling reveals the same pattern:

> Most vivid in a positive way is the story of David. There is David playing the harp to a King Saul of contradictory moods. Their alternations of love and hate are almost hard to bear. Years later I would completely identify with the lines of the spiritual: *Little David play on your harp*. But David the harpist, the poet, the singer is also a warrior who can handle slingshots against Goliath. He, the victor over giants, is like trickster Hare, in the stories told at Wangarĩ's, who could always outsmart stronger brutes. (66)

The story's attraction is partly in its familiarity, in the way it recalls and reinforces a story he has heard before in the house of his father's eldest wife. It is not a new story of freedom, but *another* story of freedom, echoing and further legitimating the impulses expressed through the trickster Hare. This does not pose an either-or choice, conserve or convert. Ngũgĩ's embrace of the biblical David does not separate him from the indigenous culture or betray its oral literary tradition; rather, it fortifies preexisting narratives about the desire to be free. The anticolonial resonance of the unlikely little David with his harp and his sling defeating the massive, sword-wielding Goliath is evident; like Ngũgĩ himself, David is a kind of rebel artist. Literacy unlocks the revolutionary potential buried in the missionary's book.

In addition to narratives of divinely sanctioned rebellion, biblical concepts were readily available to reinforce the value of African lives. Particularly powerful was the idea of a universal humanity, in spite of the troubled history of its deployment.[73] This foundational concept for the missionary enterprise was hypocritically practiced with some humans higher on the ladder than others, yet regardless of Western Christian practice, the Bible offered a means of conceptualizing humanity in ways subversive to the colonial order, ways that made "bad Africans" rather than compliant collaborators.[74] In his autobiography, *Let My People Go* (1962), Albert Luthuli, the first president of the African National Congress, responds to the claim that "natives who travel get spoilt": "perhaps the desire in any African for normal human relations—not group relations—is itself proof that he is 'spoilt.' If that is so, I can only reply that I was not spoilt abroad. I was spoilt by being made in the image of God."[75] This universal and sanctified notion of the human—made in this image of God—creates a rebellious sense of inclusion that defies apartheid's categorical grouping of human beings. That is to say not that Africans needed the

Bible in order to consider themselves human but rather that its universal vision was useful for reconfiguring group belonging and making political claims on that basis. This is also a predecessor to humanitarianism's guiding principle of universal humanity, the subject of the next chapter. Human life, in this view, is not necessarily rooted in God, but it is indeed sacred.

The Exodus story, with its emphasis on liberating "the people" at large, signals the place of mission education within anticolonial narratives as a force of communal and not merely individual uplift. Missions physically assembled collectivities that gave tangible shape to the notion of human universalism and had real potential for nationalist organizing. Mandela recalls that it was at the mission school that he began to shift from an ethnic identity to a continental one through interaction with students of other languages and backgrounds: "I began to sense my identity," he explains, "as an African, not just a Thembu or even a Xhosa."[76] In the words of Catherine Hall, "New thinking was framed by new forms of organization."[77] Njoroge's experience at the Siriana Mission School in *Weep Not Child* is suggestive of this connection:

> Here again, he met boys from many tribes. Again if these had met him and had tried to practise dangerous witchcraft on him, he would have understood. But instead he met boys who were like him in every way. He made friends and worked with Nandi, Luo, Wakamba, and Giriama. They were boys who had hopes and fears, loves and hatreds. If he quarreled with any or if he hated any, he did so as he would have done with any other boy from his village. (108)

The strength of the anticolonial project was fed by these new forms of organization, which were facilitated not by physical assembly alone, but by the cultivation of broader forms of Pan-African association through written literature. As Ajayi and Ayandele assert, literary education had a hand in "the development of uniform aspirations, values, outlooks, and desires across ethnic frontiers—a factor of great significance in the emergence of a nation."[78] The anticolonial (as well as the antiapartheid) project required strength in numbers and, thus, missions became complicit in political organizing. Luthuli's "spoiling" by Christian theology is, therefore, suggestive of the link between religious ideas and worldly freedoms for which Africans would engage in collective struggle.

This is a global pattern. In a study of nineteenth-century Jamaica, Hall shows that slaveholders and colonial settlers actually feared missionary work for that very link: "the heart of the complaint against the missions," she writes, was over "the slippage that occurred between temporal and spiritual freedom. If religious freedom were granted, what certainty was there that the claims of the enslaved would stop there?"[79] This was the case among colonized people as well as the enslaved. Granting Africans the "privilege" of human status was seen as a dangerously slippery slope between spiritual ideas and material realities:

> Missionaries believed in the unity of humankind and wanted to eman-
> cipate the local populations, beliefs not necessarily shared by adminis-
> trators and settlers who placed power and profits above Christianity. In
> many places, the settler communities stiffly resisted missionary work,
> fearing that if the indigenous peoples became Christian, then they
> would demand to be treated as equals.[80]

Some missionaries pushed these questions themselves, although more often the "equality of Africans was a matter of principle and potential, not a sugges-tion of immediate egalitarianism."[81] Ideas of individual salvation and choice, foundational to evangelical Christianity, were perceived to be dangerous for enslaved and colonized people who were not to have any individual choice. One kind of freedom could open up the desire for another. Furthermore, the discourse of universal humanity contradicted the Manichean colonial discourse. Even as they "appealed for obedience to the authorities, the mis-sionaries insisted on the right to individual salvation, and thus opened up the question of freedom of thought."[82] In other words, Christianity would "spoil" African people. Colonial fears of mission influence were justified, and the literature affirms Hall's assertion that "Christianity played a vital part in artic-ulating new claims for freedom."[83] It provided a shared language of struggle around which people of separate traditions could rally.

Ngũgĩ suggests in his essay "Literature and Society" that the Mau Mau anticolonial movement made precisely the leap that colonizers and slave-holders feared between spiritual and political freedoms. While "the colo-nial state encouraged that brand of christianity that abstracted heaven from earthly struggles," Kenyan believers reinterpreted it.[84] Ngũgĩ's decapitalization of "christianity" contributes to the sense that he is referring to the imported religion not as a unified thing in itself but as multiple and unstable, colonially conscripted yet not inherently colonial. Anticolonial fighters put that flexibil-ity to use:

> So Mau Mau took the same Christian songs and even the Bible, and
> *interpreted them for themselves*, giving these values and meaning in
> harmony with the aspirations of their struggles. Officially approved
> Christians sang of a host of angels in heaven. They sang of a spiritual
> journey in a spiritual, intangible universe where a metaphysical,

disembodied evil and good were locked in perpetual spiritual warfare for the domination of the human soul. They called on the youth to arm themselves spiritually and take up spiritual arms against an invisible satan. Led by Jesus, they would be victorious.

The Mau Mau took up similar hymns but now turned them into songs of *actual political engagement in an actual political universe.* They called for *visible* material *freedom.* The battle was no longer for some invisible new heaven but for *a real heaven on their own earth.*[85]

Here we see the slippage between freedoms of spiritual and material varieties in practice. Bhabha's description is apt: "the hybrid tongues of the colonial space make even the repletion of *name* of God uncanny."[86] Christianity provided a wealth of ideas that often had very literal consequences for the strength of the colonial order, but those ideas were not predetermined by the Western disseminators of Christianity. While it promised a world to come, better than the present one, Christianity also fostered the desire for "a real heaven on their own earth." The significant role of literacy in the capacity for critical interpretation becomes an important corollary for the usability of religious resources. These writers push us to rethink the history of concepts like universal humanity and divine emancipation, which we know to be problematic, particularly for the ways they have positioned African and other colonial subjects, but we must ask if there is, to quote Ngũgĩ, "redemptive possibility in the action of the oppressed"[87] upon colonially implicated ideas such as these. The notion of the emancipated African within the white savior narrative signifies very differently once subject to actual African agency.

Christianity, Freedom Struggles, and the Humanitarian Atlantic

In the postcolonial era, the struggle for African freedoms has taken new forms. As David Scott has argued, different eras generate different "problem-spaces," and such historical shifts call not only for new answers but for new questions, placing "a new set of demands on criticism."[88] Increasingly complex approaches to Christianity and mission history are a part of the critical demand of the twenty-first century. By the 1990s, Christianity had become a primarily nonwestern religion. Continuing to view it as the "monolithic imposition of European domination" would, as Dana Robert explains, "attribute 'false consciousness' to the majority of Christians in the twenty-first century."[89] Achille Mbembe suggests that a rethinking of the relationship between religion and progressive politics is beginning to take place: "to a certain extent, we have moved beyond a time, not so long ago, when generations after generations of leftist revolutionaries were happy to denounce religion as a *façon de parler* — a force of alienation which threatened human freedom."[90] Ngũgĩ and Achebe reflect the possibility within that shift as they articulate missions with projects of human freedom.

They model a "complex assemblage" of religious and progressive materialist thought, a way out of the idealist stand-off that blocks movement forward.[91] They build that assemblage formally as well as thematically, using the structure of the novel — and the novelistic memoir — to make divergent discourses speak to each other and with each other. They push us to think through the possibilities of moving beyond the pieties of debate, to ask how ideas can collide and coexist and be put to work in the world. Through both fictional and personal narratives, these authors suggest that Christian ethics can indeed play a role in narratives of Africa's radical transformation and not for Christians alone. In a speech called "Church, Culture, Politics," which Ngũgĩ presented in 1970 to the Presbyterian Church of East Africa in Nairobi, he opens with the confession that he is "not a man of the church . . . not even a Christian."[92] While he never strays from his critique of the church's imperialist history, he doesn't call for a separation from it. Rather, its lessons should be taken up in order to make the church relevant to the problems of postcolonial Africa: "I am stressing these things of our colonial religious inheritance," he writes, "because if the church is to mean anything then it must be a meaningful champion of the needs of all the workers and peasants of this country. It must adapt itself in form and in content to provide a true spiritual anchor in the continuing struggle of the masses in today's Africa."[93] He calls the church to a theology of liberation that, in the words of Gustavo Gutiérrez, "is open — in the protest against trampled human dignity, in the struggle against the plunder of the vast majority of humankind, in liberating love, and in the building of a new, just, and comradely society — to the gift of the Kingdom of God."[94] Ngũgĩ is thinking pragmatically about the need to make things better, the need to continue envisioning, narrating, and creating real, tangible improvement, resisting that trampling of human dignity and plunder of humankind. His primary concern is the "struggle of the masses in today's Africa" and if the church can help, all the better.

This brings us to the question of why Ngũgĩ and Achebe have returned to the issue of missions in the twenty-first century. While they have always pointed to the complexity of missions, these recent recollections are more affirmative of and even affectionate toward their Christian inheritance than they have ever been. This shift may have to do with the new locus of Christianity and the constituencies of African politics. With the enormous growth of Christianity in Africa after decolonization — led not by foreign missionaries but by homegrown evangelists—it has essentially displaced Europe as *the* Christian continent. This is a fitting time to recall what the church in Africa has been and consider what it can be, a chance to harness the emancipatory potential in the creed held by so many people on the continent today. This is especially urgent to writers so keenly aware of the ways Christianity has been coupled with the oppression of African people. For Ngũgĩ in particular, who continues to advocate a revolutionary politics of the masses, the church holds unique potential in that it assembles, organizes, and mobilizes masses of people, including the poor, excluded, and dispossessed.

The problem space of the humanitarian Atlantic calls for new African articulations of Christian ethics and material need, new imaginings of "a real heaven on their own earth." It calls for the pursuit of emancipation outside the state and creative engagement with the third sector. Both Ngũgĩ and Achebe offer a way of critiquing and rethinking Christianity, not to dismantle it entirely, but to reassemble it toward the needs of the African present as defined by African people, using the admittedly imperfect tools—and allies—available. In the secular realm, too, African people can do with humanitarianism what they have done with Christianity—take its narratives and *"interpret them for themselves,* giving [to humanitarianism] values and meaning in harmony with the aspirations of their struggles."[95]

3

The Universal Human

Missions, both sacred and secular, operate at the edges of society among the marginalized and the disempowered. Thus, humanitarian fictions are generally set on the periphery of human inclusion and even physical survival. For instance, in Graham Greene's *A Burnt-Out Case*, a passenger seeking to escape his life in Europe boards a boat heading into the Congo to disembark only at the point where "the boat goes no further."[1] There, at the remotest spot he can reach, he finds a leper colony where a group of European priests and an atheist doctor work among the quarantined, both the sick and the "burnt-out cases" who are healed but not integrated back into society. In John le Carré's *The Constant Gardener*, when a pharmaceutical company tests new drugs on impoverished Kenyans to deadly effect, the humanitarian heroine puts up a fight, proclaiming the value of lives the industry treats as disposable. In Ngũgĩ wa Thiong'o's *Wizard of the Crow* (a subject of chapter 5), the protagonist makes his first appearance "collapsed at the foot of the mountain of garbage," worn down by "the endless restraining demands of the body."[2] In settings such as these, where life is pushed to its limits, questions of human suffering and accountability come to the fore. Who is responsible for the well-being of others, and on what philosophical grounds? According to humanitarian ethics, one person's suffering is everyone's problem.

This moral imperative serves as the underlying logic of the humanitarian Atlantic, linking Africa, Europe, and North America in a network of responsibility. The idea that we are accountable not merely to those immediately surrounding us but to those who are distant and different from us presumes that we are, in some fundamental way, all the same, allowing us to know and thus act upon places distant and different from our own. In short, humanitarian action is grounded in the notion of universal humanity. As secretary general of the United Nations, Kofi Annan articulated this sensibility: "When we see an outpouring of international aid to the victims of [a catastrophe]—a great deal of it from those having no apparent link [to those victims] *except for a sense of common humanity*—that is the international community following its humanitarian impulse."[3] In this 1999 address, Annan was speaking to civil society organizations and NGOs, calling for their partnership with the UN and a third sector approach to global problems. He added that Africa, in particular, needs a unified, effective international community for support. This approach was part of a larger trend.

Alongside the faltering of the postcolonial African state, we have witnessed the rise of the third sector; where governments have failed to protect or provide for their citizens, nonprofit and nongovernmental organizations have stepped in—a phenomenon Alex de Waal calls the "internationalization of social welfare" and "responsibility."[4] If we are all fundamentally the same, then our standards of living shouldn't be so far apart. Confronting that gap means confronting power, and this fuels stories of humanitarian heroics in a world that needs saving. As Didier Fassin explains, "The humanitarian politics of life is based on an entrenched standpoint in favor of the 'side of the victims.' The world order, it supposes, is made up of the powerful and the weak. Humanitarian action takes place in the space between the two, being deployed among the weak as it denounces the powerful."[5] Therefore, the humanitarian impulse is simultaneously about a common, universal humanity and contentious relations of power. At its root, humanitarian action is defined less as a material act than as a relational one through which dramatic roles are assigned and performed, with Africa typecast as the ultimate victim. The humanitarian imagination is channeled through narratives of individual human relations, which signal universal dimensions of existence and attempt to bridge social divides, but questions arise about how the relationship among the powerful, the weak, and the humanitarian intercessor is configured.

Despite good intentions, this relationship has often failed on both practical and ethical levels, a reality Annan acknowledges. Of course, humanitarians themselves have a great deal of power in comparison to those they presume to assist. Rather than alleviating colonialism's postcolonial hangover, humanitarian intervention has often reinforced and extended the relations of imperial power, leading Mahmood Mamdani to call the international community "a post–Cold War nom de guerre for the Western powers."[6] And herein lies the paradox of humanitarian ethics. To act on behalf of another is to act on the basis of power. While humanitarianism aims to assist those who have been excluded from the inheritance of decolonization, while it claims to side with the victims and include them in a global community, it can marginalize and disempower them in turn. Universal humanism, both in theory and in humanitarian practice, is riven with tensions between liberating and dominating, caring and controlling, helping and hurting.

Theories of universal humanity have long plagued Africa specifically. Africans have often fallen outside of humanity by Western definition, and even when they have tenuously fit, it has often been at a lower rung on the civilizational ladder, with the burden placed on the Westerner to uplift the African. Yet, in spite of all this, the notion of universal humanity, so central to both religious and humanitarian missions, has been a point of genuine attraction among many African and diasporic thinkers. The question of human definition is not a point of anxiety for these writers; they are not questioning the fact of their humanity but trying to make the inclusive category live up to its name. The fact that white humanists have excluded African people from full belonging discounts those particular *proponents* of humanity but not the *concept* of humanity itself. Kwasi Wiredu's argument about cultural universals is apt: "More often than not, the alleged universals have been home-grown particulars. Not unnaturally, the practice has earned universals a bad name. But, rightly perceived, the culprits are the hasty purveyors of universals, not the idea of universals itself."[7] The idea may well be redeemable.

Within the African literature of the third sector (more than in its British and American forms), universal humanity has functioned as a valuable and even radical concept, a language of rebellion, in spite of its colonial career. Whereas some would argue that the language of universal humanity is the method of a new empire, these writers suggest that it is also a language of opposition to neocolonial power and inequity. I am interested in filling in the latter side of this conversation. Part of the problem of the postcolony that writers have continually attacked is its noninclusivity—the fact that the transformations of decolonization did not meaningfully address everyone. Samuel Moyn argues that the rise of universal human rights discourse since the 1970s grows out of that crisis of the state, out of the failure to guarantee rights on the basis of the nation.[8] This could also be said of third sector solutions more broadly; international humanitarianism responds to a crisis of national inclusion and goes over the sovereignty of the state in order to address the needs of—at least in theory—everyone, regardless of citizenship, race, religion, and so on. Novelists have taken up this dimension of humanitarian discourse to decenter and decolonize it, making use of its necessary but insufficient universalism as a concept that is "both corrupted *and* indispensable."[9]

In this chapter, I read Bessie Head and Zakes Mda as key examples; they explore the idea of universality in the context of humanitarian action in ways that are not naïve or sentimental but intensely engaged with the troubled history of its deployment. The focus here is not on the emergency branch of humanitarianism, which addresses moments of acute crisis, but on the development branch, which addresses ongoing needs. I will explore how these writers negotiate the idea of universal humanity in the context of poverty and material inequality. On that foundation, I will argue that for humanitarianism, universal humanism is both its repressive risk and its radical possibility. Stepping out of chronological order, I begin by examining a debate within Mda's *The Heart of Redness* (2000) to illustrate the relationship between universal humanism and third sector development strategies. After filling out the implications of that debate within anticolonial and postcolonial theory, I turn to Bessie Head's *A Question of Power* (1974), which, despite its early date, speaks powerfully to humanitarianism's current discontents. While Mda writes about the aftermath of apartheid and Head (as a refugee writer who fled South Africa for Botswana) addresses apartheid at a remove, both situate their texts within wider discussions of colonialism and decolonization, despite South Africa's unique historical trajectory. Mda actually writes apartheid out of *The Heart of Redness*, moving between nineteenth-century British invasion and the postapartheid era with apartheid itself existing as a temporal gap in the narrative. Head is thinking within a Pan-African framework, considering (and critiquing) various projects of black nationalism within the continent and beyond. While these writers could certainly be situated within more specific discussions of the South African timeline, I will place their texts within the anticolonial and postcolonial framework which their work seems to welcome.[10]

Humanitarian practice stems from its humanist premise, and theoretical problems have practical implications. With their focus on donor-based projects that provide water, food, and education, *The Heart of Redness* and *A Question of Power* help us think through the relationship between humanist theory and humanitarian practice. In *The Heart of Redness*, through his depiction of development debates on the ground, Mda reveals the consequences of speaking in terms of "the everyone." He gestures toward an ethical mode of identification across difference that combines universality with particularity, so often seen as bitter rivals. Head's focus on the relationships between international agents of development and the poor in Botswana (who are both recipients of and participants in development projects) builds the connection between a reimagined humanism and the possibility of a revised humanitarian practice. Both authors signal how such a humanism could be mobilized into new narratives of interpersonal and material equity. By examining the intersections between their novels and theoretical debates about humanism, I will ask: How does universalism come into conflict with humanitarianism's equalizing goals? How can humanism—with its troubling history of Euro-centrism—be decentered, and how does that enable us to reimagine human community in a way that extends beyond the state *and* beyond the rhetoric of salvation? And to that end, how might the story of human community be told differently?

Humanitarian assistance never can and never will be a sufficient solution to the unequal distribution of resources across the globe, but, to again borrow the words of Alex de Waal, "Aid exists and will not disappear."[11] Within these novels, humanitarianism—with its unsettling mix of imperialist and egalitarian tendencies—is an ambiguous but necessary ally in a nonideal world. This mode of critique never sidelines the foundational questions of international community: How do we theorize community on the basis of the human, and, if we take the human as primary, then what should we do about it? Instead, these authors offer a more critical humanism that accounts for the dangers of universalism while also preserving its progressive impulses. They displace humanism's conventional pillars—the Western, the wealthy, the white—and chart an alternative "brotherhood of man" as a process (not a preexisting condition) originating from the social margins.[12] On the one hand, their work reveals the international community to be a fiction, a euphemism for Western control and African subordination. But, on the other, they offer their own fictions of international community—using fiction, now, in the literary sense—which reimagine universalism as a legitimately inclusive foundation from which to address the needs of a diverse humanity.

The Problem of the Everyone

The Heart of Redness is set in two periods and shuttles back and forth between the historical and the contemporary, drawing links between the colonial past and the postapartheid present, jumping over apartheid itself. The historical portion deals with the cattle killing of the mid-nineteenth century when a young prophetess, Nongqawuse, advised the Xhosa people to kill their cattle and destroy their crops in order stave off British invasion.[13] The second plotline unfolds after the fall of apartheid. Camagu, a middle-aged South African, returns to his newly democratic country to vote after nearly thirty years of exile in the United States. He has spent his time abroad earning a PhD in communication and economic development, gaining experience as an "international expert" with UNESCO and other global organizations. He thus reenters South Africa as a representative of the international community and decides, upon his return, to stay and "contribute to the development of his country" (29). He begins by looking for jobs with government agencies but is repeatedly told that he is overqualified — "Too much knowledge is a dangerous thing" (29). The "big men of the government" recommend he "try the private sector" instead (30). There, too, he is rejected, "discover[ing] that the corporate world did not want qualified blacks" (30). After failing to find work in both the governmental and private sectors, he moves into the third sector to pursue a nongovernmental, nonprofit role. He does not join a major international NGO for which his qualifications would make him a good fit. Rather, after pursuing a woman to the rural seaside village of Qolorha, the home of the infamous prophetess, Nongqawuse, he settles down, joins in debates about development, and starts a cooperative with local women, volunteering as a kind of development consultant. Through the cosmopolitan figure of Camagu and the debates in which he engages, the novel tests divergent approaches to development and homes in on the problems and possibilities of identification across differences of power and privilege.[14]

Camagu enters a tense, long-standing dispute about bringing development to Qolorha, which escalates as various outsiders arrive with plans and promises. The debate has become frozen in the polarization of modernity and tradition, a fault-line suggestive of the Eurocentric trajectory of much development discourse. This parallels the historical strand of the narrative in which characters argue over conversion to Christianity and, with it, the "wonderful gift of civilization" that missionaries and colonial administrators offer (84). This formal doubling posits the development debate as a tradition that unfolds across generations, with some characters becoming mouthpieces for developmentalist and conservationist ideologies. On both sides, ideas about material change get entangled with the risk and the allure of cultural conversion. For example, one of the local development advocates, Bhonco, points to the material benefits — "When there is progress . . . there'll even be street lights" — while also welcoming cultural imperialism as part of the package: "We want to get rid of this bush which is a sign of our uncivilized state. We want developers to come and build the gambling city that will bring money to this community. That will bring modernity to our lives, and will rid us of our redness" (94, 92). "Redness" refers to the traditional use of red ochre to decorate the body and to dye clothing, and here it stands in for Xhosa cultural heritage in general. For those who favor modernity, redness is a subject of shame — a practice from which to be converted. To be for progress, in this formulation, is to be against tradition of all kinds; to advocate development is to reject local heritage and welcome in the rush of globalization (particularly Westernization). Conversely, resistance to cultural imperialism gets coupled with resistance to material forms of progress, including basic aspects of development like connecting to the electrical grid. The language of progress is also a language of destruction, and the universal pretentions of development threaten the local capacity to thrive.

Mda questions this secularized conserve-or-convert dualism. Bhonco's articulation of progress aligns the concept with colonialist condescension, but Mda leads us to ask if development projects must drive out local particularity (redness) or if they might reside together. If the notion of progress is burdened by its colonialist tendencies, what are we to do with it? In a challenge to "anti-progressive models of futurity," María Josefina Saldaña-Portillo asserts that "if one continues to recognize a need for revolutionary change in the aftermath of what fifty years of 'development' have wrought . . . then one accepts that some model of progress pertains."[15] She argues that "the problem lies not with the idea of progress per se but with the *mode* of progressive movement."[16] In *The Heart of Redness*, Mda is teasing out that distinction.

Camagu enters as a mediating character—both modern and traditional, a secular intellectual and a believer in the supernatural. He becomes a test case for development advocacy of a critically minded, genuinely democratic form. Rather than thinking in terms of the embrace or the rejection of progress, he reframes the universalist approach to progress, directing it toward the specific needs of those with whom he works. With a U.S. doctorate and a cosmopolitan sensibility, Camagu is reputed to be a figure of modernity (and thus anti-traditionalism), but he surprises the people of Qolorha with his respect for their customs—not a detached, ethnographic kind of respect but an engaged, participatory form: "they talk of Camagu in great awe. They did not expect a man with such great education, a man who has lived in the lands of the white people for thirty years, to have such respect for the customs of his people. He is indeed a man worthy of their respect."[17] Tapped into the values of the international community, Camagu becomes an advocate of development in a critical mode. He seeks a model of development that brings material benefits to Qolorha without sacrificing natural resources, cultural resources, or independence. This demand for universal standards of living does not embrace universal standards of culture. Arguments of chapter 2 about African responses to Christian missions are largely applicable here as well: as religious missions contained both colonial and anticolonial possibilities, so too does the universalism of the international community contain both neocolonial and anti-neocolonial possibilities.

This all comes together around a donor-driven water project. The scene on which I will focus unfolds the multilayered notion of universalism and its role in humanitarian discourse. Mda depicts a tense discussion regarding a water pump that has fallen into disrepair and disuse. This is perhaps the quintessential image of failed benevolence, of good intentions gone predictably

wrong. The donor of this particular water pump is a trader named John
Dalton, a white liberal "of English stock" so steeped in local culture that he
is said to have "an umXhosa heart" (8). Dalton's genealogy is suggestive of
the continuity between Christian missions and humanitarian programs. His
grandfather, Mda writes, "was a trader of a different kind. As a missionary he
was a merchant of salvation" (8). Going further back clarifies that his "own
family history was as blood-soaked as any" (9); his great-great-grandfather, a
soldier, features in the cattle-killing plotline. Also named John Dalton, he too
was an agent of conversion, working on behalf of the "Great White Chief"
whose "magnanimous wish was to convert the amaXhosa from their barbarous
ways" through the injunction to "spread British civilization" (123). Like the
double plot structure set in different centuries, the layering of names with two
generations of John Daltons makes the line between past and present fuzzy.
The shared name creates disorienting moments of slippage between the past
and present and their respective projects of improvement, inviting us to question the "magnanimous wish" embedded in the contemporary humanitarian
gesture.

The younger Dalton's aim to bring clean water to the community—which
sounds like an obvious good—becomes a subject of debate with Camagu,
who is critical of the method. Dalton is irate at Camagu's unwillingness to
invest his own efforts in the project, particularly based on their shared commitment to a blend of development and conservation of local lands. Although
they don't address humanitarianism directly, and neither is associated with
an international organization, their debate is emblematic of humanitarian
dilemmas around how to give effectively and ethically within the context of
unequal power.

Mda maps out a debate about development through outside assistance by
setting Camagu, the migrant expert, alongside Dalton, the local philanthro-
pist. Dalton is a partial outsider, distinguished not by foreignness but by privilege, both racial and economic. He comes from an advantaged place-in-the-
world[18] even though he comes from the same geographical place as the other
villagers. New to Qolorha-by-Sea, Camagu is an outsider of a different kind,
grouped racially with local people but belonging to a different clan. Of more
significance than clan, he is a foreign-educated "international expert" who
has spent the majority of his years abroad (29). A returned exile, as opposed
to a foreigner, he has deep links and loyalties to South Africa but within the
framework of a Western education and experience. With that background,
some locals see him as more foreign than he perceives himself to be, describing him as "an educated man . . . all the way from America" (150). When he
and Dalton argue over the best approach to development, Dalton condemns

Camagu as an impostor: "You come all the way from America with theories and formulas, and you want to apply them in my village" (180). This is a familiar argument against international humanitarian assistance in favor of local solutions, but it inverts the standard racial positions of insider and outsider. The face of the "international expert," this suggests, is not necessarily white, and localism is not necessarily a solution. It is possible, the novel suggests, for one from the outside to be more sensitive to the dangers of universalism and to the specificity of the local than the one who has lived there all along. Ethical engagement depends less on where these men come from than on the way each sets up and narrates his relation to the community. Different modes of identification produce different models of progress.[19]

Despite his long-term access to the local, Dalton operates on the basis of universality, which emerges most forcefully when he becomes defensive about his humanitarian efforts. Camagu critiques the foundation of the water project, explaining that it "is failing because it was imposed on the people. No one bothered to find out their needs" (179). This argument resonates with critiques of humanitarianism as the new imperialism. The language of imposition suggests that the supposed gift of development is burdensome to its recipients rather than emancipatory. Dalton finds this critique ridiculous, but rather than drawing on specific knowledge about the community and its needs — which he typically uses to justify his authority — he turns to sweeping universals, related to this community only in so far as they are related to everyone. No one bothered to find out their needs? "That is nonsense," he says. "Everyone needs clean water" (179). That is the claim I want to underline here. Everyone needs clean water. Of course, he is right, but it is more complicated than he thinks. Need poses as the obvious universal. Need testifies to the biological sameness of human beings; in order to survive, everyone does need clean water, food, and shelter. This is related to the claim often made for humanitarian care — that it operates in the field of universal ethics, not of politics[20] — but as this novel demonstrates, it is always negotiating politics, operating on a charged field of power relations. Like other critical novels of the third sector, *The Heart of Redness* refutes this division, politicizing that which is supposedly beyond politics and throwing into question the seemingly natural notion of everyone's needs.[21]

The appeal to the everyone obscures some problems and produces others — ideological, ethical, and practical. First, it encourages a dangerous mode of confidence, which is endemic to the white savior narrative. A sense of certainty and the very obviousness of the universal need for clean water blind Dalton to criticism. Obviousness doesn't invite skepticism. Camagu, however, casts doubt on this arrogant posture of certainty: "That is the main problem with you, John. You know that you are 'right' and you want to impose these 'correct' ideas on the populace from above" (179). An inflated sense of one's own rightness leads to the second problem of the discourse of the everyone: power. To speak about needs seems neutral. However, Camagu points to the specific source of those proclamations about everyone's needs, and it comes from a narrow place. The task of speaking for everyone falls on the privileged few, but this fact gets buried in the benevolent gesture of universal inclusion. For this reason, Dalton "thought he was doing [the villagers] a favor when he single-handedly raised funds for [the project] and invited government experts to get involved" (180). It doesn't occur to him that this could be an imposition. To speak of and for everyone shrouds the hierarchy through which that speaking occurs with the developer above and the populace below. In addition, this discourse reinforces the existing inequities that the project is supposed to diminish. By speaking the language of the everyone, Dalton doesn't have to consult the people who will receive his benevolence; in effect, addressing the everyone cuts those particular someones out of the circuit. Universalism becomes a method of power, a way of doing things for people without including them in the process. Thus, the ideological problem — about how humanity is theorized — produces both ethical and practical consequences. The method of assistance based not on the specific "they" or "we" but the universal "everyone" simply doesn't work, as Camagu points out: "The villagers were given a ready-made water scheme. It is falling apart because they don't feel they are a part of it" (180). The end result: the pump breaks down and doesn't get water to anyone.

Within this brief exchange, Mda dramatizes the relationship between humanitarianism's theoretical, discursive core — the way it thinks and speaks about its task — and its incapacity to carry out its proclaimed goals on a practical level. Implicit in the universal statement is a call for action. Dalton appeals to the everyone to justify his intervention: if everyone needs clean water (an indisputable premise), then the donated water pump is an obvious answer. This is more generally applicable to universalism; the implied follow-up to the "everyone needs" statement is that "we" (whoever is speaking on behalf of everyone) should do something about that need. What, then, is the proper response? Claims about the needs of everyone call for a "yes, but" response. Yes, everyone needs clean water (or nutritious food or safe housing or healthcare), but it is also more complicated than the absolute statement implies. Defenders of humanitarianism tend to get stuck on the "yes" as Dalton does. Critics tend to get stuck on the "but," insisting on the myriad problems latent in universalism. That "but" is essential, and yet it is also important that we circle back to the "yes" so that the affirmation of people's needs does not get smothered in the energy of critique. Embedded in the claim that "everyone needs clean water" is also a follow-up demand, coming not from the top of the global hierarchy but from the bottom, that everyone should *have* clean water.

As *The Heart of Redness* shows, *not* thinking in terms of the everyone holds its own set of pitfalls. The novel is attentive to postapartheid exclusion—the fact that the new nation does not meaningfully address everyone. Camagu joins a cohort of "disaffected exiles and sundry learned rejects of this new society" (26). Of course, the educated are not alone in feeling this sense of exclusion: "'Everything now . . . the fruits of liberation . . . are enjoyed only by those from exile or from Robben Island,' [Camagu] overhears a man from the group of dagga smokers complain. 'Yet we were the ones who bore the brunt of the bullets. We threw stones and danced the freedom dance'" (32). If the potential violence of humanitarianism lies in the problem of the everyone, the exclusions of the postapartheid, postcolonial nation give a different valence to that same problem. Universalism trends toward domination, antiuniversalism toward relativist neglect. Some kind of universalism is needed for this complaint of exclusion to become a meaningful claim for inclusion.

This is a sticking point in debates about development when critiques languish on the "but" and lose sight of the "yes." While Camagu, an exilic, postmodern intellectual, engages antidevelopment arguments, he doesn't stop at the point of critique or reject the discourse of the everyone. Rather, he uses those arguments in calling for a critically minded model of development. In so doing, he illustrates what I have described as the work of humanitarian fictions, especially in their ambivalence. He, too, is an advocate of development and universal access to modern services like electricity and running water. Indeed, he "assures [Dalton] that he is not belittling his efforts to develop his village. He is merely being critical of the method" (180). His appraisal of the water project does not mean pitching the whole enterprise but rethinking its method of identification through extended engagement with the local "beneficiaries" of Dalton's humanitarian efforts. Camagu's strategy is dependent upon asking questions and engaging the community in a dialogue about what they need: "Perhaps the first step would have been to discuss the matter with the villagers, to find out what their priorities are. They should be part of the whole process. They should be active participants in the conception of the project, in raising funds for it, in constructing it. Then it becomes their project. Then they will look after it" (179). *Yes*, everyone needs clean water, *but* this method is ill conceived, *and* we can do better.

Proclaiming the universality of humanity obscures difference, and yet at the same time, we need some form of universality if we are to maintain standards for justice at all. In other words, the discourse of the everyone does do essential work that cannot be dismissed as imperialist nonsense. Ernesto Laclau zeroes in on this challenge by asking what happens to "unsatisfied demands concerning access to education, to employment, to consumption goods and so on" when universalist discourse is rejected. "These demands," he explains, "cannot be made in terms of difference, but of some universal principles . . . the right of *everybody* to have access to good schools, or live a decent life, or participate in the public space of citizenship, and so on."[22] Antiuniversalism can have real consequences for justice. To speak of and on behalf of everyone obscures the unevenness of the world, but to amend that unevenness, standards for everyone are required. As Laclau puts it, "rejecting universalism *in toto* as the particular content of the ethnia of the West—can only lead to a political blind alley."[23] Camagu manages to blend a critique of top-down universalism with a universalist politics of equality. *The Heart of Redness* suggests that this is the kind of posture we must take toward development; participating in the international community involves ethically risky maneuvers across different positions of power, and we should move ahead with that in view, acknowledging how little we know of others. By raising questions of the everyone, the water-pump dilemma dovetails with debates about humanism that have been unfolding since the mid-twentieth century. I move now to these debates in order to articulate the stakes of a postcolonial universalist position.

Universal Humanism and the Problem of Difference

Used in various contexts and with various emphases, the humanist idea has consistently combined a sense of human unity—typically described as a shared essence—with a faith in human agency and even perfectibility. Humanism's origin in the Renaissance grows out of a transition from a God-centric worldview to a human-centric one, making man the agent of his own life, even of history itself.[24] This sense of agency has been linked to rationality, that uniquely human quality that supposedly separates people from animals and enables us to shape our own destinies, thus granting us a heightened sense of control. Tracing its etymological roots, Salvatore Puledda explains that Renaissance humanism took up the "ideal of *humanitas*, the Latin translation of the Greek word *paideia*, 'education.' In a confluence rich in meanings, *humanitas* came to indicate the formation and development, through education, of those qualities that make an individual a truly *human* being, that rescue 'humanity' from its natural condition and differentiate it from the barbarian."[25] Humanity, in this sense, is not merely a state of being but a destination, a goal, pursued through a narrative of rescue. In the context of literature, we might then ask: Who lies at the center of this narrative? Who determines its plot? And what kind of human community does it create?

Contrary to humanism's communal promise, both anticolonial and post-colonial theory have shown it to be a cipher for some of the most egregious offences against humanity. Recall Frantz Fanon's resonant statement in *The Wretched of the Earth* — "Leave this Europe where they are never done talking of Man, yet murder men everywhere they find them"[26] — or Aimé Césaire's in *Discourse on Colonialism*: "that is the greatest thing I hold against pseudo-humanism: that for too long it has diminished the rights of man, that its concept of those rights has been — and still is — narrow and fragmentary, incomplete and biased and, all things considered, sordidly racist."[27] He concludes, "At the end of formal humanism and philosophic renunciation, there is Hitler."[28] The love of "Man" is severed from the treatment of "men." Under colonialism, humanist claims about the all-inclusive circle of mankind served as a tool for racist delimitation, and theories of human perfectibility implied an inevitable trajectory toward Europe. Therefore, proclamations of universalism have masked violent forms of particularism.[29] Anticolonialists thus laid the groundwork for a growing critique that would reveal the consequences of a seemingly benign discourse of human inclusivity.

Nevertheless, the anticolonialist critique of European humanism was not ultimately antihumanist. Fanon and Césaire called for new, genuinely inclusive forms of humanism. Césaire argues that "at the very time when it most often mouths the word, the West has never been further from being able to live a true humanism — a humanism made to the measure of the world."[30] Fanon associates the break from colonialism with the emergence of a new kind of humanity: "After the conflict there is not only the disappearance of colonialism but also the disappearance of the colonized man. This new humanity cannot do otherwise than define a new humanism both for itself and for others."[31] He describes the reparative redistribution of wealth as the task of "reintroducing mankind into the world."[32] Decolonization bears hopes of a new era of humanity, although Fanon also anticipates its collapse. Both he and Césaire advocate a mode of international community — a capacious vision of human belonging in response to colonialism's violently antihuman practices.

Whereas Fanon and Césaire view the European rhetoric of humanity as a false universalism, a mere "pseudo-humanism," and call for a new humanism that is truly universal,[33] postcolonial critics have sharpened the critique, claiming that the problem is not false universalism but the very notion of universalism itself. According to this line of argument, the universalist drive for sameness generates the impulse to dominate and convert — in all its various forms — those who are different. With that compulsion, humanism, in some

sense, demands colonialism; therefore, colonialism can be taken as a sign
not of humanism's collapse but of its climax. In resistance to this defeat of
pluralism, postcolonial theory has often valorized difference over universality
and sameness and has, in the words of Robert Young, linked "the production
of the humanist subject [to] the general process of colonialism by which Europe consolidated itself politically as sovereign subject of the world."[34] The
discourse of human essence distorts that uneven political field, obscuring the
vastly different positions from which we enter an international community.

Even so, antihumanism is not a consensus position within postcolonial
thought. The tension between interpreting the world and changing it, between rigorous theory and effective politics, is fundamental to postcolonialism
with its roots and loyalties in both anticolonial political theory and poststructural critique, which have a vexed relation to one another, in part sympathetic
and in part antagonistic.[35] Friction arises over the question of how to critique
universal humanism without losing sight of the political horizon, how to negotiate between rigorous theory and the practical demands of the present.
According to Neil Lazarus, postcolonialism has privileged critique at the cost
of politics:

> Where postmodern and postcolonial theory have tended to react to
> the perceived indefensibility of bourgeois humanism and of colonial
> nationalism by abandoning the very idea of totality, a genuinely post-
> colonial strategy might be to move explicitly, as Fanon already did . . .
> to proclaim a "new humanism," predicated upon a formal repudiation
> of the degraded European form, and borne embryonically in the na-
> tional liberation movement.[36]

While postcolonial opposition to humanism seems to dominate the conversation, thus creating the demand for statements like Lazarus's, its presence
can be felt on a lower frequency, and major theorists have declared their
own orientations toward it. In *Orientalism*, Edward Said describes himself as
"stubbornly" continuing to apply the word humanism to his work "despite the
scornful dismissal of the term by sophisticated postmodern critics."[37] Gayatri
Spivak, generally viewed as a theorist of difference, might be considered humanism's most surprising advocate:

> It has appeared to some of my readers recently that I seem to be mov-
> ing towards some notion of universal humanity, and this has surprised
> them—I am expected to emphasize difference. . . . Contrary to the
> received assumption, it seems to me that the non-foundationalist
> thinkers are suggesting that you cannot have any kind of emancipatory

project *without* some notion of the ways in which human beings are similar.[38]

By this definition, universalism is sullied but nonetheless essential to emancipatory politics. In the context of African literature, Kwame Anthony Appiah reflects that postcoloniality's *"post*, like postmodernism's, is also a *post* that challenges earlier legitimating narratives [of nationalism, especially]. . . . But it challenges them in the name of the ethical universal; in the name of *humanism*, 'le [*sic*] gloire pour l'homme.'"[39] I want to pull at that quiet thread within postcolonial thought, and to do so, I read Bessie Head. Through analysis of her novel A *Question of Power*, along with shorter references to her other work, I aim to explore how postcolonial critiques of humanism might be mobilized in order to revise and build upon the language of anticolonial humanism.

Humanitarianism's blend of philosophical humanism and social practice positions it at the crux of these debates. Third sector humanitarianism is premised on the foundational assumptions of humanism—universalism and progress—and has mapped its rescue narratives accordingly. As "humanism's more practical-minded offspring,"[40] humanitarianism takes up the language of human development with its problematic divisions between the rescuers and the rescued, the more human and the less. In doing so, it builds a troubled mode of identification with the suffering subject:

> The one "to whom humanitarian action is addressed," as Rony Brauman [former president of Médicins Sans Frontières] puts it, "is not defined by his skills or potential, but above all, by his deficiencies and disempowerment," and this deficient being is a by-product, in Brauman's account, of the processes of identification humanitarianism solicits. . . .
>
> The humanitarian precept that beneath, behind, or before allegiances, nationality, ethnicity, or race, lies the human thus proves to be deeply problematic.[41]

Humanity is the unifying category, the catch-all term that identifies those at the top with those at the bottom. In articulating the progress narrative of human rights inclusion—a "story of free and full personality development"—Joseph Slaughter shows that "human rights law incorporates the human person as a synecdoche for human 'capacities and achievement'; [but] it also makes the human person a synecdoche for human 'weaknesses and needs.'"[42] Humanity is, therefore, both a minimalist baseline and an aspirational benchmark, a structure that has placed Europeans and Africans on opposite ends of the spectrum, with Africans supposedly lacking the agency and rationality to determine their own worlds. This has placed a ("White Man's") burden on the Westerner to raise the African to a fuller level of humanity. The humanitarian process of identification, then, is haunted by its directionality, saying of those in need, "they are like us" and "they are not enough like us." It pulls the world toward its own center without thinking very specifically about those human beings as figures with universal dimension but also with particular lives, contexts, and histories.[43] This is the process of identification that produces Dalton's altruism of imposition in *The Heart of Redness*. Humanitarianism may speak the language of care, but with universal humanism as its ideological underpinning, it has been complicit with imperial violence and, at times, indistinguishable from it.

But alternative humanisms are available. African literary theorizations of the human and the humane can help revise the conceptual limitations of humanitarian thought. The novel in particular can reinvigorate humanitarianism's anemic narratological imagination by envisioning new modes of identification with humanity at large and new ways of plotting moral and material progress. Bruce Robbins puts it nicely: "all universalisms are dirty," he writes, and "it is only dirty universalisms that will help us against the powers and agents of still dirtier ones."[44] Humanitarianism offers one such "dirty universalism"—not a solution but a potential ally, imperfect but available. By reworking the humanitarian narrative, Head articulates a model of neo-anticolonial (or anti-neocolonial) humanism that is critically minded, postcolonially informed, and peripherally situated.

Rethinking "Mankind in General"

Too often, humanitarian narratives—even the critical ones—have reflected a Western perspective, the view from the side of the "saviors." With its focus on South Africans' own development projects, *The Heart of Redness* moves away from that model. With *A Question of Power*, Head takes another step, going beyond the efforts of local elites to focus on the people who are most marginalized and who would appear least able to contribute. The novel depicts humanitarian work from the perspective of a woman, much like Head herself, who occupies multiple margins: she is born to a black father and white mother under apartheid (in violation of the Immorality Act) and becomes a refugee, "a stateless person in Botswana," where she is hospitalized for a nervous breakdown (18). Viewed from the outside, she could be a figure of pity. She embodies the subaltern as described by Spivak, cut out of "the circuits of citizenship or institutionality,"[45] thoroughly excluded from power and lacking access to resources. Through Head's writing, the subaltern speaks. While the narration is in the third person, readers have access only to Elizabeth's experiences and emotions. In representing a form of psychosis, the novel makes readers take seriously experiences that could easily be dismissed as delusions, such as the otherworldly beings who walk in and out of Elizabeth's life, often berating her. In this way, *A Question of Power* fulfills the promise Chinua Achebe associates with fiction, which operates through "imaginative identification" to "narrow the existential gap" between self and other.[46] Counterintuitively, perhaps, first-person narration would allow readers to distance themselves from Elizabeth by designating her an unreliable narrator. In this text, the objective style of the third person actually cultivates a fuller identification.

With this protagonist as its focal point, the novel examines the interactions of locals, Africans from elsewhere, and Western volunteers as they work to address the basic needs of the poor through third sector development. These interactions are often characterized by damage and disappointment, and Head enumerates the insensitivities of humanitarian volunteers to differences of culture, race, economics, experience, and history. But the novel invests a great deal of energy in the moments when community is indeed built upon, around, and within those differences. As she sorts through the problems and possibilities of identification across a steep gradient of power and privilege, Head places marginalized people at the origin of a universalist ethics that typically has its center elsewhere; in *A Question of Power*, the supposed "targets" of humanitarian benevolence become its arbiters.

Channeled through the perspective of a mentally ill protagonist, this partly surreal novel weaves together internal and external worlds—capturing, on the one hand, Elizabeth's inner turmoil as she suffers through madness and, on the other, the external world of day-to-day life in her village. The former has garnered the most attention in Head scholarship. This is exemplified by Jacqueline Rose's influential essay, "On the Universality of Madness," which analyzes Head's universalism through the lens of the protagonist's tumultuous internal narrative. Building on that work, Sonali Perera has advanced the discussion of Head's ethical imagination by turning outward, focusing on the external narrative of communal labor and situating the novel in relation to Marxism.[47] Following Perera's lead, my analysis will privilege the external narrative but with the goal of understanding the novel's implications for humanitarian thought. By exploring how Head negotiates ethics in a transnational context, I will show how universal humanism embodies humanitarianism's most common pitfalls and its most hopeful possibilities.

While Head highlights human difference as a problem for universalism, she also suggests that difference makes it vital. The protagonist and central consciousness is a figure of alterity; Elizabeth does not fit in either of her parents' racial categories or communities and thus lives a borderline existence. To be "Coloured" under apartheid is to be legally defined by what one is not—"a person who is not a white person or a native," according to the Population Registration Act of 1950.[48] Stigmatized as a "half-breed" and "Coloured dog," who threatens to "contaminate . . . pure black skin" as well as white, her very humanity comes under question (127, 129, 127). Although she finds safety in Botswana, her volatile mental health alienates her. In foregrounding difference, the novel is very much in keeping with the oppositional postcolonial values and critiques which would emerge over the next two decades. Yet it is the person marked by difference who clarifies that universalism is urgently needed. In A *Question of Power*, Elizabeth's perspective emerges from her experience of violent particularisms that categorize and segregate: "In South Africa she had been rigidly classified Coloured. There was no escape from it to the simple joy of being a human being with a personality. There wasn't any escape like that for anyone in South Africa. They were races, not people" (44). Such fractures in humanity leave her—Coloured, mad, stateless, rural, single, female—to slip between the cracks. But this problem, she suggests, entraps everyone, misfits and otherwise. Furthermore, these exclusionary tendencies apply to liberationist movements as well as to oppressive regimes. In resistance to apartheid, Elizabeth aspires to identify with humanity at large rather than any particular group, including black nationalists who, in many ways, share her resistant stance: "'I've got my concentration elsewhere,' she said. 'It's on mankind in general, and black people fit in there, not as special freaks and oddities outside the scheme of things, with labels like Black Power or any other rubbish of that kind'" (133). The challenge of international community, then, lies in building coalitions that supersede human differences while also allowing those differences room to live and breathe.

Through the universalist vocabulary she weaves throughout the novel, Head positions her work in direct conversation with humanist philosophy. Examples include "humanity, compassion, tenderness," "awakening love of mankind," "the simple joy of being a human being with a personality," "the dignity of man," "the wonderful strangeness of human nature," "people as God-like," "mankind in general," "lovers of mankind," and so on (19, 35, 44, 63, 72, 109, 133, 202). It seems surprising that Head so often uses masculine nouns to signal the universal when forging "the brotherhood of man" in this novel consistently involves women as its main players. On the one hand, this masculine language runs counter to her inclusive aims; at the same time, it mirrors the language of the male humanists who came before her, both colonial and anticolonial, and thus places her work more explicitly in that conversation, a conversation that extends to postcolonial era humanitarians and the vocabulary of human rights. Head's linguistic strategy, here, illustrates Mikhail Bakhtin's notion that "characteristic for the novel as a genre is not the image of man in his own right, but precisely the *image of a language*."[49] By reflecting the image of humanist language, the novel is able to riff on it and revise it.

Both historically and ideologically, Bessie Head's work is positioned between anticolonial and postcolonial theorists; *A Question of Power* was published in 1974. Writing shortly after Botswana's independence and in search of a better future for African people, Head eschews nationalism, embracing transnational connection as the preferred measure of community.[50] With a keen sensitivity to the problematic deployments of so-called universal humanism in Africa, she nonetheless insists on the necessity of thinking beyond various particularisms to address "mankind in general" (134). Her antineocolonial novels echo some of the humanism of Fanon and Césaire but rework it to prefigure the critiques that postcolonial and poststructural theory would raise. Essentially, she decenters humanism in order to redeem it. She shows that humanism, to borrow Appiah's phrase, "can be provisional, historically contingent, antiessentialist (in other words, postmodern), and still be demanding."[51] And she suggests that, in this form, humanism has the potential to build a genuine community internationally.

Head situates *A Question of Power* in the space of postcolonial disillusionment within a new, exclusive order, an order that has failed to account for everyone. In light of insufficient provision by government and private sector commerce, the impoverished rural village of Motabeng becomes a testing ground for third sector activity: "Motabeng village was full of IVS [International Volunteer Service] and Peace Corps, as they formed almost the entire staff of the Motabeng Secondary School" (24). In contrast to most of the African novels in *Humanitarian Fictions*' archive, this one presents a number of white characters with substantial speaking roles, including Europeans, an American, and a South African. While the white savior narrative features one charismatic hero, Head presents multiple humanitarian figures of various dispositions, compelling and compromised to varying degrees. This cast enables Head to explore the many possibilities of humanitarian relationships as they play out in connection to her refugee protagonist. Head's evaluation of humanitarian action depends on the kinds of human relations it establishes; an ethical humanitarianism is only possible on the basis of a rigorously ethical humanism, and that is not the humanism most easily and immediately available to foreign humanitarians. "Actually existing humanitarianism,"[52] Head might suggest, has some serious soul-searching to do.

Several characters in A *Question of Power*—the majority of foreign volunteers and aid workers, in fact—embody an imperialist humanism. The humanitarian presence in the village is, in large part, a colonial resettlement. Funded by their own government, a group of Danish farm instructors and their families set up the kind of fortress that would come to characterize humanitarianism as the new empire. The Danish "built large, modern houses for the people they sent over and took care of every detail of their lives, down to the last ounce of petrol" (71). They drive around in Land Rovers and spend their evenings "denigrating their pupils. Apparently they had a high standard of culture and civilization in Denmark" (71). In spite of their impulse to universalize access to farming and food, they set themselves apart.[53] They are as committed to defining their distinction from the "natives" in space, in style, and in language as were their colonial predecessors. Humanitarianism in this expression does indeed appear to be the grinning mask of a new empire.

The arrogance of the missionary mentality—evident in the missionary who tells Elizabeth when she is a child that she may "get insane just like [her] mother" (16)—finds its echo in the humanitarian volunteers who populate the village of Motabeng. There is, for example, the English manager of a farming development project, who "was so intensely reserved and aloof that no conversation ever went beyond his work and his crops" (70). As a Quaker, he demonstrates the type of Christian universalist motivation that fails to produce any sensitivity to the people around him. Detachment from local life characterizes his behavior across the board: "He said he didn't like the lager beer Eugene brewed because there were an awful lot of drunkards in Botswana and he was encouraging it. He didn't like any music but the great choral music of the cathedral churches of England he had on tape" (70). His tone ranges from disinterest to disdain. With Elizabeth, "he was in the habit of replying to her every query with rude and sarcastic remarks. His attitude clearly said: 'Yes, insect, and what do you want now? Can't you see that I'm a very busy man?'" (71). Eurocentric superiority pervades his communication, all within this supposedly egalitarian project, ironizing the promises of humanism.

This brand of self-importance takes its shrillest form in Camilla, a Danish landscape designer turned agricultural volunteer. Shortly after Elizabeth joins the vegetable gardening project, associated with the Motabeng Secondary School and run by volunteers, both local and foreign, she goes to the Danish gardens to learn their new methods. Her teacher is a local trainee named Small-Boy. As he turns the soil, Small-Boy confidently instructs Elizabeth, who jots down notes. The process of one trainee instructing a newer one is working, even though the English project manager came up with this system in order to extract himself from it. But the lesson is soon interrupted when foreign power reasserts itself in the form of Camilla, who bursts through the gate, seeking to catch the workers off guard, idling about as "natives" are wont to do: "If someone doesn't come down here during practical work time," she announces—"someone" being a white person—"these trainees will just sit under the trees and play dice" (74). Before even observing what is happening, she launches into a harsh series of corrections: "Small-Boy! Didn't I tell you not to leave the manure on top of the bed? You must turn it at once!" (75). She has failed to notice that he is in the midst of that very process and has just explained it to Elizabeth. In this scene, Head illustrates the centripetal force of the humanitarian benefactor: "All life had to stop and turn towards [Camilla]. Her voice had an insistent command to it, yet it was no command of life. It was a scatter-brained assertion of self-importance" (75). Herein, humanism and egoism are enmeshed. She brings the training process to an immediate halt, grabbing Elizabeth's notebook and inscribing her own incoherent notes. With her authoritarian approach to teaching, she overwrites learning into oblivion. In effect, she negates real improvement with her pretentions to expertise.

Through the figure of Camilla, *A Question of Power* points to the unintended consequences of humanitarian assistance and its guiding ideology. This mode of universalism exacerbates fractures within humanity rather than fostering any kind of global unity, yet the humanitarian benefactor can remain gleefully oblivious to the problem. She is, "after all, . . . here to help the natives" (77). Her brand of universal humanism espouses the view that she, being more human than "the natives," has the right and responsibility to fix them, even if she has little faith in their capacity to change. It is a problem of universalism on the one hand—the idea that the whole world can use her brand of help—and of particularism on the other—the idea that African people occupy a category distinct from her own humanity. The idea of aid is ironized in this scene in which the offer of help actually makes things much worse: "All of a sudden," after Camilla's jarring entrance, "the vegetable garden was the most miserable place on earth. The students had simply become humiliated little boys shoved around by a hysterical white woman who never saw black people as people but as objects of permanent idiocy" (76). The workers we first encounter in the garden are not voiceless or powerless, but Camilla's intervention makes them so. This is the mode of humanitarian identification outlined previously; for Camilla, humanitarian beneficiaries are, to reiterate Brauman's argument, "not defined by [their] skills or potential, but above all, by [their] deficiencies and disempowerment."[54] This universalism perpetuates inequality.

We might ask, in light of Camilla's damaging behavior, whether an ethical form of transnational assistance is even possible; can goodwill expressed across differences of race, culture, status, and history ever be anything but ignorant?[55] Can the outsider ever really presume to know the needs of the local, let alone offer meaningful help? Camilla taps into a limitation of humanitarian interaction more broadly, a limitation that affects even Head's more sympathetic characters. For instance, Tom, an American Peace Corps volunteer, is notable in his contrast to most other volunteers: "He [takes] up lodgings with the farm students in their dormitory"—breaking the imperial divide that continues to organize the spatial relationship between humanitarian visitors and locals—and forms a close friendship with Elizabeth. Yet he, too, is prone to an American swagger that blurs into disrespect. When Elizabeth invites him into her home, he immediately feels "quite at ease," washes his full torso in the kitchen sink, and drips water onto the floor, "unconsciously" muddying it with his boots (113). Humanitarian arrogance is a role that even the finer volunteers slip into inadvertently.

Although international altruism in A *Question of Power* is often neocolonialist, it also contains anti-neocolonial possibilities. This is best exemplified by Eugene, an Afrikaner refugee working to build "educational programmes for developing countries"; he is the founder of the Motabeng secondary school and offers "youth-development work-groups" to teach practical "skills in building, carpentry, electricity, printing, shoe-making, farming and textile work" (56, 68). Elizabeth first gets to know him when he offers to take care of her son while she is in the hospital following a nervous breakdown. "We are both refugees," he tells her, "and we must help each other" (52). Head names Eugene's "humanity" as the quality that sets him apart and makes him such an attractive figure in contrast to other humanitarians, even those who advance Eugene's programs. Take, for example,

> The Englishman [who] did all the right things through an impatience
> for progress. He lacked the humanity of the Eugene man who had
> originated the projects. In his pamphlet writing, the Eugene man
> totally blurred the dividing line between the élite who had the means
> for education and the illiterate who had none. Education was for all.
> He always turned up with something for *everyone*. (71–72)

Here, Head's language of moral evaluation is on display. James Phelan claims that this kind of evaluation is fundamental to fiction as a mode of communication: "individual narratives explicitly or more often implicitly establish their own ethical standards in order to guide their audiences to particular ethical judgments."[56] In the case of A *Question of Power*, that ethical guidance is especially pronounced, demonstrating that critical humanitarian fictions are morally minded texts. The Englishman depicted in this scene illustrates the deep-seated flaws of the international community. He indexes the rationale for arguments against development as, in Arturo Escobar's words, "a top-down, ethnocentric, and technocratic approach, which treat[s] people and cultures as abstract concepts, statistical figures to be moved up and down the charts of 'progress.'"[57] Against this hierarchical universalism, Eugene models a radically inclusive approach to humanity. This is an admirable ethics of the everyone. He is sensitive to the individuals who make up that collective, rather than targeting some vague totality in the name of progress. By blurring the lines of status and entitlement, this universalism subverts the neocolonial order.

As an ethical model of transnational assistance, Eugene also clarifies the geopolitical coordinates of the novel's decentered humanism. Universalism's provenance is not the imperialist First World. In Eugene, universalism is a sign of his Africanization. "In this respect," in his attention to *everyone*, Eugene

> was an African, not a white man, and the subtlety of it spread to his
> conduct in everyday life. She had spent a day in his house. At lunch-
> time a group of labourers had walked into his house and sat down
> at table with him. They were Batswana. They had picked up their
> spoons, quietly bent their heads and eaten their food in a humble
> manner. He was so identical with them in gesture and posture that,
> startled, Elizabeth thought: "How is it his movements and gestures
> are so African? There's such a depth of knee-bending in him, it's an
> unconscious humility." (72)

This scene of international community is located not in the grand halls of a Western metropolis but around a table of workers in a rural African village, a marginal place that does not appear on the world map. The humanism Head uplifts is not European humanism. It is Afrocentric in source (linked to the continent rather than a particular region, nation, or town), yet not necessarily or exclusively centered upon Africa and African people. For that reason, it is a decentered humanism, rather than merely recentered. This is the kind of ethical orientation that Eugene has picked up, which Head describes as his "humanity." With Camilla, "all life had to stop and turn toward her," but Eugene offers a decentering practice of humility, deflecting attention from the self (75). This is a scene of humanitarian identification, but the expected direction of adaptation is reversed. His development projects' strength comes not out of making African people more like himself, but out of making himself sincerely, seamlessly, almost indistinguishably more like them — "identical," even. This illuminates the error in seeing humanism as a European philos-ophy. Head suggests that real, genuine humanism is an African philosophy.

And yet this does not eliminate the risk. A *Question of Power* presses on fundamental questions of both postcolonial studies and humanitarian discourse about relations between those with power and resources and those without. By Head's representation, people of goodwill, both local and foreign, are never fully good, or fully heroic, or fully able to extract themselves from the vectors of colonial history, but her decentered humanism offers a way to think about approaching an ethical version of international community even if it is never fully within our grasp. Spivak suggests that this tension defines the nature of ethics itself. According to Spivak's definition, the test case for ethics is an encounter between self and other—an attempt at communication that narrows the gap between them, even though it is a gap that can never be fully closed. While there is always a gap, always something that does not get across in interactions—especially as communication occurs across differentials of power—Spivak claims that it should be our constant goal to try to close it. The pursuit of justice is thus centrally concerned with the effort to hear the other. Although ethical singularity (or the closing of that interpersonal gap) is never fully achieved—it can merely be "*approached* when responses flow from both sides"[58]—it is the horizon for which we must continually strive: "a fully just world is impossible, forever deferred and different from our projections, the undecidable in the face of which we must risk the decision that we can hear the other."[59] Rather than one person managing to speak for or represent the other, Spivak imagines a collectivity based on *mutual* speaking, not merely listening to or speaking for.[60] This profound kind of engagement is necessary to the transformation of society—without it, she tells us, "nothing will stick."[61] A *Question of Power* stages conversations between privileged humanitarians and impoverished locals to suggest that this kind of conversation—which does not foreclose difference—is necessary for "establish[ing] the brotherhood of man." Decentered humanism strives for mutual eating, mutual speaking, and mutual power.

Desecularizing the Human, Relocating the Divine

At stake in in this version of humanism is a notion of what humanitarian care would look like if it were to be developed from the bottom up, changing the terms of the typical salvation narrative. For white people like Eugene, this requires alignments and affinities that challenge the conventions of whiteness. As Said puts it, "Being a White Man" in the colonies "was a very concrete manner of being-in-the-world, a way of taking hold of reality, language, and thought."[62] Eugene has acquired a different manner of being-white-in-the-world. As a model of learned, bottom-up humanitarian effort, he has already taken on the humble style of being that Head endorses, the "depth of knee-bending" associated with those he assists. The novel also explores the process of getting there, and in doing so posits a narrative of something akin to conversion. Whereas the white savior narrative is about bringing God into dark places, Head insists that God is already in Africa. As she writes elsewhere, "Africa was never 'the dark continent' to African people."[63] Africa (in a broad, continental sense within Head's usage) becomes a source of enlightenment—the very seat of the divine. At times, in its sweeping statements on morality and human suffering, the narration feels downright scriptural. Its spiritual tenor is supplemented by a series of condensed conversion narratives.

The first subject of conversion in A *Question of Power* is Elizabeth herself, who becomes a mouthpiece for the text's humanist ethics. Her experience of madness is philosophically generative, working through the very real tensions that she confronts in her waking life and thinks about within the context of Africa at large. The novel positions her as a visionary: "Africa had nothing, and yet, tentatively, [Elizabeth] had been introduced to one of the most complete statements for the future a people could ever make: Be ordinary. Any assumption of greatness leads to a dog-eat-dog fight and incurs massive suffering. She did not realize it then, but the possibilities of massive suffering were being worked out in her" (39). Global humanitarian crises, as the apex of "massive suffering," are her domain, but facing them requires self-abnegation rather than individual transcendence: "Be ordinary" rather than "Be great." She attains this insight through a dream world that defies rationality. She is visited repeatedly by "the poor of Africa." In one of her hallucinatory visions, a man approaches her accusingly:

> "You have never really made an identification with the poor and humble. This time you're going to learn how. They are going to teach you," and he flung his arm dramatically into the room. They were the poor of Africa. Each placed one bare foot on her bed, turned sideways so that she could see that their feet were cut and bleeding. They said nothing, but an old woman out of the crowd turned to Elizabeth and said: "Will you help us? We are a people who have suffered." She nodded her head in silent assent. (31)

Elizabeth here receives "the call" to assist the suffering, to play a humanitarian role within a narrative of African development. In this passage, the form of help is not evident, but it does imply that the prerequisite will be *"identification with the poor and humble"* who, with their worn-down bodies and stoic plea, epitomize the image of the humanitarian subject. Certainly, Elizabeth herself is a person who has suffered, but here, too, there is a gap in communication and relative power. This identification is not automatic, nor is it facilitated by Elizabeth alone. It must be learned, and "they are going to teach" her. Roles are mixed up between the giver and the receiver, the teacher and the learner, the supposedly knowing and the supposedly ignorant. The standard racialization of those roles—white benefactors and black beneficiaries—is also displaced. Identification in the case of a character like Camilla is about making the impoverished subject more like the "civilized" self. In this scene, the direction of identification is reversed, disrupting relations of authority that characterize humanist thought and humanitarian action—both of which are problematically centered on and determined by the wealthy West. This goes beyond the reversal we saw with Eugene: the white benefactor is now absent. What Elizabeth uncovers is a humanitarian theology, which becomes the central component of Head's decentered humanist philosophy.

For Head, theorizing the human and theorizing the divine go hand in hand. The moral orientation of A *Question of Power* is based on the lessons of "the poor of Africa," lessons which Elizabeth learns and shares. The image of African suffering is intimately familiar within the humanitarian repertoire, but here, the humanitarian subject, typically defined by deficiency, is invested with divine wisdom. In a conversation with her American friend, Tom, Elizabeth explains,

> "There's some such thing as black people's suffering being a summary of everything the philosophers and prophets ever said. . . . They said: 'Never think along lines of I and mine. It is death.' But they said it prettily, under the shade of Bodhi trees. It made no impact on mankind in general. It was for an exclusive circle of followers. Black people learnt that lesson brutally because they were the living victims of the greed inspired by I and mine and to hell with you, dog. Where do you think their souls are, then, after centuries of suffering? They're ahead of Buddha and Jesus and can dictate the terms for the future, not for any exclusive circle but for mankind in general." (134)

A *Question of Power* links the humanitarian discourse of long suffering to that of major world religions. This suggests that the best ethical possibilities for a new humanism lie with those who are not consulted—humanitarianism's recipient populations—and places them in the position not only of epistemic privilege but of spiritual authority. They can see the moral demands of the future and articulate them to the well-meaning but often insensitive humanitarians who show up in their villages. In a field that is dominated by international experts,[64] Head turns from professionalized knowledge to spiritual wisdom, and in doing so suggests the power of religious modalities for thinking about greed, inequity, and interpersonal care.[65]

Following "the call," Elizabeth passes on this wisdom. When she finishes explaining to Tom her philosophy of "mankind in general," rooted in the on-going history of African suffering, the outcome is depicted as another scene of conversion: Tom "had a way of sailing straight up to heaven when anything touched his heart. He turned towards her a face flaming with light. He said under his breath: 'Oh, oh, oh. That's right. Yes, that's right'" (135). Tom experiences a kind of religious awakening, propelling him toward heaven, illuminating his face. Here the foreign humanitarian is converted to a local version of universal humanism founded not on reason but on reverence. Head thus replaces the hubristic, reasoning subject of humanism with a humble, caring subject as the goal to which we should aspire. Reason (the capacity that was supposed to bring man to his pinnacle) is susceptible to the logic of capitalist greed and colonialist violence—self-interest is reasonable. What is needed for a genuine form of international community, then, is the primacy not of reason but of reverence, not secularism but a renewed and redirected sense of the sacred.[66]

The religious dimension lies not only in the form of conversion but in the content of the belief system which Elizabeth advocates. Through Elizabeth's reflection, Head poses the fundamental questions of religion:

> What is love?
>   Who is God?
>   If I cry, who will have compassion on me as my suffering is the suffering of others? (70)

The text explores the nature of God and the implications for humans and their relations to both God and to one another, and Elizabeth wrestles with these questions throughout. Whereas Head's answers do not add up to any orthodox doctrine—certainly not to the Christianity missionaries taught her—she does draw on fundamental ideas of the Bible in order to articulate her own theology. The Christian elements of this theology also mingle with Buddhist and Hindu beliefs in which Head had a long-standing interest.[67] Thus the sources for Head's religiosity are multilayered and creatively mixed. Even as she affirms New Testament doctrine to a degree, Head is analyzing it within that broader framework. Although "Christianity and formal church going were never going to be an expansive way of life for me," she explains in a personal essay, "I value that vivid, great short story teller, Jesus Christ, and the foundation he laid for such terms as mankind, the human race and love of one's neighbor."[68] Interestingly, what she finds in religion is a model *storyteller* who uses narrative to articulate an inclusive vision of humanity. Through this influence, a critically selective version of Christian humanism permeates her novels as well as her essays. She proclaims a partial faith, to use John A. McClure's apt term. Like postsecular narratives more generally, Head's novels "affirm the urgent need for a turn toward the religious even as they reject (in most instances) the familiar dream of a full return to an authoritative faith."[69] For Head, particular orientations of religious consciousness are needed, including moral seriousness, a focus on universal love, and a posture of reverence.

This is also the case in Head's first novel, *When Rain Clouds Gather* (1968). With its straightforward narrative form, it does not strike the philosophical pitch of *A Question of Power*, but it too draws us into a religious consideration of human suffering. To harness reverence, it is necessary to define the god deserving of it. This brings us to a third moment of conversion, which connects humanitarianism directly to questions of divinity. It involves an interaction between Gilbert Balfour, an English humanitarian who is in the village to assist with agricultural development and food production techniques, and Dinorego, a local elder with whom Gilbert develops a close bond. The scene occurs when Gilbert questions his own humanitarian impulse and universalist faith:

> What was he looking for? What was he doing? Agriculture? The need for a poor country to catch up with the Joneses in the rich countries? Should superhighways and skyscrapers replace the dusty footpaths and thorn scrub? It might be what he had in mind; at least, he said this to excuse himself for the need to live in a hurricane of activity. But the real life he had lived for three years had been dominated by the expression on Dinorego's face, and God and agriculture were all mixed up together after these three years. Yet it was a real God this who stalked his footsteps along the dusty pathways, who listened with quiet interest to the discussions on agriculture. Gilbert had no clear explanation of how he had become certain of this, but there was a feeling of great goodness in this country.[70]

This scene combines a faltering faith in progress — represented by those superhighways and skyscrapers — with a new faith in the God who seems to reside in those dusty footpaths and in a poor old man like Dinorego. Gilbert's Western-centric agenda gives way to a new reverence for this place; the secular gods of the West are displaced by "great goodness in this country." There is a version of transcendence in his kind of work, but it is attached neither to Gilbert himself nor to the grand project of improving Africa; rather, the transcendent lies within the dusty local footpaths and the bare feet that walk them daily. In poor, rural Botswana, Gilbert — a secular humanitarian — finds God. He, too, is a convert.[71]

All this talk of God, it must be noted, is accompanied by frequent warnings against the very concept of God. For example, in A *Question of Power*, Elizabeth is "appalled" and "frightened" by the phrase, "Glory be to God on high," because it "implie[s] that there was still something up there, unseen, unknown to account for" (109), and when people act on behalf of God on high, they all too often disregard the human beings around them. But, rather than claiming that there is no God, Elizabeth relocates the divine, bringing it from heaven down to earth: "God is people. There's nothing up there. It's all down here" (109). While this sounds a lot like secularization, there is a unique shift taking place here. Secular humanism addresses the problem of God with a philosophy that says "it's all down here," but that does not, in fact, escape the dangers of "God on high." In transferring the central determinant of history from God to man (a "universal" humanity that is, indeed, gendered), humanism gives man complete power, tempting him to transcendence. Head is just as wary of men acting *as* God as she is of men acting *on behalf* of a distant God in heaven. Men who aspire to become gods themselves have no reverence for others, and thus they propagate suffering as they disidentify with ordinary human beings. To be transcendent in this sense is to aim for ascendency over other men, a move exemplified by both the "big man" of postcolonial authority and the humanitarian who poses as a savior.[72] Thus, within secular humanism, the elimination of God does not eliminate the *problem* of God but merely transfers it with serious consequences for humanity. As Michael Hardt and Antonio Negri put it, "There is a strict continuity between the religious thought that accords a power above nature to God and the modern 'secular' thought that accords that same power above nature to Man. . . . Like God, too, this transcendent figure of Man leads quickly to the imposition of social hierarchy and domination."[73] To be transcendent is to identify oneself with God and thus to disidentify with ordinary human beings on earth, particularly the poor and suffering. This version of human aspiration for transcendence has often appeared in literary representations of the postcolony, figured in both the physical expansion of postcolonial leaders and their excessive projects of splendor.[74] Particularly in *When Rain Clouds Gather*, Head berates those African inheritors of the postcolony whose wealth defies the limitations of human consumption, those figures who exemplify a phenomenon Tejumola Olaniyan has described as the "postcolonial incredible"—"too improbable, astonishing, and extraordinary to be believed."[75]

For Head, the uneven distribution of wealth after independence is indeed astonishing. She associates the "postcolonial incredible" with Solomon of the Old Testament, who "decked himself up in gold and . . . built a house that was a hundred cubits in length and fifty cubits in breadth and thirty cubits in height. Gold candlesticks, cherubims, and pomegranates adorned this house, which had forty bathrooms" (*Rain Clouds*, 215). She contrasts Solomon with "the God with no shoes," not unlike the hungry peasants of Botswana:

> Then came a God who was greater than Solomon, but he walked around with no shoes, in rough cloth, wandering up and down the dusty footpaths in the hot sun, with no bed on which to rest his head. And all that the followers of this God could do was to chronicle, in minute detail, the wonder and marvel of his wisdom.
>
> There were two such destinies which faced Africa—that of the followers of Solomon and that of a man with no shoes. But the man with no shoes had been bypassed, scorned, and ridiculed while the Solomons stalked the land in their golden Chevrolets. Who would eat then if all the gold and pomegranates went into the house of Solomon? Who would bathe if all the water went into his forty bathrooms? Who would have time to plough if everyone had to join the parade to watch Solomon pass by in his Chevrolet of molten gold, his top hat and silk shirt, glittering in the African sun? For that's all that Solomon wants—a lot of gapers and marvellers. And things were mixed up because there were too many Solomons and too many men with no shoes, and no one could be certain who would win out in the end— except that the man with no shoes was often too hungry to stand in the parade these days. (*Rain Clouds*, 215–16)

This model of asceticism responds to the polarizing excesses of neocolonial life—"too many Solomons and too many men with no shoes"—and drama-tizes the ironic notion that a messiah would come in a form so closely resem-bling the humanitarian subject. That in itself is a call to respect those who are often seen merely as numbers in the vast projects of the international community. Redemption lies, contrary to expectation, in the humble form of a shoeless peasant. The lesson Head takes from the biblical description of Christ is not about his death but about his everyday life, not about salvation but about sufficiency—an antidote to the transcendent man of postcolonial power and to the man-turned-savior of the white savior narrative. The eth-ics of sufficiency is divine in that it does not seek to attain a position above others, as is implicit in the ethics of salvation, but to "just be a person" who only needs—and thus only takes—so much. In the context of the neocolonial politics of hoarding (a global, not merely African, phenomenon, to be clear), there is something radical in the pursuit of just enough, something messianic in the ethics of sufficiency.

The God with no shoes is also a model for the thorough identification with the poor that Head is calling for. If God is the equal of the poorest people, then one offers reverence to God through reverence for them. In other words, there is a close identification here, even to the point of interchangeability, between God and the poor. Head's postcolonial humanism thus operates on the basis of a simultaneous deflation and exaltation of humanity. Even as they dethrone the distant God in heaven, these novels propose the desecularization of the human. Head explains elsewhere: "I have used the word God, in a practical way, in my books. I cannot find a substitute word for all that is most holy but I have tried to deflect people's attention into offering to each other what they offer to an Unseen Being in the sky. When people are holy to each other, war will end, human suffering will end."[76] Head shares the primary value of humanitarianism: the human should not be made to suffer.

Head's humanitarian theology, a philosophy of God and humanity, places supreme value on the ordinary, the simple, the merely sufficient. The ethical injunction of her work—"be the same as others in heart; just be a person"—is drawn from the identification with the poor (*Question*, 26). Reverence for the otherworldly, for something above or beyond humanity, has produced violence of varying degrees, but Head's earthly reverence aims to prevent it: "the basic error seemed to be a relegation of all things holy to some unseen Being in the sky. Since man was not holy to man," she writes, "he could be tortured for his complexion, he could be misused, degraded and killed" (206). Since people are willing to commit their lives and their resources to an "unseen Being in the sky," Head seeks to turn that reverence to human beings themselves, and she articulates this theology through Elizabeth: "There is only one God and his name is Man. And Elizabeth is his prophet" (206). The capitalization of Man, here, mirrors the capitalized God of monotheistic religions. Head makes a subtle but significant distinction between man claiming to be God and her own claim that God is Man.

This ethical model of being is not naively utopian as is often the case when people talk about the love of "mankind in general"; it doesn't expect to transform the world into one big happy family of man. Head has shown humanity to be far too complex for that and far too greedy. She isn't hoping to convert those who aspire toward the gilt "material possessions and dazzling raiments" of a King Solomon (*Rain Clouds*, 215). Rather this ethical model of being is for people of good intentions who often get mixed up in the ugliness of the white savior narrative—in the way it segregates the world while also claiming its oversimplified unity, in its willingness to destroy in order to convert, in its blindness to people that accompanies its humanist rhetoric, in its unwavering confidence and triumphalist approach to progress. The claims here are smaller, aiming to recast ignorant goodwill into critically minded goodwill.

Even Camilla, it turns out, is capable of change, but this is dependent on Elizabeth's compassion, on her ability to see Camilla as "crazily, pathetically human" (*Question*, 78). When Camilla hears Elizabeth's critique of her (Camilla's) racialism, she takes it as transformative advice. Afterward, Elizabeth "met a totally changed woman with a soft, subdued air, as near as a woman of her type could ever come to brooding reflection," comparable, on a smaller scale, to Eugene (86). She seems to be converted. Head recommends a decentered, desecularized humanism as an ethical and theological orientation for people like Camilla—of good but often ignorant will—as an alternative structure of thinking and believing to that of the white savior narrative, available for those who seek it.

The Earthly and the Enchanted

Bessie Head's work incites a crisis of humanitarian faith by throwing its power into question, even as she values altruistic practice. This encourages the mode of self-critique that has been a hallmark of postcolonial studies. Head's decentered, desecularized humanism is an alternative to grand narratives of African salvation by Western humanitarian means. It is a humanism, to echo Césaire's phrase, "made to the measure of the world"—a sharply stratified world. This highlights the implicit affinity between postcolonial theory and humanitarian ethics. These systems of thought, which are largely in conflict, both insist that lives pushed to the periphery are, in fact, primary. African novels of the third sector, like *A Question of Power* and *The Heart of Redness*, open up a conversation with postcolonial critique and humanitarian commitment. As I claimed in the introduction, this is a tentative alliance worth cultivating, and a more critical humanism can help.

The move toward desecularization in African novels about humanitarianism contrasts with the task of African literature about religious missions as elaborated in the preceding chapter. Ngũgĩ and Achebe have shown how mission students and anticolonial fighters took otherworldly claims about justice in the next world and made them secular and worldly, calling for "a real heaven on their own earth."[77] They secularized heaven by materializing it. In a related but distinct move, Head brings heaven to earth in a practice of enchantment. The texts featured in chapter 2 addressed the demand to be treated as human and not merely be called human; they attempted to bring the implications of humanity, the idea of being made in the image of God, into a worldly politics, in some sense disenchanting the notion of humanity and secularizing its implications. Head desecularizes that project without dematerializing it, insisting on the necessity of the sacred for *this* world. As opposed to their worldly heaven, Head posits a heavenly world.

Relocating the divine responds to the inequities inscribed in the fiction of the international community, and it offers a way of reframing the turn to enchantment in contemporary anglophone African fiction. The move away from social realism toward what is often described as magical realism—exemplified by Zakes Mda[78]—might be better understood as *reverent* realism, drawing on indigenous African views of the spirit world as well as world religions. Mda offers enchanted visions of both the urban and rural poor, from tin and cardboard shacks that glow in multicolored splendor to miraculous conception on horseback (in *Ways of Dying* and *The Heart of Redness*, respectively). When Camagu moves to Qolorha, he is driven by an enchanted mode of desire for a woman he likens to a "mother spirit" (*Heart*, 28); he is seeking an experience of divinity in the South African countryside. Although Camagu arrives in Qolorha as a semiforeigner with secular expertise, it is his reverence for local people, practices, and belief systems that earns him their respect (98–99). His postcolonial humanism locates divinity and spiritual wisdom in a rural village of southern Africa.

Both Mda and Head contribute to a project of revising the humanist foundation that guides humanitarian action, and in changing the philosophical base, they offer insight for transforming the structure built upon it. Secular humanitarianism contains many traces of the religious missions that preceded it. In their reverent forms of humanism, these authors critique that religious residue while also replacing it with new ways of encountering the divine.

4

The Benevolent Gift

If the problem of the twentieth century was the problem of the color line, as Du Bois so memorably declared at its inception, the poverty line may be the problem of the twenty-first. According to Mahmood Mamdani, decolonization brought about "deracialization without democratization" of authority or resources.[1] In other words, a black elite inherited formerly white positions of power and privilege without the restructuring of colonial society toward which many had aspired. As Frantz Fanon predicted, promises of a better life for all would give way to a postcolony that would be "only an empty shell, a crude and fragile travesty of what might have been."[2] Ongoing inequity is exhibited in the excessive wealth of the few and the intractable poverty of the many, nations of "ten millionaires and ten million beggars," in Mwangi wa Githinji's striking phrase.[3] In the wake of decolonization, African fiction has represented the disappointment resulting from broken promises of redistribution. Ngũgĩ wa Thiong'o, Chimamanda Ngozi Adichie, and Ben Okri have compared the bellies of Big Men, round from overindulgence, to those of hungry children, round from malnutrition. Awi Kwei Armah and Yvonne Vera have shown the arrival of the postcolony to be saturated with a sense of nonarrival, an ongoing waiting room for real transformation. Zakes Mda, Bessie Head, and Chris Abani have focused on the men, women, and children who have been excluded from the reshuffling of postcolonial and postapartheid power. The changes that took place with the fall of empire were incomplete because they were not inclusive: the redistribution of power and resources did not meaningfully incorporate everyone, leaving many without having even their basic needs — like food, clean water, shelter, healthcare, and safety — met. Such unmet needs are the focus of humanitarians in the postcolonial era, demarcating a shared problem space with writers of African fiction.

This is, fundamentally, a problem of distribution: Who has what, and how do they acquire it? What should be given, and how should it be parceled out? Humanitarianism responds to this problem through the structure of the benevolent gift. Poverty and hunger have come to define the image of Africa within the global imagination, making over the dark continent as the poor continent—the primary target of global benevolence. An "Official American" in Norman Rush's short story collection *Whites* captures this sentiment when she describes Botswana as "a poor relation, someone nice who refuses gifts at first, someone you like."[4] It is a sentiment often applied to the continent at large, a poor relation within the global "family of man." Humanitarianism is, by definition, a project of giving that connects people across the globe. Whereas the human rights narrative focuses on the individual rights-bearing subject, the humanitarian narrative revolves around relationships between those in the position to give and those in the position to receive. Humanitarianism asks: If we are part of an international community, then what responsibilities do we have toward people across the globe? In particular, what obligations do the relatively rich have to the very poor? The logic of the gift is therefore built into the humanitarian premise of universal inclusion and care.

The problem of giving and receiving is also a central concern of the literature of the third sector. Like the concept of universal humanity, which emerged in chapter 2 and became the subject of chapter 3, the humanitarian gift echoes Christian discourse. Christian theology is, at its core, about the absolute, unreturnable gift of salvation. The narrative of saving others through sacrificing oneself gets mapped onto the social world through religious missions, and it becomes secularized through humanitarian missions. Emerging from a Christian theory of the gift, humanitarian giving is an especially loaded transaction. In the theological gift relation, the giver is also the god. Human indebtedness is therefore expressed through worship. The hierarchical humanitarian relationship becomes similarly enchanted, with a special, even transcendent status attached to the giver.

To get at the history of this relation, I will look first at Tsitsi Dangarembga's *Nervous Conditions* (1988) to signal how literary responses to religious missions have engaged questions of the material world and foreseen the attractions and limitations of humanitarian aid. In contrast to chapter 2, my focus is not on the spiritual or intellectual dimensions but on the material, viewing Christian mission stations like humanitarian relief centers, in which cultural power mingles with material aid. As David Rieff explains, "In practical terms,

all the elements of the humanitarian enterprise — tending the sick, improving sanitation and housing, and upgrading education — were fundamental
to the enterprise of European missionaries in Asia, Africa, the Middle East,
and Latin America."[5] The colonial mission station offered gifts of both spiritual and material varieties, and African literature about missions anticipates
many of the negotiations that would also occur around secular humanitarian
benevolence. Dangarembga draws out the dialectic between emancipation
and domination in aid relationships, meditating on the unresolvable tension
between the desire for freedom and the urgent needs of the body.

The real stakes of this chapter lie in contemporary forms of humanitarian
aid, in what Michael Barnett calls the age of liberal humanitarianism (which
began with the end of the Cold War in 1989).[6] Nuruddin Farah's *Gifts* (1993)
interrogates the structure of giving within this era. Expressing a desire to preserve notions of responsibility and assistance, Farah suggests that what we call
giving is often a misnomer for more devious kinds of transactions. Alternative
structures of global care might be found by changing the terms of exchange
and the terminology with which it is described. Finally, an analysis of Philip
Caputo's *Acts of Faith* (2005) takes us into a twenty-first-century setting that
looks disturbingly similar to the age of empire. As an American war correspon-
dent, Pulitzer Prize–winning journalist, and novelist, Caputo is best known for
his memoir about the Vietnam war, and he enters this conversation as a critic
of his own country's presence abroad. Often compared to Joseph Conrad and
Graham Greene, Caputo creates characters who face "hard moral choices
in circumstances stripped of the usual guideposts and of external restraints."[7]
Like Dangarembga, he chastens the expectations of aid, but with a focus on
the relief worker through whom he cultivates a darker but less damaging humanitarian sensibility. *Acts of Faith* illuminates the ugly power dynamics that
are threaded through the humanitarian encounter of giver and recipient and,
like *Gifts*, encourages an undoing and rebuilding of that relation.

Together, these novels scrutinize and revise the concept of the benevolent
gift. If, as Erica Bornstein has claimed, "giving may well be an ethos of our
time,"[8] then it is worth assessing how literature has reflected the emergence
and effects of that ethos. *Nervous Conditions*, *Gifts*, and *Acts of Faith* help us
think through the following questions: How does the concept of the gift operate on the exceptionally unequal landscape of humanitarianism? What kinds
of relationships does it set up between humanitarian givers and their supposed
beneficiaries? How do people navigate and find agency within those relationships, and how does literature complicate and reimagine the conceptual
underpinnings of the gift? These are also the dilemmas that animate debates

about giving in philosophy, anthropology, and international politics, and this chapter will situate the literature within this broader context.

Distribution, Domination, and the Dilemmas of Aid

The UNICEF ads that have been popping up lately on my computer screen proclaim, "You have the power. Make a direct impact with your monthly donation." "You have the power. Kids need your help more than ever." "You have the power to give children the nutrition they need." As this refrain implies, the question of care is also a question of power. For people in the Global North, this is a common appeal, delivered through digital advertising, television commercials, and mailings. It often arrives through the voices of celebrities who plead with viewers to "reach into your pocket and pull out 50 cents," for example. In other words, it doesn't take much: "It's never been easier to save the life of a child."[9] Others suggest the easy path is not nearly enough. In *Living High and Letting Die*, philosopher Peter Unger argues not only that well-off people should donate to charitable organizations like UNICEF, CARE, and Oxfam but that "it's *seriously* wrong not to."[10] This isn't your run-of-the-mill donation appeal. For Unger, one must give the majority of one's current wealth and future income. While this may sound like heroic giving, Unger insists (following Peter Singer's earlier assessment) that it is not heroic or even noteworthy but a basic moral requirement. This upsets the "traditional distinction between duty and charity," according to which charity is a praiseworthy, elective act of generosity.[11]

Yet reframing the obligation of the giver doesn't necessarily change the experience of the recipient. The Unger-Singer formulation begs the question of whether humanitarian aid is truly effective; it assumes effectiveness and builds an argument from there. Implicit in their claims is a narrative: we can start from donation and arrive at meaningful change. The premise that charitable organizations can solve global problems begins to look flimsy once we take humanitarianism's track record into account. Among scholars, there is, by and large, a consensus that "actually existing humanitarianism"[12] has been ineffective. Even with all the donations that have gone into fighting poverty, the horizon of global equality continues to slip further into the imagined future. While noting that, compared to a century ago, fewer people (especially in Asia) are "living in what the World Bank calls 'extreme poverty,' an income of less than a dollar a day," Kwame Anthony Appiah insists that "Africa has been left behind, and it is Africa that presents the greatest challenge to our development experts—and to our sense of global obligations."[13] Although he agrees about the urgency of the problem, he argues that Unger's response "blocks thought about the complexity of the problems facing the global poor."[14] Taking humanitarian donation for a solution to poverty overpromises and oversimplifies. This line of thinking is related to white saviorism's narrative imagination—the notion that a straightforward solution is in our grasp if we are willing to step up to the moral challenge. This narrative uplifts the act of giving as an adequate response to global inequity, even a satisfactory replacement for government services and citizen entitlements. In some cases, the narrative calls for grand sacrifice on the part of aid workers and donors; in others, it emphasizes the ease of giving in order to encourage a wide donor base. "You have the power."

One of the predominant sentiments among critics of humanitarianism is that its discourse needs to be cut down to size. Giving is supposed to save people, to change the world, to usher in a new order of global care. However, in *A Bed for the Night: Humanitarianism in Crisis*, David Rieff worries that this is a "waste of hope," and he calls for a chastening of humanitarian promises and expectations.[15] He points out that, at its core, humanitarianism is defined by very modest assurances and quotes a poem by Bertolt Brecht to suggest that aid "won't change the world . . . But a few men have a bed for the night."[16] There is something to be said for a humanitarianism of moderated promises and plans. A bed for the night isn't much, but it does meet a real need. In a related vein of critique, Alex de Waal argues that "most current humanitarian activity in Africa is useless or damaging and should be abandoned" but that it is nonetheless "too noble an enterprise" to be neglected.[17] While de Waal is less pessimistic than Rieff and argues that, with significant reform, humanitarianism could achieve more, he contends that its transformation must begin from a reduced estimation of its capacity and effects. He recommends that "the first maxim must be: do no harm. Aid at least can shed its illusory aspirations and provide some modest material benefits in the context of African political initiatives."[18] A chastened aid narrative, combined with a heightened awareness of the damage goodwill can do, is a necessary step toward creating a more effective mode of international assistance.

Fiona Terry offers a useful amendment to the "do no harm" refrain that has become familiar within the scholarship on reform. She argues that aid not only promises too much but that it *inevitably* does a measure of harm: "doing no harm is not possible because humanitarian action will always generate winners and losers. The best that aid organizations can do is *minimize* the negative effects of their action."[19] She, too, argues for a chastening of our expectations of humanitarian care, calling us to set our sights on a "second-best world": "We can never construct the best world in which our compassion can immediately translate into an end to suffering, but we can try to build a second-best world based on hard-headed assessments of needs and options."[20] Terry proposes a very worldly humanitarianism that operates not above politics in some otherworldly ethical realm, but in the nonutopian space of *this* world.

Studies of aid's ineffectiveness force us to ask not only what it means to give a gift but what it means to see it through. A more equalizing strategy for humanitarian organizations is blocked by their limited accountability to the populations they serve. One problem with the structure of the gift is that it does not require follow-through. An American character in Rush's *Whites* illustrates this shortcoming in his explanation of why development workers like to stay in Botswana surrounded by "drought [and] poor people":

> "It's because it isn't our country and we can't help what happens. We can offer people advice and we get paid for it. We get good vacations, we eat off the top of the food chain, we get free housing. Hey!, but we're not responsible for what happens if Africa goes to hell, *because we've done our best*. Also, at the same time, we're not responsible for what happens in America, either, really—because, hey!, we weren't home when it happened. Say we get fifteen per cent compliance on birth control here, which is what we do get and which is terrific by Third World standards. O.K., *it's not enough*. But what can we do, we tried. We told them. But *we're too late*. We all know it, but somebody pays us to keep up the good work, so we say fine." (104)

Gifts, in contrast to entitlements, are not to be questioned. The gift is about emotion, not reason; gratitude, not critical response. Based on the etiquette of giving and receiving, bad gifts can self-perpetuate, letting givers off the hook with relative ease. Rush highlights the "top of the food chain" benefits of humanitarian practice: a lifestyle that aid workers can't access at home plus the psychological insulation of knowing "we've done our best." Even for donors who don't receive the material benefits of aid work, there is the giver's glow—the feeling of self-satisfaction that comes from the act of benevolence, apart from the outcome. Giving meets an emotional need whether or not it is publicly displayed. As Chris Tiffin and Helen Gilbert explain, "Even if the donation is anonymous, the gift is performed to the audience of self. Thus, virtually all forms of personal benevolence, even the most apparently altruistic, involve a structural relationship that situates the donor as a dominant, self-approving figure."[21] Domination inevitably produces harm, but for the dominant that often remains invisible.

The problem of domination is not exclusive to humanitarianism but is embedded in the structure of the gift in general. This leads us to ask whether the charitable mode of giving can be effective at all.[22] Based on his seminal anthropological studies, Marcel Mauss claims that reciprocity must be built into the gift structure so it can function as a practice of solidarity. Although it appears to be "free and disinterested," the gift, in fact, always involves self-interest and triggers obligation; because "power resides in the object given," it must be balanced by a return gift.[23] The trouble arises when that obligation cannot be met. When it goes unreciprocated, the gift "makes the person who has accepted it inferior," and, therefore, charity is "wounding."[24] The problem is intensified within the humanitarian relationship where power is, from the start, so remarkably unequal; the benevolent gift, which cannot be recipro-cated, is a "wounding" gift.

With international aid, the gift relation is projected on a massive scale. Even with the best of intentions, even with the most morally rigorous ap-proach to aid, power is built into its gift design. Didier Fassin explains that "a radically unequal order . . . is the mark of the humanitarian relationship—a structural fact, in other words, regardless of the motivations of actors."[25] This doesn't come down to "individual choices" but to the system in which "the gift can have no counter gift."[26] Giving without the possibility of return puts the recipient in a position of perpetual indebtedness. Therefore, aid is inevitably plagued by the problem of power, a key factor in producing the unavoidable harm Terry warns against. This calls for persistent vigilance over dynamics that can be mitigated but not eliminated. Like the religious missions from which it emerged, secular humanitarianism resides at the crux of emancipation and domination, as Barnett elaborates:

> Humanitarians frequently act without asking the recipients what they want, a neglect that they generally justify on the grounds that time is urgent or that their needs are obvious. While humanitarians might claim that they do not violate anyone's liberty because they do not carry guns or use the force of law, they arrive in highly deprived envi-ronments with various privileges and resources that make any notion of consent inherently problematic.[27]

That unevenness of power is not a reason not to act but a reality to continually confront. This is the inescapable context of humanitarianism, and a better humanitarianism needs to think not only about the inequity that motivates action but the inequity that is generated and entrenched by that action. The problem is not merely an issue of ideology; it is about the efficacy of aid. Challenging the ideology of the gift has the potential to make humanitarian giving more ethical *and* more effective.

Of course, the stakes are especially high for recipients. The humanitarian fictions studied in this chapter—and throughout this book, in fact—are characterized in part by their very worldliness. These stories are about bodies worn down from thankless labor, malnutrition, nakedness, and inadequate shelter. Their authors are thinking about the most basic human needs, how those needs are met, and the implications. What does it mean to meet one's needs through the charity of others? Does it inevitably imply a surrender of agency and independence? This is where humanitarianism comes into contact with one of the central concerns within the African novel, which, from its inception, took up and adapted a European form associated with modernity. In the words of Abiola Irele, "It may be argued that the fundamental theme of modern African literature written in the European languages is that of the cleavage of consciousness provoked by the historic encounter with Europe."[28] Humanitarianism continues to provoke this "cleavage of consciousness," as the novels in this chapter will demonstrate. The writers engage with the critiques of altruism that I have described, but in taking up those critiques they also attempt to think beyond them toward alternative theorizations of global giving practices. They draw us into the dilemmas of aid to wrestle with the tensions between emancipation and domination, conservation and conversion, African empowerment and disempowerment, grand promises and disappointing realities.

Religious Missions and Material Conditions

Tsitsi Dangarembga's *Nervous Conditions* is staked upon these tensions. Set in colonial Rhodesia (which would become Zimbabwe), the novel begins in 1968 and follows the coming-of-age of thirteen-year-old Tambu Siguake, who leaves her village for a mission school, seeking a better life. She narrates in a voice that is disillusioned and critically retrospective. Joseph Slaughter reads the novel as a "dissensual *Bildungsroman*"—a narrative of expected human rights integration (which would enable the full development of the human personality) that is ultimately characterized by hyperbole and disappointment. It displaces the teleological plot of the human rights development narrative with a "sense of no ending."[29] Whereas Slaughter reads it as a narrative of human rights development, I will read *Nervous Conditions* as a narrative of humanitarian development, focusing not on self-actualization but on the needs of the body and the relationship of aid. In this story of disillusionment, Dangarembga explores the global church as a nongovernmental, nonprofit source of development, foreshadowing the ongoing problems of humanitarian aid that would be evident at the time of the novel's publication in 1988.

When the story opens, Tambu is living in poverty and longing for a way out. Up to this point, her successful uncle, Babamukuru, the headmaster at a mission school, has sponsored her brother's education as a source of uplift for the family. When her brother dies, Tambu takes on the mantle of family uplift, receiving the chance to attend the mission school as her uncle's ward. She is thrilled at the opportunity, and expects to find "mental, and eventually, through it, material emancipation," freedom "from the constraints of the necessary and the squalid."[30] What she instead finds at the mission station is a world of new constraints. As I have argued in previous chapters, one of the hallmarks of the literature of the third sector is the plot reversal it enacts upon the white savior imagination. In Slaughter's words, Dangarembga is "rehistoricizing [Tambu's] personal story of development as the story of an illusion."[31] In place of the total emancipation she expects, Tambu finds alienation from her family, home, and culture, indebtedness to missionary benefactors, a cap on success allowed within the colonial system, and increasing exposure to racism exemplified by the overcrowded segregated dorm room where she arrives at the end of the novel. The narrative of emancipation becomes a narrative of disappointment, and the sense of movement and uplift is ultimately replaced by images of confinement and limitation. Literary critics have thus read the novel as a story of cultural and psychological alienation.[32]

It is also a story of the humanitarian gift. This is a novel of conditions in both the psychological and material senses, and I am interested in how the urgency of material need constantly presses on Tambu's consciousness. I want to tease out the story of needs from the story of rights that Slaughter articulates, because urgent need is the foundation for understanding the gift exchange in the humanitarian context. The human rights narrative—according to which Tambu should become an emancipated, rights-bearing subject—does indeed fail, but this is complicated by the way her more abstract political rights are entangled with the immediacy of meeting basic needs for food, water, and clothing. In *Nervous Conditions*, the social starting point is extreme poverty, and the Tambu we meet in the beginning is the embodiment of the humanitarian subject—the malnourished African child. Hers is a body shaped by deprivation:

> When I stepped into Babamukuru's car I was a peasant. You could see that at a glance in my tight, faded frock that immodestly defined my budding breasts, and in my broad-toed feet that had grown thick-skinned through daily contact with the ground in all weathers. You could see if from the way the keratin had reacted by thickening and, having thickened, had hardened and cracked so that the dirt ground

its way in but could not be washed out. It was evident from the corru-
gated black callouses on my knees, the scales on my skin that were due
to lack of oil, the short, dull tufts of malnourished hair. This was the
person I was leaving behind. (58)

This passage highlights how the conditions of poverty become readable
through the body—the thickened, cracked feet that do not know shoes, the
brittle texture of skin and hair that signals a lack of protein and thus a limited
diet. The journey to the mission will dramatically transform the body's signals.
Tambu will transform in other ways, too, as she gets more closely wrapped up
in colonial culture, but in terms of meeting physical needs, this is a narrative
of progress.

The primary motivation for Tambu's transformation is the intense pressure
of fundamental needs, and therefore we must fold together the cultural and
material narratives at hand while assessing the psychological consequences.
She expects to be "emancipated" from the persistent nagging of the physical:

This new me would not be enervated by smoky kitchens that left eyes
smarting and chests permanently bronchitic. This new me would
not be frustrated by wood fires that either flamed so furiously that the
sadza burned, or so indifferently that it became mbodza. Nor would
there be trips to the Nyamarira [River], Nyamarira which I loved to
bathe in and watch cascade through the narrow outlet of the fall where
we drew water. Leaving this Nyamarira, my flowing, tumbling, musical
playground, was difficult. But I could not pretend to be sorry to be
leaving the water-drums whose weight compressed your neck into your
spine, were heavy on the head even after you had grown used to them
and were constantly in need of refilling. (59)

These are conditions Tambu cannot work her way out of—she has certainly
tried—and thus she welcomes external assistance, even at the cost of the river
she loves so dearly. The back-and-forth of this passage illustrates the conflicting pulls of freedom and sufficiency, psychological and physical health. The
river itself is a site of ambivalence, linking lighthearted joy with the hardships
of life without plumbing.

Dangarembga wrote *Nervous Conditions* in the 1980s, following a massive
surge of images for humanitarian fundraising not unlike that we see of the
malnourished, water-drum-toting Tambu. The novel depicts the body of the
humanitarian subject, and while this imagery resonates with televised representations of hunger, it does a different kind of work. In his powerful essay,

"How to Write about Africa"—a facetious prescription for Western writers—Binyavanga Wainaina draws our attention to the problem of "The Starving African":

> Among your characters you must always include The Starving African, who wanders the refugee camp nearly naked, and waits for the benevolence of the West. Her children have flies on their eyelids and pot bellies, and her breasts are flat and empty. She must look utterly helpless. She can have no past, no history; such diversions ruin the dramatic moment. Moans are good. She must never say anything about herself in the dialogue except to speak of her (unspeakable) suffering.[33]

This is an old standby of the humanitarian imagination (and it will be a central figure in the following chapter). Wainaina's satire crystallizes a common critique of the representation of Africa in Western writing in many forms—books, film, news, and, of course, humanitarian fundraising efforts. Dangarembga takes up the same subject, but she addresses *a* (nearly) starving African rather than *The* Starving African, a flat, singular figure. Her image of hunger includes the physical signs standard in representations of malnutrition but in a context that changes the stakes.[34]

Tambu receives aid within a narrative of her own striving. She is not wandering helplessly, waiting for Western benevolence. Before her brother dies and the mission school scholarship becomes available to her, she sets up her own business, growing and selling maize to raise funds for her education. In contrast to The Starving African, she has a past and a history. In fact, the plot is dedicated to the extended documentation of her history, spoken in her own unruly voice. Wainaina's Starving African "must never say anything about herself" outside of her suffering, but Tambu presents a full, multidimensional self-image, positioning her experience as worthy of an entire novel (that would eventually evolve into a trilogy).[35] The Starving African is static, but this is a narrative of becoming in which Tambu develops the voice with which to critique her conditions. In this way, Dangarembga writes over the silence produced by the humanitarian "machinery of compassion,"[36] emphasizing the role of African agency and the much fuller life that often gets written out of the representation of need. This is the story of humanitarian giving told from the perspective—and through the agency—of the recipient.

Tambu's experience illustrates the tension between the desire for emancipation and the desire for enough. The problems the mission school addresses are urgent. Consider the contrast between the "peasant body" and the mission school body. Tambu knows what the mission offers after seeing her brother, Nhamo, return following a period spent there: the "change in appearance was dramatic. He had added several inches to his height and many to his width, so that he was not little and scrawny any more but fit and muscular" (*Nervous*, 52). This description appears just a few pages before Tambu references her own "thickened" feet, calloused knees, and "malnourished hair" (58). As the comparison makes clear, Nhamo's changed appearance is the manifestation of a changed life. But there are other disquieting dimensions to his healthier look: "Vitamins had nourished his skin to a shiny smoothness, several tones lighter in complexion than it used to be. His hair was no longer arranged in rows of dusty, wild cucumber tufts but was black, shiny with oil and smoothly combed" (52). This is a body healed by humanitarian gifts—it is also a body whitened by those gifts. Health gets linked to lighter skin and straighter hair. Eating with a fork also means, for the first time, eating enough. Even as the mission student approaches the colonial culture, he is moving out of colonially imposed conditions of the material variety. At the same time, his improved conditions are colonially enabled. There is a shuttling back and forth, here, which illustrates the humanitarian "paradox of emancipation and domination."[37] To become the recipient of the humanitarian gift is to enter a morass of unsettling influences. Derek Wright thinks of that influence in terms of the "cultural byproducts" of aid.[38] Culture and conditions are a joint package.

Tambu will undergo the same kind of transformation as her brother, adding support to James Ferguson's claim that "yearnings for cultural convergence" can stem from "an aspiration to overcome categorical subordination."[39] When she arrives at Babamukuru's home, signs of "civilized" culture are also signs of a new place-in-the-world. She is intimidated by the gracious dining room, for example, with its large table and abundant seating: "That table, its shape and size, had a lot of say about the amount, the calorie content, the complement of vitamins and minerals, the relative proportions of fat, carbohydrate and protein of the food that would be consumed at it. No one who ate from such a table could fail to grow fat and healthy" (*Nervous*, 69). By making bodies and furniture speak so vividly to material conditions, Dangarembga primes us to read a setting for the way it signals needs, their fulfillment, and social status; inequity is woven into the literary landscape. In many ways, the mission is a cage, but resisting it is complicated by the fact that in it, Tambu is healthy, well fed, and well dressed.

The gift extended to Tambu invites other, less calculable, problems, manifested partly in her cousin Nyasha's own nervous condition—a life-threatening eating disorder—which reverses and ironizes Tambu's trajectory from starvation to sufficiency. The improved conditions she finds in mission schools are themselves nervous conditions—contingent, indebting, and tenuously held. She avoids displeasing her uncle for fear of losing the basic resources he provides, because he, as the giver of gifts, also controls them. The mission is thereby framed not as a source of sustenance that Tambu has a *right* to claim but as a gift and a blessing that could be revoked at any time and for which she should be grateful. Change is specific, not structural; having her needs met today makes no guarantee for tomorrow. Furthermore, social uplift is contingent upon the favor of missionaries who select beneficiaries they view as "useful to their people" (14). When, years earlier, Babamukuru was offered a scholarship to study in England, "to decline it would have been a form of suicide. The missionaries would have been annoyed by his ingratitude. He would have fallen from grace with them and they would have taken under their wings another promising young African in his place" (14). This system operates not on the basis of fairness but on favor, which unfolds in layers that ripple outward from the mission. Babamukuru must be grateful to the missionaries; Tambu must in turn be grateful to him.

In this context, she is forced to negotiate how much control is worth forfeiting. Would it be better to return to grinding poverty for the sake of self-determination? Should she reject a well-rounded meal for the sake of those higher-level needs like independence and pride?[40] These are questions without satisfactory answers.[41] The life of her mother—for whom the "poverty of blackness" is compounded by the "weight of womanhood" (*Nervous*, 19)—is not a romantic alternative by any means. Self-actualization is also blocked by the constraints of material deprivation, and thus her mother is hardly a figure of independence. This is not a scenario of real choice but a forced impasse. These issues become a subject of debate within human rights discourse. Some argue that "first generation rights"—political and civil individual rights—should be deferred in the interest of material and economic rights (called "second generation rights"), which are most urgent and become the necessary base for individual liberty. Others argue that the order should be the reverse.[42] For Tambu, the fulfillment of material rights comes at the expense of individual liberties, and it is not an easy trade-off. Neither option is without serious cost. The novel resides within the anxiety of meeting needs through compromising sources, thereby producing a sense of unease without a straightforward resolution—in essence, a nervous condition. For Tambu, charity is indeed "wounding."[43]

The language of the white savior narrative empowers the giver, and *Nervous Conditions* shows how that language infiltrates the voices of African recipients. A giver of gifts doesn't have to be concerned with structural transformation or even with real success, since it is an act not of obligation but of benevolence; it is the thought—not the effect—that counts. Tambu learns this lesson not from the missionaries themselves but from her grandmother:

The Whites on the mission were a special kind of white person, special in the way that my grandmother had explained to me, for they were holy. They had come not to take but to give. They were about God's business here in darkest Africa. They had given up the comforts and security of their own homes to come and lighten our darkness. It was a big sacrifice that the missionaries made. It was a sacrifice that made us grateful to them, a sacrifice that made them superior not only to us but to those other Whites as well who were here for adventure and to help themselves to our emeralds (103).

What gets built up around the missionaries is a narrative—a narrative of what they could have had and what they have chosen instead, a narrative that characterizes them as heroic, brave, and selfless. The missionaries' relationship to Shona locals is a function of the savior narrative attached to them, which distinguishes "the special kind of white person" from the standard. Giving consolidates their authority. Sacrifice earns them status, and humility makes them holy. Tambu's grandmother teaches this lesson and Tambu then imports its vocabulary directly into her own—"God's business here in darkest Africa," "lighten our darkness," "big sacrifice," "self-denial and brotherly love" (103). The text, in this way, speaks the language of white saviorism.

But as Tambu shifts from the mode of informing to interpreting, she introduces a doubleness into that language. This shift begins when she describes missionaries' superiority and contrasts them with white profiteers, because in that sentence she drops the tone of objectivity. She claims ownership of "our emeralds" and sarcastically describes the white people who "help themselves" to them. From there, she breaks down the distinction between white groups: "The missionaries' self-denial and brotherly love did not go unrewarded. We treated them like minor deities. With the self-satisfied dignity that came naturally to white people in those days, they accepted this improving disguise" (103). They, too, are helping themselves to African resources. Filtered through Tambu's voice, the keywords of white saviorism come to signify differently. They communicate on two tracks—one sincere, one ironic. Through an act of narration, "other 'denied' knowledges enter upon the dominant discourse and estrange the basis of its authority—its rules of recognition."[44] This doubling of language unsettles the grandmother's speech, too, even though she appears to have been sincere. Terms like holiness, darkness, and sacrifice then operate on two levels, with the notion of disguise hovering around the denotative meaning. The passage offers a lesson in reading. It demonstrates how "perspectival orientations shape readers' engagement with a narrative."[45] This point applies not only to the novel itself but to the white savior narrative that it embeds. In other words, Tambu's perspective shapes readers' engagement with the white savior narrative; it dissuades readers from taking that narrative's terms at face value. Through this use of perspective, Dangarembga affirms Mieke Bal's "privileging [of] focalization as the most important concept in postcolonial narratology"; focalization helps readers be "politically aware and ethically sensitive."[46] Before narrating to an audience, however, Tambu must cultivate that awareness and sensitivity in herself.

Although she was selected and groomed to be a "good African," loyal to the benevolent whites, Tambu becomes increasingly rebellious toward the end of the novel and throughout the sequel, *The Book of Not*. *Nervous Conditions* closes by signaling the "process of expansion" which enables Tambu to become a critical narrator: "Quietly, unobtrusively and extremely fitfully, something in my mind began to assert itself, to question things and refuse to be brainwashed, bringing me to this time when I can set down this story" (204). She narrates her story some years after the plot's conclusion (though she doesn't specify how many years) and can thus bring critical perspective to bear on her younger, naive self. The doubling of white savior language she ultimately achieves had to be learned over time, once she gained distance from the scene of the gift. The gift narrative is also a gauntlet narrative. One does not pass through unscathed, but domination and dependency are not the inevitable end. Gifts can function to purchase loyalty to, and thus perpetuation of, an unjust system, but that transaction does not necessarily work. For material assistance to escape its constraining effects, it would have to take the power dynamics of the gift into critical account. This also means that, in critiquing the structure of the gift, we should not elide the agency of people navigating the costs and benefits of receiving.

The Postcolonial Language of *Gifts*

Nuruddin Farah's *Gifts* negotiates the politics of giving and receiving on personal and global levels, linking questions of the international community to matters of local communities. It, too, confronts the tension between the critique of aid and the urgency of material needs. Farah enters the question of foreign aid by recounting the story of Duniya, a nurse who lives a modest life in Mogadiscio, the Somali capital, with her children. We are introduced to her discomfort with receiving gifts when she accepts a ride from Bosaaso, an acquaintance with whom her relationship builds over the course of the novel. When he asks about her hesitancy to accept the gift of a ride, her response links the personal to the political, comparing individual stakes to global ones: "Because unasked-for generosity has a way of making one feel obliged, trapped in a labyrinth of dependence. You're more knowledgeable about these matters, but haven't we in the Third World lost our self-reliance and pride because of the so-called aid we unquestioningly receive from the so-called First World?"[47] This mix of scales (individual decisions made on the basis of global transactions) suggests that Duniya's environment is so inundated by the structure of First World giving and Third World receiving that it becomes metonymic for gift relationships in general. This is also evident in the way Farah intersperses the main narrative with other kinds of texts—news briefs following most chapters and editorial articles embedded within. This textual collage expands the dialogic form of the novel, putting literary discourse into conversation with the public discourse on international aid. By integrating nonfictional genres that represent famine, starvation, and international aid in Somalia, Farah "extends the universe of reference for his novel" into the discursive realm of journalists, policy analysts, and development experts, bringing fiction into nonfictional debates about the internationalization of social welfare and aid.[48]

This is a field of debate in which the novel's Somali characters are very much engaged—it is not merely the terrain of the "international experts" and world news. While the third-person narrator of *Gifts* focuses on Duniya's personal experience and emotional life, the insertion of other textual forms adds the impersonal, objective tone of news reporting as well as the polemical, even combative tone of political argument. In this way, Farah combines narrative scales so that stories of nations, of global leaders, and of ordinary people cohere. In addition to displaying a mix of styles, these embedded texts attest to a variety of positions on aid. They document actress Liv Ullman's "mission of mercy" as a Goodwill Ambassador for UNICEF, presidential pandering in order to secure aid from Western nations, rejected and failed donations such as Ronald Reagan's gift of spoiled milk to Poland, and Poland's retort in the form of donated blankets for New York's homeless. Arguments about the imperialist nature of aid's application, the production of dependency, and the depletion of African agency and pride are delivered primarily through the editorial publications of Taariq, Duniya's ex-husband. He argues that aid perpetuates famine and cultivates inequity by providing just enough stability to prevent total crisis: "Foreign food donations create a buffer zone between corrupt leaderships and the starving masses. Foreign food donations also sabotage the African's ability to survive with dignity" (Farah, 196). In other words, if famine were allowed to progress to its logical conclusion, bad leaders would be overthrown; according to this argument, aid blocks revolution that would change the circumstances of the people in a systemic way rather than offering a temporary fix.

This argument also draws attention to the intangible dimensions of the humanitarian relation: What does the gift mean for one's sense of self? How can survival and dignity coexist? Farah depicts a diversity of intention and effect, which Taariq also observes in an editorial:

> Every gift has a personality—that of its giver. On every sack of rice do-
> nated by a foreign government to a starving people in Africa, the char-
> acteristics and mentality of the donor, name and country, are stamped
> on its ribs. A quintal of wheat donated by a charity based in the Bible
> Belt of the USA tastes different from one grown in and donated by a
> member of the European Community. You wouldn't disagree, I hope,
> that one has, as its basis, the theological notion of charity; the other,
> the temporal, philosophical economic credo of creating a future
> generation of potential consumers of this specimen of high quality
> wheat. (197)

Taariq's analysis shows the power embedded in donor relations and also complicates it. Whereas giving always involves power, the structure of power it
sets up is not always the same. That is not to say that good intentions suffice.
Both the Bible Belt and the European Community, in this example, are acting
in the name of good intentions, but there is more to be distinguished in the
mode of intent, depending on the philosophical framework from which the
donation emerges, the roots of those intentions. This challenges the theoretical tendency to think of the gift as a consistent, inevitable structure.

Gifts also pushes us to broaden our understanding of the network of donation. Too often, the discussion of humanitarian giving gets stuck on Europe
and the United States with the white savior as the quintessential giver. But that
is just one version of a far more diverse field of care. Donors include foreigners
from various countries with diverse sensibilities. In contrast to Europeans, for
example, the Chinese doctors at Duniya's clinic are noted for their humility:
"No pomp, no garlands of see-how-great-we-are" (20). And this isn't an exclusively foreign enterprise. Somalis are donors, too, including those newly
returned after years abroad. Duniya takes in an orphaned baby; her daughter
donates blood; Dr. Mire, with whom she works, has returned to Somalia from
the United States "to donate his services to the government and the people
of their country, accepting no payment, only an apartment, conveniently located and modestly furnished" (17); Bosaaso is back in the country under the
same arrangement, volunteering for the Ministry of Economic Planning. By
distributing the role of giver across many characters rather than concentrating
it in a single character or character type (like the foreign humanitarian), Farah
shows that the structure of the gift is not singular or unidirectional but comes
in a variety of configurations and personalities.

Moreover, Farah makes clear in *Gifts* that global forms of aid are entering a culture which has its own preexisting modes of distribution and care, independent giving systems as a protection in times of need. "Most Africans," Taariq explains, "are (paying?) members of extended families, these being institutions comparable to trade unions. Often, you find one individual's fortunes supporting a network of needs of this larger unit. . . . Those who have plenty, give; those who have nothing expect to be given to" (197). Again, local practices of giving force a rethinking of the gift structure. Those who "have nothing" are dependent, yes, but not trapped, indebted, or undignified. Although Taariq acknowledges that the expectation of receiving can go problematically far, the novel offers a functioning example of this kind of family network through the relationship between Duniya and her brother, which I will come to shortly. Or, there is the example of *Qaaraan*, a Somali tradition of "passing round the hat for collections . . . when you are in dire need of help" (196). The system has checks and balances; to qualify for assistance one has to be considered a "respectable member of society" and one cannot "appl[y] for more" in the short term (196). By building up this rich context of African giving systems and local agency, Farah provides a corrective to the singularity and simplicity of the white savior narrative, focusing on Somalis active in the process of caring for themselves, their families, and communities. Assembling numerous versions of the story of donating and receiving, *Gifts* wrests the position of donor from the ownership of the West.[49]

Taariq's article "Giving and Receiving: The Notion of Donations" includes a description of the humanitarian context to which the novel responds. If, as Taariq argues, every gift has the personality of its giver, television representations of hunger in Africa are both reflecting and in turn recreating a problematic personality: "No doubt, television is a personality creator, and donors have their smiling pictures taken, alternating with scenes of Ethiopian skeletons. For the first time Africa has been given prime time TV coverage, but alas, Africa is speechless, and hungry" (199). Ironically, at the very moment that African people enter the realm of global concern they are silenced and flattened, juxtaposed against the full faces of donors. Conrad's African bodies come to mind again, those bunches of angles languishing under the trees, "shadows of disease and starvation,"[50] almost entirely voiceless: "In Conrad's *Heart of Darkness*," Taariq recalls, "the one and only moment the African is given a line to speak, the poor fellow is made to employ an incorrect grammatical structure. That was of prime and all-time literary significance" (Farah, 198). Taariq points to a disconnect between voice and body. While *Heart of Darkness* notes the physical suffering of African people, it represents the starving body in a silent, dehumanized form: "They were not enemies, they were not criminals"—that's all well and good, but it goes much further—"they were *nothing earthly* now,—nothing but black shadows of disease and starvation, lying confusedly in the greenish gloom."[51] *Heart of Darkness* is about hunger, too, but this scene takes the African body beyond the earthly and thus beyond politics. Without voice, they are also outside of language, that distinguishing characteristic of human identity and belonging. In contrast, we saw that Dangarembga's representation of the vocal humanitarian subject in *Nervous Conditions* highlights the social making of that body, drawing attention to the human relations that produced such inequity (particularly the dispossession enacted by colonialism). *Gifts*, too, takes on these humanitarian images and situates them within a narrative that is constantly pointing to the social production of inequality.

Duniya is determined not to be trapped in the kind of relationship those images reflect and produce. Through her character, the novel explores a strategy of response to the critiques Taariq lays out regarding the reinforcement of Western power and the disempowerment of African subjects. Farah's mix of genres is again significant as it reveals how individual lives (the quintessential subject of novels) are shaped by political arguments. Duniya feels that the costs of aid are too high; free gifts, like the "overpriced aid package from the European Community" (20), come with long strings attached. To maintain self-reliance and pride, she assumes the aid of others must be rejected and makes a family policy of it: "If there was one thing Duniya couldn't stand, it was her children bringing home unauthorized gifts of food, or money, given to them by Uncle So-and-so or Aunt So-and-so" (26). Her position is understandable and represents a common response to the sense of obligation embedded within the gift. But Farah's answer is not so straightforward. The novel begins with Duniya breaking her own rule, accepting that ride against (what she thinks is) her better judgment. Her narrative is about the process of becoming vulnerable, about opening oneself up to receive. While the novel incorporates the critique of aid as imperialism and dependency production, it also complicates our assumptions about how the recipient is positioned in the postcolonial gift structure. Like the various personalities of giving, there are various personalities of receiving. This makes room for agency within the act of accepting the gift.

Even with its critique of dependency, *Gifts* has little faith in an isolating self-reliance that depends only on one's own hands to tug on one's own metaphorical bootstraps. The glorification of self-reliance buys into another myth that also obscures the network of social relations.[52] The argument that the poor should independently support themselves assumes that the rich already enjoy that independence, that the "haves" are self-made. The novel makes clear that this is an illusion, projecting a sense of social and economic autonomy that does not in fact exist. If the rich don't get there on their own, why should the poor? If the misfortunes of some are related to the fortunes of others, as Farah suggests they are, then the solution cannot be found in isolation. That kind of rugged individualism fails to account for the ways human beings are inevitably interconnected. The novel builds up a different language around giving and receiving by showing how people are interdependent in ways that obligate them to one another. It is not necessarily the recipient who is indebted to the donor. Obligation positions donors very differently than the framework of benevolence.

Farah's novel illustrates that alternative framework through the relationship between Duniya and the one person whose generosity she has always accepted freely, her wealthy brother Abshir. He explains the logic that makes this possible:

> "You are a woman and younger than me. . . . I suppose these facts are central to our gift relationship, yours and mine." . . .
>
> . . . "If you were a boy, you wouldn't have been married off to a man as old as your grandfather in the first place, and in the second, you might have got a scholarship to a university of your choice, because you were brilliant and ambitious. An injustice had been done. It has been my intention to right the wrong as best I could." (242)

Abshir suggests that a gift relationship can genuinely aim to transform existing power relations rather than reinforce them. But it must be situated within a critique of the social network of inequity production. Failing to take that historical background into account means fundamentally misperceiving the present exchange. Abshir recognizes that what he has gained as a man is not unrelated to what Duniya has been denied as a woman. This interaction makes visible what Olakunle George describes as "the network of relations that determines (and thereby, narrativizes) the body in pain."[53] Assumptions about the meaning of that "network of relations" are the foundation for making sense of the person in need. It is a question of how the story of Abshir's gift gets told. In making visible those unjust relations and in trying to "right the wrong" from which he has benefited, Abshir is actually the indebted one. His gifts unveil the injustice that produced their inequity rather than concealing it. Furthermore, within this framework, Abshir gives without the implication that his gifts are a solution to the problem. The fact that Duniya has never felt indebted or undignified upon receiving his gifts suggests that the personality of the gift is indeed flexible; it can reflect and produce different kinds of relationships.

Duniya's perception of the individual recipient role is shaped by international aid; conversely, the meaning of international aid can be shaped by the individual gift relation with her brother. To understand the global aid relationship, we must contextualize it and remember that Western meddling creates the desperate context in which people come to need aid. By taking African lands, generally the base of economic livelihood, and eroding indigenous social, cultural, and political structures, colonialism displaced the foundations of African societies, the resources and methods which had enabled communities to survive and thrive independently.[54] This uneven relationship continues after decolonization with Western governments, businesses, and financial institutions exploiting African nations while also claiming to assist. The context changes the terms.

Farah is constantly playing with the terms, giving new meaning to "gifts" of various kinds. In a flashback, Bosaaso remembers an argument between his late wife, Yussur, and a Danish aid worker, Ingrid, "about the philosophical and cultural aspects of giving and receiving gifts" (47). The debate grows out of what Yussur sees as Ingrid's misuse of language when she describes a used china set she has just sold to her for ten American dollars, "equivalent in local currency to more than a senior civil servant's salary" as "more or less a gift" (48). Yussur connects this to another major criticism of aid as an essentially self-interested gesture on the part of the powerful:

> "My husband told me only recently that the United States, the world's richest country, between 1953 and 1971 donated *so-called* economic assistance worth ninety million dollars to Somalia, one of the world's poorest. Over sixty million of this *so-called* aid package was meant to finance development schemes, including teacher-training and a water supply system for the city of Mogadiscio. But do you know that nearly twenty million dollars were accounted for by food grown in the USA by American farmers, given to us in sacks with the words DONATED BY THE USA TO THE REPUBLIC OF SOMALIA written on them? And of course from that we have to deduct the salaries of Americans working here and living like lords in luxury they are not used to at home. Why must we accept this intolerable *nonsense*?" (49, emphasis added)

This echoes critiques of aid that we have heard before—the benefits for "donors," the luxurious lives of aid workers, the misrepresentation of the extent of the gift. What is distinct, however, is the emphasis Yussur places on the problem of language itself. Terms like "economic assistance" and "aid package" become nonsensical when matched up with what their work actually looks like. According to what system of meaning are goods from which the givers

profit "donated"? And what kind of relationship to the recipients does that misleading language produce? The language of the gift is forcing the terms of gift
giving and receiving onto another kind of transaction. A system that poses as
disinterested benevolence is in fact beneficial to the United States, its farmers,
and aid workers. Yussur goes on to drive home the point: "What I'm trying to
say, my dear Ingrid, is that a language is the product of a people's attitude to
the world in which they find themselves. Now can you understand why it irks
me to hear you describe the china for which we paid ten US dollars as a gift?"
(49). Yussur isn't turning down the content of the so-called gift. She wants the
china set but according to different terms of exchange; she wants to call it what
it is and take it on that basis, not on the pretense of a gift. Humanitarian aid,
this interaction implies, if it is to function at all, must be called by its proper
name, and "gift" is not it.

As Ngũgĩ insists in *Something Torn and New*, the problem of terms is,
indeed, applicable to the global network of giving. The standard language of
Western donation obscures a divergent reality: "the continent's relationship
to the world has thus far been that of *donor* to the West. Africa has given her
human beings, her resources, and even her spiritual products through African writing in European languages. We should strive to do it the other way
around."[55] Within this historical context, it is a bitter irony to think of the West
as perpetual donor to Africa. Recalibrating the terms opens up new possibilities for more equitable exchange. At the beginning of *Gifts*, Duniya rejects
assistance because of its implications as a massive, international transaction in
the form of aid, but by the end she has entered into a reciprocal relationship of
giving which the novel affirms. To "feel obliged, trapped in a labyrinth of dependence" (Farah, 22) is not the only possibility or personality for receiving. In
linking the personal and the global, Farah suggests that this model might also
scale up, that international assistance might be reshaped in a related form.
It is thus significant that Duniya moves toward accepting assistance within
the context of a different language and a different set of relational dynamics
defined by independence and reciprocity. The terms of exchange—and the
historical network of relations in which they are inscribed—matter.

Humanitarian Technologies of the Self

By upending the discourse of donation, *Gifts* calls for a reckoning on the side
of donors and humanitarians. Such is the work of *Acts of Faith*. For Philip Caputo, an exploration of the power dynamics circulating through the international "machinery of compassion" (*Acts*, 310) tempers overblown expectations
and triggers a moral reckoning within the "giver." The authority of altruism

that missionaries enjoyed, as represented in *Nervous Conditions*, would find its ultimate expression in the humanitarian encampments of the postcolonial era, as Caputo's novel shows. The book emerged from his experience as a journalist reporting on humanitarian aid during the Second Sudanese Civil War. With *Acts of Faith*, Caputo connects that context to his novelistic interests in "political corruption, greed, and the tendency of faith, whether in religion or a secular ideology, to curdle into fanaticism."[56] Preceding the narrative is a list of major and minor characters including missionaries, aid workers, and philanthropists along with military men and mercenaries. From there, the third-person narrator moves, chapter by chapter, among the major characters' perspectives and experiences as they work, fight, and survive the vicissitudes of war. The sprawling, intricate form of this novel attests to the complexity of Caputo's subject.

Shifting among such a range of perspectives can have a dizzying effect, but *Acts of Faith* is grounded by an anchor character and leading focalizer, Fitzhugh Martin, described in the "Cast of Characters" as a "mixed-race Kenyan" and "former UN relief worker." Although his is just one among several perspectives, he serves as the thread that takes us from beginning to end. In the opening chapter, "Introductory Rites," he is interviewed by an American journalist and provides the framework for making sense of the story and its characters. This section serves as a preface, located before the main text, but set, in plot time, after it has all unfolded. Described as a Kenyan "of all races," Fitzhugh has a unique perspective. He is an outsider in Kenyan society "without a tribal allegiance or a claim to any one race" and an outsider among the mostly white, Western humanitarian staff with whom he works (13). Despite their differences, Fitzhugh was drawn to relief work for reasons not unlike those of his white colleagues. As a soccer player with the Harambee Stars, he "saw something of the world, and what he saw—namely the shocking contrast between the West and his continent—convinced him to do something more with himself than chase a checkered ball up and down a field. He'd heard a kind of missionary call, quit soccer, and became a United Nations relief worker, first in Somalia and then in Sudan" (13).[57] Upon leaving Kenya and seeing Europe and the United States, Fitzhugh enters the network of the humanitarian Atlantic. His turn to third sector work is based on a new understanding of global injustice that hits close to home, showing the West in stark contrast to "*his* continent." In this example, the African aid worker is also inspired by the "missionary call" and driven by the moral cause. But, as was the case with the missionaries I addressed in chapter 1, Fitzhugh's real motivation isn't quite as valorous: "That was the story he told, but it wasn't entirely true: a serious knee injury that required two operations was as responsible for his leaving the sport as a Pauline epiphany" (*Acts*, 13). Being Kenyan doesn't make him an ideal relief worker or resolve the messy ethics of giving; he isn't a hero but a regular human, pulled by conflicting desires and motivations, enchanted by the biblical language of epiphany. Fitzhugh is nonetheless the voice of conscience in the novel, even if he acts in ways that fail to live up to his morals. On the one hand, he participates in the conventional humanitarian discourse: "He meant to do all in his power to save the southern Sudanese from the curses of the apocalypse" (14), and he is magnetically drawn to "*a place where a few people can make a big difference*" (32). On the other hand, he has a level of self-awareness and a capacity for critique that eludes many others.

For example, Fitzhugh's existence within the UN, "the army of international beneficence" (14), is strained. He loves the work but hates the institutional context in which he must do it. The UN base had

> the look of a military installation, ringed by coils of barbed wire. The field managers and flight coordinators and logistics officers — to his eyes a mob of ambitious bureaucrats or risk-lovers seeking respectable adventure — drove around like conquerors in white Land Rovers sprouting tall radio antennae; they lived and worked in tidy blue and white bungalows, drank their gins and cold beers at bars that looked like beach resort tiki bars, and ate imported meats washed down with imported wines. (14)

Regardless of what aid workers think of their efforts, to hungry locals their base is a center of consumption. In this novel, aid is scaled up into massive, highly bureaucratized organizations. UN workers' "special" status is akin to that of the missionaries in *Nervous Conditions*, but they have taken that status to new levels, leaving behind the simple living that was common among missionaries. This is the kind of aid that, in *Gifts*, appears in the news reports but that characters do not encounter directly. In *Acts of Faith*, the UN base is a public spectacle that projects the irony of giving before suffering witnesses. The barbed wire surrounding their compound makes literal the violent division between cosmopolitan givers and African recipients. Aid workers' resemblance to their European predecessors is conspicuous: "They were the new colonials," living in the same bungalows and drinking the same wine, "and Fitzhugh grew to loathe them as much as he loathed the old-time imperialists who had pillaged Africa in the name of the white man's burden and the *mission civilisatrice*" (14). The base seems a kind of vortex, devouring resources in dubious proportion to what it gives out. The UN workers seem to thrive on grandeur, distinguishing themselves not only from the people they serve but from local workers in their own industry. These are "special whites" in terms of material status but certainly not moral status in the eyes of the community. Through Fitzhugh's focalization, this critique is coming from a person who is both within and outside the system, and he maintains faith in the moral cause at the heart of humanitarian care: "Relief work—what a bland phrase, as if it were merely another form of labor. But it wasn't. It reaffirmed the human bond. It was the marshaling of resources to organize compassion into effective action, for without action, compassion degenerated into a useless pity" (271). The UN marshals resources and organizes action, yet the distance between the organization's employees and the targets of their "compassion" blocks the real affirmation of "the human bond."

Often the bureaucracy itself seems to get in the way of really thinking and caring about others. The example with which Book 1 opens, the trigger for Fitzhugh's firing, occurs when the UN food stores get overstocked. Following protocol, UN employees take away the excess to burn it, and on the journey to its destruction they carefully protect the donated food from hungry people:

> Mindful that cremating tons of food would make for bad press, the High Commissioners had the dirty work done under the cover of darkness at a remote dump site, far out in the sere, scrub-covered plateaus beyond Loki. Truck convoys would leave the UN base before dawn with armed escorts, their loads covered by plastic tarps; for the Turkana, men as lean as the leaf-blade spears they carried, knew scarcity in the best of times and were consequently skilled and enthusiastic bandits. (16)

Aid in places of scarcity is an envied resource, and this does generate serious challenges for distribution, but in following distribution plans too closely, the UN withholds food—with armed force, no less—from those who need it as badly as those their mandate tells them to assist. The brutal irony becomes even more painful to Fitzhugh when he visits a Sudanese province that had recently been attacked by the government army with a slash-and-burn method that destroys food sources and leaves citizens worse off than the rebel army, the government army's supposed target. Those who had escaped death in the attack are dying of starvation afterward. Fitzhugh is there to do a "needs assessment" but is not equipped to do anything about the needs he finds (17). Once Fitzhugh puts this in perspective—"*My goodness*, he thought . . . *a tenth of the surplus that had been put to the match could have saved them all*"—he assists Father Malachy Delany, an Irish missionary, in outing the UN scandal (18). This incident reveals how the gift is bound up by the rules and regulations of humanitarian bureaucracy, its morality undercut by its mandate.

Still, Fitzhugh is an altruistic idealist with a strong sense of the right way and the wrong way to do aid. After being fired from the UN, he hopes to find a better humanitarian framework and joins a nongovernmental organization to fly aid into Sudan. His trajectory is driven by a pursuit of the moral cause, with the hope of matching the noble idea to material practice. He works under the leadership of Douglas Braithwaite, also a former UN employee, who now manages the independent airline contracted by International People's Aid. Fitzhugh is initially inspired by the confident American who seems to have a strong ethical sensibility that resonates with Fitzhugh's frustrations with the UN. When another pilot, Tara, tells Douglas that she thinks it should be left to the southern Sudanese to "sort themselves out," his heated response seems to outline a better model of assistance. The task of the humanitarian is not to do the sorting himself, he argues, but "to pitch in and help them do the sorting" (71). Tara retorts, "You don't make a good carpenter by building his house for him," asserting that aid is ultimately disabling. But Douglas has already considered that:

> "Right. You give him a hammer, show him how to use it. But then you don't stand back and feel real good about yourself and say *tsk-tsk* when he bends a nail or whacks his thumb. Sometimes your arm has to get sore with his. Sometimes your sweat has to drip on the ground with his. Sometimes you have to swing it *for* him, not sit in the air-conditioning like [the UN workers he so loathes] with maps and pins and fax machines." (71)

This is an ethics of solidarity, not of pity, projecting a humanitarianism that is about much more than handouts; swinging the hammer means getting alongside the recipients rather than sitting so comfortably above them. Fitzhugh is excited by this rare gesture of equality between the helpers and the helped, and he jumps in enthusiastically: "And you don't eat Danish ham and drink French wine while the other guy gets by on his porridge and bad water. . . . And when the job's done, you leave with the shirt on your back, not a hundred thousand in back pay" (71). Fitzhugh envisions a different mode for the humanitarian "gift," and ultimately, his attraction to Douglas is more about his (Fitzhugh's) own philosophy of aid.

Through Fitzhugh's lament against the lavishness of the UN and through counterexamples of international do-gooders who actually do good, *Acts of Faith* affirms an ascetic practice of humanitarian ethics which combines simple living and solidarity with local people. There is Father Jim Rigney, for instance, an American missionary who had built churches, clinics, schools, had dug wells, and had "lived ascetically, in a small mud-brick house out in the Masai-Mara, . . . beloved by his congregations and seen as a champion of the oppressed" until he was murdered for political reasons (6). His house is the same kind as the houses of the Kenyans who attend his church, a stark contrast to the barbed wire fortress of UN luxury living. The Irish missionary Malachy has adapted so fully to the local context that "anyone who saw him, clapping his hands to tribal songs, leading chants of call and response, had to wonder who had converted whom" (16). He lives closely among the Turkana, speaking their language and taking on their practices. The humanitarian figures the novel most values combine a leftist political sensibility, focused on global injustice, with an ascetic religious sensibility. Their asceticism is fully grounded in this world, not the next, modeling a kind of "unworldly engagement with the world."[58] The secular Fitzhugh embeds the spiritual language of the missionaries into his own philosophy: "Relief work *was* a religion, at least to his way of thinking. In a way it was an act of faith that infused his actions with spiritual value," freedom "from the inner tyrant who kept demanding, *I want, I want, I want*" (*Acts*, 20). What makes these religious men so compelling for Fitzhugh is not the religious specificity of their creed or the relationship it establishes between God and humanity; rather it is the relationship among people—to the self and to others—through the restraint of personal greed. This is a way of managing the tension between altruistic giving and self-centered grasping. Fitzhugh becomes a mediator of the various languages of aid that circulate in the novel.

Although he is not religious, Douglas Braithwaite initially seems to voice a secular version of ascetic altruism; he turns out to be far less sincere than Fitzhugh first believes. Fitzhugh hopes to find a transformative version of assistance with Douglas, but the sins of the fine-wine-drinking UN workers ultimately pale in comparison to Douglas's transgressions. He starts out as a seemingly heroic humanitarian giver, risking his life flying aid into Sudan to help the displaced and dispossessed of war; he turns out to be one of the monstrous antiheroes—a gunrunner, embezzler, and murderer. For the first part of the novel, his good intentions contrast with those of his partner, Wesley Dare, who, defined as a mercenary in Caputo's "Cast of Characters," never denies that he is in Africa for the money. Over the course of the story, however, the distinction between these characters' motives becomes increasingly blurred and eventually we discover that Douglas is the more wildly self-serving of the two. As his business grows more and more profitable, he becomes an "aid entrepreneur" (261) and eventually a gunrunner and war profiteer, in the end orchestrating the murder of several characters in order to cover up his illicit operations and a related embezzlement scheme. After successfully preventing his plot from being exposed, he and his partner continue "using the delivery of humanitarian aid to conceal their 'criminal activities,'" namely supplying weapons to a rebel army (659).The difference between good and evil becomes indistinguishable for the character himself:

> [Douglas] was like an actor who had become the role he was playing, but with this difference: The self-deception was not artful but as natural and unconscious as the feathers on the birds he observed. It was the absence of craft that granted him the power to deceive others. In his attractive costumes — the successful entrepreneur of aviation, the man of compassion, the crusading idealist — the murderer was invisible. So were the naked appetites and ambition that had driven him. And this was hidden too: the derangement wrought by his *faith in the rightness of his actions*. (648, emphasis added)

It is faith in the *"rightness* of the mission" (270) that enables Douglas to take the risk of flying aid to those in need, to view himself as one of the "airborne knights, rescuing the peasants" (270), and ultimately to carry out extreme violence while still believing his own performance as "the man of compassion, the crusading idealist" (648). The power of giving can be inspiring but also terrifying. The language matters but it is not enough; theorizing about solidarity with local people, which Douglas does well, does not suffice to keep greed in check.

As we have seen in previous examples, profit and philanthropy, avarice and altruism, are embedded in the position of the giver. What Douglas uniquely demonstrates is that this issue is more complicated than hypocrisy. In Douglas, "the contradiction between the idealist and the relentless entrepreneur was too great for Fitzhugh to resolve" (514). The issue isn't that one side, the idealist or the entrepreneur, is more real than the other. Douglas is both the "cutthroat" profiteer and "a moral man, a man of compassion, who had risked a great deal, even his life, to bring succor to the starving, the sick, the defenseless" (514). The protected status of the giver — the "special kind of white person"[59] — enables a character like Douglas to advance the most perversely self-serving agendas in a way that is beyond even his own understanding. In *Horn of Africa*, Caputo presents the danger thus:

> It was the gleam of something darker than madness — belief, an absolute belief in the rightness of one's religion or political dogma or personal destiny, the faith that creates saints and demons alike, that inspires both the martyr and the murdering bigot, that gives a man the power to destroy others because he is willing to risk his own destruction in its name.[60]

The disintegrating line between missionary and mercenary becomes a familiar trope in the literature of the third sector.[61] We get the sense that these are
in fact related and overlapping types of global actors—wandering misfits in
pursuit of glory of which, like profit, one can never have enough. In some
cases, the missionary is a mask for the mercenary; alternatively, the two can
exist simultaneously and persuasively within one person. Each enables the
other while also undercutting the other.

By Caputo's representation, this is a specifically (though not exclusively)
American mode of being in the world. It is written into the way Douglas carries
himself, foreshadowing the threat to come. When they meet, Fitzhugh immediately recognizes the man as an American based on "the way he [stands],
chin cocked up, shoulders slouched just a little, projecting the relaxed bellig-
erence of a citizen of the nation that ran the world" (Acts, 23). When Edward
Said referred to the White Man as "an idea, a persona, a style of being," he
had British colonials in mind.[62] In the latter half of the twentieth century, this
"style of being" gravitated toward the United States. Embracing the rhetoric
of mission, the U.S. takes the posture of the benevolent world power. We also
see this in Quinette, an evangelical Christian who goes to Sudan on a mission
to free enslaved people. Fitzhugh observes, "She and Douglas [are] alike in
many ways; so American in their narcissism, in their self-righteousness, in
their blindness to their inner natures, in their impulse to remake the world
and reinvent themselves, never realizing that the world wishes to remain as
it is and that oneself is not as malleable as one likes to think" (Acts, 664).
Although they do not represent the United States officially, they have unconsciously absorbed its sense of global authority. They give not as humans to
humans but as Americans to Africans. The dynamics of state power thus shape
seemingly independent acts of giving in the NGO sector.

While the white savior was traditionally male, the role is not, in fact, confined by gender. By including Quinette, who so explicitly embraces the discourse of humanitarian salvation, Caputo doesn't let white women off the
hook. Adapting Said, we can say that being a White Woman in Africa is also
"a very concrete manner of being-in-the-world."[63] In Quinette, we see the
psychology of the giver play out violently. Her good deeds contain an uglier
edge: "The emergency had summoned all the discordant strains in her nature
to play in concert: her egoism and her desire for self-sacrifice; her need to
be of service and also at the center of attention; her pity for the victimized
and her pride in being their savior; and the lead violinist in this symphony
of motives was her jealousy" (Acts, 547). Ultimately, she sends a woman into
slavery out of jealousy. But long before she becomes explicitly cruel, her work
on behalf of others targets her own needs and insecurities. Altruism becomes

a kind of perversion, and the difference between helping and hurting becomes irreversibly confused. There is a reason this American drama unfolds on African grounds. Quinette projects herself into the available plotline of the white savior narrative. She positions herself as the humanitarian hero who sacrifices now for glory later: "Maybe thirty or forty years from now, this crusade would be on the History Channel, and she would be able to tell her grandchildren that she'd been in it, been part of something altogether noble and so much bigger than herself" (214). She plays into the tropes of an existing story in order to be able to tell that story again. This is the performance that the structure of the gift enables — uplifting oneself through a project "bigger" than oneself — and women prove as adept at this as men.

The way people respond to Quinette, however, challenges the meaning of the gift and the giver. As a reward for her grand sense of sacrifice, she expects "reciprocity. She loved Africa and wanted it to love her back" (222). Material reciprocity is not possible, but emotional reciprocity is. She envisions herself reporting back to her church, telling her story from "the podium, describing the scene and her own exalted emotions and grateful arms encircled her" (153). The reality, however, is that people don't feel the indebtedness that Quinette — and many theorists of the gift — expect. Therefore, they do not even verbally reciprocate: "What could she tell [people back home] now? That the people just sat and stared when they heard they were free?" (153). Still, reciprocity isn't a deal breaker because Quinette can continue to rely on the story she tells herself "that God had summoned her . . . that He was leading her to something, step by step" (499). The savior narrative protects its hero from the bruising of reality.

Such a bruising, however, would be valuable. As an African observer of these American "do-gooders," Fitzhugh becomes the voice of humanitarian disenchantment. Much like the author himself, for whom Fitzhugh seems to be a kind of mouthpiece, this character synthesizes the meaning of events in the narrative. Through working with Douglas, he becomes complicit, but he is not dragged down entirely. He eventually puts together the pieces of Douglas's scheme, quits, and sets up his former employer to be caught, although he knows that justice will be incomplete. By the end Fitzhugh is deeply disillusioned:

> When he looked back on the past three years of work and risk, he couldn't see what difference he had made. . . . He was reminded of the warning on side-view mirrors — CAUTION: OBJECTS IN THE MIRROR ARE CLOSER THAN THEY APPEAR. It was just the opposite in the mirror of Sudan. Whatever one's object was — to end a famine, to bring peace,

to heal the sick—it was farther away than it appeared, seemingly within one's grasp but always beyond it. (648)

His expectations for aid have been undercut by its outcomes. "Making a difference" is illusory, apparently accessible but always escaping into the distance. Furthermore, Fitzhugh finds that simply doing moderate good—nothing on the scale of ending famine, bringing peace, or healing the sick—requires compromise with evil. To bring Douglas to some justice, at least to get him to stop what he is doing, Fitzhugh must make a deal with a man who is "something of a devil . . . but a minor devil compared with our American friend" (657). The ethics of the greater good, by the end of the novel, becomes an ethics of the lesser evil, since to remain above it would be to do nothing, to accept the status quo. In *Acts of Faith*, aid is unsavory business.

Fitzhugh's idealism has dissolved into a cynical realism. By the end, his narrative allows us to understand the position he advocates in the first pages of the book: "That's how the African thinks of good and evil. It's foolish to try and separate the two. Foolish *and* dangerous. You have to give in to it, the oneness, I mean, but not entirely. No! You submit without surrendering. That's the difficult trick. That's how the African survives, physically and otherwise" (6). It seems, initially, a "sweeping generalization" (6), but by the end of the novel it becomes clear there is more to it than that. The mesh of good and evil, as it turns out, is not so much about Africa itself as about the vectors of global power that collide there. To "submit without surrendering" is a strategy needed by both locals and foreigners to negotiate the field of greed and violence in which humanitarianism finds its home. Fitzhugh clarifies with an anecdote about the well-respected missionary, Father Jim, whom he considers to be a model of successful contribution—up to a point:

A political missionary as much as one who ministered to the soul. . . . An apostle of human rights who became known in Kenya for his intemperate public denunciations of official greed and nepotism and brutality. Bandits in Savile Row suits, Father Jim called cabinet members and members of parliament, fattening themselves while people in the villages he served went without clean water or electricity or proper medical care. (6)

Father Jim refuses to politely ignore the relations of power in which his parishioners are inscribed. This seems like a good thing, since obscuring power is a frequent problem in theories of aid, but by amending that problem, he becomes a target for murder. To government leaders, Father Jim strikes a chord that the apolitical discourse of charity would not. According to Fitzhugh and to the locals with whom he works, Father Jim is doing real good, and yet that is ultimately defeated by the brutality of the elites he pits himself against. In Fitzhugh's view, he dies because he doesn't submit.

This is part of what it means to be white in Africa. Both Father Jim and Malachy demonstrate that not everyone who is white in Africa embodies the White Man style of being. The diversity of positions is part of what the large cast of characters in *Acts of Faith* helps us to see. But there are patterns of whiteness that affect even the most admirable white characters. As Fitzhugh explains, Father Jim "did things that needed doing and said things that needed saying, but . . . he did them in *the way white guys do things over here*, head-on, and he said them so loudly, so directly, even after he got a couple of death threats, even after the head of his own order sent him a letter, asking him to back off just a little" (6–7, emphasis added). Although Father Jim is the rare good humanitarian in the novel, his style is a manifestation of whiteness, which subtly molds his work and makes him vulnerable to unanticipated consequences. The threats are not empty, and he is killed by a member of parliament whom he had tried to bring to justice. The good is here defeated by an insistence on the best: "He could have submitted to the evil without surrendering to it. But he didn't," Fitzhugh laments (8). To get anywhere, it is necessary to accept the second-best option; the first, this suggests, is utopianism and often the naive optimism associated with whiteness. The novel's exploration of humanitarianism is a journey into moral messiness. Even Fitzhugh's language attests to that ambiguity. When interviewed, he "doesn't answer directly" but speaks "in the metaphorical language he favors" (5), the language of the literary, which, in Teju Cole's phrase, should "leave the reader not knowing what to think."[64]

Built into the novel's theorization of aid is the inevitability of failure. The moral imperative is about making things less bad rather than dramatically better, recognizing that a "first-best" world is inaccessible and thus striving for "second-best."[65] To circle back to Fiona Terry's argument, "The best that aid organizations can hope to do is *minimize* the negative effects of their action."[66] As *Acts of Faith* demonstrates, this concession is partly about forces beyond one's own control, but for the agent of humanitarianism it is also about the forces within. This is where the kind of soul-searching that is common to religious practice comes into play, even in the secular religion of relief work, as is the case for Fitzhugh. It enables him to be aware of and to free himself from "the inner tyrant who [keeps] demanding *I want, I want, I want*" (20). Religious discourse insists on the evil within the self, and for Douglas, the failure of that recognition allows him to carry out the cruelties he enacts. Fitzhugh tries to explain how the man could have fallen so far: "Greed, believing in something too deeply, but in the end . . . there is something missing in him. He lacks a moral imagination when it comes to himself. He's so certain of his inner virtue that he believes anything he does, even something this terrible, is the right thing" (651). Douglas doesn't recognize the evil within, the inseparability of God and the Devil (649). Fitzhugh does, as do the humanitarian missionaries whom the novel affirms for their ascetic modes of thinking and living. This is akin to what Foucault calls technologies of the self. He situates the concept in centuries-old practices of Christian monasticism, explaining that it is "a matter of dislodging the most hidden impulses from the inner recesses of the soul, thus enabling oneself to break free of them."[67] Applying this practice to aid workers also changes the stakes of questions the white savior narrative takes for granted: Who needs to be freed and from what kind of darkness? How does being white shape and constrain one's perspective? And what does that mean for the giving relationship?

From this evaluation of individual humanitarians' devastating moral failures, Caputo develops a theory applicable to humanitarian thought more broadly: "Anyone who does not acknowledge the darkness in his nature will succumb to it. He will not take precautions against its prompting, nor recognize it when it calls" (*Acts*, 648). *Acts of Faith* asks us to understand humanitarianism as a noble project plagued by its own moral ambivalence. In *The Dark Sides of Virtue*, David Kennedy argues that it is only in engaging its dark sides that humanitarianism can minimize its harm and maximize its benefits. *Acts of Faith* thus articulates a "posture or sensibility for humanitarian work"[68] that would allow it to anticipate and deal more effectively with the moral messiness that it can never fully escape. According to this model, the sharp critique of humanitarianism's "evils" is not its end but its necessary starting place. The moral dimension to preserve is not the sense of God-given mission but the knowledge that the humanitarian self can do wrong in the very act of doing good.

Questions of Power

The meaning we ascribe to the practice of giving matters. Is it driven by benevolence? Or is it obligation? Or an acknowledgment of debt? Does it offer salvation or mere survival? Is the capacity to give earned through individual effort, or is it a social position endowed by imperial structures of power? The same goes for receiving. Is it a position of indebtedness or entitlement? Is accepting a gift a surrender of agency or an assertion of one's own value? Should it evoke feelings of gratitude? Shame? Satisfaction? Indifference? Is the state of need a natural position or an imposed one? The answers to these questions matter because they define the texture of the humanitarian relationship.

The third sector novel is a space of experimentation that plays with those questions. Through narration and dialogue, it tests out multiple languages of aid and multiple languages of critique. In so doing, this literature helps us understand the myriad effects of white saviorism while also illuminating the possibilities and risks of alternative approaches to giving. It offers an extended mode of thinking through the significance of humanitarian principles and their complexities, including the social, political, emotional, and psychological nuances of the humanitarian encounter on both sides—those who give and those who receive. As Dangarembga, Farah, and Caputo show, the power bound up with the gift has persistently compromised global responses to African needs. These writers disenchant benevolence and give the lie to the humanitarian fiction of "special whites," showing how the effects of this fiction play out. This expands and refines our conception of what it means to be white in Africa as well as what it means to be African in the humanitarian encounter.

Importantly, in their response to poverty, these authors continue to think in the global frame, suggesting that it is a world problem, not just a nation problem. The point of contention isn't that humanitarianism connects the wrong places on the map, but that it misunderstands and misrepresents the nature of the relationships among them. The critique of the gift doesn't eliminate the obligation to give; instead, it requires a more honest, theoretically and historically informed discourse around donors and recipients. Ngũgĩ's point is worth reiterating here: Africa has, for centuries, been "donor to the West . . . [having] given her human beings, her resources, and even her spiritual products."[69] In a similar conceptual turn, Bruce Robbins breaks the habitual use of the word "beneficiaries," which typically describes recipients of aid, and argues that it is better suited for the so-called "benefactors" who are linked to suffering people "not merely as potential rescuers but also as beneficiaries of the system that produces that suffering."[70] In their conceptual reversal of donor and beneficiary, Ngũgĩ and Robbins remind us of the West's own criminal indebtedness. The novels studied in this chapter, and critical humanitarian fictions more generally, help us reenvision the humanitarian relationship in, to borrow Robbins's phrase, "an estranged and uncomfortable way."[71] Dangarembga, Farah, and Caputo defamiliarize the language of the gift, which preserves the innocence of the givers and inscribes the recipients in debt. By multiplying the meaning of giving beyond the benevolent structure of the gift, these novels uncover a more intricate network of transactions and flows.

This reveals the density of the humanitarian Atlantic network, which has been mapped by the circulation not only of aid but of European colonizers, enslaved Africans, and the goods and wealth produced by those movements. The imbalanced flow of wealth continues today. In *The Black Atlantic*, Paul Gilroy takes "the image of ships in motion across the spaces between Europe, America, Africa, and the Caribbean" as a way of focusing attention not only "on the middle passage [but on] the various projects for redemptive return to an African homeland, on the circulation of ideas and activists as well as the movement of key cultural and political artifacts."[72] With the humanitarian Atlantic, we might begin from the cargo ship or airplane carrying aid to Africa, but like Gilroy's extension beyond the slave ship, the crossings here go well beyond the delivery of the gift. In addition to flows of aid workers and missionaries, sacks of grain and medical supplies, we can add relational, psychological, and emotional flows. The sides of the Atlantic are linked by self-righteousness and self-effacement, gratitude and indifference, excitement and fear, pride and shame, hope and desperation, greed and generosity, loathing and love. There are also flows of narrative from journalists and humanitarians as well as authors who challenge the dominant image of an Africa in need of saving.

Remembering the troubled layers of this transatlantic relationship complicates the significance of giving and receiving aid, showing the dangerous power of the gift structure but also the agency and sophistication of people who accept it. On the one hand, the anxiety of indebtedness is real and places undue pressure on potential recipients of aid to sacrifice material wellbeing for the sake of independence. On the other hand, that sense of disempowerment is premised on the fiction of benevolence. By overestimating the power of Western giving, we overestimate the powerlessness of African people in the recipient position. Redefining the personality of the gift through the dense network of the humanitarian Atlantic alters the terms of exchange in the aid relationship, deflating Western hubris and unveiling the African agency that was there all along.

5

The Nongovernmental Organization

In a scene from NoViolet Bulawayo's *We Need New Names*, a boy named God-knows rallies his friends in a game of pretend: "Wayyyt, wayyyt, wih neeeeed tuh tayk a pictchur, whereh ease mah camera? Godknows cries, making like he is the NGO man, and we laugh and we laugh and we laugh. Godknows runs and picks up one of those bricks with the holes in them and holds it like it's a camera and takes and takes and takes pictures."[1] The other kids know the routine and quickly pose for the brick turned camera. This imitation is suggestive of the presence of NGOs in the lives of the hungry children in Zimbabwe whom the novel depicts. The humanitarian worker has become a kind of stock character available for imaginative play. Godknows's act of imagination displays the perceptiveness of children about the adults they encounter. What is an "NGO man"? An English-speaker who takes pictures. That is his characteristic action and the camera is his characteristic prop. Their play reveals that these children are used to being captured in NGO images, and picture taking (rather than aid giving) dominates those interactions. The young narrator, Darling, explains in a preceding scene, "They just like taking pictures, these NGO people, like maybe we are their real friends and relatives and they will look at the pictures later and point us out by name to other friends and relatives once they get back to their homes" (54). In Darling's world, the term "NGO people" functions as a general identity category. While local NGO workers have names, the white foreigners never do. They are a blank mass. They are, in their actual presence, peripheral figures, but they have enough of an emotional impact to come up as frequent references in the talk of children and that of their parents. NGOs are constantly representing Africa to the world. What if their own image were reflected back to them? The pretend brick camera invites readers to view NGOs through a new lens. Nongovernmental organizations may have a tight grip on African image-making, but the imaginative world of a novel can take hold of the camera in ways that defamiliarize those now ubiquitous images.

The preceding chapter focused on the structure of the gift and the inequalities inscribed within the aid relationship. This chapter will move to the nongovernmental organization — the institution that manages the aid relationship and funnels humanitarian sentiment into humanitarian action. It will also consider the role of the humanitarian worker as the individual emissary of the NGO. A staple in Western humanitarian narratives, white saviors have often filled this position, epitomizing the nonstate actor in the Western imagination. Already, we have seen white saviors decentered in African narratives; this chapter will take an additional step, underscoring the fact that foreign humanitarians are far less present in daily life than the popular humanitarian imagination would suggest.[2] In spite of myriad constraints, people living in poverty or suffering through crisis do organize independently, creating a local third sector to address the needs of their communities. African literature reflects that, and in so doing, it can help us understand how the dynamics around NGOs play out within African contexts, outside the conventional narrative of foreign intervention. In this final chapter, I will examine two novels, both published in 2006, which capture these dynamics — Chimamanda Ngozi Adichie's *Half of a Yellow Sun* and Ngũgĩ wa Thiong'o's *Wizard of the Crow*. These are not humanitarian novels in any obvious sense, which is, in fact, why I turn to them here; they show the scope of humanitarian fictions, how extensively they can break from the patterns of the white savior narrative while still sharing its interest in third sector forms of assistance. Within these novels, aid in its usual, Western sense is peripheral at best. In many cases, humanitarian fictions turn romantic saviors tragic, revealing their destructive effects. These novels, however, are not about saviors, failed or otherwise. Instead, they chart a network of third sector care that lies under the radar of its major international networks, thus reconceptualizing the NGO as a grassroots effort rather than a foreign intervention.

As a reading of these novels will highlight, the NGO is a channel of action and of communication. As a channel of action, it envisions progress through nonstate intervention, ideally operating independently of governments and declining to take sides in political conflicts.[3] A not-for-profit enterprise, the NGO relies on donors for funding and thus on global goodwill. It operates not on behalf of a particular constituency but on the principle of humanity. Humanitarian action is supposed to be apolitical and transcendent, lying not merely outside of state interests but above and beyond them. Secondly, the

NGO is a channel of communication. Funding operations on the ground requires persuading a foreign audience to support those operations, and NGOs have formed one of the most powerful voices by which Africa is represented to the West. The interconnected networks of journalism and humanitarian fundraising project an image of Africa as the ultimate humanitarian subject.[4] Their modes of storytelling not only feature foreign players but are bound to external audiences. On the one hand, this means catering to Western tastes for the kind of "Africa" they want to see, adapting for the postcolonial era what Chinua Achebe described as "a particular way of looking (or, rather, not looking) at Africa and Africans" that is rooted in the colonial "arsenal of derogatory images."[5] On the other hand, it means actively shaping those tastes. As marketers, NGOs have created desire and demand for a particular kind of looking (or not looking), which flattens Africa into a singular, suffering place. As James Ferguson puts it, "When we hear about 'Africa' today, it is usually in urgent and troubled tones. It is never just Africa, but always the crisis in Africa, the problems of Africa, the failure of Africa, the moral challenge of Africa to 'the international community.'"[6] NGO fundraising campaigns have supplied much of the vocabulary for these conversations. Yet Western donors are not the only audience. As exemplified by the kids who play NGO in *We Need New Names*, African people also receive and creatively respond to NGOs' messages.

Taken together, *Half of a Yellow Sun* and *Wizard of the Crow* show the rise and the ubiquity of the visual and verbal rhetoric of the NGO. In their handling of humanitarian actions and communications, these novels help us reevaluate how the story of state failure and humanitarian response is told. These are stories of state crisis in which characters must seek third sector avenues for their livelihood and survival. In the worlds Adichie and Ngũgĩ depict, where poverty, hunger, and violence are pressing, foreign NGOs and humanitarians are a point of common reference but not a significant presence. This draws attention to the smaller-scale alternatives to international aid that are centered on African agency and often led by women. The altruistic characters in these novels redefine the relationship between humanitarian saviors and humanitarian subjects. Thinking beyond the nation as the organizing principle of care and affiliation puts us in an international humanist framework. But thinking beyond the nation doesn't necessarily mean going outside of it.

Without focusing on humanitarianism in a conventional sense, Adichie and Ngũgĩ follow local characters as they organize around health, hunger, and poverty, supporting their communities through volunteer work, enabling us to fill out the story of third sector practices of care. By doing so, they teach us to disarticulate the humanitarian from the white savior and the Western

NGO. Nonetheless, the characters are navigating the sphere of international NGOs which, even when they are not physically present, are consciousness shaping. This chapter reveals not only how Africa has entered global consciousness through the discourse of the NGO but how that discourse has affected African consciousness of the globe. *Half of a Yellow Sun* and *Wizard of the Crow* grapple with the same tensions that pervade NGOs, particularly the relationship between ethics and politics. By situating these humanitarian fictions outside the typical "aid-centric"[7] frame, Adichie and Ngũgĩ complicate the third sector approach, which defines itself apolitically. They repoliticize the nonstate.

Tensions in NGO Discourse

The story of the NGO is also a story of the African state. Among scholars and within the humanitarian community, discussions of humanitarian crises and the explosive growth of NGOs in the 1980s and '90s are typically framed in terms of governmental failure. Often, this takes the form of an origin story that Julie Fisher summarizes thus: "NGOs are founded as a result of governmental failure to address precisely those areas where governments have historically held a comparative advantage in Europe and the United States."[8] One abdicates; the other arrives. Noting that NGO arrival is not an exclusively Western phenomenon, Stephen Ndegwa describes an inverse relationship between the state and the NGO whereby "the decline of the state in Africa has also provided entry points for both foreign and local NGOs to embark on development work—for instance, when states have been unable to provide adequate services such as healthcare, education, and agricultural and credit extension."[9] In other words, as the public sector contracts, the nonstate sector expands. NGOs represent an alternative that is supposed to entail freedom and flexibility unavailable to state bureaucracies. In addition to filling social service gaps, NGOs are valued for their "ability to challenge unequal relationships and pursue transformative agendas through their people-centered approaches."[10] They can leverage their own relative power "to articulate neglected and marginalized interests and issues that are being ignored by the state actors and the economy."[11] Egalitarian in spirit, they focus on unmet needs and marginalized people, promising to transform what the state does not or cannot. Their promise lies less in what they *are* than what they are *not*: governmental.[12]

Some critics have complicated the failed state argument and situated it in the context of Western power, insisting that we cannot accurately speak about the failure of the African state without addressing the role played by the West. Ian Smillie, for example, emphasizes the colonial history that left

newly independent governments "ill-equipped both politically and economically" to support their populations.[13] Smillie also questions the timeline in
the failed-state narrative: "it is too facile to say that non-profit organizations
have sprung up because of state and market failure. The tens of thousands of
small community-based organizations that are often missed in the surveys of
Asia, Latin America and Africa were there long before the state and market
existed in forms that could succeed or fail."[14] Our view of nonstate actors
and interventions varies depending on where we look—at the global or the
local, starting with colonial history or with the postcolonial present. It is also
important not to paint African governments with too broad a brush, as if they
were a singular institution, destined for failure. Firoze Manji and Carl O'Coill
argue that, while Western neoliberal policies would eventually eviscerate the
African state, its early accomplishments should not be forgotten as they so often are in development discourse based on a "largely ideologically motivated
caricature of the state as being 'inefficient' and unable to deliver effective
services."[15] This argument provides a check on some of the neocolonial biases
that show up in critiques of the African state's "ignorance, corruption, and
lack of accountability."[16]

Despite scholars' interventions, NGOs' own discourse tends to avoid the
intricacies of historical and political contextualization. The third sector's identity lies in proclaimed ideological and institutional difference from the state.
This gives humanitarian organizations a sense of outsider status, "living in
a world of ethics, constantly battling the forces of evil and indifference."[17]
Humanitarianism, as articulated by the NGO community, has often set itself
outside of and above political interests, operating in the realm of virtue, driven
by "moral sentiments," which "link affects with values."[18] Underpinning this
approach is a set of core principles first articulated by the International Committee of the Red Cross and now widely accepted. As summarized by Michael
Barnett, these include "impartiality, for they must give aid based on need,
not on who is being helped or where they live; neutrality, for they must avoid
appearing to act in ways that favor one side or another; and independence,
for they must be unconnected to any party with a stake in the conflict. These
principles rendered humanitarians apolitical."[19] This orientation shapes humanitarianism as a project and a narrative form. Its action is driven by moral
principles that seem above reproach and applicable regardless of historical
and social contexts. Part of the reason the savior can swoop in is because he
is outside of and above politics; his universal ethics can override local sovereignty. However, as humanitarian workers well know, implementing moral
principles is far messier than any savior narrative suggests.

One common critique of NGOs points to their cooptation by donor states.

The relationship between humanitarianism and the state has, by many accounts, grown more complicated in the last few decades. Global powers, especially the United States, have taken up the discourse of humanitarianism, and NGOs have "found themselves being explicitly used by states as a tool for their political and strategic objectives."[20] According to Didier Fassin, "humanitarian reason" has become a language of state self-justification: "On both the national and the international levels, the vocabulary of suffering, compassion, assistance, and responsibility to protect forms part of our political life."[21] This vocabulary even lends itself to the contradictory notion of humanitarian war when violent intervention becomes a means of protection. On a more basic level, it is an issue of donor power with NGOs receiving funds from official sources such as USAID (United States Agency for International Development). When they become dependent on governmental funding, Cornelia Beyer explains, "NGOs can be understood as an extension of the state."[22] According to this line of critique, NGOs become pawns, reinforcing rather than undoing the global hierarchy that is their lifeblood. More radical critics like Issa Shivji argue that NGOs perpetuate the "saga of domination, exploitation and humiliation of the continent by European and American imperial powers."[23] No one has put this as vividly as Tejumola Olaniyan, who has described "the African radical image" of NGOs as "representatives of the hypocrisy of western liberalism whose proboscis would suck you dry and then rub some Vaseline into the wound so that you can be available for more sucking."[24] By this account, NGO power and imperial power go hand in hand.[25]

The power dynamics between NGOs and African states are also contentious.[26] In the emergency environment of war, militants can coopt aid in order to support their own aims and potentially prolong the conflict. In terms of development aid, African states have seen NGOs as both a resource and a threat. Ndegwa writes that "African governments have come to view NGOs as socioeconomic assets but also more warily as political challengers whose benevolence needs to be directed and coordinated in order not to undermine the state."[27] According to many critics, undermining the state is precisely their effect, aligning their work with the neoliberal aim to shrink the state in favor of the private sector. By providing public services such as education, healthcare, and water, they can be "used as an excuse and a scapegoat for the withdrawal of the state."[28] This suggests that NGOs weaken the state's responsibility and capacity to provide for its own citizens. For this reason, as Aziz Choudry and Dip Kapoor describe it, NGOs "act to absorb cuts in services" and function "as a safety valve or lid on more militant opposition against such politics."[29] The problem, then, is not that they are too political; it is instead that they depoliticize issues that demand political answers.[30] Their very identity as apolitical can thus impede long-term solutions.

This all raises questions of authority and accountability, leading scholars to ask, "Whose interests do these NGOs represent?"[31] The nonstate solution depends heavily on donors—both private and governmental—and thus directs NGO interests and accountability "upward" to those who control the finances rather than "downward" to the constituents who are supposed to benefit.[32] Dependence on donors means NGOs are "increasingly pulled further away from the poor groups that they claim to represent and in whose name many now raise huge funds."[33] This also involves overlooking the root causes of poverty and depoliticizing plans to address it. Calling development a "grand illusion," Lina Suleiman finds that "NGOs develop more according to external demands than in response to local public interests and discourse."[34] Their increasing professionalization and emphasis on technology and data also concentrate power within the imported "expert"; the fact that "knowledge is largely drawn from Western sources and assumptions" sends messages about "whose knowledge matters, where it comes from and who controls it."[35] Often, this limits NGOs' effectiveness because interventions are not necessarily those best suited to their locations or desired by people who live there.[36] The big question here is about the locus of authority and determination. Who owns the problem and who should have a say in how to solve it? Representing this strand of thought, Alex de Waal argues that "we should be careful not to reinforce the humanitarians' moral ownership of other people's suffering."[37] Solutions, he claims, must be political, and they "cannot come from anyone other than Africans themselves."[38] I lay out these debates as a prelude to show how Adichie and Ngũgĩ enter the conversation. African writers don't offer solutions and are often skeptical of solution claims regardless of the source. They do, however, envision forms of moral ownership that are locally based and politically engaged.

The Aesthetics and Politics of Emergency Aid

Many of the complex dynamics around NGOs became evident during the Biafran War (1967–70), which was a turning point for international humanitarianism. In his reflections on Biafra collected in *There Was a Country*, Chinua Achebe lays out a definition from the Failed States Index (now called the Fragile States Index) that he sees as "relevant to the Nigerian situation": "[A failed state] is one that is unable to perform its duties on several levels: when violence cascades into an all-out internal war, when standards of living massively deteriorate, when the infrastructure of ordinary life decays, and when the greed of rulers overwhelms their responsibilities to better their people and their surroundings."[39] All of these elements came into play amidst a devastating civil war:

The Nigeria-Biafra conflict created a humanitarian emergency of epic proportions. Millions of civilians—grandparents, mothers, fathers, children, and soldiers alike—flooded the main highway arteries between towns and villages, fleeing the chaos and conflict. They traveled by foot, by truck, by car, barefoot, with slippers, in wheelbarrows, many in worn out shoes. Some had walked so long their soles were blistered and bleeding. As hunger and thirst grew, so did despair, confusion, and desperation.[40]

This kind of image was essential to making Biafra a globally acknowledged moral emergency and a humanitarian tipping point. Though "for months the international community ignored Biafra in the same way it ignored other conflicts in the decolonizing world," images of Biafran desperation did break into global consciousness.[41] For aid organizations to mobilize resources, messaging is a primary concern, and the new ubiquity of television at the time of the war changed the game. Kevin O'Sullivan writes that "the relief effort thrust non-state actors to the forefront of public and official thinking about aid. Biafra was the first 'televised famine,' the first real test of the West's response to crisis in postcolonial Africa, and one of the largest disaster relief efforts of its kind in history."[42] During the Biafran war, what would become the quintessential humanitarian image—the starving African child—got its global start. In the new postcolonial context, the "white man's burden" had grown passé. The African was no longer uncivilized; the African was starving. Responses by NGOs "tended to reduce the complexity of the crisis to simple, easily consumable ideas. . . . The urgency of 'saving' replaced 'civilising' as the buzzword for Western intervention in the Third World."[43] As Mahmood Mamdani might put it, talk of Biafra "entered the arena of grand narratives."[44] In so doing, it "generated a sense of adventure" for Western humanitarians,[45] who took on a role not unlike that of missionaries addressed in earlier chapters and solidified the image of the starving African who could be saved by Western benevolence. Biafra is one of the pivotal places in humanitarian history for the way it centered NGOs on the world stage and for the profound challenges it posed for those organizations.[46]

This is the setting for Chimamanda Ngozi Adichie's *Half of a Yellow Sun*, yet here we see the humanitarian landscape without humanitarians. Through chapters that cycle among three focalizing characters—Olanna, an Igbo heiress turned academic; Richard, a white British writer; and Ugwu, a villager who moves to Nsukka to work as a houseboy—Adichie highlights the personal, quotidian experiences of the Biafra-Nigeria conflict. War is all encompassing, but it contains a multitude of experiences from which the novel selects a representative few. Richard fills the role of a white foreigner who witnesses war as an outsider; Olanna experiences war as a well-off Nigerian with connections and resources; Ugwu is poor and rural, a Nigerian of a background opposite to Olanna's. Also central are Olanna's twin sister, Kainene, who remains in the wealthy circles of her parents that Olanna rejects, and Olanna's "revolutionary lover" (in Kainene's words), Odenigbo, who teaches at the university in Nsukka. The novel traces their experiences leading up to and during the war and in its immediate aftermath. According to John Marx, "*Half of a Yellow Sun* presents life in the failed state as a grueling version of normal through recourse to description of what we once called 'private life.'"[47] It explores what it is like to live through humanitarian crisis on a day-to-day basis as both helper and helped.

Adichie embeds within the novel an abbreviated humanitarian narrative. Interspersed throughout the text, it appears in eight segments, each numbered and labeled "The Book: The World Was Silent When We Died." With two exceptions, these insertions follow Richard's chapters, and until the end of the novel we are led to think he is the writer. Adichie thus plays with a trenchant pattern of narrative expectations regarding who tells the humanitarian tale, only later revealing the writer to be Ugwu, whom we first come to know as Odenigbo's illiterate houseboy. The title alone, "The World Was Silent When We Died," makes a humanitarian plea. It demands a response to violence while also critiquing the international community's failure to respond. Marx situates it in a category he calls "failed-state fiction."[48] It is also failed-*nonstate* fiction. The title of the inserted book lays responsibility not at the feet of the Nigerian leadership but with the world at large. By calling the world to account, this book immediately joins a public debate over the international community's response. It also reflects critically on writing as a process. As Emmanuel Mzomera Ngwira points out, the inserted sections do not reproduce the text itself but instead highlight the task of the author in "selecting material and writing the book," putting the reader "'in' the writing process."[49] By placing a former servant from a rural village in this role, Adichie questions the power relations embedded in storytelling. Ngwira argues that this is Adichie's "attempt to rethink this 'epistemological power of the Western subject' over the African story."[50] The form—splicing an independent narrative into the main narrative of *Half of a Yellow Sun*—also draws explicit attention to the *act* of representing humanitarian crisis, an act in which Adichie herself is engaged. This reminds us that narration is never neutral but always involves a series of choices.

The title "The World Was Silent When We Died," which Richard selects before handing the project over to Ugwu, comes from a conversation with

Kainene's friend Colonel Madu, who seeks to recruit Richard to write in support of Biafra for the Propaganda Directorate, which would "send [his] pieces
to our public relations people overseas."[51] Richard initially hesitates because
Madu "would not have asked [him] if [he] were not white," but Madu is able
to persuade Richard of the plan's logic: "Of course I asked you because you are
white. They will take what you write more seriously because you are white"
(305). The generic "they" he uses here calls attention to the international
nonstate. A "public relations" campaign targets the public in general more
than governments. It is a project of image-making, of shaping a narrative,
and Madu suggests that the language of international community is more
persuasive from the pen of a European writer. He breaks it down for Richard:

> "Look, the truth is that this is not your war. This is not your cause.
> Your government will evacuate you in a minute if you ask them to. So
> it is not enough to carry limp branches and shout *power, power* to show
> that you support Biafra. If you really want to contribute, this is the way
> that you can. The world has to know the truth of what is happening,
> because they simply cannot remain silent while we die. They will
> believe a white man who lives in Biafra and who is not a professional
> journalist." (305)

This is the power of the white savior narrative; it legitimates some storytellers
and delegitimates others. Madu works within that system. For Richard, one
line will continue to echo: *"They simply cannot remain silent while we die rang
in his head"* (305). This captures much of the spirit of humanitarian storytelling: if you inform them, they will care. And the method of delivery matters to
make hearers into believers. Biafran military leaders were indeed aware of the
power of "international sympathy" and "the political credibility that accompanies aid."[52] Within the economy of global sentiment, Richard is useful. He
takes on the project and turns Madu's line into his book title but with added
disillusionment. He describes his planned book to Ugwu thus: It is about "the
war, and what happened before, and how much should not have happened.
It will be called 'The World Was Silent When We Died'" (396). The change
of tense and mood—from the hopeful, future-facing present tense ("They
cannot remain") to the resigned past tense ("The World Was")—turns the
story tragic. Ultimately, Richard decides, "The war isn't my story to tell, really"
(425). The plan for the book was his, but the process of writing it, documented
throughout the novel, is Ugwu's.

Ugwu opens on a tragic humanitarian image, which Olanna witnessed
and relayed to him, the kind commonly used to provoke sympathy and spur
action:

For the prologue, he recounts the story of the woman with the calabash. She sat on the floor of a train squashed between crying people,
shouting people, praying people. She was silent, caressing the covered
calabash on her lap in a gentle rhythm until they crossed the Niger,
and then she lifted the lid and asked Olanna and others close by to
look inside.

   Olanna tells him this story and he notes the details. She tells him
how the bloodstains on the woman's wrapper blended into the fabric
to form a rusty mauve. She describes the carved designs on the woman's calabash, slanting lines crisscrossing each other, and she describes
the child's head inside: scruffy plaits falling across the dark-brown
face, eyes completely white, eerily open, a mouth in a small surprised
O. (82)

This image could be considered gratuitous in its representation of victim-
hood. It is dramatic and highly aestheticized in the geometric imagery of the
calabash's design, in the O-shaped mouth, and in the blending colors of blood
and fabric. This is a story of suffering told beautifully, creating a mix akin to
what Karen Halttunen calls the "pornography of pain," a concept that draws
attention to the roles of the observer and the observed.[53] Similarly, Barnett
critiques the humanitarian "politics of pity" as a problem of authoritative perspective: "Those that presume the authority to represent the suffering of others
frequently (mis)appropriate the pain in ways that celebrate the deliverer and
limit the capacity of the victims to express in their own words their suffering
and sorrow."[54] On the surface, the image of the mother with the calabash fits
neatly into the humanitarian portfolio, but the perspectives within the story
suggest otherwise. The mother invites others to look; as a witness, Olanna testifies to that pain; Ugwu passes on the women's message. This representation
doesn't celebrate the deliverer of aid or lock the victims in silent suffering. It
does, nevertheless, demand to be seen.

   This depiction of suffering stands in contrast with what Mamdani calls the
"assault of images without context" — the kind of humanitarian representation
in which "there is no discussion of history or politics: no context, no analysis
of causes."[55] Such images stand alone, severed from their political surroundings, even "driv[ing] a wedge between your political and moral senses, to
numb the former and appeal to the latter."[56] Harnessing that moral appeal,
Biafra was an origin moment for what would become a photographic habit.
As O'Sullivan explains, "The crisis in Biafra offered many individuals their
first glimpse of postcolonial Africa, and the image it created—of suffering,
devastation and the need for immediate relief—eclipsed the debate about

justice or the politics of need."[57] NGOs, celebrated for and identified by their *non*governmentality, rally around a discourse that separates moral impulse from political analysis.

But Ugwu's story does not make this illusory separation. Instead, he suggests that to adequately care about that desperate mother, we must understand the larger story — both the political narrative and the human story of life that is more than war. This book within a book inserts humanitarian crisis into a new frame. Ugwu takes the individualized image of war in the form of that mother and places her on a sociopolitical map: "For the book cover, though, he draws a map of Nigeria and traces in the Y shape of the rivers Niger and Benue in bright red. He uses the same shade of red to circle the boundaries of where, in the Southeast, Biafra existed for three years" (82). This is the story of a country, a political formation.[58] It represents a politics with a past. The second section of The Book shifts back in time from the image of postcolonial crisis to the history of British colonization, arguing that the fault lines of the civil war were drawn by the British who "preferred the North" where "the Hausa-Fulani were narrow-featured and therefore superior to the negroid Southerners" (115). In the South, "missionaries were allowed in to tame the pagans," while the North remained Muslim, "as civilized as one could get for natives" (115). "Nigeria was born" by fusing North and South after contentiously dividing them; when Nigeria gains independence, as described in part 3 of The Book, it happens on shaky ground like "a collection of fragments held in a fragile clasp" (155). Ugwu situates the humanitarian crisis of the late twentieth century in the historical context of colonial violence, implying that we can't understand Biafra without including that backstory. Critics of humanitarian discourse often point to its dehistoricization and depoliticization, its failure to take context into account. The problem demands going beyond what Kwame Anthony Appiah calls "explosions of feeling,"[59] and developing what Teju Cole describes as "constellational thinking" that can "connect the dots [and] see the patterns of power behind the isolated 'disasters.'"[60] Ugwu's book offers that kind of thinking, a political story in which there is no "pure" humanitarian space. It connects the dots between the grief-stricken mother and the global powers that create the conditions for violence, starvation, and psychological trauma.

For the epilogue, Ugwu writes a poem that, delivered in second person, directly implicates the reader, beginning from its title, "Were You Silent When We Died?" The first stanza asks:

Did you see photos in sixty-eight
Of children with their hair becoming rust:

Sickly patches nestled on those small heads,
Then falling off, like rotten leaves on dust? (375)

These were the images that many hoped the world wouldn't tolerate. The poem speaks on one level to people who did see the "photos in sixty-eight" and on another level to the younger generations who don't need to have seen those particular photos to recognize the genre they inaugurated. It aims at Americans in particular with its reference to the "gloss-filled pages of your *Life* [*Magazine*]" (375). In articulating the language of humanitarian concern, the insider voice has displaced the outsider. Ugwu's poem changes the terms of the humanitarian plea from "we must help them" to "you must help us" or, more accurately, "you should have helped us." As Ngwira describes it, "the reader's 'fly-on-the-wall' position is significantly destabilized by a direct mode of address which draws the reader from the position of an observer to that of an addressee."[61] The moral tenor also shifts from a triumphant spirit of doing right to a tragic spirit of having done terrible wrong. The poem ends on the image of "Naked children laughing, as if the man / Would not take photos and then leave, alone" (375). This implies that nonaction was built into the relationship all along. The photographer was not going to make a meaningful difference. The same goes for those American readers of *Life*: "starvation brought Africa into Nixon's American campaign and made parents all over the world tell their children to eat up" (237). The language of humanitarian concern entered the U.S. household, but it didn't change the plight of the starving African who has served as an object lesson for well-fed American kids. The visual rhetoric of humanitarianism made the world see but not act, signaling its inefficacy. The question the poem asks — "Were you silent?" — has already been answered, but posing it as a question makes it a plea to readers to do better. Even if the image fails, we must still confront its reality.

Agents of the Third Sector

Ugwu's book occupies a small space within a lengthy novel, which represents humanitarian crisis more expansively. Local characters are engaged in both third sector volunteerism and public sector politics. Foreign humanitarians and their campaigns, however, occupy only the very edges of *Half of a Yellow Sun*. For example, the notorious Count Von Rosen — the "Swedish aristocrat" who flew aid and "bombed Nigerian targets" (310, 311) and is often referenced in humanitarian histories — receives one page of text describing a chance meeting with Richard. When Richard drops off two American journalists at the airport (where relief planes are only occasionally able to land), three planes arrive and their supplies are quickly transported to lorries: "Pilots were screaming. 'Hurry up, you lazy boys! Get them off! We're not going to be bombed here!' . . . There was an American accent, an Afrikaans accent, an Irish accent" (373). These men are not seen but merely heard. This lies in contrast to the globally circulating narratives of humanitarian relief, which feature brave souls such as O'Sullivan describes: "How better to portray the selfless heroism of NGOs than through the dangerous—and sometimes deadly—act of landing at Uli airstrip in darkness and under the attentions of Federal fighter planes?"[62] Surely their adventures could merit an enticing plotline, but in this novel, they are forgettable, a blip on the narrative radar.

Similarly, leading aid organizations, the Red Cross and Caritas, are referenced a number of times but not actively characterized. Like the "NGO people" in We Need New Names, they are referred to offhandedly as "the Red Cross people" or "the Caritas people" (Adichie, 281, 283). Their services are far from heroic.

> The Red Cross irritated Ugwu; the least they could do was ask Biafrans their preferred foods rather than sending so much bland flour. When the new relief centre opened, the one Olanna went to wearing a rosary because Mrs. Muokelu said the Caritas people were more generous to Catholics, Ugwu hoped the food would be better. But what she brought back was familiar, the dried fish even saltier, and she sang, with an amused expression, the song the women sang at the centre.
> *Caritas, thank you,*
> *Caritas si anyi taba okporoko* [Caritas says we should eat stockfish]
> *na kwashiorkor ga-ana.* [and kwashiorkor will go away.]
> She did not sing on the days she came back with nothing. (283)[63]

Far from the "vulnerable but always grateful pauper,"[64] Ugwu is irritated by NGOs' failure to ask for Biafran input or to think much about the quality of the food they provide. There is an interesting aloofness in the song women sing, recounting the instructions from Caritas, which promise to solve the problem. These instructions outline a simple solution that in reality is far from simple. In fact, references in Half of a Yellow Sun are often about NGOs' inability to provide: on the ground, the Red Cross is blocked by the military and is forced to "suspend relief flights" (279, 347). Often, the relief center isn't even functioning: Olanna goes there one day only to find that "the gate was locked, the compound empty, and she waited around for an hour until the crowd began to disperse. On Tuesday, the gate was locked. On Wednesday, there was a new padlock on the gate" (271). This center of humanitarian care is vacant and austere. Aid organizations in the novel are an inconsistent source of (at best) insufficient supplies, and they constitute a nearly faceless entity. The peripheral role of humanitarian characters in *Half of a Yellow Sun* demonstrates how narrative technique directs readers toward what is most worthy of attention. Alex Woloch describes novels' "distribution of attention" among minor characters and protagonists: "Each moment," he writes, "magnifies some characters while turning away from others."[65] There is a sense of tension here among "different characters who jostle for limited space within the same fictive universe."[66] The white savior narrative poses a "distribution" problem in its fascination with the foreign humanitarian. As a corrective, novels like *Half of a Yellow Sun* redistribute attention by repositioning the NGO and its representatives. This happens not only by making them minor characters but by making them vague characters who lack both narrative space and descriptive specificity. Within this "economy of characterization,"[67] it doesn't much matter who the NGO is. What matters is how they function in the lives of the protagonists in whom readers are invested. When a white savior or foreign aid worker is the protagonist, interest funnels toward his or her experience rather than the outcome of the humanitarian intervention. But here, no matter how valiant an intervention may be, it only takes on significance in relation to the recipients.

The decentering and demotion of the foreign nonstate actor (at the level of the individual humanitarian and the NGO) suggests a mismatch between the story abroad and the reality on the ground; this is also evident in the representation of people who need humanitarian assistance. The victims of war and recipients of aid in *Half of a Yellow Sun* are not only people in poverty who would already have been considered candidates for aid. They are also people of privilege. Before the war, Olanna is a participant in the culture of charity. She volunteers regularly with the St. Vincent de Paul Society and serves as the organizational secretary (229). Her volunteerism resembles a religious rite. Odenigbo "liked to tease her about religion's not being a social service, because she went to church only for St Vincent de Paul meetings, when she took Ugwu with her for the drive through dirt paths in nearby villages to give away yams and rice and old clothes" (107). Donating food and used clothing to rural Africa is typically associated with the Global North as if aid were something foreign, but here the practice of charity is locally rooted and locally directed. Olanna is part of the transnational culture of assistance, linked through a faith-based organization even though she doesn't subscribe closely to the faith itself. There is nothing grand or adventurous about this practice, no rhetoric of salvation. It is simply part of quotidian life, sandwiched in a list of other activities: "she added new material to her lectures, cooked long meals, read new books, bought new records. She became secretary of the St Vincent de Paul Society, and after they donated food to the villages she wrote the minutes of their meetings in a notebook. She cultivated zinnias in her front yard and, finally, she cultivated a friendship with her black American neighbor" (229). "Charity trips" do not receive a place of pride in her narrative (229).

Once the war begins and as it escalates, we witness the process of the donor being reduced to a recipient. Relative wealth insulates characters to an extent, but it does not save them. Olanna and Odenigbo end up living in a single room without electricity or running water, where they struggle to protect their daughter (born to Odenigbo and another woman, then adopted by Olanna), who shows increasing signs of malnutrition. For Olanna, dependence on aid comes as a shock: "Olanna stood awkwardly among the men and women and children, who all seemed used to standing and waiting for a rusted iron gate to be opened so they could go in and be given food donated by strangers. She felt discomfited. She felt as if she were doing something improper, unethical: expecting to get food in exchange for nothing" (267–68). As a woman of the privileged class, who subscribes to an ethic of individualist self-sufficiency, she feels miscast in the role of humanitarian subject. This denaturalizes the image of the aid recipient and leads an educated global readership to identify with the protagonist not as an object of pity but as a peer. Even the kind of woman who collects clothing and food to donate to impoverished villagers can get "used to" waiting to receive such donations herself: "It was not until Saturday that the gate [of the relief center] swung open and Olanna surprised herself by how easily she joined in the inward rush of the crowd, how she moved nimbly from queue to queue, dodged the swinging canes of the militia, pushed back when somebody pushed her" (271–72). The Olanna who can shove her way through a crowded relief center is a far cry from the Olanna we first meet. Her world devolves from one of comfort and plenty to one of deprivation and desperation. *Half of a Yellow Sun* reminds us that these are circumstantial positions, not natural, permanent, or inevitable. In contrast to the humanitarian subject defined by her otherness, Olanna works as a bridge character, linking the Biafran story to a privileged Western readership. Generally, a white savior type fills this role based on the assumption that "a foreign protagonist, some American who [American readers] can identify with as a bridge character . . . can get people to care about foreign countries, to read about them, ideally, to get a little bit more involved."[68] Olanna is neither white nor American, but as a member of the global donor class, she is especially relatable to that class. Through Olanna, Adichie breaks down the division of donor and recipient, showing both to exist within the same person.

The novel similarly complicates the representation of the ultimate humanitarian subject—the starving African child. When war sets in, kwashiorkor
becomes a common point of reference and concern for the characters. Familiar not only to victims but to observers, images of child starvation became a
form of leverage during the Biafran war, pushing donors to give and NGOs
to act.[69] An Oxfam trustee has explained the strategy behind this method of
appeal: "many donors join us because of an emotional response to poverty—to
the sight of a pitiful baby dying—and not because they know anything about
land reform or the politics of aid."[70] *Half of a Yellow Sun* engages readers'
sympathy through similar images, including that of Olanna and Odenigbo's
daughter who becomes ill from malnourishment: "Her face had lost its fat and
was eerily adult, sunken and thin skinned" (266). As her daughter loses weight
and chunks of hair, Olanna worries desperately that she will die. Characters'
use of the generic name Baby deindividualizes this child and reinforces her
tie to the image of the suffering African infant. (Only Kainene calls her by her
given name, Chiamaka.) This Biafran Baby can stand in for the Biafran baby
more generally. Liisa H. Malkki clarifies that the appeal of the generic child as
humanitarian subject lies partly in the embodiment of neutrality: "The child
is often made to appear as the exemplary human, and as politically harmless
and neutral."[71] Children take on unique persuasive power "in contemporary
discourses of humanitarianism and liberal internationalism where childlike
innocence is a way of making recipients of humanitarian assistance a tabula
rasa, innocent of politics and history, innocent, in a way, about causes of war
and enmity. This is the need for help neutralized. Pure need."[72] The child is
thus neatly aligned with the discourse and values of the NGO.

But, as critics including Malkki note, depoliticization has consequences;
the nongovernmental organization can do damage by extracting government
from its message when, in reality, the political and the ethical are mutually
constitutive. To suggest otherwise is to wrench the meaning of the starving
child not only from her political context but from the personal context of family, culture, and history. The power of the baby, in particular, Fassin asserts,
lies in "the moral quality of innocence and the social quality of vulnerability":
"Who could oppose the principle of saving the lives of newborns?"[73] The
problem lies partly in the affective response that this generates: "this emotional mobilization," Fassin writes, "is fragile and ambiguous. . . . Above all,
the affective emphasis reifies children as victims in a way that removes them
far from the social reality in which they live."[74] In the white savior narrative,
the baby is a stock character who serves a narrative purpose, telling the audience how to feel and providing moral clarity. The blankness of the baby helps
justify the motivations and endorse the actions of the white savior because

the innocence of the recipient lends innocence to the giver. By placing a malnourished Biafran baby at the center of her novel, Adichie indexes the humanitarian message and repackages it. Aside from the name, this Baby is not generic. Instead, the suffering child is situated in a rich context; she has a history, a family, a distinctive personality.

The complexity of the positions within the humanitarian relationship is also revealed through Olanna's twin sister, Kainene. In contrast to Olanna, Kainene never separated herself from her father's world of wealth and political influence. Early on in the war, insulated by her wealth and connections, Kainene leverages the crisis for her own good. The war opens opportunities for her business, which in turn opens conflict with Olanna. Before Port Harcourt's fall, Kainene explains to Olanna, "I was an army contractor, and I had a license to import stockfish. I'm in Orlu now. I'm in charge of a refugee camp there. . . . Are you silently condemning me for profiteering from the war? Somebody has to import the stockfish, you know" (343). This is one of the primary foods distributed at relief centers, and Kainene has indeed benefited from the needs of others. Tying this back to Olanna's experience at the relief center and the women's song about stockfish allows us to see aid in a more constellational perspective. It reveals the politically contingent, morally compromised network through which life-sustaining aid is delivered and shows the blurred line between providing and profiteering.

As the war hits closer to home, however, Kainene's stance evolves, and ultimately, she spends her days working in the refugee camp rather than overseeing its administration from a distance. When suppliers are blocked from delivering to the refugee camp, "Kainene launche[s] a Plant Our Own Food movement, and when she join[s] the men and women and children in making ridges, Olanna wonder[s] where she had learned to hold a hoe" (389). Manual labor is a new world for Kainene. Part of this conversion is about self-protection. She throws herself into the work after witnessing one of servants decapitated by shrapnel. Here, altruism is partly but not entirely self-serving, and she fully commits to the work of supporting refugees:

> "There's a man from Enugu who has a fantastic talent for making
> baskets and lamps. I'll have him teach others. We can create income
> here. We can *make a difference!* And I'll ask the Red Cross to send us a
> doctor every week."
>   There was a manic vibrancy about her, about the way she left for
> the refugee camp each day, about the exhaustion that shadowed her
> eyes when she returned in the evenings. She no longer spoke of Ikejide
> [who was killed]. Instead, she spoke about twenty people living in a

space meant for one and about the little boys who played war and the women who nursed babies and the selfless Holy Ghost priests. (319)

Kainene, who once so comfortably inhabited the discourse of business and profit, now takes up the humanitarian discourse of "making a difference." It seems that her transformation is genuine even if it is not disinterested. Absorbing herself in humanitarian work keeps her own losses from overwhelming her; it is a way of coping with her own hurts, as humanitarian action perhaps always is in some sense. In Barnett's words, "Humanitarianism is about meeting the needs of others and meeting our own needs. . . . Some are motivated by a feeling of power and superiority, some by guilt, some by the possibility of religious redemption and salvation, some by a desire to demonstrate goodness to themselves and to others."[75] This applies not only to the foreign humanitarian but also to the local; all are reckoning with the conflicting motivations at stake in "making a difference." Self-interest may be inevitable, but not all self-interest is the same. In this case, healing the self through care for others is a way of mitigating harm on both sides of the giving relationship.

Ultimately, readers of *Half of a Yellow Sun* are left with the impression that while men are the dominant players in war, women lead in relief efforts. Near the end of the war, before Kainene disappears when seeking food, she and Olanna spend their days at the refugee camp, where conditions grow increasingly dire. Olanna gathers children under trees and teaches daily lessons: "they were Biafra's future, after all" (389).[76] Olanna, too, is among the desperate: "She worried about . . . how her periods were sparse and no longer red but a muddy-brown, how Baby's hair was falling out, how hunger was stealing the memories of the children" (389). She simultaneously shares the refugees' suffering and seeks to alleviate it through teaching. Kainene wrangles the Red Cross into providing for the refugee camp: "I finally got the Red Cross to give me some [protein tablets] last week. We don't have enough, of course, so I save them for the children" (348). This picture of day-to-day care is far less heroic than the salvation narrative of foreign intervention would have it. But it captures a more realistic picture of the kind of care people encounter in the face of humanitarian crisis. It also reveals the gender dynamics at stake. Men and women do not experience need equally: "Women are largely responsible for household water, sanitation and hygiene management; they bear a disproportionate burden when these basic services are lacking, and face health, security and psychological vulnerabilities due to inadequate access and decision-making control."[77] Women also tend to play a larger role in coping with and supporting others through crisis. The desperate mother with her daughter's head in a calabash is emblematic of one dimension of this story—women's suffering—as is the secondhand trauma Olanna experiences as a witness. But the strength and centrality of women as mothers, leaders, and organizers is fundamental to this story as well. An examination of local rather than international practices of humanitarian care places women at the center of the narrative. This is also evident in *Wizard of the Crow*, where women, though often overlooked and unheard by men, are the heartbeat of community care and political resistance in a context where the formal humanitarian sector is even more distant.

NGO Consciousness and the Humanitarian Script

Whereas *Half of a Yellow Sun* shows the emergence and expansion of secular NGO discourse around the Biafran War, Ngũgĩ wa Thiong'o's *Wizard of the Crow* marks the NGO framework's expansion beyond any particular time, place, or event. This novel depicts a world infused with the language of the NGO apart from the organizations themselves. The NGO has escaped contextual boundaries. This is reflected partly through the generality of the setting. *Wizard of the Crow* takes place in the fictional African country of Aburĩria, with most of the action unfolding in its capital, Eldares. As Simon Gikandi has shown, this fictionalized nation correlates in many ways with Kenya, satirizing "the nasty politics of [the Moi] period" and more specifically the 1980s.[78] But through the abstraction of an invented name and its mythic mode of storytelling (rooted in Gikuyu folklore), Aburĩria also functions as a composite representative of the African nation, an examination of neocolonial meddling, government corruption, capitalistic greed, and rampant inequality that are recognizable beyond the author's own country. The timeline is similarly vague and thus flexible.[79] For example, while there are direct parallels to the structural adjustment era of the 1980s and '90s, the representation of dictatorship gives the novel a kind of timelessness; the Ruler, the second of independent Aburĩria, has been "on the throne so long that even he [can]not remember when his reign began."[80] Elsewhere, a character positions the setting more precisely at "the beginning of a new millennium, the third millennium since Christ was born" (59). This endows the contemporary with epic grandeur. Ian MacDonald situates the story in "the near future," in a period of "technological estrangement" in which genetic engineering and "technobiological bodies" have transformed human capabilities.[81] In sum, *Wizard of the Crow* speaks to a range of times and places. It also explores different positions within the Aburĩrian hierarchy. The narrative follows a split but intersecting trajectory: first, the machinations of the Ruler, along with his ministers; and second, the developing friendship of two commoners, Kamĩtĩ and Nyawĩra, who take on the mantle of the Wizard of the Crow. By combining these two narrative tracks, Ngũgĩ indicts Aburĩrian elites—as well as the Europeans and Americans who support them—for producing the suffering he shows among common people. He invites us to interrogate the relationships between poverty and power and between the third sector and the state.

While it lacks the historical specificity of *Half of a Yellow Sun*, this novel, too, maps a humanitarian landscape with few humanitarians—in this case, the site of development rather than emergency aid. The problem is not war or catastrophe but the perpetual day-to-day travails of poverty, unemployment, hunger, and lack of sanitation services. As the nation's political leaders gallivant around the globe for designer shopping, plastic surgery, and high-profile meetings, the majority of citizens struggle. Although Aburĩria is generalized through an invented name and a nameless dictator known simply as "the Ruler," it is not one-dimensional. Kamĩtĩ provides an overview in a surreal scene in which he breaks "free of the body" and flies over the country as a bird:

> From his vantage point, he had a bird's-eye view of the northern, southern, eastern, western, and central regions of Aburĩria. The landscape ranged from the coastal plains to the region of the great lakes, to the arid bushlands in the east; to the central highlands and northern mountains. People differed as much in the languages they spoke as in the clothes they wore and how they eked out a living. (*Wizard*, 38–39)

Kamĩtĩ sees that it is a land of many differences. It is also a land united by struggle, which he frames as a nearly universal experience: "Some fished, others herded cattle and goats, and others worked on the land, but everywhere, particularly in towns, the contours of life were the same as those in Eldares. Everywhere people were hungry, thirsty, and in rags. In most towns, shelters made out of cardboard, scrap metal, old tires, and plastic were home to hundreds of children and adults" (39). This is the humanitarian problem space in its quotidian form. With wealth for the few and poverty for the many, Aburĩria is a place of brazen inequality, as Kamĩtĩ observes: "He found it ironic that, as in Eldares, these shacks stood side by side with mansions of tile, stone, glass, and concrete" (39). Citizens are keenly aware of this discrepancy and wonder how bad things can get: "can conditions become worse that this?" "The streets they passed told the same old story. The potholes had multiplied; there was garbage everywhere for want of collection" (76). These are signs that state infrastructure is failing. Basic services are unattended to, and the multiplication of trash has additional consequences for sanitation and health.

So, when the state fails to provide, what do people do about it? What are the alternatives? The private sector is a dead end. Kamĩtĩ struggles desperately to provide for himself and find a job, but—even with his impressive education, including a BA in economics and an MBA—it is next to impossible without elite connections. His experience is shared by the masses. Near the end of the novel, a large group of "the dispossessed" stages a march demanding "a clean atmosphere so that people can have clean air to breathe, clean water to drink, and clean spaces to live and enjoy. They reject the rule of the viper and the ogre. Their songs end up in chorus with the other parts of the globe: Don't let them kill our future" (748). This is a critique of their political leaders—"the viper and the ogre"—as well as a call to the world at large to help them on the path to a better future. With this novel, MacDonald argues, Ngũgĩ's "populism has moved from the nationalist to the global scale, broadening his earlier, more provincial, representations of resistance."[82] The struggle of local characters in *Wizard of the Crow* is linked "with the other parts of the globe" (748), and in calling out to the world to listen, characters are making a humanitarian plea. It isn't apolitical, and they are also calling their government to account, but their outlook for state revolution or reform isn't exactly optimistic. Both the private and the public sectors are corrupt, and characters find that those channels do not solve or suffice. This is the kind of scenario that drives people to seek a third path. By representing this scenario, Ngũgĩ creates a different narrative around the third sector, focused on how people attempt to meet their own needs; this is a third sector driven by struggle rather than benevolence.

That is not to say Western benevolence has fallen out of the conversation. As was the case in *Half of a Yellow Sun*, aid is very much part of the public discourse, including frequent references to NGOs and appeals to "the world" for help. Upon the rumored arrival of international funding to Aburĩria, numerous "NGOs sprang up" to claim "a share" (245). The logic of international nongovernmental aid has entered common consciousness, but in actuality, such aid is largely absent. What aid does exist is coopted by government and operates as a façade. The aid relationship links the international community not to the general populace but to the leaders of government and business— heads of the public and private sectors.

The state leaders' narrative is all about securing international funds for ridiculous projects while simultaneously working to suppress the voices of the people. Global aid here operates through state transactions rather than nonstate forms of assistance. Many Aburĩrians hope that the delegation from the Global Bank (essentially a stand-in for the World Bank) will assist the poor, but these "missionaries," as they are often called (135, 159, 160), are dedicated not to humanity but to "money and market" (681). The project the government ministers propose is called "Heavenscrape or simply Marching to Heaven" (16). This satirizes President Daniel arap Moi's attempt to construct

Africa's tallest building in 1989 in Nairobi's Uhuru Park with the backing of the World Bank, a project Wangari Maathai and the Green Belt Movement resisted.[83] In Ngũgĩ's hands, the narcissistic project is taken to celestial extremes as leaders plan to "raise a building to the very gate of Heaven so that the Ruler could call on God daily to say good morning or good evening or simply how was your day today, God? The Ruler would be the daily recipient of God's advice, resulting in a rapid growth of Aburĩria to heights never before dreamt by humans" (16). In other novels, we have seen the danger associated with men who are the supposed "recipient[s] of God's advice," working, so they say, on behalf of the people at large. This is a theme of humanitarian fictions. In this iteration, Ngũgĩ draws a resemblance between white saviors and African dictators. Sounding a more business-minded note, one of the Ruler's top advisors is "waxing ecstatic about how the benefits of the project could trickle down to all citizens" (17). Marching to Heaven mixes and mocks the humanitarian language of transcendence and the neoliberal discourse of trickle-down economics. Contrary to the promises of humanitarian assistance, Nyawĩra predicts that aid for this project would produce a crisis and describes it in humanitarian terms: "Marching to Heaven will swallow our land. Where shall we take shelter from the sun and rain? It will snatch water from the mouth of the thirsty and food from the mouth of the hungry. Skeletons will people our country. How shall we get back to the body, the mind, and the soul of the nation?" (208). This connects humanitarian need to state greed, and international aid is implicated in a global system of consumption. As Joseph McLaren argues, Ngũgĩ pushes "critics of the so-called 'failed African states'" to reckon with the ways in which "the West and global capital are implicated."[84]

The problem is not limited to intergovernmental lending organizations like the Global Bank; it also goes for the international third sector. Rather than operating independently, NGOs in the novel melt into a larger aid industry driven by state and corporate interests. This complicates the assumptions about NGOs' function that often underlie critiques of African state failure. In shortsighted attempts to ameliorate conditions, NGOs open up space for governmental abuse and for the rise of a corporate world order. Tajirika, a vicious businessman and corrupt political climber, implores the Ruler to play it strategically: "Corporate capital was aided by missionary societies," and "NGOs will do what missionary charities did in the past. . . . With the privatization of Aburĩria, and with the NGOs *relieving us* of our social services, the country becomes your real estate" (746, emphasis added). In this ironic inversion of relief work, *Wizard of the Crow* aligns with many critiques of NGOs (and their missionary forerunners) for their complicity with both capitalist industry and governmental power. According to this argument, after the Cold War,

NGOs gave states the option of "shedding their welfare 'burden.' The state now claimed that basic protections and services were properly in the purview of, and more efficiently delivered by, NGOs, faith-based agencies, and even the private sector."[85] Issa Shivji describes this as a "reproduction of the colonial mode," suggesting the very premise of the third sector is a myth: "NGOs are neither a third sector, nor independent of the state. Rather they are inextricably imbricated in the neoliberal offensive, which follows on the heels of the crisis of the national project."[86] In *Wizard of the Crow*, this is, indeed, the case. The international third sector—purportedly nongovernmental and nonprofit—has been coopted by the intersecting interests of government and profit. As the unwitting allies of public corruption and private greed, global NGOs have no meaningful presence in the lives of the people. This suggests that critiques of the postcolonial African state must look not only to the state itself but to the international network that underwrites it, linking powerful people in the most powerful places to the most powerful people in the least powerful places.

Aburīrian elites use both actual suffering and images of suffering to their own advantage. The Ruler and his henchmen fatten themselves off the public's poverty. The rounded belly serves as an equivocal sign of overconsumption, on the one hand, and of kwashiorkor, on the other. Under "corporonialism," the hunger of the Aburīrian people becomes a tool through which the government solicits international interest and the financial influx that can come with it.[87] The strategic use of suffering and sympathy for political gain that was an issue in Biafra (exemplified by Colonel Madu in *Half of a Yellow Sun*) is here taken to its logical extreme. Government leaders not only exploit the people's suffering but preserve it as a kind of currency. Managing the poor is not about public services but about optics:

> The government also had to be mindful not to upset tourism by
> sweeping too many beggars off the streets. Pictures of beggars or wild
> animals were what many tourists sent back home as proof of having
> been in Africa. In Aburīria, wild animals were becoming rare because
> of dwindling forests and poaching, and tourist pictures of beggars or
> children with kwashiorkor and flies massing around their runny noses
> and sore eyes were prized for their authenticity. If there were no beg-
> gars in the streets, tourists might start doubting whether Aburīria was
> an authentic African country. (*Wizard*, 35)

Tourism in Africa is tied to the visual rhetoric of white saviorism. For Western visitors educated in NGO fundraising appeals, Africanness is equated with poverty and malnutrition. Westerners appear more interested in looking than in helping, and Aburīrian officials are eager to satisfy their voyeuristic desires. The government has learned to speak the NGO lingo, crafting a "humanitarian" scene of poverty and malnourishment as a global public attraction. This reveals the troubling economics of the humanitarian Atlantic. There is a sense that various actors—news outlets, tourists, NGOs, governments—are colluding to articulate and reinforce a discourse that equates Africanness with wretchedness. According to that equation, help must come from the outside, and by keeping "beggars in the streets," the government in the novel courts that help. In this way, the commodified image of African suffering takes on a life of its own beyond the grasp of its original disseminators. This point applies not only to the Aburīrian government but to common people in need of assistance.

In *Wizard of the Crow*, humanitarianism is a lens through which foreigners look and locals perform. Sharply attuned to the rhetoric of relief, the citizens of Aburīria enter into a humanitarian transaction in which they act out the role of beggars as a way of engaging Western sympathies. This mode of engagement is a staple of daily life around the hotels of wealthy tourists, and it comes to a pinnacle with the arrival of the Global Bank "missionaries":

> The rumor circulating in the country was that the delegates might actually be bringing a lot of cash to give to the poor; after all, it was not called the Global Bank for nothing. So in addition to invited guests who arrived in chauffeur-driven Mercedes-Benzes and others answering the call of duty, scores of others, barefooted but armed with expectations, waited outside the gates of Paradise [the hotel where the mission is convening] for a share of largesse. (73)

The contrast between the barefooted and the Benz-ed illustrates the stark inequality in the global order, but as people wait for foreign "largesse," they maintain a degree of difference from the picture of the "authentic African country" sought by tourists (35). They are stronger—"*armed* with expectations"—and more savvy. The point that the visitors "might actually" help signals that the poor are hopeful but also wary. Their sophistication becomes more evident as the scene continues: "There were always beggars loitering around those kinds of hotels at all hours of day and night. But that night they were there in unusually large numbers, looking for all the world to see like wretchedness itself. The blind seemed blinder than usual, the hunchbacked hunched lower, and those missing legs or hands acted as if deprived of other limbs" (73). Aid is theater, and the givers are not alone on the stage. The language in this passage consistently points to a gap between appearance and reality, between spectacle and substance, between hope and experience: beggars are "*looking* for all the world to see *like* wretchedness itself." And their infirmities become exaggerated, the blind blinder, the weak weaker. Outside onlookers can't tell the difference. For them, this charade *is* African authenticity.

This invites a reexamination of familiar images and narratives produced by NGOs, hinting at the covert meanings that may underlie the overt marketing messages—meanings over which the suffering subjects may have more control than onlookers (including critics) assume. Such a reexamination puts a twist on Homi Bhabha's notion of colonial mimicry according to which the colonizer seeks "a reformed, recognizable Other, *as a subject of difference that is almost the same, but not quite*."[88] In Bhabha's description, the colonized subject approximates the image of the colonizer, becoming "*almost the same, but not white*."[89] In the case of *Wizard of the Crow*, African people are not mimicking the image of the Westerner but the image of African difference. They are almost the same as the humanitarian image of the African as the West's radical Other, but *not quite*. In that gap and in their critical consciousness lies a subtle threat. To apply Bhabha's words, this scene plays with the "area between mimicry and mockery" which reveals that "mimicry is at once resemblance and menace."[90] By acting out their given roles, the people of Aburīria become recognizable to a global humanitarian gaze while also tricking the eye.

Wizard of the Crow represents sophisticated ways that people exert their own agency within humanitarianism's ideological and narratological framework. The poor work within the system by speaking the language of popular humanitarian concern, both visually and verbally: "The way they carried themselves was as if they thought the Global Bank had come to appreciate and even honor their plight. So they sang, *You are the way; we are the world! Help the poor! Help the poor!* in different languages because the delegates were assumed to have come from all corners of the globe" (73–74). In singing the title line of the song "We Are the World," they capture the trademark sentiment of the famed 1985 famine relief fundraiser, Live Aid.[91] Lilie Chouliaraki calls this global humanitarian rock concert and its 2005 reprisal "crucial performances of the humanitarian imaginary, insofar as they use the global appeal of rock to disseminate and legitimize the moral imperative of solidarity."[92] Aid has a distinct tune and lyrics, which form a shared vocabulary between the African poor and the Western rich. Like English, this is a colonial language, emanating from the Western powers but escaping their control. It is also a theatrical language, performed by the Aburīrian poor who know not to ask in their own words but in the script provided for them by the white savior narrative. They know their Western audience, and they make the street their stage. For readers, this global theater of aid breaks the fourth wall. As players pick up their masks, they both dramatize and denaturalize the narrative of humanitarian salvation.

Even though the beggars in the scene are producing a spectacle, the need they perform is both real and urgent. The beggars might play up their ailments to fit the humanitarian picture of the suffering African, but this is a way of representing real problems, not inventing them. The performance of disability, for example, extends existing disabilities rather than making them up: "those missing legs or hands acted as if deprived of other limbs" (*Wizard*, 73). This isn't fraud but embellishment, although the extent of that embellishment becomes more ambiguous as the scene goes on. These "actors" seem to know that without the performance, assistance is even less likely. This is a matter of audience. The continent is globally legible through the rhetoric of the NGO. What would "Africa" be without the spectacle of poverty? In the eyes of "the world," the poor of Africa are an object of consumption as well as concern: "The foreign journalists were particularly interested in the scene [in Eldares], for they believed that a news story from Africa without pictures of people dying from wretched poverty, famine, or ethnic warfare could not possibly be interesting to their audience back home" (74). The international "community" demands a highly visible form of need in order to perceive it and be moved by it, but that isn't necessarily enough. Despite the dazzling performance, the "missionaries" pass the crowd of beggars with little interest.

In sum, international humanitarianism in *Wizard of the Crow* is a spectacle without substance, a script performed by both givers and recipients. The recipients, however, see it for the fiction it is. This illustrates the meaning of humanitarian fiction in two senses: it shows how humanitarian promises turn up empty and how life imitates narrative. Humanitarianism offers such a familiar script that one can play aid as a child plays house. The actors and the terms of the relationship are already laid out. A realistic approach to aid means operating under the assumption that there will be no aid. The performance dissipates when the police attack the crowd "with their riot gear" (75). Order is restored and the demands of the poor are temporarily quelled: "A miracle appeared as the beggars dispersed. Those with humps fled upright; the blind could see once again; the legless and armless recovered their limbs as they scurried from the gates of Paradise" (75). This performance introduces a sense of insincerity and cynicism into the aid relationship, this time on the part of the supposed beneficiaries. Here, I mean insincerity not in a negative sense but in a positive, protective sense. People "at the receiving end of humanitarian attention know quite well that they are expected to show the humility of the beholden rather than express demands for rights," Fassin asserts, and Ngũgĩ shows that they can use this knowledge strategically to their advantage.[93] If aid is indeed coming, the deferential pose of the beggars will position them well to receive it. But it's best they don't believe in that deference. If they are prepared to receive nothing, they are not fully invested. The beggars in the novel are embodying the position of the weak, the fragile, and the vulnerable, but they gain agency through their performance as they knowingly play the role. Their identity, then, is not equated with their casting in the humanitarian drama.

Debating Aid through the Micro-NGO

Engagement with humanitarianism in *Wizard of the Crow* isn't exclusively about performance; NGO values are also sincerely applied. In the scene described above, the humanitarian interaction is tied to a fixed and ready script, but for the main characters, the language of humanitarian care remains promising in a new configuration. Whereas the spectacle of aid is global, the actual work of nongovernmental, nonprofit aid is local. Ngũgĩ situates the ethics of humane care in local life. The fundamental question of humanitarianism is, How do we care for people who are suffering and in need? That is also the question at the heart of the novel, and the paired protagonists, Kamĩtĩ and Nyawĩra, illustrate and debate various ways of answering it. The fact that this becomes evident through a process of debate is significant. Bottom-up visions of humanitarianism are, if they are to be taken seriously, also in need of interrogation. Ngũgĩ depicts African characters engaged in that process. This also relates to his audience. In contrast to the early novels that I addressed in chapter 2, Ngũgĩ wrote *Wizard of the Crow* in Gikuyu first and translated it into English afterward. This suggests that humanitarian debates are not only for Western readers or English-speaking, cosmopolitan Kenyans but for Gikuyu speakers who might never have been out of Kenya.

The "we" in the question above (How do we care for people who are suffering and in need?) is typically assumed to be a relatively wealthy "we" with the haves giving to the have-nots. This assumption constrains our sense of what care looks like. Ngũgĩ expands it. When Nyawĩra gets in a near-fatal car crash, her experience echoes the parable of the good Samaritan. She feels taken aback by "the number of cars that simply passed her by; no one had stopped to see if anyone was hurt or needed help. The people who hurried to her rescue were the barefooted, mostly. One unloaded his donkey cart to rush her to the nearest medical center many miles away" (79). Altruism is not the purview of the wealthy. In this novel, poverty and social marginalization are strongly correlated with the morality of care. In the New Testament parable, the Samaritan assists a man who has been robbed, beaten and left for dead after others of higher status—a priest and a Levite, "the first two categories of the social hierarchy that dominated post-exilic Judaism"—pass by.[94] This runs counter to the positioning of the Samaritan as "a hated [person], despised as a foreigner and a heretic, one of the lowest in the hierarchy."[95] The story is about challenging the expectations and relational dynamics of inclusion and exclusion. In its conjuring of the parable, Nyawira's story contradicts the assumption that people at the top of the social ladder—racially, ethnically, financially, or otherwise—are the natural humanitarians.

For Kamītī and Nyawira themselves, benevolence is also correlated with poverty. After the car crash, Nyawira chooses to renounce the life of wealth her father has planned for her to instead live among common people, aiming to "build a new tomorrow" (80). This functions as a conversion moment built on existential questions: "If she had died, what would she have left behind as her legacy to the living? There had to be more to life than fast cars, parties, and beauty parlors" (79). Nyawira's transformation saves her from the moral decrepitude associated with wealth in this novel. In fact, wealth is so rotten that, for Kamītī, cash literally stinks; the more he acquires, the more intolerable the stench becomes. He, too, alters his early views on money, value, and shame. In reckoning with his own poverty and inability to attain a job, Kamītī rethinks the position of the beggar, realizing that "prayer after all is a form of begging and it was the cornerstone of all religions" (49). Begging transforms from a thing of shame into a spiritual practice: "Yes, prayers are blessed. Begging is blessed. Among the followers of Buddha, the holiest are known by their vows of poverty, and they are sustained in the path of holiness by begging. Didn't Buddha himself renounce the trappings of wealth for a life of begging and purity?" (49). At this point, early in the novel, Kamītī still hopes to find work, but the spiritual principle of poverty continues to influence his thinking. Buddhism provides an alternative to the moral cesspool of materialism, and it is not colonially implicated in the ways Christianity is, a problem we see in descriptions of Global Bank representatives as missionaries and in the Ruler's self-appointment as a Christ figure. Buddha's story hinges on the renunciation of wealth and the ethic of nonattachment. While, in contrast to the Buddha, Kamītī doesn't come from wealth, this worldview provides resources for confronting the material world, particularly through the ethics of nongrasping. As Kamītī puts it, "The Buddhist attitude toward property attracted me" (211). Enlightenment depends on a detachment from the "human defilement" of money (211). Decoupling wealth from superiority means that Kamītī does not have to see his poverty as indicative of failure or inadequacy. And therefore, to be seen begging should not trigger shame. For Kamītī and Nyawira, living a moral and meaningful life requires detachment from the pursuit of wealth, whether one is rich or poor.

This attitude toward money leads Nyawīra and Kamītī to nonprofit work. The explicit language of humanitarianism soon enters their relationship. They stumble into this project accidentally. Fleeing from police, they take cover in Nyawīra's house, and Kamītī makes a sign to scare the police away, warning that this is the home of a powerful wizard. Oblivious to the ruse, people soon seek out the wizard's help, and Kamītī follows through as advertised. Nyawīra is teasing when she first suggests that Kamītī "form [his] own NGO." "NGO? Of witchcraft?" he replies. "'Yes. And soothsaying. Magic healing. You'll become a consultant for everything to do with magic,' Nyawīra [goes] on, laughing at her own suggestions" (122). The moniker turns out to be rather apt. The Wizard of the Crow does come to play the part of an NGO, serving people whom the state has failed to secure. Although the term NGO is dropped briefly and lightly here, it continues to resonate in both the work he does and his attitude toward care and profit.

For example, after receiving a visit and a payment from the police constable, Kamītī has money and a potential source for much more income. Playing Wizard could be wildly profitable, but he sees money (and smells it) as a "source of foulness" (123). Still, the work he did to get that money was positive, advising the police officer to "never molest a beggar, a diviner, a healer, a wizard, or a witch. If you ever do any harm to the helpless, this magic will turn against you" (118). Nonetheless, his unease with the money is so strong that Kamītī attempts to quit, but an opportunity for kindness pulls him back in. As he leaves the house to dispose of the money from the police officer, he finds "a man standing outside the door," a "stranger [who] looked frail, ill, and tired":

> This must be the shrine of the Wizard of the Crow, the man said, and without waiting for confirmation proceeded to unburden himself of his problems. He was suffering, he said, from a big stomachache.
>
> "I do not want to claim that I am bewitched. I have no money and therefore I cannot go to the hospital. All I want from you are a few roots and leaves to chew to make the pain go away."
>
> Kamītī tried to deny that he was the Wizard of the Crow, but the words stuck to his tongue. (130)

Under the pretense of fetching the leaves and roots requested, he departs, intending never to return, but he reevaluates and decides to help the sick man. Although Kamītī isn't a real wizard, and thus could be read as a kind of scam artist—Gikandi describes him as "a fake"[96]—his help is more genuine than it seems at first glance.[97] He studied plants medicinally in an herbology course in India, so his use of plants is not unfounded. Even his most fanciful technique—mirror scratching—has effects attributable not to the action itself but to Kamĩtĩ's ability to truly see people, especially their underlying vulnerabilities. In this way, his process is real. After Kamĩtĩ instructs the old man to take the leaf-and-root tea with food, the man replies: "Food? Did you say food? You think I have eaten anything for days? If the medicine depends on food, then it is no good to me" (131). So Kamĩtĩ cooks up a meal and feeds him. In a final gesture of care, he gives the man the money he has earned as the Wizard: "Then suddenly an idea struck him: to renounce his role as the Wizard of the Crow, he had to dispense with the income derived from it. And what better way to achieve this than an act of kindness? So he dug into his bag and took out the entire bundle of notes [he had received previously as payment] and gave it to the old man as part of the medicinal treatment" (131). At this point, he is still trying to renounce this role that has been thrust upon him, but after providing genuine help, word spreads, and he becomes resigned that "he had better accept his role as healer" (132). Donating the money secures his position. The Wizard of the Crow has become something of a micro-NGO, distributing resources to the hungry and the sick while eschewing the paths of profit and power.

It is striking how much *Wizard of the Crow* plays with the language of humanitarianism—through references to moral transcendence, benevolent saviors, wounded bodies and souls, universal humanity, the alleviation of suffering—without ever representing the work of international NGOs. As critical as the novel is of international humanitarianism, it suggests there is something truly compelling about the nonstate, nonprofit orientation. The function of the Wizard as micro-NGO branches beyond Kamĩtĩ himself, and he and Nyawĩra work jointly to serve people in need: "To the destitute, they offered a bowl of soup, beans, and rice or *ugali*. And to all who came there for the holy day, they talked about healthy living. . . . The needy and the curious were drawn to the shrine" (275–76). They engage in humanitarian work without the title or the foreign connections, establishing a nonprofit of sorts, a third-sector community service that fills a gap where the public and private sectors have failed. And like the humanitarian tradition, their project interweaves dimensions of morality and spiritual transcendence with material assistance. Nyawĩra's home, which the two share, is both a shelter and a shrine. In contrast to the opaque bureaucracy of NGOs in *Half of a Yellow Sun*, this micro-NGO foregrounds a moral philosophy that develops through ongoing conversations around the fundamentals of the humanitarian sensibility. By envisioning the NGO as a pair of individuals rather than a massive, faceless organization, it becomes a place of liveliness and debate.

For Kamĩtĩ, the transcendent, universal view of humanity is especially important, and he speaks the language of universal humanity that is spoken by
NGOs the world over. He sets his work apart with values higher than power
or profit, upholding the sanctity of human life. When Kamĩtĩ first theorizes
universal humanity, he is himself in the position of the humanitarian subject.
After a long, fruitless day of job hunting, he has "collapsed at the foot of the
mountain of garbage" (38). His body is nearly mistaken for a piece of trash,
disposable and worthless. Since he has taken the mystical form of a "bird self,"
hovering above his body, he considers letting the garbage collectors bury his
body in trash in order that he might be free of it: "That way my soul shall be
free to roam across land and all over this sky. Yes, to go wherever it wishes
without the endless restraining demands of the body. I am thirsty, I want water
to drink; I am hungry, I want food to eat; I am naked, I need some clothes;
I am out in the rain, I need some shelter; I am ill, I must find a doctor" (39,
40). The universal human is found by seeking the lowest common denom-
inator, the most stripped-down form of being. Kamĩtĩ is here presented as
that desperate humanitarian subject on the verge of obliteration, akin to the
category Fassin describes as "the bare life that is to be saved . . . the *zoē* [bare
life] of 'local populations' who can only passively await both bombs and humanitarian workers."[98] But Kamĩtĩ does not "passively await." He is *both* the
body of humanitarian need and the voice of humanitarian care, both the
desperate spectacle and the compassionate spectator. Claiming his body is a
way of claiming his fundamental value as a human being: "I am human, I am
a human being, a soul, and not a piece of garbage, no matter how poor and
ragged I look, and I deserve respect, he heard himself say time and again as
he descended to and repossessed his body" (40). His claim to dignity and life
demands only an affirmation of being human. In this configuration—"I am
a human being, a soul"—the human and the soul are one. The body itself is
sacred, not just the spirit that transcends it.

This language of reverence for life inspires and infuses Kamĩtĩ's role as the
Wizard of the Crow. While he advocates an apolitical humanism, Nyawĩra
pushes back. Together, they grapple with the fundamental values and tensions that animate humanitarian organizations and the discussion surrounding them. Debates about humanity and humane care are staged through their
unfolding dialogue as the two gradually form a partnership. The way Ngũgĩ
grants access to these characters' perspectives prioritizes their political positions over their interiority. Getting to know their minds is less about unique,
individual experience and more about their sociopolitical context and the
possibilities of response. As Divya Dwivedi, Henrik Skov Nielsen, and Richard

Walsh explain, this is a common strategy in postcolonial narratives: "Focaliza-tion is often more importantly about the socially constructed aspects of politi-cal situations than the idiosyncrasies of individual subjectivity; it provides for the irreducible role played by beliefs, allegiances, and historical and ideologi-cal positionality in the unfolding of social and political struggles."[99] The "ideo-logical positionality" of the characters in *Wizard of the Crow* drives much of the action and dialogue. Through most of the novel, Kamĩtĩ is averse to poli-tics, inclined instead to the neutrality of the humanitarian stance. In contrast, Nyawĩra, a central player in the Movement for the Voice of the People, argues for the necessity of politics: "The water I drink, the food I eat, the clothes I wear, the bed I sleep on, are all determined by politics, good or bad. Politics is about power and how it is used. Politics involves choosing sides in the struggle for power. So on which side are you?" (86–87). She and Kamĩtĩ are navigating one of humanitarianism's key dilemmas—the question of whether ethics can be separated from politics. Kamĩtĩ seeks an ethically concentrated neutral space: "Must one always be on this or that side?" he asks Nyawĩra; "I believe in humanity, divine, indivisible. We all need to look deeply in our hearts and the humanity in us will be revealed in all its glory" (87). This is the funda-mental principle of humanitarianism, as Fassin declares: "'Saving strangers'— in other words, people one does not know—simply on the grounds of their common humanity is the supreme mission that humanitarian organizations undertake."[100] But through Nyawĩra's response, we see that Kamĩtĩ's humani-tarian language—and humanitarian language in general—is neither realistic nor entirely right. Nyawĩra prevents us from taking this celebratory language of humanity at face value. She asks Kamĩtĩ, "And this glorious humanity you wax so poetic about, what turns it against itself? Original sin?" (87). It is a concept in need of genuine consideration and critical interrogation.

Kamĩtĩ's approach is more spiritual and more private, Nyawĩra's more secu-lar and overtly political; through the pairing of these characters, the language of care isn't articulated in a single voice but is multiple and subject to ongoing debate. Both characters are morally attuned and committed; they care deeply about the same problem—a corrupt system that multiplies wealth for the elite and leaves the masses with almost nothing. The question is how to respond. After Kamĩtĩ retreats into the wilderness, Nyawĩra tries to persuade him to return and help her:

> "Maybe we are different. You are drawn to the ministry of wounded
> souls, I to the ministry of wounded bodies. I may not know which is
> the better ministry. But this I know: human beings are free to choose

how they use the gifts given to them by God, nature, sun, fate, call it
what you like, I mean that transcendent power that you say governs all
our lives, whether we use it to seek personal salvation or a collective
deliverance." It was not a question, but again Kamĩtĩ squirmed under
the implication. (212)

This suggests that his approach may be too withdrawn and individualist, despite the value it places on humanity in general. The "ministry of wounded
bodies" and the "ministry of wounded souls" are contrasted throughout the
novel and tied to the language of salvation: "There are two kinds of saviors,"
Nyawĩra tells Kamĩtĩ: "those who want to soothe the souls of the suffering and
those who want to heal the sores on the flesh of the suffering. Sometimes I
wonder which is right" (94). The plot tests out that query.

Kamĩtĩ attempts to live out his theory of humanist neutrality and ends up
in retreat. He flees to the wilderness after he finds he has become "an ac-
cessory to the very evil that revolted [him]" (207). Serving people regardless
of their identity means helping the greedy as well as the needy. Again, he is
confronting the tensions of the NGO—this time, the risk of being coopted
by higher powers and causing unintended damage. Even the Ruler demands
Kamĩtĩ's services. Kamĩtĩ "thus reluctantly becomes the surreptitious connection between the world of power, its demonic excesses, and the singular logic
of those who oppose it."[101] This reveals the trouble with neutrality, and Kamĩtĩ
is engaged in the same kind of identity struggle that NGOs undergo, caught
between the interests of the powerful and the needs of the powerless. This is
not to say he is in the same position or receives the benefits of the Western
humanitarian, employed by a well-funded NGO; even so, he wrestles with
the dilemma of the nonprofit, nongovernmental project as it gets swept up in
the global tides of power. In this case, the government explicitly coopts him,
initially requesting "a price for [his] services to the State" (*Wizard*, 369). He
refuses, using the language of the third sector: "You are guardians of the State,
and I am a guardian of life" (369). Once he is taken into custody, he maintains
this line of thought: "my powers are for protecting the laws that govern the
body and the soul, and yours are to protect the laws that govern society," he
tells one of the ruler's top ministers; "I look not for those that break the law of
society but those that destroy the law of life. I fight illness; you fight criminals"
(406–7). He positions himself much like the NGO, operating in service of
human life as something apart from and transcending the state. But, also like
the NGO, he isn't immune to cooptation by state power. Both Kamĩtĩ and
Nyawĩra are grappling with the fundamental question of how to live a meaningful, ethical life. He has aimed for service without political struggle—"a

decent life apart from politics" (129) — but the novel suggests the need for politicization as represented by Nyawīra and her leadership within the Movement for the Voice of the People. As Shivji argues about NGO activists, "We have to choose sides. . . . Put simply, we cannot be neutral."[102] That is, indeed, what Kamītī finds.

Over the course of the novel, the characters' opposing positions — humanist spiritualism and political activism — grow toward one another. Kamītī and Nyawīra see the merit in the alternative view and modify their own, arriving at a middle ground that values the transcendent while tipping toward Nyawīra's earthly politics. As her discourse evolves, it comes to approximate Kamītī's; she explains, for instance, that "the life of even the least among us should be sacred, and it will not do for any region or community to keep silent when the people of another region and community are being slaughtered" (726). Notions of spiritual reverence that undergird the humanitarian ethics of care now infuse her language — including the biblical injunction to care for the "least of these" — which nonetheless remains a call to political engagement. While both characters' positions evolve, Kamītī's moves further, suggesting the primary importance of political thought and effort. More specifically, he must "learn to listen to the voices of women" (83). Eventually, he does, and this adds texture to his view of universal humanity, diversifying and politicizing it; he joins the Movement for the Voice of the People, of which Nyawīra is the chair. Effective reverence for human life, Ngũgĩ shows, must be political. This is also embodied by Nyawīra and Kamītī's collaborative relationship, which turns romantic. Together, they respond to failure of the state through the third sector, while continuing to make public sector demands to hold the state accountable. At the end of *Wizard of the Crow*, Nyawīra affirms that "today our relationship is much stronger because to the bond of love we have now added that of politics" (763). Love without politics does not suffice. This is a lesson not only for Kamītī but for the NGO philosophy in general. This suggests that the humanitarian mode of care in which the "life of even the least among us [is] sacred" (726) occurs not outside the state but in conflict with it, since the state is so heavily implicated in the desecration of life. Part of the job of the nonstate actor is not to ignore the state or circumvent it but to hold it accountable.

Resituating the Third Sector

International NGOs dominate the global discourse about Africa today, and African authors write back. They, too, are telling humanitarian stories and engaging third sector discourses. Their humanitarian fictions, however, attempt to create a truer picture of the contexts in which NGOs work and of the populations they are supposed to serve. Like Godknows in *We Need New Names*, they take up the camera and create their own modes of humanitarian looking. These authors represent the same settings and situations as NGOs do but attach them to different plots, character types, voices, and points of view. On the one hand, *Half of a Yellow Sun* and *Wizard of the Crow* show the power of NGOs in shaping Western consciousness of Africa and African consciousness of the West. On the other, they underscore foreign NGOs' limited presence and capacity. Both celebrations and critiques of humanitarianism tend to overestimate the role of international organizations in the day-to-day life of people in need. The familiar worry about global NGOs creating dependent African populations appears overblown once we consider how keenly aware African people are that NGOs are not actually dependable. To frame the problem of humanitarianism in terms of African dependency is to again magnify the presence and importance of the Western savior, despite critiquing the method and language of salvation. In contrast, by marginalizing humanitarian organizations (including those that provide desirable resources), these novels foreground the agency of people in need, even when their agency is partly expressed by calling on the world for help. Foreign humanitarians might be absent, peripheral, useless, or damaging, but the third sector operates with or without them. We misunderstand the actual humanitarian scene when we overlook practices of care that are happening on the ground among African people themselves. International NGOs are part of the story of survival but never its center. And survival has a very different tenor than salvation.

Also evident is the way that, when humanitarian subjects call upon NGOs for help, they do so with savvy and strategy. This reveals how the white savior narrative lives and moves in the world. Picking up the conventions of that narrative, African people can appeal to Western vanity by playing their assigned roles. Even seemingly obsequious interactions with NGOs can thus be read as ambiguous. This is a realm of performance and masking. The appearance of powerlessness can belie a much more dynamic mode of agency hidden under the surface. Adichie's and Ngũgĩ's humanitarian fictions critique the role of the white savior while also complicating the role of the starving (or otherwise struggling) African. In depicting conditions of material desperation, their novels do not leave us with the sense that people without power are powerless or that people who depend on assistance from others are fully dependent. Positions within the aid relationship are circumstantial, not existential. The NGO sensibility—organizing help where the state falls short—is not necessarily a top-down endeavor. It can also spring from the bottom as an expression of independence, limited in resources but not in commitment or moral insight.

In representing humanitarian landscapes without foreign humanitarians, both novels perform a kind of unscripting. By embedding local voices to narrate the crisis and the call for help, by following impoverished characters who don't fit standard casting of humanitarian subjects, and by unveiling the performance within humanitarian interactions, Adichie and Ngũgĩ draw attention to NGO discourse as a script and then revise it. This is not just about roles that are played, then cast aside. Characters also take ownership of the humanitarian terms, showing an investment in the NGO idea itself. These authors' insistence on the political does not mean a return to the national frame or a rejection of global models of care. They depict an interconnected world based on mutual responsibility. Even as they repoliticize the nonstate, challenging humanitarian notions of ethics and neutrality, they encourage a universalist view of humanity. The notion that life should be sacred applies to emergency situations when life is directly threatened as well as to endemic problems associated with poverty that hobble life in the long term. Adichie and Ngũgĩ critique the world — not just the state — for its inattentiveness, suggesting that responsibility for human welfare is indeed global.

To affirm the sacredness of life, as these novels do, demands an assessment of power. Such a view must engage with sources of life's desecration, including imperialism (of both colonial and neocolonial eras), government corruption, and private greed. In other words, the ethical aspiration needs grounding in a political analysis. In terms of humanitarian storytelling, this means situating needs within their social, historical, and political contexts. It also means prioritizing awareness not only of the powers NGOs are up against but the powers that frame their own existence. When we think about NGOs primarily as institutions, we direct our attention to organizations that are backed by a staff, resources, and a substantial donor base. When we think instead about the NGO as a sensibility, micro-humanitarian practices rise to the surface — tiny communities (Olanna and Kainene, Nyawĩra and Kamĩtĩ) that organize around a moral mandate.

I have used the term "humanitarian subjects" to refer to the recipients of humanitarian aid — those who are subject *to* NGO power. But "subject" also works in the grammatical sense, functioning as the actor in a sentence, not the recipient of the action. Humanitarian fictions can transform our sense of what constitutes humanitarian action and whose values guide it — the typical humanitarian subject can also be the humanitarian actor. Studies of NGOs often conclude with a call to incorporate more African voices. On a practical level, that requires NGOs to engage with actual constituents. On a theoretical level, literature can contribute; in condensed form, it gives access to a range of African voices that index those missing from dominant global conversations about aid.

Epilogue

Rearticulating the Humanitarian Atlantic

I began from the argument that humanitarianism has a narrative problem and that literature could help us assess the implications, while also making space for alternatives. Collectively, the novels studied here rearticulate the humanitarian Atlantic that links Africa, Europe, and North America through a discourse of global ethics, providing new language and new modes of relation. This doesn't give us ready answers, but reading these novels in conjunction does provide a field of concepts and narrative strategies to draw on. In general, this literature's critique of humanitarianism, while vigorous, is not dismissive. The humanitarian commitment to care for the marginalized and dispossessed speaks to the most urgent questions of poverty, war, and global inequity that we face today. But, as David Kennedy asserts, "Our ideals can be compromised by the words we use to express them, just as our deeds can in turn betray our words."[1] This also goes for our narratives. It has been the aim of *Humanitarian Fictions* to assess the problem of words and narratives and to assemble, through the discourse literature provides, a more ethical humanitarian lexicon. So, what is the new language the novels have offered, and what are the new narrative tactics?

A review of the structuring concepts for each chapter suggests that humanitarianism's core frameworks are imperially inclined but ultimately redeemable. First, the moral cause can blind its actors to the damage they inflict, but it can also give depth to the consideration of suffering. A reverent worldview, though not traditionally religious, can be more humane than a fully secularized conception of humanity. Second, the emancipated African of this literature is certainly not the one missionaries envisioned, nor is this figure compliant with the expectations of the Western humanitarian. But global modes of care can, indeed, be liberating when negotiated—either explicitly or covertly—by African agency. Third, the universal human is often a false universal, a rhetorical façade that covers a stratified humanity. But both anticolonial and postcolonial projects of emancipation have found enormous resonance in universal humanism and have never let its Western articulations have the last word. Fourth, the notion of the benevolent gift elides the realities of Western power and exploitation of Africa. Novelists remain invested in practices of giving while removing them from the framework of benevolence; there is nothing inherently wrong with the recipient position, and situating it in a social and historical context alters the dynamics of disempowerment. Finally, the NGO is both necessary and insufficient. It can address acute needs, but its tendency to deflect political problems into apolitical frames is profoundly limiting. Looking at nongovernmental practices of care on the ground, we are reminded that the West has no ownership of the humanitarian position and instead supplements local practices that are already, and more consistently, in place.

On the whole, this suggests that the fundamental concepts of humanitarian ethics are redeemable through the agency of African thinkers, both real (the authors themselves) and fictional (the characters, including some depicted by Western authors). The recovery and revision of those concepts depends on a departure from the white savior sensibility that haunts mainstream humanitarian storytelling. In this epilogue, I will return briefly to the five elements with which I defined the white savior narrative (based on Lyotard's elements of grand narrative) and reflect on what *Humanitarian Fictions* has offered in their place. Synthesizing this literature does not reveal a singular alternative with a prescribed character type, plot trajectory, genre, or style. Instead, like a language, the literature of the humanitarian Atlantic provides building blocks that can be assembled in numerous ways. This adds up to a distinct humanitarian sensibility because, to return to the words of Fanon, "To speak a language is to take on a world, a culture."[2] The culture of white saviorism is rooted in the stories it tells, and those stories in turn reinforce the culture.

This begins from casting. The protagonist of the white savior narrative was white (of course) and traditionally male. He was highly capable, sincerely motivated, heroically brave, rightly confident, and generously benevolent. He stood in contrast to minor white characters whose greed helped dramatize the savior's goodness. That model of humanitarian leadership is a fiction. But the humanitarian fictions studied here—using "fiction" now in the literary sense—force a reckoning for that kind of character or eliminate him completely. In so doing, they theorize whiteness in its global context. In these stories, white protagonists—both men and women—begin from a place of inadequacy. They travel to Africa on the basis of a white savior fantasy, and their confidence reveals itself to be the delusion of narcissism. They are oriented toward the self, not others. Whiteness is, from one perspective, an opportunity for personal gain; it is also a danger and a liability. To be white in Africa is to have relative power not accessible elsewhere. To be white is often to trample, to be blind without knowing it. But whiteness is no more singular than blackness. Characters range from the cruel tyrant (Nathan of *The Poisonwood Bible*) to the oblivious racist (Camilla of *A Question of Power*) to the shortsighted universalist (Dalton of *The Heart of Redness*) to the figure of exemplary, ethical humility (Eugene of *A Question of Power*). White characters who are able to reckon with the problem status of whiteness, often through a process of cultural conversion, are able to make meaningful contributions. But the default of whiteness, based on its alignment with power, is to hurt, not to help. Therefore, any genuinely ethical practice of care across boundaries of race, nation, and continent will begin from humility and hesitation.

Much of this literature sidelines white characters, removing them from the center of humanitarian story. This applies to religious missionaries in *The River Between*, for example, and to secular humanitarians in *Half of a Yellow Sun*. Their displacement reminds us that, viewed from Africa, white saviors were never the center anyway. Sometimes white humanitarians are fully absent in this literature. When present, they often are faceless, distant, and unfeeling. Western donors form a vague "world"—as in calling to "the world for help"—that most often does not respond. African characters are instead the key players in sorting out humanitarian questions of equity, safety, and ethics. This isn't, however, a case of black heroes replacing white ones. Typically, these humanitarian characters are nonheroic, engaged in day-to-day struggle without the drama of salvation or rescue. We also see the centrality of women in leading community practices of care—not in ways that are grand enough to register as humanitarianism in its mainstream sense, but authors such as Bessie Head, Chimamanda Ngozi Adichie, and Ngũgĩ wa Thiong'o endorse their work as primary manifestations of humane ethics. This suggests that we must look for humanitarian practice in places where it is less obvious, and we must think about humanitarianism intersectionally, not just in terms of nation and race, but also in terms of gender and other social markers such as ethnic group, class status, and educational background. This requires consideration of diversity among African people themselves, beyond the black-white, African-Western binaries.

The white savior plot featured a dangerous voyage into the heart of darkness. In critical humanitarian fictions of the Western variety, this element often lingers in a reduced form. Africa is still a place of danger and adventure even if the action unfolds amidst suffering rather than savagery. An important distinction here is that many aspects of the dangerous voyage are revealed to be a projection of the white narcissistic mind. Characters like Quinette in *Acts of Faith* and B.J. in *Girls at Play*, for example, illustrate the radical difference between Africa as an imagined destination versus Africa as an actual location. Alternatively, we have white characters like Eugene in *A Question of Power* who don't have a journey at all; they are established immigrants and fixtures in local life. In the African novels, too, protagonists are often facing danger; the threat comes not from Africa itself but from power and greed emanating often (though not exclusively) from the West. In *Wizard of the Crow*, for instance, Kamĩtĩ and Nyawĩra face a world ravaged by "imperial corporonialism."[3] In *Nervous Conditions*, Tambu navigates the disquieting domain of "special" whites as well as their African inheritors.[4] Danger in such novels has a social and political context; it is not some essential, ontological threat of the African landscape. I am reminded of Bessie Head's statement that "Africa was never 'the dark continent' to African people."[5] Humanitarian fictions by African writers make that truth especially clear.

Straying from the adventure plot, these novels don't conform to any particular genre, and they range widely in technique. Some stick closely to an individual protagonist and focus on interiority; some shift among multiple perspectives and include large casts of characters. Some focus narrowly on a particular location, representing village life, for example, while others sprawl over vast spaces of land and time. Across the board, they are about suffering, but they are also about family, about friendship, about love. From the early iterations to the contemporary, they are often about the banalities of day-to-day life and about the fractures within African communities. *Things Fall Apart*, for example, encompasses all of these. Even in the case of a war novel like *Half of a Yellow Sun*, much of the plot is devoted to daily life and relationships, a pattern that continues in the midst of violent conflict. In contrast to the white savior narrative, then, these humanitarian fictions do not cohere around one genre with predictable tropes. To talk about African need and humanitarian aid is to talk about a vast range of issues and experiences.

The third element by which I defined the white savior narrative was the great goal — to save souls or lives, to make history and change the world. White saviorism promises transformative progress and a dramatic plot to achieve it. In some cases, the literature shows the goal to be thoroughly corrupt, perverse, and self-serving. *Heart of Darkness* — especially through Kurtz's treatise on "humanizing, improving, instructing"[6] — is the ultimate example, although it is also the most pessimistic. Conrad's cynicism about progress comes partly from the fact that his narrative is far less invested in African people than others in this archive; it is easier to reject progress when people in need remain distant and abstract. Other authors offer a good dose of skepticism about progress while also sharing core aspirations of humanitarianism minus the grandeur of salvation. They are invested in transformative change, in creating a more humane, equitable world. In *A Question of Power*, when characters build communal gardens to grow food, the goal is for everyone to have *enough*, which is both basic and radical. *Gifts* envisions fair systems of resource distribution on both micro and macro scales. *The Heart of Redness* seeks a mode of development that brings advantages like clean water and electricity while still honoring (and thus not converting) local life. African characters pursue many of humanitarianism's commitments, and they do so on behalf of others, often in cases where their relative privilege is negligible or nonexistent. Their aim is not salvation but sufficiency for *everyone*.

As opposed to the romantic spirit of white saviorism, these novels are realist in orientation, which is not to say they are strictly realist in style. Examples include Conrad's disorienting sentences that mirror the limited vision of the characters and Head's disorienting descriptions of mental illness. Also illustrative is Ngũgĩ's use of images that take truths to their logical—but reality-bending—extremes when, say, the body of a voraciously greedy Ruler inflates to the size of a room. There is an instructive moral dimension to this mode, as is common in the folktales on which Ngũgĩ draws.

Infusing their realism with a sense of reverence, these humanitarian fictions break the boundaries between religious and secular worldviews. There is often a spiritual dimension to the moral cause they represent, but it is attached to an ascetic form of Christianity—in John A. McClure's term, a "partial faith"—or a Buddhist practice of nongrasping.[7] This is the case for migrant missionaries in *Acts of Faith* and *The Poisonwood Bible*; Malachy and Brother Fowles are men of faith without much mission sensibility. It is also the case for African protagonists (local and migrant), particularly in *A Question of Power* and *Wizard of the Crow*. This suggests that a better humanitarianism does not necessarily leave its religious roots but articulates its faith apart from orthodoxy. Divorced from the discourse of salvation, religious frameworks can be valuable because they provide models of not wanting or taking too much. Sufficiency, rather than abundance, becomes aspirational. These stories are often about small, incremental forms of progress without a solution or definitive end, but they are nonetheless invested in making the world better and in imagining a different distribution of resources and power. As sharply as they depart from the white savior narrative, the spirit of "making a difference" stays on, although it is no longer simplistic or naïve.

This brings us to the question of tone. The tone of these novels—and of

characters whose style of being they endorse—breaks away from the authoritative, confident, optimistic ethos of the white savior narrative. Their collective
discourse is dominated by uncertainty. Doubt produces hesitation and opens
debate. Sometimes these authors are deeply pessimistic; they are often hopeful, but it is a cautious, tempered hope, hinged on African agency and not
foreign intervention. In other words, they maintain humanitarian aspiration
but without the unthinking enthusiasm. Often, they achieve this through use
of perspective—the child narrator in We Need New Names who responds to
the camera of the "NGO people" by turning the lens back on them, for example, or the shifting perspectives in The Poisonwood Bible and Acts of Faith.
These texts are contemplative, producing questioning and thinking, often at
an explicitly philosophical pitch. Waiyaki in The River Between, Elizabeth in
A Question of Power, and Tambu in Nervous Conditions embody this orientation. African characters who participate in humanitarian projects are not just
acting or feeling—the verbs that dominate the white savior sensibility. They
are *thinking* people—theorists as well as activists. This is evident when they
respond to Western intervention and when they imagine their own futures
apart from external assistance.

These are also novels of discussion, in which characters debate the discourse of humanity and projects of material improvement. Think of Elizabeth
and Tom in A Question of Power, Camagu and Dalton in The Heart of Redness, or Kamītī and Nyawīra in Wizard of the Crow. These conversations occur
within African communities and across boundaries, and characters often undergo a process of questioning and learning. Dispensing with moral certitude,
this literature advocates a posture of humanitarian humility. In contrast to
the white savior narrative's "explosions of feeling,"[8] these are novels of ideas,
provocations to thought. Humanitarian fictions, thus, resonate with Jeanne-
Marie Jackson's call to view "the African novel as a source of *thinking about
thinking*, a site of agile negotiation between private minds and public spaces."[9]
Many Western readers turn to African literature for the catharsis of sympathy,
but what they get here is something more more difficult and less satisfying.
These humanitarian fictions provide no sense of security that the world will
get better and things will be OK. They build a humanitarian relationship not
just of sympathy or hope but also of questioning and debate, leaving us in a
space of uncertainty. They abide by Teju Cole's prompting that a novel should
"leave the reader not knowing what to think."[10]

Whereas the white savior narrative simplifies and singularizes, the humanitarian fictions I have studied here complicate and deconstruct. They break
down the familiar structure of oppositions that undergird white saviorism.
Africa, for the most part, is not a place of darkness, and the West is not the

source of light. Good and evil are messy; doing the right thing is not clear-cut. Among the most important binaries this literature breaks is that of benefactor and beneficiary. African characters are often the givers, white characters the receivers. This alters the accompanying categories of powerful and powerless, showing agency on the side of the oppressed. The repositioning of benefactor and beneficiary can happen in terms of small-scale interactions—such as the hospitality of the poor in Bessie Head's work—or in terms of international relations and colonial history—like the flows of the humanitarian Atlantic, which Farah shows are dominated not by Western gifts to Africa but by the reverse. Reframed humanitarian positions also emerge when authors reveal the white savior narrative to be a channel of intercultural performance. African people knowingly engage with the West through the lens of white savior fictions; understanding the narrative and its scripted roles can be a strategy of survival, a way of exerting agency in highly constrained circumstances. Of course, this challenges the role of African people as passive beneficiaries within that narrative. It also challenges critiques of Western humanitarians that overemphasize their power and influence over African subjects.

Breaking the division between ethics and politics is another essential theme of the humanitarian Atlantic. Whereas the Western humanitarian imagination typically thinks of transatlantic connection in terms of ethical imperatives that transcend politics, these humanitarian imaginings show how the map is stitched together first through power. This includes the history of colonialism and enslavement; it also includes a neocolonial present that continues to funnel resources disproportionately to the West, particularly the United States. These texts consistently politicize ethics and contextualize it within social and historical worlds. In this way, they break the discourse of purity that imagines a humanitarian space where ethics can act freely without the entanglement of politics. They depict an Africa that is tied to and engaged with the West, but they show those connections to be much more complicated than a narrative of Western altruism for a needy Africa would suggest.

Parallel with that politicization, these novels break the history-future binary by which humanitarian discourse focuses on progress to the exclusion of the past. Western engagement with Africa, they suggest, is not a matter of voluntary, altruistic commitment to the future, but the obligatory outcome of a tragic history. Chinua Achebe's words capture that shared perspective: "Because the West has had a long but uneven engagement with the continent, it is imperative that it understand what happened to Africa. It must also play a part in the solution. A meaningful solution will require the goodwill and concerted efforts on the part of all those who share the weight of Africa's historical burden."[11] The Atlantic triangle is defined not only by humanitarian crossings but by its inhumane history. White saviorism forgets that. Better narratives of African improvement will speak a language of futurity that is grounded in an understanding of the past. They must ask questions about how and why we are connected (historically, socially, politically) *and* what we should do about it. To jump to the latter question without giving serious attention to the former is to practice the risky maneuver of "ignorant goodwill."[12]

In sum, these novels demystify and reinvent the vocabulary of global care to suggest that the humanitarian Atlantic can be crossed in more ethical, more effective ways. They situate humanitarian representation within a political network of social relations, and they negotiate the tension between utopian desire and real-world necessity. Their language is universalist but not imperialist, progress-oriented but not salvation-based, postsecular but nonmissionary, invested in giving but not in the frame of benevolence. They show the entanglement of ethics with social, political, and historical forces. They prioritize humanity but draw more on the language of sacredness than sameness. They are open to third sector projects but also make claims upon the state. Although the international community is inadequate and, in many ways, illusory, critical humanitarian fictions affirm that, in this irreversibly globalized world, some version of transatlantic care must endure.

Acknowledgments

This book has been long in coming, and its roots go far back. More people than I can mention here have shaped my ideas, well before they found their way onto the page. This is a book about humanitarianism in Africa. I study from a distance experiences of war, poverty, and hunger. I have witnessed them only as an outsider and a guest to those who have known them firsthand. Traveling to Angola and to refugee camps in Namibia and Zambia with an NGO over the last two decades, I have witnessed the arrogance, ineffectiveness, and even cruelty of some "benevolent" Westerners, signals of altruism's most troubling tendencies. As a white person in Africa, I am implicated in that, as is my family history. My paternal grandparents were missionaries in Angola, and while that history has enriched my life with experiences and friendships I wouldn't have had otherwise, it has long been a source of deep embarrassment. Encountering postcolonial studies and African literature in college gave me the tools to understand why, and my conversations with Angolan people added depth to that understanding. But working with Angolan teachers and community leaders has also forced me to put aside my preconceptions of anti-imperial agency to see the complex negotiations that occur around Western "gifts" of both secular and spiritual varieties. It has revealed how insignificant foreign humanitarianism is in comparison to the daily efforts by which African people care for one another.

I, too, have been the beneficiary of that care. I would especially like to thank the Abel family, the Capeio family, and the Huambo family for their incredible warmth and hospitality. In Angola and Namibia, they have been models of humanitarian efforts. I have learned a great deal from the intelligence and humor of Adriano and Elvis Huambo, and I have loved laughing together reading *Wizard of the Crow*. Pastor Bernardo Capeio has shown me a depth of socially committed faith that I have never witnessed stateside; this shaped questions I have asked in this book about African engagements with Christianity. Dina Justina chose to care for my father when he was at his most vulnerable as a young child and she was barely older. She and Helena Nahei are on my mind every time I read Bessie Head because they have exemplified radical practices of care for orphans and refugees, even when they were refugees themselves.

My dad, J. Andrew Cole, who was born and raised in Angola, taught me to love books and to seek better stories about Africa than mainstream American culture offered. When I went to college, he was eager to discuss everything I was learning in my classes, and he referred to it as "our education." I wish he had lived to see this book. My mom, Lynn Cole, has also invested deeply in my education since the very beginning. Her confidence in me is enthusiastic and unwavering, and she often tells me it's not just because she's my mother. Even if that were the case, what a privilege it is to have that kind of backing. I also find that love in my siblings—Rachel, Ross, Stephanie, and Ben—and I can always count on their interest, support, and laughter (with me and at me). The Rom-Paustian family, too, has embraced and encouraged me in all things. I am especially indebted to Dan Paustian, whose presence has sustained me through every step of the writing process. A running coach once told me that training for a marathon means passing through pockets of despair, when the miles seem to stretch endlessly and the finish line feels impossibly distant; that goes for writing a book, too. I thank Dan for standing by me through the pockets of despair and for celebrating the high points at every opportunity.

I have been fortunate to have incredible teachers throughout my education. This includes those who gave me an early foundation in reading and writing: Lori Widlicka, Eva Tarini, Carolyn Schoeller, Lynn Drew, and Sherry Medwin. Literacy is a gift. My professors at the University of Wisconsin opened new worlds to me, including the challenges and pleasures of intellectual life: Heather Dubrow, Dean Makuluni, Cyrena Pondrom, Scott Straus, Henry Turner, and Craig Werner. Tejumola Olaniyan oversaw my senior thesis at Wisconsin, served as a reader on my dissertation committee, and continued to mentor me through 2019, the year of his untimely death. He was an exuberant critic who always made me better, and his memory continues to push me. Rebecca Walkowitz, whom I also met at the University of Wisconsin, has been my role model, mentor, and advocate for nearly twenty years. More than anyone, she taught me to write, and her lessons echo in this book as well as in my teaching.

I met wonderful people at Rutgers, where I studied for my PhD and began this project. Years after taking a class with Sonali Perera, I'm still thinking through questions she raised; her endlessly detailed feedback, her sincerity, and her fierce investment in her students were pivotal for me. Every conversation I have with Stéphane Robolin adds depth to my work and my worldview. I am always touched by his perceptiveness, his warmth, and his generous listening. John McClure was my advisor throughout graduate school, and much of my best thinking emerged from talks in his office. He helped me find my voice and trust it. I am continually inspired by his wisdom, ethical sensibility, and ordinariness in Bessie Head's beautiful sense of the term. (John will know what I mean.) I am grateful to Cheryl Robinson and Courtney Borack, who made the literature department run and whose office was a refuge, as was the apartment I shared with Teagan Bradway and Joshua Crandall, whose friendship was a highlight of graduate school. In the years since, Teagan has been a constant source of feedback, advice, commiseration, and fun and has read more of my drafts than anyone. The book is far better for it.

I have also found an intellectual home with the African Literature Association and my ALA crew: Nicole Cesare, Uchechi Okereke-Beschel, and Bernard Oniwe. Their friendship has been life giving. I will always appreciate the welcoming leadership of the ALA, including the mentors I knew before joining—Tejumola Olaniyan and Stéphane Robolin—and those I met, whose generosity and encouragement have meant a great deal to me. Olakunle George's scholarship influenced this book's core arguments early on, and his incisive feedback enabled me to strengthen them, particularly by refining the theoretical frameworks. Jeanne-Marie Jackson's astute reading pushed me to draw out the narrative implications of the project and to sharpen the parameters of its archive.

I have benefited from the warm support of the English Department chairs at North Central College—Martha Bohrer, Jennifer Jackson, and most recently, Jennifer Joan Smith, whose cheerleading can be heard well beyond our office walls. I am most indebted to Sohinee Roy, whose critical feedback and warm support have been crucial to this project.

Starting this book and seeing it through has depended on the privilege of time and resources. I have received support from a Jacob K. Javits Fellowship, an SAS Mellon Grant, a Charlotte W. Newcombe Fellowship, a Rutgers University Graduate Fellowship, and North Central College research grants, including a Sabbatical Leave Award.

A version of chapter 2 was published in 2014 in *Research in African Literatures*. A version of chapter 3 was published in 2017 in *Humanity: An International Journal of Human Rights, Humanitarianism, and Development*. While both essays have been expanded and substantially revised for the context of the book, they benefited enormously from the insightful feedback of the journals' anonymous reviewers as well as the editors, including Joseph Slaughter and Molly Reinhoudt.

Fordham University Press has also offered wonderful support. In particular, I thank my acquiring editor Tom Lay for his confidence in this book and all his help in carrying it though, including his selection of outstanding readers who saw the good in my manuscript and shared crucial ways to improve it. As project editor, Kem Crimmins beautifully orchestrated the book's production process and ensured that all the pieces came together. I am grateful to Nancy Basmajian for bringing her vast knowledge and impressive eye for detail to the copyediting process. Finally, I thank Femi Johnson for allowing his exquisite painting, *Muse Morning*, to grace the cover of this book.

Notes

Introduction: The White Savior Narrative and the Third Sector Novel

1. *Kony 2012*, dir. Jason Russell, *YouTube*, uploaded by Invisible Children, Inc., 5 March 2012, 26:15.

2. For examples, see Mahmood Mamdani, "What Jason Didn't Tell Gavin and His Army of Invisible Children," *Daily Monitor*, 13 March 2012; and the series of articles in the *New York Times* Room for Debate section, "Kony 2012 and the Potential of Social Media Activism," 9 March 2012, especially the responses by TMS Ruge and Angelo Izama.

3. Teju Cole, "The White-Savior Industrial Complex," *The Atlantic*, 21 March 2012, n.p.

4. There has long been discussion over the use of capital or lowercase letters for racial labels, particularly black/Black. Arguments for capitalization gained momentum in 2020, following George Floyd's murder and the increased visibility of the Black Lives Matter Movement, and capitalizing the B in Black subsequently became a norm in mainstream American publishing. Explanations for the change often refer to a shared history, identity, and culture among African Americans. This logic, applied to a minoritized group in the United States, does not apply in the same way to a majority black continent made up of thousands of ethnic groups that have their own histories, identities, and cultures. I worry about overextending an American norm to an African context, and for that reason, I will follow the majority of the African scholars and novelists I cite in this book, using the lowercase for racial designations (black and white, blackness and whiteness) and uppercase for ethnic designations (Igbo, Shona, Xhosa, etc.). On the debate over capitalization in the U.S. context and what it reveals regarding "larger perplexities about the meaning of race," see Kwame Anthony Appiah, "The Case for Capitalizing the B in Black," *The Atlantic*, 18 June 2020, n.p.

5. Gayatri Chakravorty Spivak, *A Critique of Postcolonial Reason* (Cambridge, MA: Harvard University Press, 1999), 284.

6. On Kipling's White Man, see Edward Said, *Orientalism* (1978; New York: Vintage, 1994), 226–28.

7. Achille Mbembe, *Critique of Black Reason*, trans. Laurent Dubois (Durham, NC: Duke University Press, 2017), 12.

8. Michael Ignatieff, *The Warrior's Honor: Ethnic War and the Modern Conscience* (New York: Metropolitan, 1997), 4; Michael Barnett, *Empire of Humanity: A History of Humanitarianism* (Ithaca, NY: Cornell University Press, 2011), 220.

9. Alex de Waal, *Famine Crimes: Politics and the Disaster Relief Industry in Africa* (Oxford: James Currey, 1997), 221; David Rieff, *A Bed for the Night: Humanitarianism in Crisis* (New York: Simon and Schuster, 2002), 24, 170.

10. Didier Fassin, *Humanitarian Reason: A Moral History of the Present* (Berkeley: University of California Press, 2012), 207.

11. On television and journalism, see Ignatieff, *The Warrior's Honor*. On celebrity humanitarian advocacy, see Lilie Chouliaraki, *The Ironic Spectator: Solidarity in the Age of Post-humanitarianism* (Cambridge: Polity, 2013); and Lisa Ann Richey, ed., *Celebrity Humanitarianism and North-South Relations: Politics, Place, and Power* (London: Routledge, 2016). On films set in both Africa and the United States, see Matthew W. Hughey, *The White Savior Film: Content, Critics, and Consumption* (Philadelphia: Temple University Press, 2014).

12. Cole, "White-Savior Industrial Complex," n.p.

13. V. Y. Mudimbe, *The Invention of Africa: Gnosis, Philosophy, and the Order of Knowledge* (Bloomington: Indiana University Press, 1988).

14. Gaurav Desai, *Subject to Colonialism: African Self-Fashioning and the Colonial Library* (Durham, NC: Duke University Press, 2001), 4.

15. Desai, 4.

16. Abiola Irele, "Narrative, History, and the African Imagination," *Narrative* 1, no. 2 (May 1993): 169.

17. Michael Maren, *The Road to Hell: The Ravaging Effects of Foreign Aid and International Charity* (New York: Free Press, 1997), 11.

18. Rieff, *Bed for the Night*, 66, 76.

19. On NGO imperialism, see Issa G. Shivji, *Silences in NGO Discourse: The Role and Future of NGOs in Africa* (Nairobi: Fahamu, 2007). For influential, opposing views on official aid, see Jeffrey D. Sachs, *The End of Poverty: Economic Possibilities for Our Time* (New York: Penguin, 2005); Dambisa Moyo, *Dead Aid: Why Aid Is Not Working and How There Is a Better Way for Africa* (New York: Farrar, Straus, Giroux, 2009); and William Easterly, *The White Man's Burden: Why the West's Efforts to Aid the Rest Have Done So Much Ill and So Little Good* (New York: Penguin, 2006).

20. On military humanitarian intervention and "humanitarian government," see Michel Feher, *Powerless by Design: The Age of the International Community*

(Durham, NC: Duke University Press, 2000); Barnett, *Empire of Humanity*; Michael Barnett and Thomas G. Weiss, *Humanitarianism Contested: Where Angels Fear to Tread* (Abingdon, UK: Routledge, 2011); and Fassin, *Humanitarian Reason*.

21. Noam Chomsky, "Humanitarianism Imperialism: The New Doctrine of the Imperial Right," *Monthly Review*, 1 September 2008, n.p.

22. On the problematic use of the term "beneficiary," see Hugo Slim, *Humanitarian Ethics: A Guide to the Morality of Aid in War and Disaster* (New York: Oxford University Press, 2015), 2, 212. For a study that flips standard assignment of the term, see Bruce Robbins, *The Beneficiary* (Durham, NC: Duke University Press, 2017).

23. Chinua Achebe, "Africa's Tarnished Name," in *The Education of a British-Protected Child* (New York: Anchor, 2009), 80.

24. I apply the term *third sector* somewhat anachronistically in this book, reaching back well before it was in use. Amitai Etzioni coined the term in 1973 and used it within a domestic rather than international context, including various actors within civil society such as religious, cultural, and community-based organizations.

25. Barnett, *Empire of Humanity*, 19.

26. For examples in the context of literature, see James Dawes, *The Novel of Human Rights* (Cambridge, MA: Harvard University Press, 2018); and Eleni Coundouriotis, *The People's Right to the Novel: War Fiction in the Postcolony* (New York: Fordham University Press, 2014).

27. Peter Stamatov, *The Origins of Global Humanitarianism: Religion, Empires, and Advocacy* (New York: Cambridge University Press, 2013), 14.

28. Barnett, *Empire of Humanity*, 54.

29. Barnett, 64.

30. Even if missionaries have fallen out of fashion since the Victorian era, they continue to maintain a following. In fact, there are more missionaries at work in the world today than ever before, and they continue to wield a massive support network and following (see Julian Pettifer and Richard Bradley, *Missionaries* [London: BBC Books, 1990]). There is also a whole industry of Christian publishing with a keen interest in humanitarian work in the name of God, including texts written by and about Americans in Africa, such as *Another Man's War: The True Story of One Man's Battle to Save Children in the Sudan* (Nashville, TN: Thomas Nelson, 2009) by Sam Childers, and coauthored books by African survivors and Western advocates such as *Girl Soldier: A Story of Hope for Northern Uganda's Children* by Faith J. H. McDonnell and Grace Akallo (Grand Rapids, MI: Chosen Books, 2007).

31. Andrea Paras and Janice Gross Stein, "Bridging the Sacred and the Profane in Humanitarian Life," in *Sacred Aid: Faith and Humanitarianism*, ed. Michael Barnett and Janice Gross Stein (New York: Oxford University Press, 2012), 226, 229.

32. See Heather D. Curtis, *Holy Humanitarians: American Evangelicals and Global Aid* (Cambridge, MA: Harvard University Press, 2018); and Michael Barnett and Janice Gross Stein, eds., *Sacred Aid: Faith and Humanitarianism* (Oxford: Oxford University Press, 2012). For an alternative take from a Christian perspective,

see Daniel J. Mahoney, who derides the humanitarian "religion of humanity" as the "subversion of Christianity and authentic political life"; Mahoney, *The Idol of Our Age: How the Religion of Humanity Subverts Christianity* (New York: Encounter, 2018), 7.

33. Jean-François Lyotard, *The Postmodern Condition: A Report on Knowledge*, trans. Geoff Bennington and Brian Massumi (Minneapolis: University of Minnesota Press, 1984), 36.

34. Lyotard, xxiv.

35. Joseph Conrad, *Heart of Darkness* (New York: Modern Library, 1999), 61.

36. These organizations even show up in literature. In NoViolet Bulawayo's *We Need New Names* (New York: Little, Brown, 2013), white characters appear in T-shirts reading "Invisible Children" and "Save Darfur," a sign of the humanitarian message's mass production and circulation (11, 269).

37. Mahmood Mamdani, *Saviors and Survivors: Darfur, Politics, and the War on Terror* (New York: Doubleday, 2009), 21.

38. See Fiona Terry, *Condemned to Repeat? The Paradox of Humanitarian Action* (Ithaca, NY: Cornell University Press, 2002).

39. Graham Greene, *The Heart of the Matter* (New York: Penguin, 1999), 110.

40. Susan Sontag, *Regarding the Pain of Others* (New York: Picador, 2003), 71.

41. Said, *Orientalism*, 3.

42. Achille Mbembe, "On the Power of the False," *Public Culture* 14, no. 3 (2002): 631.

43. Mbembe, 631–32.

44. This is inspired by articulations of the Black Atlantic by Paul Gilroy and Brent Hayes Edwards. The humanitarian Atlantic overlaps with networks of slavery, abolitionism, and black internationalism.

45. Examples of the former include James Dawes's *The Novel of Human Rights* and Crystal Parikh's *Writing Human Rights: The Political Imaginaries of Writers of Color* (Minneapolis: University of Minnesota Press, 2017). Examples of the latter include Elizabeth S. Anker's *Fictions of Dignity: Embodying Human Rights in World Literature* (Ithaca, NY: Cornell University Press, 2012), Joseph Slaughter's *Human Rights Inc.: The World Novel, Narrative Form, and International Law* (New York: Fordham University Press, 2007), Elizabeth Swanson Goldberg's *Beyond Terror: Gender, Narrative, Human Rights* (New Brunswick, NJ: Rutgers University Press, 2007), and Debjani Ganguly's *This Thing Called the World: The Contemporary Novel as Global Form* (Durham, NC: Duke University Press, 2016).

46. Mīkoma Wa Ngũgĩ, *The Rise of the African Novel: Politics of Language, Identity, and Ownership* (Ann Arbor: University of Michigan Press, 2018), 13.

47. James Ferguson, *Global Shadows: Africa in the Neoliberal World Order* (Durham, NC: Duke University Press, 2006), 2.

48. Ferguson, 3.

49. Neil Lazarus, "The Politics of Postcolonial Modernism," in *Postcolonial*

Studies and Beyond, ed. Ania Loomba et al. (Durham, NC: Duke University Press, 2005), 424.

50. Coundouriotis, *People's Right to the Novel*, 224.

51. Anker, *Fictions of Dignity*, 35.

52. Rita Barnard, "Fictions of the Global," *NOVEL: A Forum on Fiction* 42, no. 2 (2009): 213.

53. Kwame Anthony Appiah, foreword to *Nervous Conditions* by Tsitsi Dangarembga (New York: Seal, 2004), vi.

54. Ngũgĩ wa Thiong'o, *Decolonising the Mind: The Politics of Language in African Culture* (London: James Currey, 1986).

55. Tejumola Olaniyan, "The Paddle That Speaks English: Africa, NGOs, and the Archaeology of an Unease," *Research in African Literatures* 42, no. 2 (Summer 2011): 55.

56. Kwame Anthony Appiah, *In My Father's House* (Oxford: Oxford University Press, 1992), 155.

57. Eleni Coundouriotis's *The People's Right to the Novel* is a notable exception. While humanitarian narrative is critical to her book's framework, it is secondary to the genre of the war novel with "War [being] the topic of humanitarianism par excellence" (3). My focus, in contrast, is on the humanitarian narrative itself, with war occasionally factoring in; I emphasize the aid relationship and the kinds of stories it generates.

58. Joseph Slaughter, "Foreword: Rights on Paper," in *Theoretical Perspectives on Human Rights and Literature*, ed. Elizabeth Swanson Goldberg and Alexandra Schultheis Moore (London: Routledge, 2012), xiii.

59. Dawes, *Novel of Human Rights*, 200.

60. Kenneth Burke, *Counter-statement* (Berkeley: University of California Press, 1931), 105, 106.

61. Homi K. Bhabha, *The Location of Culture* (London: Routledge, 1994), 142, 141.

62. Ferguson, *Global Shadows*, 20.

63. Bhabha, *Location of Culture*, 172.

64. Chinua Achebe, *There Was a Country* (New York: Penguin, 2012), 58.

65. Achebe, 58.

66. Didier Fassin, "Humanitarianism as a Politics of Life," trans. Rachel Gomme, *Public Culture* 19, no. 3 (2007): 511.

67. Lyotard, *Postmodern Condition*, xxiv.

68. Chinua Achebe, "The Truth of Fiction," in *Hopes and Impediments: Selected Essays* (New York: Anchor, 1988), 143.

69. Nicholas Kristof, "Westerners on White Horses . . . ," *New York Times*, 14 July 2010, n.p.

70. Cole, "White-Savior Industrial Complex," n.p.

71. Spivak, *Critique of Postcolonial Reason*, 416.

72. Martin Luther King Jr., *Strength to Love* (Minneapolis, MN: Fortress, 2010), 39.

Chapter 1: The Moral Cause

1. Jonathan J. Makuwira, *Non-governmental Development Organizations and the Poverty Reduction Agenda: The Moral Crusaders* (London: Routledge, 2014), 16.

2. Michael Barnett, *Empire of Humanity: A History of Humanitarianism* (Ithaca, NY: Cornell University Press, 2011), 53–54.

3. See, for example, *Holy Humanitarians: American Evangelicals and Global Aid* (Cambridge, MA: Harvard University Press, 2018), a study of the *Christian Herald* by Heather D. Curtis.

4. Andrea Paras and Janice Gross Stein, "Bridging the Sacred and the Profane in Humanitarian Life," in *Sacred Aid: Faith and Humanitarianism*, ed. Michael Barnett and Janice Gross Stein (New York: Oxford University Press, 2012), 213, 224.

5. The African literary response to missions has been rich and extensive. To give it adequate space, I save its analysis for the following chapter.

6. Examples written over several decades include Eloise Knapp Hay, *The Political Novels of Joseph Conrad* (1963); J. Hillis Miller, *Poets of Reality: Six Twentieth-Century Writers* (1965); Hunt Hawkins, "Conrad's Critique of Imperialism in *Heart of Darkness*" (1979); John A. McClure, *Kipling and Conrad: The Colonial Fiction* (1981); Benita Parry, *Conrad and Imperialism: Ideological Boundaries and Visionary Frontiers* (1983); Andrea White, "Conrad and Imperialism" (1996); Kenneth Graham, "Conrad and Modernism" (1996); Ian Watt "Conrad's *Heart of Darkness* and the Critics" (2000); and Susan Stanford Friedman, "Periodizing Modernism: Postcolonial Modernities and the Space/Time Borders of Modernist Studies" (2006).

7. Joseph Conrad, *Heart of Darkness* (New York: Modern Library, 1999), 10.

8. The Congo is part of Kingsolver's personal history, as it was for Conrad. Although her home base has always been in the United States, she spent much time abroad as a child, including one year in a remote Congolese village where her father volunteered as a physician.

9. In an interview given at the time he was writing *Acts of Faith* (a novel I will address in chapter 4), Caputo acknowledged "the writer I'm most conscious of, the one who I sometimes, if I read him, can hear him speaking, actually talking to me, is Conrad" (Michael Neiberg, Thomas G. Bowie, Jr., and Donald Anderson, "A Rumor of War: A Conversation with Philip Caputo at 58," *War, Literature, and the Arts* 12, no. 1 [2000]: 9).

10. Patrick Brantlinger, "Victorians and Africans: The Genealogy of the Myth of the Dark Continent," *Critical Inquiry* 12, no. 1 (Autumn 1985): 229.

11. Brantlinger, 175.

12. See Anna Johnston's *Missionary Writing and Empire, 1800–1860* (Cambridge: Cambridge University Press, 2003), for an extensive, archival account of the forms of missionary writing. Her focus is on the London Missionary Society and missionaries to India, Polynesia, and Australia. On missionary journals in the Nigerian context, see J. D. Y. Peel, *Religious Encounter and the Making of the Yoruba* (Bloomington: Indiana University Press, 2000), chap. 1.

13. John Chisholm Lambert, *The Romance of Missionary Heroism: True Stories of the Intrepid Bravery, and Stirring Adventures of Missionaries with Uncivilized Man, Wild Beasts and the Forces of Nature in All Parts of the World* (1907; Shawnee, KS: Gideon House, 2017), 10.

14. Julian Pettifer and Richard Bradley, *Missionaries* (London: BBC Books, 1990), 23.

15. Johnston, *Missionary Writing and Empire*, 7.

16. Pettifer and Bradley, *Missionaries*, 22.

17. Peel, *Religious Encounter*, 19.

18. Peel, 17.

19. See Johnston, *Missionary Writing and Empire*, 6–8; and Pettifer and Bradley, *Missionaries*, 81–87.

20. John Chisholm Lambert, 81.

21. Lambert, 82.

22. Lambert, 82.

23. Brantlinger, *Victorian Literature and Postcolonial Studies*, (Edinburgh: Edinburgh University Press, 2009), 22.

24. Brantlinger, 23.

25. R. M. Ballantyne, *The Coral Island* (Oxford: Oxford University Press, 1990), 288.

26. Ballantyne, 284.

27. Charlotte Brontë, *Jane Eyre* (Oxford: Oxford University Press, 1999), 531.

28. Conrad, *Heart of Darkness*, 5.

29. In fact, Gideon House Books continues to publish *The Romance of Missionary Heroism* with this pitch to readers on the back cover: "It is sometimes difficult for those of us steeped in the comforts and ease of today's modern world to grasp what a life of radical faith can look like. . . . This collection . . . reminds us of the hefty price missionaries must be willing to pay to prepare previously untilled soil for the Gospel of Jesus Christ."

30. Barnett, *Empire of Humanity*, 75. In *The Idol of Our Age: How the Religion of Humanity Subverts Christianity* (New York: Encounter, 2018), Daniel J. Mahoney argues that through this discourse, or "religion of humanity," "humanitarianism subverts Christianity and the moral law and leaves nothing but confusion in their place" (1, 2). This polemic critiques universal humanism from a starkly different angle than postcolonial critics do. I expand on the discourse of humanity in chapter 3. Other scholars suggest that contemporary humanitarianism is far less secular than Mahoney takes it to be, as demonstrated in *Sacred Aid: Faith and Humanitarianism*, edited by Michael Barnett and Janice Gross Stein (Oxford: Oxford University Press, 2012).

31. Teju Cole, "The White-Savior Industrial Complex," *The Atlantic*, 21 March 2012.

32. This special status of "virtuous" travelers is noted by African writers as well. In Tsitsi Dangarembga's *Nervous Conditions*, for example, the narrator depicts the

position of power that missionaries come to occupy through the denial of the selfish motivations. I deal with this issue in chapter 4.

33. Conrad, *Heart of Darkness*, 30. Carola M. Kaplan, in noting the breakdown of binaries throughout the text, claims that "the gang of virtue is indistinguishable from the gang of greed" ("Colonizers, Cannibals, and the Horror of Good Intentions in Joseph Conrad's *Heart of Darkness*," in *Joseph Conrad*, ed. Harold Bloom [New York: Chelsea House, 2003], 67). While I find the parallelism she makes between the "gang of virtue" and the "gang of greed" useful, the claim I want to make is a bit different, essentially that they are *almost* indistinguishable, but the difference of designation is indeed significant, since the narratives that get attached to them have consequences.

34. On the modernist aesthetics of paradox, ambiguity, and uncertainty in Conrad's text, see Walter Göbel, "The Birth of Modernism in the 'Heart of Darkness,'" in *Conrad in Germany*, ed. Walter Göbel, Hans Ulrich Seeber, and Martin Windisch (New York: East European Monographs, 2007), 107–21. On the uncertainties produced through the dense narrative layers of the novella, see Peter Brooks, "An Unreadable Report: Conrad's *Heart of Darkness*," in *Joseph Conrad's* Heart of Darkness (Modern Critical Interpretations), ed. Harold Bloom (New York: Chelsea House, 1986), 105–27. The unknowable quality of Conrad's Congo stands in contrast to popular mission narratives which combined missionary work with exploration and information gathering. Livingstone's epic of travel literature was also a text of ethnography, geography, and tropical disease pathology. A large part of his task was to map the uncharted places of the earth. He was a collector of knowledge and as such was a key player in the work of imperial expansion. Bringing "light" to the "dark" places of the earth has been a project for the mapmaker as well as the missionary. Bringing the gospel abroad also meant bringing home knowledge of those locations.

35. Mikhail Bakhtin, *The Dialogic Imagination*, ed. Michael Holquist, trans. Caryl Emerson and Michael Holquist (Austin: University of Texas Press, 1981), 334.

36. Bakhtin, *Dialogic Imagination*, 334.

37. Bakhtin, 338.

38. Paul Theroux, *Girls at Play*, in *On the Edge of the Great Rift Valley: Three Novels of Africa* (New York: Penguin, 1996), 248.

39. Lambert, *Romance of Missionary Heroism*, 78.

40. Lambert, 88.

41. J. Hillis Miller, *Poets of Reality: Six Twentieth-Century Writers* (Cambridge, MA: Harvard University Press, 1965), 6.

42. John A. McClure, "The Rhetoric of Restraint in *Heart of Darkness*," *Nineteenth-Century Fiction* 32, no. 3 (December 1977): 310.

43. V. Y. Mudimbe, *The Invention of Africa: Gnosis, Philosophy, and the Order of Knowledge* (Bloomington: Indiana University Press, 1988), 47–48.

44. For another take on the concept of vision in *Heart of Darkness* and the strategy of "excessive examination," see Rebecca L. Walkowitz, "Conrad's

Naturalness," in *Cosmopolitan Style: Modernism beyond the Nation* (New York: Columbia University Press, 2006).

45. Alex de Waal, *Famine Crimes: Politics and the Disaster Relief Industry in Africa* (Oxford: James Currey, 1997), xvi.

46. David Rieff, *A Bed for the Night: Humanitarianism in Crisis* (New York: Simon and Schuster, 2002), 67.

47. Barnett, *Empire of Humanity*, 37.

48. Liisa H. Malkki, *The Need to Help: The Domestic Arts of International Humanitarianism* (Durham, NC: Duke University Press, 2015), 53.

49. Malkki, 10.

50. Barbara Kingsolver, *The Poisonwood Bible* (New York: Perennial, 1998), 9, 10.

51. Heather D. Curtis, *Holy Humanitarians: American Evangelicals and Global Aid* (Cambridge, MA: Harvard University Press, 2018), 33.

52. Conrad criticism post-1975 (the year of Achebe's lecture that condemned Conrad as a "bloody racist") is also always written *after* Achebe. Nicolas Tredell describes criticism on *Heart of Darkness* in terms of "two epochal phases: before and after Achebe" (*Joseph Conrad: Heart of Darkness* [New York: Columbia University Press, 1998], 71).

53. Mudimbe, *Invention of Africa*, 47.

54. McClure, "Rhetoric of Restraint," 312.

55. Kurtz's transformation has often been described in terms of "going native," partly on the basis of Marlow's own description, but John McClure has shown that this "theory of reversion" is highly problematic, both for the blame it places on African cultures for violence and for what it fails to see in the text itself—Marlow's own attribution of blame wavers. See John A. McClure, *Kipling and Conrad: The Colonial Fiction* (Cambridge, MA: Harvard University Press, 1981), especially 131–36.

56. Philip Caputo, *Acts of Faith* (New York: Vintage, 2005), 261.

57. Tim Jeal is better known as a biographer than as a novelist, most notably for his biographies of Livingstone and Stanley. This investment in the history of nineteenth-century missions is evident in *For God and Glory* (also published as *The Missionary's Wife*), which reads very much as a historian's novel. Jeal looks more favorably on missionaries than do the other novelists I deal with, but he writes with the historical hindsight that necessarily brings scrutiny to their projects, no matter how noble one takes their intentions to have been.

58. Paul Theroux, *Girls at Play*, 223.

59. Theroux, 274, 275.

60. Chinua Achebe, *The Education of a British-Protected Child* (New York: Anchor, 2009), 79.

61. Rob Nixon, "Preparations for Travel: Naipaul's Conradian Atavism," in *London Calling: V. S. Naipaul, Postcolonial Mandarin* (Oxford: Oxford University Press, 1992), 90.

62. See also Inga Clendinnen's essay, which argues that the heart of darkness "trope has infiltrated so deeply into Western consciousness that the phrase 'heart

of darkness' resonates for people who have read no Conrad at all" (Clendinnen, "Preempting Postcolonial Critique: Europeans in the *Heart of Darkness*," *Common Knowledge* 13, no. 1 [2007]: 3).

63. Brantlinger, "Victorians and Africans," 196.

64. Chinua Achebe, *No Longer at Ease* (New York: Anchor, 1994), 45–46.

65. Rieff, *Bed for the Night*, 67.

66. De Waal, *Famine Crimes*, xvi.

67. Barnett, *Empire of Humanity*, 6.

68. David Kennedy, *The Dark Sides of Virtue: Reassessing International Humanitarianism* (Princeton, NJ: Princeton University Press, 2004), xviii.

69. Kennedy, xiv.

70. Barnett, *Empire of Humanity*, 239.

71. Ngũgĩ wa Thiong'o, *Moving the Centre: The Struggle for Cultural Freedoms* (Oxford: James Currey, 1993), 6.

72. Achebe, *Education*, 54.

Chapter 2: The Emancipated African

1. Michael Barnett, *Empire of Humanity: A History of Humanitarianism* (Ithaca, NY: Cornell University Press, 2011), 55.

2. Olakunle George, *Relocating Agency: Modernity and African Letters* (Albany: SUNY Press, 2003), 86.

3. David Attwell, *Rewriting Modernity: Studies in Black South African Literary History* (Athens: Ohio University Press, 2005), 9.

4. Attwell, 67.

5. Olakunle George, *African Literature and Social Change: Tribe, Nation, Race* (Bloomington: Indiana University Press, 2017), 46, 102.

6. For a related analysis of the development of black South African theater in the context of missions, see Bhekizizwe Peterson, *Monarchs, Missionaries, and African Intellectuals: African Theatre and the Unmaking of Colonial Marginality* (Johannesburg: Wits University Press, 2000).

7. Apollo Amoko, "Autobiography and *Bildungsroman* in African Literature," in *The Cambridge Companion to the African Novel*, ed. F. Abiola Irele (Cambridge: Cambridge University Press, 2009), 195.

8. This joke has often been attributed to Desmond Tutu and, before him, to Jomo Kenyatta, but it operates as a widely known and repeated adage.

9. This argument resonates with critiques of NGOs, which will be the subject of chapter 5. Many scholars claim that NGOs depoliticize political problems that would be better addressed through the state.

10. J. D. Y. Peel, *Religious Encounter and the Making of the Yoruba* (Bloomington: Indiana University Press, 2000), 6.

11. V. Y. Mudimbe, *The Invention of Africa: Gnosis, Philosophy, and the Order of Knowledge* (Bloomington: Indiana University Press, 1988), 47.

12. Mudimbe, 47.

13. Homi K. Bhabha, *The Location of Culture* (London: Routledge, 1994), 131.

14. Bhabha, 141.

15. Ogbu Kalu, "Protestant Christianity in Igboland," in *Christianity in West Africa: The Nigerian Story*, ed. Ogbu Kalu (Ibadan: Daystar, 1978), 315.

16. Lamin Sanneh quoted in Dana Robert, *Converting Colonialism: Visions and Realities in Mission History, 1706–1914* (Grand Rapids, MI: William B. Eerdmans, 2008), 3–4.

17. Olúfẹ́mi Táíwò, *How Colonialism Preempted Modernity in Africa* (Bloomington: Indiana University Press, 2010), 52.

18. Táíwò, 57.

19. I lay this debate out in more detail in Megan Cole Paustian, "'A Real Heaven on Their Own Earth': Religious Missions, African Writers, and the Anticolonial Imagination," *Research in African Literatures* 45, no. 2 (Summer 2014): 1–25.

20. J. F. Ade Ajayi and E. A. Ayandele, "Writing African Church History," in *The Church Crossing Frontiers: Essays on the Nature of Mission, in Honor of Bengt Sundkler*, ed. Peter Beyerhaus and Carl F. Hallencreutz (Stockholm: Almquist and Wiksells, 1969), 98.

21. Chinua Achebe, "The Novelist as Teacher," in *Hopes and Impediments: Selected Essays* (New York: Anchor, 1988), 105.

22. Chinua Achebe, *Things Fall Apart* (New York: Anchor, 1959), 74.

23. Ngũgĩ wa Thiong'o, *The River Between* (London: Heinemann, 1965), 55.

24. On female circumcision and the imperialism of Western feminist responses, see *African Women and Feminism: Reflecting on the Politics of Sisterhood*, ed. Oyèrónkẹ́ Oyêwùmi (Trenton, NJ: Africa World, 2003); and Wairimũ Ngarũiya Njambi, "Rescuing African Women and Girls from Female Genital Practices: A Benevolent and Civilizing Mission," in *Burden or Benefit? Imperial Benevolence and Its Legacies*, ed. Helen Gilbert and Chris Tiffin (Bloomington: Indiana University Press, 2008), 160–79.

25. Kwame Anthony Appiah, *Cosmopolitanism: Ethics in a World of Strangers* (New York: Norton, 2006), 111.

26. Bhabha, *Location of Culture*, 162.

27. Ngũgĩ wa Thiong'o, *Dreams in a Time of War: A Childhood Memoir* (New York: Pantheon, 2010), 113.

28. Alison Searle, "The Role of Missions in *Things Fall Apart* and *Nervous Conditions*," *Literature and Theology* 21, no. 1 (March 2007): 60.

29. Nelson Mandela, *Long Walk to Freedom* (New York: Little, Brown, 1994), 38.

30. Ngũgĩ wa Thiong'o, *In the House of the Interpreter* (New York: Anchor, 2012), 12–13.

31. In his study of the West African colonial intelligentsia, Philip S. Zachernuk aims to displace the tendency among critics to frame African encounters with Western culture in terms of a binary choice, conserve or convert, wherein conversion becomes a form of surrender to the supposed injunction of the mission, which

declares, in the words of Basil Davidson, "ABANDON AFRICA, ALL YE WHO ENTER HERE" (qtd. in Zachernuck, *Colonial Subjects: An African Intelligentsia and Atlantic Ideas* [Charlottesville: University Press of Virginia, 2000], 7). Gauri Viswanathan, too, has sought to extract conversion from the language of complicity and colonized consciousness, arguing that in many cases, conversion in colonial contexts was not a "knee-jerk reaction to failed political solutions, as mass conversions tend to be read" but a "form of political and cultural criticism" (Viswanathan, *Outside the Fold: Conversion, Modernity, and Belief* [Princeton, NJ: Princeton University Press, 1998], 213).

32. Chinua Achebe, *The Education of a British-Protected Child* (New York: Anchor, 2009), 37.

33. Julian Pettifer and Richard Bradley, *Missionaries* (London: BBC Books, 1990), 98–99.

34. John L. Comaroff and Jean Comaroff, *Of Revelation and Revolution*, vol. 2, *The Dialectics of Modernity on a South African Frontier* (Chicago: University of Chicago Press, 1997), 217.

35. Bruce Robbins, *Feeling Global: Internationalism in Distress* (New York: New York University Press, 2003), 4.

36. Robbins, 4, 75.

37. George, *Relocating*, x.

38. Simon Gikandi, "The Role of Colonial Institutions," in *Encyclopedia of African Literature*, ed. Simon Gikandi, s.v. "colonialism, neocolonialism, and postcolonialism" (London: Routledge, 2003), 172.

39. Missionary orthographies in Roman script were preceded in parts of Africa by ancient scripts — Egyptian hieroglyphics and Ge'ez — and later by the use of Arabic script for Hausa, Wolof, Somali, and centuries-old Swahili writing traditions. See Albert Gérard, *African Language Literatures: An Introduction to the Literary History of Sub-Saharan Africa* (Washington, DC: Three Continents, 1981).

40. Searle, "Role of Missions," 60.

41. The primary text for translation was the Bible, but second to that was *The Pilgrim's Progress*, which became a major presence in the Christian textual tradition within Africa. For more on the influence of *The Pilgrim's Progress* in African language translations, see Isabel Hofmeyr, "Dreams, Documents, and 'Fetishes': African Christian Interpretations of *The Pilgrim's Progress*," in "Signs, Texts, and Objects within African Christian History," special issue, *Journal of Religion in Africa* 32, no. 4 (November 2002): 440–56; and "Reading Debating/Debating Reading: The Case of the Lovedale Literary Society, or Why Mandela Quotes Shakespeare," in *Africa's Hidden Histories: Everyday Literacy and Making the Self*, ed. Karin Barber (Bloomington: Indiana University Press, 2006), 258–77. For more on language learning and translation, see Paul Laudau's essay "Language," in Norman Etherington's edited collection *Missions and Empire* (Oxford: Oxford University Press, 2005); and Lamin Sanneh's *Translating the Message: The Missionary Impact on Culture* (Maryknoll, NY: Orbis Books, 1989), as well as

"'They Stooped to Conquer': Vernacular Translation and the Socio-cultural Factor," *Research in African Literatures* 23, no. 1 (1992): 95–100. On education and literacy, see Sanneh's sixth chapter in *West African Christianity: The Religious Impact* (London: Hurst, 1983), Leon de Kock's *Civilising Barbarians: Missionary Narrative and African Textual Response in Nineteenth-Century South Africa* (Johannesburg: Witwatersrand University Press, 1996), and Andrew Porter's *Religion versus Empire? British Protestant Missionaries and Overseas Expansion, 1700–1914* (Manchester: Manchester University Press, 2004).

42. Sanneh, "'They Stooped to Conquer,'" 96.

43. Frantz Fanon, *Black Skin, White Masks*, trans. Charles Lam Markmann (New York: Grove, 1967), 38.

44. Sanneh, *Translating the Message*, 125.

45. Other indigenous language novelists in this position include Thomas Mofolo (Sesotho); Henry Masila Ndawo and A. C. Jordan (Xhosa); John Langalibalele Dube, R. R. R. Dhlomo, and C. L. S. Nyembezi (Zulu); Daniel Olorunfemi Fagunwa and Adekanmi Oyeldele (Yoruba); Pita Nwana (Igbo); and Stephen A. Mpashi (Bemba). See Gérard, *African Language Literatures*. A full account of the mission influence on African writing would have to consider the African language traditions that often preceded fiction in European languages. Many of the African language texts of the nineteenth and early twentieth centuries grappled with the relationship between local cultures and Christianity.

46. Simon Gikandi, *Maps of Englishness: Writing Identity in the Culture of Colonialism* (New York: Columbia University Press, 1996), xix; see also Ngũgĩ wa Thiong'o (Cambridge: Cambridge University Press, 2000), 21.

47. Jesse Chipenda, quoted in Lawrence W. Henderson, *Development and the Church in Angola: Jesse Chipenda the Trailblazer* (Nairobi: Acton, 2000), 45.

48. Henderson, 43.

49. I should note that in focusing on literary figures I am dealing with a subset of the colonized African population, a group of people who were at least curious about elements of what missions had to offer. Their level of engagement cannot be generalized and should not be extended to any kind of universal statement about missions and African people.

50. Olakunle George, "The 'Native' Missionary, the African Novel, and In-Between," *NOVEL: A Forum on Fiction* 36, no.1 (Autumn 2002): 18.

51. Gikandi, *Maps*, 34.

52. Gikandi, *Ngũgĩ*, 39.

53. Ngũgĩ, *Dreams*, 111. Gikandi describes the desire for education and the fear that it "marked an irreversible move away from the existing foundation of identity and community" as major themes of Ngũgĩ's works throughout his career (*Ngũgĩ*, 40).

54. Other noteworthy examples include Mongo Beti's *Mission to Kala* (1957), Noni Jabavu's *The Ochre People* (1963), and Tsitsi Dangarembga's *Nervous Conditions* (1988).

55. Porter, *Religion versus Empire?*, 317.

56. Ngũgĩ wa Thiong'o, *Moving the Centre: The Struggle for Cultural Freedoms* (Oxford: James Currey, 1993), 137, 139.

57. Ngũgĩ, 137.

58. Paulo Freire, *Pedagogy of the Oppressed*, trans. Myra Bergman Ramos (New York: Seabury, 1973), 15.

59. Freire, 15.

60. Freire, 61.

61. My focus is on anglophone literature by writers from British colonies, but as the work of Sarah Robbins and Ann Ellis Pullen suggests, these are relevant issues within the colonial context more broadly and would merit consideration in a comparative framework. The Portuguese colonialists in particular saw African literacy as a liability; in Angola, for example, "local Portuguese officials were highly suspicious of missionaries' efforts to learn the local language and to provide literacy skills (both reading *and* writing) to the students in mission schools" (Robbins and Pullen, *Nellie Arnott's Writings on Angola, 1905–1913: Missionary Narratives Linking Africa and America* [Anderson, SC: Parlor, 2011], xviii).

62. Noni Jabavu, *The Ochre People* (London: John Murray, 1963), 75.

63. This is related to what Dana Robert describes as a practice of "converting colonialism." She explains that those who converted to Christianity used the new faith to help navigate the strictures of colonial rule and to create alternative structures of governance. Along with missionaries, these Christians sought to "convert colonialism" by coopting aspects of it that seemed compatible with their goals while changing prejudicial elements to accommodate biblical values (Robert, *Converting Colonialism*, 5).

64. Gikandi, *Ngũgĩ*, 40.

65. For an example of this argument as it appears within Ngũgĩ's work, see J. F. K. Mugambi, ed., *Critiques of Christianity in African Literature* (Nairobi: East African Educational Publishers, 1992).

66. Achille Mbembe, *Critique of Black Reason*, trans. Laurent Dubois (Durham, NC: Duke University Press, 2017), 101.

67. Chinua Achebe, *Arrow of God* (New York: Anchor, 1969), 189, 13.

68. See Marshall Berman, *All That Is Solid Melts into Air: The Experience of Modernity* (New York: Penguin, 1982) on "making oneself at home in modernity" (5).

69. For an example, see Hofmeyr, "Reading." She points to an incongruous "proclivity for quoting Shakespeare" among the leadership of the African National Congress, arguing that "Shakespeare, in short, became a way of talking about politics" (259).

70. Ngũgĩ wa Thiong'o, *Weep Not Child* (London: Heinemann, 1987), 43. Jomo Kenyatta himself, the Black Moses of *Weep Not Child*, was interested in the ways Kenyans took ownership of Biblical interpretation, becoming authorities of the text, capable of contesting missionary readings on Biblical grounds. In *Facing Mount Kenya* (New York: Vintage, 1965), he describes the conflicts that arose when

missionaries condemned and attempted to outlaw local beliefs and practices without understanding the values and social functions which made them important.

71. Ngũgĩ wa Thiong'o, *A Grain of Wheat* (1967; rev. ed., London: Heinemann, 1986), 85.

72. Mbembe, *Critique*, 101.

73. I deal in depth with the problem of the universal human in chapter 3.

74. On colonial compliance and the "rise of the 'model kafir'" narrative and its subversion in nineteenth-century South African literary production, see Leon de Kock, *Civilising Barbarians*. For an exploration of "fault-lines in the family of man," see Catherine Hall, *Civilising Subjects: Metropole and Colony in the English Imagination 1830–1867* (Chicago: University of Chicago Press, 2002).

75. Albert Luthuli, *Let My People Go* (New York: McGraw-Hill, 1962), 85.

76. Mandela, *Long Walk*, 33.

77. Catherine Hall, *Civilising Subjects*, 105.

78. Ajayi and Ayandele, "Writing African Church History," 99.

79. Hall, *Civilising Subjects*, 102.

80. Barnett, *Empire of Humanity*, 67.

81. Gustav Sjablom, qtd in Barnett, *Empire of Humanity*, 69.

82. Hall, *Civilising Subjects*, 105.

83. Hall, 105.

84. Ngũgĩ wa Thiong'o, "Literature and Society: The Politics of the Canon!," in *Writers in Politics: A Re-engagement with Issues of Literature and Society*, rev. and enl. ed. (Oxford: James Currey, 1997), 20.

85. Ngũgĩ, 20–21, emphasis added.

86. Bhabha, *Location of Culture*, 144.

87. Ngũgĩ, *Moving the Centre*, 6.

88. David Scott, *Refashioning Futures: Criticism after Postcoloniality* (Princeton, NJ: Princeton University Press, 1999), 8.

89. Robert, *Converting Colonialism*, 2.

90. Mbembe, qtd. in Gayatri Spivak, "Religion, Politics, Theology: A Conversation with Achille Mbembe," *Boundary 2* 34, no. 2 (2007): 150.

91. William E. Connolly, *Capitalism and Christianity, American Style* (Durham, NC: Duke University Press, 2008). My thinking on this subject has also been influenced by John A. McClure, who offers another way of envisioning and articulating such an assemblage in *Partial Faiths: Postsecular Fiction in the Age of Pynchon and Morrison* (Athens: University of Georgia Press, 2007).

92. Ngũgĩ wa Thiong'o, "Church, Culture and Politics," in *Homecoming* (Brooklyn, NY: Lawrence Hill Books, 1972), 31.

93. Ngũgĩ, 34.

94. Gustavo Gutiérrez, *A Theology of Liberation*, trans. Sister Caridad Inda, John Eagleson, and Matthew J. O'Connell (Maryknoll, NY: Orbis, 1988), 12.

95. Ngũgĩ, "Literature and Society," 20.

Chapter 3: The Universal Human

1. Graham Greene, *A Burnt-Out Case* (New York: Viking, 1961), 16.
2. Ngũgĩ wa Thiong'o, *Wizard of the Crow* (New York: Anchor, 2006), 38–40.
3. Kofi Annan, "The Meaning of International Community," address to DPI/NGO Conference, 15 September 1999, 3 (emphasis added).
4. Alex de Waal, *Famine Crimes: Politics and the Disaster Relief Industry in Africa* (Oxford: James Currey, 1997), 66, 214.
5. Didier Fassin, "Humanitarianism as a Politics of Life," trans. Rachel Gomme, *Public Culture* 19, no. 3 (2007): 511.
6. Mahmood Mamdani, *Saviors and Survivors: Darfur, Politics, and the War on Terror* (New York: Doubleday, 2009), 12.
7. Kwasi Wiredu, *Cultural Universals and Particulars: An African Perspective* (Bloomington: Indiana University Press, 1996), 2.
8. See Samuel Moyn, *The Last Utopia: Human Rights in History* (Cambridge, MA: Belknap, 2010).
9. Jacqueline Rose, "On the Universality of Madness," *Critical Inquiry* 20, no. 3 (1994): 401.
10. In her essay "Rehearsals of Liberation: Contemporary Postcolonial Discourse and the New South Africa," *PMLA* 110, no. 1 (January 1995), Rosemary Jolly explains that although South Africa won independence from Britain in 1961, apartheid meant the "suspension of a postcolonial era for the majority of South Africans" (22). For the majority of the population, postcoloniality did not arrive until 1994. In *Citizen and Subject: Contemporary Africa and the Legacy of Late Colonialism* (Princeton, NJ: Princeton University Press, 1996), Mahmood Mamdani argues that apartheid was not exceptional within Africa but a form of indirect rule which fits into the same genealogy as the other colonies. As a suspended form of decolonization, the postapartheid does parallel the postcolonial in many ways that literature has captured. See also Annamaria Carusi, "Post, Post and Post: Or, Where Is South African Literature in All This?," *Ariel* 20, no. 4 (October 1989): 79–95.
11. Alex de Waal, "Democratizing the Aid Encounter in Africa," *International Affairs* 73, no.4 (1997): 638.
12. Head, *Question*, 158.
13. In *Bulletproof*, Jennifer Wenzel offers an extensive exploration of the cattle killing and the ways it has been taken up within contemporary writing. This includes a chapter on *The Heart of Redness*, its complex temporality, and what Wenzel calls its ethics of retrospection (Wenzel, *Bulletproof: Afterlives of Anticolonial Prophecy in South Africa and Beyond* [Chicago: University of Chicago Press, 2009]). Mda's use of history has also been a point of some contention. Andrew Offenburger ("Duplicity and Plagiarism in Zakes Mda's *The Heart of Redness*," *Research in African Literatures* 39, no. 3 [October 2008]: 164–99) accuses Mda of borrowing too extensively from his historical source to the point of plagiarism. See also Mda, "A Response to 'Duplicity and Plagiarism in Zakes Mda's The Heart of Redness' by Andrew Offenburger,"

Research in African Literatures 39, no. 3 (2008): 200–203. For a theorization of temporalities within the novel, see Benita Parry, "The Presence of the Past in Peripheral Modernities," in *Beyond the Black Atlantic: Relocating Modernization and Technology*, ed. Walter Goebel and Saskia Schaibo (London: Routledge, 2006), 13–28.

14. For a different approach to the problem of development in the novel, see Paul Jay, "The Cultural Politics of Development in Zakes Mda's *The Heart of Redness*," in *Global Matters: The Transnational Turn in Literary Studies* (Ithaca, NY: Cornell University Press, 2010), 137–53.

15. María Josefina Saldaña-Portillo, *The Revolutionary Imagination in the Americas in the Age of Development* (Durham, NC: Duke University Press, 2003), 6.

16. Saldaña-Portillo, 6.

17. Zakes Mda, *The Heart of Redness* (New York: Picador, 2000), 98–99. For example, when he returns to his hotel room and finds a snake coiled on his bed, he stops the staff from killing it. This echoes and rewrites scenes from Achebe's novels, which depict tensions around the sacred python, such as the moment in *Things Fall Apart* when the radical convert Enoch kills and eats a python. Locals in *The Heart of Redness* are surprised that Camagu doesn't act more like a convert. For a reading of Camagu as an "interstitial" intellectual, see Michael Titlestad and Mike Kissack, "'The Foot Does Not Sniff': Imagining the Post-anti-apartheid Intellectual," *Journal of Literary Studies* 19, no. 3–4 (December 2003): 255–56.

18. James Ferguson uses the term *place-in-the-world* "with 'place' understood as both a location in space and a rank in a system of social categories (as in the expression 'knowing your place')" (*Global Shadows: Africa in the Neoliberal World Order* [Durham, NC: Duke University Press, 2006], 6).

19. For related arguments about the scales (local to global) of assistance that have influenced my own analysis, see Tejumola Olaniyan, "The Paddle That Speaks English: Africa, NGOs, and the Archaeology of an Unease," *Research in African Literatures* 42, no. 2 (Summer 2011): 46–59, and Bruce Robbins, *Feeling Global: Internationalism in Distress* (New York: New York University Press, 2003). Both authors suggest that the distance between the agents and recipients of assistance is not as damning as it may seem, since it is a problem that affects assistance at large, which is always operating across different levels of power, even at the local scale.

20. On the false binary of ethics versus politics, see Michael Barnett, *Empire of Humanity: A History of Humanitarianism* (Ithaca, NY: Cornell University Press, 2011), 6.

21. This move is indeed characteristic of critical humanitarian fictions generally. Examples include *Heart of Darkness*, *The Poisonwood Bible*, and *Acts of Faith*, which reveal the third sector to be compromised by its entanglement with the interests of Western states. Achebe and Ngũgĩ show the negotiation of both colonial and anticolonial politics through the channel of the mission school. And in chapter 4, I will argue that Tsitsi Dangarembga's *Nervous Conditions* and Nuruddin Farah's *Gifts*

situate the suffering body and the benevolent gift within a network of sociopolitical relations that that humanitarian imagery tends to obscure.

22. Ernesto Laclau, "Universalism, Particularism and the Question of Identity," in *The Identity in Question*, ed. John Rajchman (New York: Routledge, 1995), 100–101, emphasis added.

23. Laclau, qtd. in Bruce Robbins, "Race, Gender, Class, Postcolonialism: Toward a New Humanistic Paradigm?," in *A Companion to Postcolonial Studies*, ed. Henry Schwarz and Sangeeta Ray (Malden, MA: Blackwell, 2000), 526.

24. Salvatore Puledda, *On Being Human: Interpretations of Humanism from the Renaissance to the Present*, trans. Andrew Hurley (San Diego, CA: Latitude, 1997), 19. For more on human unity, agency, and history, see Kate Soper, *Humanism and Anti-humanism: Problems of Modern European Thought* (London: Hutchinson, 1986).

25. Puledda, 9. On the bildungsroman narrative of human rights incorporation, see Joseph Slaughter, *Human Rights Inc.: The World Novel, Narrative Form, and International Law* (New York: Fordham University Press, 2007).

26. Frantz Fanon, *The Wretched of the Earth*, trans. Constance Farrington (New York: Grove, 1963), 311.

27. Aimé Césaire, *Discourse on Colonialism*, trans. Joan Pinkham (New York: Monthly Review, 1972), 37.

28. Césaire, 37. Wole Soyinka explains that "the Atlantic slave trade remains an inescapable critique of European humanism," one which came long before the Holocaust. He argues that insisting on the Holocaust as *the* moment of that critique—and Césaire, to be clear, is not making that claim—is "proof that the European mind has yet to come into full cognition of the African world as an equal sector of universal humanity" (Wole Soyinka, *The Burden of Memory, the Muse of Forgiveness* [New York: Oxford University Press, 1999], 38).

29. That is not to say that European philosophical traditions, including humanism, were entirely defunct. These thinkers are more precise and more subtle in their response. Césaire, although he has sometimes been painted as an advocate of a pre-European past, insists that this is not his claim; rather, "it was our misfortune to encounter that particular Europe" (Césaire, *Discourse on Colonialism*, 45).

30. Césaire, 73.

31. Fanon, *Wretched*, 246. On the revolutionary discourse of the New Man and its coincidence with Western development discourse in the Latin American context, see Saldaña-Portillo, *Revolutionary Imagination*.

32. Fanon, *Wretched*, 106. In *Black Skin, White Masks*, too, a text all about the malignant division of humanity by race, Fanon ends on the note of humanism: "man is a yes. . . . Yes to life. Yes to love. Yes to generosity. . . . No to the butchery of what is most human in man: freedom" (*Black Skin, White Masks*, trans. Charles Lam Markmann [New York: Grove, 1967], 222).

33. Césaire, *Discourse on Colonialism*, 37.

34. Robert Young, *White Mythologies: Writing History and the West* (London: Routledge, 1990), 124–25. Major theorists of this tradition of dethroning humanism's

sovereign subject include Heidegger, Althusser, Barthes, Foucault, and Derrida. For a mapping of the history of the humanism debate, see Puledda, *On Being Human*. See also James Clifford, *The Predicament of Culture: Twentieth-Century Ethnography, Literature, and Art* (Cambridge, MA: Harvard University Press, 1988), chap. 4.

35. That genealogy is the subject of some debate. Simon Gikandi explores the relationship among anticolonialism, postcolonialism, and poststructuralism in detail in "Poststructuralism and Postcolonial Discourse," marking a fundamental break in which postcolonial discourse aligns itself with poststructuralism over and against anticolonial thought. He challenges Robert Young's claim that antihumanism, the project of dismantling the very category of Man, developed from anticolonialists' politicization of the universal "Man," despite their attachment to new forms of humanism. Gikandi, "Poststructuralism and Postcolonial Discourse," in *The Cambridge Companion to Postcolonial Literary Studies*, ed. Neil Lazarus (Cambridge: Cambridge University Press, 2004), 97–104.

36. Neil Lazarus, *Nationalism and Cultural Practice in the Postcolonial World* (Cambridge: Cambridge University Press, 1999), 143.

37. Edward Said, *Orientalism* (New York: Vintage, 1994), xxiii.

38. Gayatri Spivak, qtd. in Robbins, "Race," 566.

39. Kwame Anthony Appiah, *In My Father's House* (Oxford: Oxford University Press, 1992), 155.

40. Robbins, "Race," 558.

41. Lynn Festa, "Humanity without Feathers," *Humanity: An International Journal of Human Rights, Humanitarianism, and Development* 1, no. 1 (Fall 2010): 13.

42. Slaughter, *Human Rights, Inc.*, 149, 148.

43. See Shivji's *The Concept of Human Rights in Africa* (London: Codesria, 1989) for a view of the tensions around applying Western- generated human rights discourse within the African context.

44. Robbins, *Feeling Global*, 75.

45. Gayatri Chakravorty Spivak, *A Critique of Postcolonial Reason* (Cambridge, MA: Harvard University Press, 1999), 310.

46. Chinua Achebe, "The Truth of Fiction," in *Hopes and Impediments: Selected Essays* (New York: Anchor, 1988), 145.

47. Sonali Perera, *No Country: Working-Class Writing in the Age of Globalization* (New York: Columbia University Press, 2014), 145. See also Desiree Lewis, *Living on a Horizon: Bessie Head and the Politics of Imagining* (Trenton, NJ: Africa World, 2007), 9.

48. Parliament of South Africa, *Population Registration Act*, Act No. 30 of 1950, https://www.sahistory.org.za/sites/default/files/DC/leg19500707.028.020.030 /leg19500707.028.020.030.pdf.

49. Mikhail Bakhtin, *The Dialogic Imagination*, ed. Michael Holquist, trans. Caryl Emerson and Michael Holquist (Austin: University of Texas Press, 1981), 336.

50. On Head's transnationalism within Southern Africa, see Rob Nixon, "Border Country: Bessie Head's Frontline States," *Social Text* 36 (Autumn 1993): 106–37.

51. Appiah, *In My Father's House*, 155.

52. Alex de Waal uses this phrase in *Famine Crimes*, 66. This concept draws on the terminology of "actually existing socialism," which distinguishes the current reality from an ideal form. Speaking of "actually existing humanitarianism" enables defenders of humanitarianism to confront its limitations without rejecting the potential of the idea behind it. See de Waal's introduction to *Famine Crimes* and David Rieff, *A Bed for the Night: Humanitarianism in Crisis* (New York: Simon and Schuster, 2002).

53. This is a common theme within both literary and nonfictional critiques. See, for example, Michael Maren, *The Road to Hell: The Ravaging Effects of Foreign Aid and International Charity* (New York: Free Press, 1997), which combines memoir with political critique.

54. Brauman, qtd. in Festa, "Humanity without Feathers," 13.

55. Spivak discusses the problem of "ignorant goodwill" in *A Critique of Postcolonial Reason*, 416.

56. James Phelan, *Experiencing Fiction: Judgments, Progressions, and the Rhetorical Theory of Narrative* (Columbus: Ohio State University Press, 2007), 10 (italicized in original).

57. Arturo Escobar, *Encountering Development: The Making and Unmaking of the Third World* (Princeton, NJ: Princeton University Press, 1995), 44.

58. Spivak, *Critique*, 384.

59. Spivak, 199.

60. Gayatri Chakravorty Spivak, "Can the Subaltern Speak?," in *Marxism and the Interpretation of Culture*, ed. Cary Nelson and Lawrence Grossberg (Urbana: University of Illinois Press, 1988), 295.

61. Spivak, *Critique*, 383.

62. Said, *Orientalism*, 227.

63. Bessie Head, *A Woman Alone: Autobiographical Writings*, ed. Craig MacKenzie (London: Heinemann, 1990), 299.

64. On the flooding of various international "experts" into the Third World, see Escobar, *Encountering Development*, chap. 2.

65. For a fuller exploration of "the impulse to reopen relations with the religious," see John A. McClure, *Partial Faiths: Postsecular Fiction in the Age of Pynchon and Morrison* (Athens: University of Georgia Press, 2007). He explains that this impulse returns "as it always has, when worldly life becomes intolerable. And it returns with a specific, historically supercharged force, as secular modernity's promises of peace, prosperity, and progress fail to materialize and as reason itself begins to undermine secular rationalism's claims to exclusive authority on matters of truth" (10).

66. Achille Mbembe explains that reason has been an especially prickly concept in defining African humanity. The universal human was defined by a capacity to reason, but Africans were "supposed not to contain any sort of consciousness and to have none of the characteristics of reason or beauty. . . . Because of this radical difference, it was deemed legitimate to exclude them, both de facto and

de jure, from the sphere of full and complete human citizenship: they had nothing to contribute to the work of the universal" ("African Modes" 245). The not-yet-sufficiently human could become human only through the erasure of difference.

67. In *Living on a Horizon: Bessie Head and the Politics of Imagining*, Desiree Lewis centralizes the issue of spirituality in Head's work which has otherwise received little critical attention. She argues that "spirituality shapes her distinctive notions of humanism and explorations of subjectivity and consciousness. Head consequently invests spirituality with a powerful critical force" (11). Head's personal exploration of Eastern thought is fleshed out in Gillian Stead Eilersen's biography, *Bessie Head: Thunder behind Her Ears—Her Life and Writings* (Johannesburg: Witwatersrand University Press, 1995).

68. Head, *Woman Alone*, 96.

69. McClure, *Partial Faiths*, 6.

70. Bessie Head, *When Rain Clouds Gather* (Evanston, IL: McDougal Littell, 1968), 214.

71. In an essay entitled "God and the Underdog," Head describes her own encounter with the British volunteer on whom Gilbert's character, at least in this scene, is based. He is "deeply moved by a vision of God through an old Batswana man" (*Woman Alone*, 45–46).

72. Kurtz in *Heart of Darkness* is a prime example of that version of man's transcendence. Through this critique, Head offers another perspective on the mission "heroes" I addressed in chapter 1.

73. Michael Hardt and Antonio Negri, *Empire* (Cambridge, MA: Harvard University Press, 2000), 91 (italicized in original).

74. Ngũgĩ's 2006 novel, *Wizard of the Crow*, which I analyze in chapter 5, contains noteworthy examples, including a project to "raise a building to the very gates of heaven so that the Ruler could call on God daily?" (16).

75. Tejumola Olaniyan, "'Living in the Interregnum': Fela Anikulapo-Kuti and the Postcolonial Incredible," in *Arrest the Music! Fela and His Rebel Art and Politics* (Bloomington: Indiana University Press, 2004), 2.

76. Head, *Woman Alone*, 99.

77. Ngũgĩ wa Thiong'o, "Literature and Society: The Politics of the Canon!," in *Writers in Politics: A Re-engagement with Issues of Literature and Society*, rev. and enl. ed. (Oxford: James Currey, 1997), 21.

78. For an exploration of magical realism in the works of Zakes Mda, situated within a broader discussion of its application in postcolonial literature, see Derek Alan Barker, "Escaping the Tyranny of Magic Realism? A Discussion of the Term in Relation to the Novels of Zakes Mda," *Postcolonial Text* 4, no. 2 (2008): 1–20. David Attwell analyzes Mda's work in order to understand what he sees as "the experimental turn" in contemporary South African fiction. See Attwell, *Rewriting Modernity: Studies in Black South African Literary History* (Athens: Ohio University Press, 2005), chap. 6.

Chapter 4: The Benevolent Gift

1. Mahmood Mamdani, *Citizen and Subject: Contemporary Africa and the Legacy of Late Colonialism* (Princeton, NJ: Princeton University Press, 1996).

2. Frantz Fanon, *The Wretched of the Earth*, trans. Constance Farrington (New York: Grove, 1963), 148.

3. Mwangi wa Gĩthĩĩnji, *Ten Millionaires and Ten Million Beggars: A Study of Income Distribution and Development in Kenya* (London: Routledge, 2019).

4. Norman Rush, *Whites* (New York: Vintage, 1984), 19.

5. David Rieff, *A Bed for the Night: Humanitarianism in Crisis* (New York: Simon and Schuster, 2002), 64–65.

6. Michael Barnett, *Empire of Humanity: A History of Humanitarianism* (Ithaca, NY: Cornell University Press, 2011), 161-170.

7. Philip Caputo, "Putting the Sword to the Pen," *South Central Review* 34, no. 2 (Summer 2017): 18.

8. Erica Bornstein, *Disquieting Gifts: Humanitarianism in New Delhi* (Stanford, CA: Stanford University Press, 2012), 15.

9. "UNICEF USA: Save a Child for Only 50 Cents a Day," *YouTube*, performed by Alyssa Milano, uploaded by UNICEF, 4 September 2013.

10. Peter Unger, *Living High and Letting Die: Our Illusion of Innocence* (New York: Oxford University Press, 1996), 7.

11. Peter Singer, "Famine, Affluence, and Morality," *Philosophy and Public Affairs* 1, no. 3 (Spring 1972): 235.

12. Alex de Waal, *Famine Crimes: Politics and the Disaster Relief Industry in Africa* (Oxford: James Currey, 1997), 66. For explanation of the term "actually existing humanitarianism," see chapter 3, note 52.

13. Kwame Anthony Appiah, *Cosmopolitanism: Ethics in a World of Strangers* (New York: Norton, 2006), 172.

14. Appiah, 171.

15. Rieff, *Bed for the Night*, 28.

16. Rieff, epigraph.

17. De Waal, *Famine Crimes*, xvi.

18. Alex de Waal, "Democratizing the Aid Encounter in Africa," *International Affairs* 73, no.4 (1997): 639.

19. Fiona Terry, *Condemned to Repeat? The Paradox of Humanitarian Action* (Ithaca, NY: Cornell University Press, 2002), 224.

20. Terry, 216–17.

21. Chris Tiffin and Helen Gilbert, eds., *Burden or Benefit? Imperial Benevolence and its Legacies* (Bloomington: Indiana University Press, 2008), 4.

22. For Derrida, the real gift cannot even *exist*. A true gift would have to incur no sense of debt or obligation, which, he argues, is impossible. To even recognize "the gift *as* a gift" is to "annul" it: "The simple identification of the gift seems to destroy it" (Jacques Derrida, *Given Time: I. Counterfeit Money*, trans. Peggy Kamuf [Chicago: University of Chicago Press, 1992], 14).

23. Marcel Mauss, *The Gift: The Form and Reason for Exchange in Archaic Societies*, trans. W. D. Halls (London: Routledge, 1990), 4.

24. Mauss, 83.

25. Didier Fassin, *Humanitarian Reason: A Moral History of the Present* (Berkeley: University of California Press, 2012), 253.

26. Fassin, 253, 233.

27. Barnett, *Empire of Humanity*, 35.

28. Abiola Irele, "Narrative, History, and the African Imagination," *Narrative* 1, no. 2 (May 1993): 161–62.

29. Joseph Slaughter, *Human Rights, Inc.: The World Novel, Narrative Form, and International Law* (New York: Fordham University Press, 2007), 269.

30. Tstitsi Dangarembga, *Nervous Conditions* (New York: Seal, 2004), 87, 93.

31. Slaughter, *Human Rights*, 230.

32. The title refers to Jean-Paul Sartre's preface to Frantz Fanon's *The Wretched of the Earth*. Dangarembga's epigraph reads, "The condition of the native is a nervous condition." For several perspectives on alienation and the novel's relation to Fanon, see Charles Sugnet, "*Nervous Conditions*: Dangarembga's Feminist Revision of Fanon," in *The Politics of (M)Othering: Womanhood, Identity, and Resistance in African Literature*, ed. Obioma Nnaemeka (London: Routledge, 1997), 33–49; and Ann Elizabeth Willey and Jeanette Treiber, eds., *Negotiating the Postcolonial: Emerging Perspectives on Tsitsi Dangarembga* (Trenton, NJ: Africa World, 2002), especially the essays by Zwicker, Andrade, Willey, Geller, Wixson, and Basu.

33. Binyavanga Wainaina, "How to Write about Africa," *Granta* 92 (Winter 2005): n.p.

34. For an extended examination of food and hunger in the novel, see Hershini Bhana, "The Political Economy of Food: Hunger in Tsitsi Dangarembga's *Nervous Conditions*," *Proteus* 17, no. 1 (2000): 18–24; Heidi Creamer, "An Apple for the Teacher? Femininity, Coloniality, and Food in *Nervous Conditions*," *Kunapipi* 16, no. 1 (1994): 349–60; and Derek Wright, "'More Than Just a Plateful of Food': Regurgitating Colonialism in Tsitsi Dangarembga's *Nervous Conditions*," *Commonwealth* 17, no. 2 (1995): 8–18. On the gendered dimensions of growing, preparing, serving, and eating food, see Kelli Donovan Wixson's essay in Willey and Treiber, *Negotiating the Postcolonial*.

35. Dangarembga published *The Book of Not* in 2006 (Banbury, UK: Ayebia Clarke) and *This Mournable Body* (Minneapolis, MN: Graywolf) in 2018.

36. Philip Caputo, *Acts of Faith* (New York: Vintage, 2005), 310.

37. Barnett, *Empire of Humanity*, 11.

38. Derek Wright, *The Novels of Nuruddin Farah* (Bayreuth: Eckhard Breitinger, 1994), 133.

39. James Ferguson, *Global Shadows: Africa in the Neoliberal World Order* (Durham, NC: Duke University Press, 2006), 20.

40. This is related to the basic needs approach to development which was influential in the 1980s. For an introduction to this approach, see Stewart, *Planning to Meet Basic Needs* (London: Macmillan, 1985); and Paul Streeten et al., *First*

Things First: Meeting Basic Human Needs in the Developing Countries (Oxford University Press, 1981).

41. I am reminded of Bruce Robbins's caution about academic critique of modernity and progress:

> Those who urgently need to "change their lives" do not speak lightly of progress, even if they rightly distrust the universalized, inevitabilist gradualism that has been its frequent ideological form. While it presents itself as metropolitan self-critique, the unreflective scorn for modernity among Western intellectuals actually functions as metropolitan self-aggrandizement. Like a certain left-wing antiprofessionalism, aimed obliquely at the new place women and people of color have made for themselves in the academy, this apparent self-critique denigrates in the metropolis precisely that which is now being desired and demanded by intellectuals on the periphery. This is kicking away the ladder one has climbed oneself; it ensures that the necessarily higher ground from which the critique emanates remains in metropolitan hands and defines the metropolis's continuing superiority. (*Feeling Global*, 112)

42. Dambisa Moyo makes the first kind of argument in *Dead Aid: Why Aid Is Not Working and How There Is a Better Way for Africa* (New York: Farrar, Straus, Giroux, 2009), although she does so from a neoliberal perspective and not the socialist view from which this argument originated (see 42). Alex de Waal offers an alternative argument, claiming that to change system which produces poverty, it is necessary that citizens be able to hold their governments accountable for providing the needs of their populace. That of course demands some measure of democracy. David Scott has offered related insights about the deferral of individual rights. See *Refashioning Futures: Criticism after Postcoloniality* (Princeton, NJ: Princeton University Press, 1999), 149–50.

43. Mauss, *Gift*, 83.

44. Homi K. Bhabha, *The Location of Culture* (London: Routledge, 1994), 165.

45. Divya Dwivedi, Henrik Skov Nielsen, and Richard Walsh, "Introduction," in *Narratology and Ideology: Negotiating Context, Form, and Theory in Postcolonial Narratives* (Columbus: Ohio State University Press, 2018), 19.

46. Mieke Bal, "In the Absence of Post-," in Dwivedi et al., *Narratology and Ideology*, 248, 249.

47. Nuruddin Farah, *Gifts* (New York: Arcade, 1993), 22.

48. In his exploration of multitextuality and the notion of the gift in Farah's novel, Francis Ngaboh-Smart points to the centrality of an external anthropological text, Marcel Mauss's *The Gift*. He argues that, through the acknowledgment of Mauss at the front of the book, Farah "extends the universe of reference for his novel" (Ngaboh-Smart, "Dimensions of Giving in Nuruddin Farah's *Gifts*," *Research in African Literatures* 27, no. 4 [1996]: 145). Tim Woods, "Giving and Receiving: Nuruddin Farah's *Gifts*, or, The Postcolonial Logic of Third World Aid," *Journal of Commonwealth Literature* 38, no. 1 (2003): 91–112, also addresses Farah's use of

The Gift, linking it to implications for foreign aid. Kirsten Holt Petersen, "Charity Wounds Him Who Receives: Nuruddin Farah's *Gifts*," in *Emerging Perspectives on Nuruddin Farah*, ed. Derek Wright (Trenton, NJ: Africa World, 2002), 591–610, situates the novel in relation to Derrida's model of the pure gift.

49. For another literary example of undoing the standard roles of Western giver and African receiver, see Peace Corps writer Marla Kay Houghteling's short story, "Ma Kamanda's Latrine," in *Living on the Edge: Fiction by Peace Corps Writers*, edited by John Coyne (Willimantic, CT: Curbstone, 1999). When Ma Kamanda's rural Sierra Leonean town welcomes a Peace Corps teacher, she has a latrine built for the visitor and writes in the wet cement, "A GIFT TO THE U.S. GOVERNMENT FROM THE PEOPLE OF PUNUMBA" (256), a biting ironization of the power dynamics and representational optics of aid.

50. Joseph Conrad, *Heart of Darkness* (New York: Modern Library, 1999), 20.

51. Conrad, 20, emphasis added.

52. See James Ferguson, *Give a Man a Fish* (Durham, NC: Duke University Press, 2015), for another angle on the myth of self-reliance and the almost ubiquitous critique of "handouts."

53. Olakunle George, *Relocating Agency: Modernity and African Letters* (Albany: SUNY Press, 2003), 2.

54. The texts I analyze in chapter 2 pivot on this history of destabilization and loss. Through tracing the arc between Chinua Achebe's early novels, *Things Fall Apart* and *No Longer at Ease*, we see the traditional wealth of a family degenerate into poverty and hunger. Ngũgĩ's *Weep Not Child* and *The River Between* document the loss of lands and the aspiration for their recovery, and his memoir reveals this to be the experience of his own family as well. His father's land, and thus his wealth, is signed away under the new colonial legal system.

55. Ngũgĩ wa Thiong'o, *Something Torn and New* (New York: BasicCivitas Books, 2009), 127–28. For a reading of this passage within the wider context of the book and its relation to current aid debates, see Cilas Kemedjio, "Of Aid and the African Renaissance," a contribution to the *Critical Investigations into Humanitarianism in Africa* blog, 14 April 2010.

56. Caputo, "Putting the Sword to the Pen," 24.

57. Arundhati Roy would likely describe this as the depoliticization of resistance: "NGOs," she argues, "employ local people who could be activists in resistance movements, but instead feel they are doing some immediate creative good while earning a living" ("Help That Hinders," *Le Monde Diplomatique*, November 2004). Although the United Nations is an intergovernmental organization and not an NGO, it draws the same type of worker.

58. John A. McClure, *Partial Faiths: Postsecular Fiction in the Age of Pynchon and Morrison* (Athens: University of Georgia Press, 2007), 186.

59. Dangarembga, *Nervous Conditions*, 103.

60. Philip Caputo, *Horn of Africa* (New York: Dell, 1980), 66.

61. For a nonfictional example, take Greg Mortenson, founder of the Central

Asia Institute and author of the wildly successful *Three Cups of Tea*. In 2011, he was asked by the watchdog group, American Institute of Philanthropy, to step down from his position at the head of the Central Asia Institute based on reports of false representation of the schools he had built and the use of donor funds for his own personal enrichment. In *Three Cups of Deceit* (New York: Anchor Books, 2014), John Krakauer, adventure writer and disillusioned former supporter of Mortenson's organization, quotes the former treasurer of its board of directors explaining that "Greg regards CAI as his personal ATM" (7). It is an instance that reveals this literature's basis in reality.

62. Edward Said, *Orientalism*, 226. This is in the context of an analysis of Rudyard Kipling with reference to the novel *Kim* and the poem "A Song of the White Men."

63. Said, *Orientalism*, 227.

64. Teju Cole, "The White-Savior Industrial Complex," *The Atlantic*, 21 March 2012.

65. Terry, *Condemned to Repeat?*, 217.

66. Terry, 224.

67. Michel Foucault, *Ethics: Subjectivity and Truth*, ed. Paul Rabinow (New York: New Press, 1997), 221; see "Self Writing" and "Technologies of the Self."

68. David Kennedy, *The Dark Sides of Virtue: Reassessing International Humanitarianism* (Princeton, NJ: Princeton University Press, 2004), xiv.

69. Ngũgĩ, *Something Torn*, 127.

70. Bruce Robbins, *The Beneficiary* (Durham, NC: Duke University Press, 2017), 31.

71. Robbins, 5.

72. Paul Gilroy, *The Black Atlantic: Modernity and Double Consciousness* (London: Verso, 1993), 4.

Chapter 5: The Nongovernmental Organization

1. NoViolet Bulawayo, *We Need New Names* (New York: Little, Brown, 2013), 64.

2. Alex de Waal opens his study of famine and humanitarianism by pointing out that it is actually "inappropriate to begin an account of famine by examining humanitarian action [when] relief is generally merely a footnote to the story of how people survive famine" (*Famine Crimes: Politics and the Disaster Relief Industry in Africa* [Oxford: James Currey, 1997], 1). The novels I study in this chapter essentially give international humanitarians their proper place as a footnote.

3. On the principles of independence and neutrality, first articulated by the International Committee of the Red Cross, see introductions by Fiona Terry in *Condemned to Repeat? The Paradox of Humanitarian Action* (Ithaca, NY: Cornell University Press, 2002) and Michael Barnett in *Empire of Humanity: A History of Humanitarianism* (Ithaca, NY: Cornell University Press, 2011).

4. On the relationship between journalists and relief organizations, see de Waal, *Famine Crimes*, 82–85.

5. Chinua Achebe, *The Education of a British-Protected Child* (New York: Anchor, 2009), 79.

6. James Ferguson, *Global Shadows: Africa in the Neoliberal World Order* (Durham, NC: Duke University Press, 2006), 2.

7. The term "aid-centricity" comes from Fiona Terry, *Condemned to Repeat?*, 5.

8. Julie Fisher, *Nongovernments: NGOs and the Political Development of the Third World* (West Hartford, CT: Kumarian, 1998), 47.

9. Stephen N. Ndegwa, *The Two Faces of Civil Society: NGOs and Politics in Africa* (West Hartford, CT: Kumarian, 1996), 21.

10. Nicola Banks, David Hulme, and Michael Edwards, "NGOs, States, and Donors Revisited: Still Too Close for Comfort?," *World Development* 66 (2015): 710.

11. Cornelia Beyer, "Non-governmental Organizations as Motors of Change," *Government and Opposition* 32, no. 4 (September 2007): 521.

12. See also Jonathan J. Makuwira, *Non-governmental Development Organizations and the Poverty Reduction Agenda: The Moral Crusaders* (London: Routledge, 2014); George Kaloudis, "Non-governmental Organizations: Mostly a Force for Good," *International Journal on World Peace* 34, no. 1 (March 2017): 81–112; and Jennifer N. Brass et al., "NGOs and International Development: A Review of Thirty-Five Years of Scholarship," *World Development* 112 (2018): 136–49.

13. Ian Smillie, *The Alms Bazaar: Altruism under Fire — Non-profit Organizations and International Development* (London: Intermediate Technology, 1995), 2.

14. Smillie, 25.

15. Firoze Manji and Carl O'Coill, "The Missionary Position: NGOs and Development in Africa," *International Affairs* 78, no. 3 (2002): 575–76.

16. Fisher, *Nongovernments*, 2.

17. Barnett, *Empire of Humanity*, 6. For more on NGOs' identity as "alternative," see Anthony J. Bebbington, Samuel Hickey, and Diana C. Mitlin, eds., *Can NGOs Make a Difference? The Challenge of Development Alternatives* (London: Zed, 2008), 3–5, 31.

18. Didier Fassin, *Humanitarian Reason: A Moral History of the Present*, trans. Rachel Gomme (Berkeley: University of California Press, 2012), 1.

19. Barnett, *Empire of Humanity*, 2.

20. Barnett, 32.

21. Fassin, *Humanitarian Reason*, 2.

22. Beyer, "Non-governmental Organizations," 533.

23. Issa G. Shivji, *Silences in NGO Discourse: The Role and Future of NGOs in Africa* (Nairobi: Fahamu, 2007), 3.

24. Tejumola Olaniyan, "Postmodernity, Postcoloniality, African Studies," in *African Literature: An Anthology of Criticism and Theory*, ed. Tejumola Olaniyan and Ato Quayson (Malden, MA: Blackwell, 2007), 640.

25. For a critique of these kinds of critiques, see Hugo Slim's *Humanitarian Ethics: A Guide to the Morality of Aid in War and Disaster* (New York: Oxford

University Press, 2015), 183–230, in which he challenges arguments about humanitarianism's power and complicity.

26. African governments' responses to NGOs are wide ranging and, according to Julie Fisher, include repressing, ignoring, coopting, taking advantage of, passively accepting, and cooperating (*Nongovernments*, 40–43).

27. Ndegwa, *Two Faces*, 22.

28. Beyer, "Non-governmental Organizations," 533.

29. Aziz Choudry and Dip Kapoor, *NGOization: Complicity, Contradictions and Prospects* (London: Zed, 2013), 6.

30. For more, see Manji and O'Coill, "Missionary Position," as well as Shivji, *Silences in NGO Discourse*.

31. Kaloudis, "Non-governmental Organizations," 107.

32. Banks, Hulme, and Edwards, "NGOs, States, and Donors," 709; Makuwira, *Non-governmental Development Organizations*, 86–87.

33. Banks, Hulme, and Edwards, "NGOs, States, and Donors," 710.

34. Lina Suleiman, "The NGOs and the Grand Illusions of Development and Democracy," *Voluntas* 24 (2013): 257.

35. Choudry and Kapoor, *NGOization*, 14, 16.

36. Sarah Michael argues that large NGOs based in the Global North overpower small local NGOs and in so doing, undermine development in Africa. See *Undermining Development: The Absence of Power among Local NGOs in Africa* (Bloomington: Indiana University Press, 2004).

37. De Waal, *Famine Crimes*, 217.

38. De Waal, 214.

39. Chinua Achebe, *There Was a Country* (New York: Penguin, 2012), qtd. 250.

40. Achebe, 169.

41. Barnett, *Empire of Humanity*, 134.

42. Kevin O'Sullivan, "Biafra's Legacy: NGO Humanitarianism and the Nigerian Civil War," in *Learning from the Past to Shape the Future: Lessons from the History of Humanitarian Action in Africa*, ed. Christina Bennett, Matthew Foley, and Hanna B. Krebs (London: Overseas Development Institute, October 2016), 5.

43. O'Sullivan, 9.

44. Mahmood Mamdani, *Saviors and Survivors: Darfur, Politics, and the War on Terror* (New York: Doubleday, 2009), 21.

45. O'Sullivan, "Biafra's Legacy," 9.

46. Numerous studies feature Biafra as a watershed in NGO history. Following the Biafran War, some Red Cross doctors broke away to form Médecins Sans Frontières (in English, Doctors Without Borders) in protest of the ICRC's policy of neutrality and silence in the face of human rights violations.

47. John Marx, "Fiction and State Crisis," *NOVEL: A Forum on Fiction* 42, no. 3 (2009): 526.

48. Marx, 529.

49. Emmanuel Mzomera Ngwira, "'He Writes about the World That Remained

Silent': Witnessing Authorship in Chimamanda Ngozi Adichie's *Half of a Yellow Sun*," *English Studies in Africa* 55, no. 2 (2012): 47, 48.

50. Ngwira, 44.

51. Chimamanda Ngozi Adichie, *Half of a Yellow Sun* (London: Harper, 2006), 304.

52. Terry, *Condemned to Repeat?*, 42. See Terry (42–47) on the legitimacy that humanitarian discourse and action can bring to political movements and leaders. See also Barnett on turning "sympathy into political capital" (*Empire of Humanity*, 134).

53. Karen Halttunen, "Humanitarianism and the Pornography of Pain in Anglo-American Culture," *American Historical Review* 100, no. 2 (April 1995): 304.

54. Barnett, *Empire of Humanity*, 34.

55. Mamdani, *Saviors and Survivors*, 56.

56. Mamdani, 57.

57. O'Sullivan, "Biafra's Legacy," 11.

58. Ian Smillie explains that the humanitarian framework prevented other nations from viewing Biafra in political terms: "While the rapid escalation of relief activities helped Biafra to survive the late summer and early autumn of 1968, it essentially transformed a potential country into little more than an object of pity. Interpreted largely through the eyes of relief agencies, Biafra became a humanitarian problem rather than a political problem, excusing the UN and virtually every Western government from direct involvement. . . . The emphasis on Biafra's suffering, used by the relief agencies for fundraising purposes, perhaps damaged its chances for recognition and for the international political support that might really have saved it" (*Alms Bazaar*, 105–6).

59. Kwame Anthony Appiah, *Cosmopolitanism: Ethics in a World of Strangers* (New York: Norton, 2006), 170.

60. Teju Cole, "The White-Savior Industrial Complex," *The Atlantic*, 21 March 2012, n.p.

61. Ngwira, "Witnessing Authorship," 51.

62. O'Sullivan, "Biafra's Legacy," 9.

63. Translation by Uchechi Okereke-Beshel.

64. Barnett, *Empire of Humanity*, 34.

65. Alex Woloch, *The One vs. the Many: Minor Characters and the Space of the Protagonist in the Novel* (Princeton, NJ: Princeton University Press, 2003), 15, 12.

66. Woloch, 13.

67. Woloch, 103.

68. Nicholas Kristof, "Westerners on White Horses," *New York Times*, 14 July 2010, n.p.

69. For example, Marie-Luce Desgrandchamps explains that with pictures of "malnourished children splashed across the Western media in July 1968, pressure mounted on the ICRC to find solutions and be more effective." Desgrandchamps, "'Organising the Unpredictable': The Nigeria-Biafra War and Its Impact on the ICRC," *International Review of the Red Cross* 94, no. 888 (Winter 2012): 1417.

70. Veronica Booth, qtd. in O'Sullivan, "Biafra's Legacy," 11.

71. Liisa H. Malkki, *The Need to Help: The Domestic Arts of International Humanitarianism* (Durham, NC: Duke University Press, 2015), 79.

72. Malkki, 82.

73. Fassin, *Humanitarian Reason*, 179, 167.

74. Fassin, 180.

75. Barnett, *Empire of Humanity*, 14–15.

76. On children as "embodiments of the future," see Malkki, *Need to Help*, 95–98.

77. Georgia L. Kayser et al., "Water, Sanitation, and Hygiene: Measuring Gender Equality and Empowerment," *Bulletin of the World Health Organization* 97 (2019): 438.

78. Simon Gikandi, "Review: The Postcolonial Wizard," *Transition* 98 (2008): 165, 158.

79. For an extended analysis of time and narrative form, see Robert L. Colson, "Arresting Time, Resisting Arrest: Narrative Time and the African Dictator in Ngũgĩ wa Thiong'o's *Wizard of the Crow*," *Research in African Literatures* 42, no. 1 (Spring 2011): 133–53.

80. Ngũgĩ wa Thiong'o, *Wizard of the Crow* (New York: Anchor, 2006), 5.

81. Ian P. MacDonald, "The Cybogre Manifesto: Time, Utopia, and Globality in Ngũgĩ's *Wizard of the Crow*," *Research in African Literatures* 47, no. 1 (Spring 2016): 67, 72.

82. MacDonald, 59.

83. Ndegwa, *Two Faces*, 35.

84. Joseph McLaren, "From the National to the Global: Satirical Magic Realism in Ngũgĩ's 'Wizard of the Crow,'" *Global South* 2, no. 2 (Fall 2008): 152.

85. Barnett, *Empire of Humanity*, 165.

86. Issa Shivji, *Silences in NGO Discourse*, 29.

87. Ngũgĩ coins the term corpolony to encapsulate the "corporate colony" of contemporary life, in which the nation can "be wholly managed by private capital" in "the new global order" (*Wizard*, 746). Corporonalism explicitly combines the colonial and the corporate while also indexing the corporeal, the body that consumes the world. This colonialism is fundamentally about bodies—who eats more and who eats less, who grows and who starves.

88. Homi K. Bhabha, *The Location of Culture* (London: Routledge, 1994), 122.

89. Bhabha, 128.

90. Bhabha, 123.

91. The song "We Are the World" was written by Michael Jackson and Lionel Richie and performed by a collective of musicians called USA for Africa. For an analysis of Live Aid, see Lilie Chouliaraki, *The Ironic Spectator: Solidarity in the Age of Post-humanitarianism* (Cambridge: Polity, 2013), chap. 5.

92. Chouliaraki, 106.

93. Fassin, *Humanitarian Reason*, 3–4.

94. Michel Gourgues, "The Priest, The Levite, and the Samaritan Revisited: A Critical Note on Luke 10:31–35," *Journal of Biblical Literature* 117, no. 4 (Winter 1998): 713.

95. Patrick Colm Hogan, "Christian Pharisees and the Scandalous Ethics of Jesus: Teaching Luke's Gospel at the End of a Millennium," *College Literature* 26, no. 3 (Fall 1999): 101. Hogan shows that Samaritans were also "reviled" as "a racial out-group": "Jews of Jesus' time at least in part defined themselves against Samaritans as an 'out-group,' due to the Samaritans' 'distinct religious tradition' and supposedly 'impure blood line'" (101, quoting Massey).

96. Gikandi, "Postcolonial Wizard," 159.

97. After he has already become the Wizard and is worried that he is a fraud, Kamĩtĩ's parents reveal that his grandfather "had been a holy seer, a spiritual leader working with forces fighting the British in the war of independence" (294). His father explains that he hid this background from Kamĩtĩ to "remove this burden from [his] shoulders." "A seer," he explains, "lives in self-denial in the service of others" (295). For Kamĩtĩ, it turns out, this is a seemingly inevitable calling.

98. Fassin, *Humanitarian Reason*, 231.

99. Divya Dwivedi, Henrik Skov Nielsen, and Richard Walsh, *Narratology and Ideology: Negotiating Context, Form, and Theory in Postcolonial Narratives*, ed. Dwivedi, Nielsen, and Walsh (Columbus: Ohio State University Press, 2018), 20.

100. Fassin, *Humanitarian Reason*, 232.

101. Gikandi, "Postcolonial Wizard," 159.

102. Shivji, *Silences in NGO Discourse*, 65.

Epilogue: Rearticulating the Humanitarian Atlantic

1. David Kennedy, *The Dark Sides of Virtue: Reassessing International Humanitarianism* (Princeton, NJ: Princeton University Press, 2004), xx.

2. Frantz Fanon, *Black Skin, White Masks*, trans. Charles Lam Markmann (New York: Grove, 1967), 38.

3. Ngũgĩ wa Thiong'o, *Wizard of the Crow* (New York: Anchor, 2006), 760.

4. Tstitsi Dangarembga, *Nervous Conditions* (New York: Seal, 2004), 103.

5. Bessie Head, *A Woman Alone: Autobiographical Writings*, ed. Craig MacKenzie (London: Heinemann, 1990), 29.

6. Joseph Conrad, *Heart of Darkness* (New York: Modern Library, 1999), 40.

7. John A. McClure, *Partial Faiths: Postsecular Fiction in the Age of Pynchon and Morrison* (Athens: University of Georgia Press, 2007).

8. Kwame Anthony Appiah, *Cosmopolitanism: Ethics in a World of Strangers* (New York: Norton, 2006), 170.

9. Jeanne-Marie Jackson, *The African Novel of Ideas: Philosophy and Individualism in the Age of Global Writing* (Princeton, NJ: Princeton University Press, 2021), 2.

10. Teju Cole, "The White-Savior Industrial Complex," *The Atlantic*, 21 March 2012, n.p.

11. Chinua Achebe, *There Was a Country* (New York: Penguin, 2012), 2.

12. Gayatri Chakravorty Spivak, *A Critique of Postcolonial Reason* (Cambridge, MA: Harvard University Press, 1999, 416.

Works Cited

Achebe, Chinua. *Arrow of God*. 1964. New York: Anchor, 1969.
———. *The Education of a British-Protected Child*. New York: Anchor, 2009.
———. "An Image of Africa: Racism in Conrad's *Heart of Darkness*." 1977. In *Hopes and Impediments: Selected Essays*, 1–20. New York: Anchor, 1988.
———. *No Longer at Ease*. 1960. New York: Anchor, 1994.
———. "The Novelist as Teacher." In *Hopes and Impediments: Selected Essays*, 40–46. New York: Anchor, 1988.
———. *There Was a Country*. New York: Penguin, 2012.
———. *Things Fall Apart*. 1958. New York: Anchor, 1959.
———. "The Truth of Fiction." In *Hopes and Impediments: Selected Essays*, 138–53. New York: Anchor, 1988.
Adichie, Chimamanda Ngozi. *Half of a Yellow Sun*. London: Harper, 2006.
Ajayi, J. F. Ade. *Christian Missions in Nigeria, 1841–1891: The Making of a New Élite*. Evanston, IL: Northwestern University Press, 1965.
Ajayi, J. F. Ade, and E. A. Ayandele. "Writing African Church History." In *The Church Crossing Frontiers: Essays on the Nature of Mission, in Honor of Bengt Sundkler*, edited by Peter Beyerhaus and Carl F. Hallencreutz, 90–108. Stockholm: Almquist and Wiksells, 1969.
Amoko, Apollo. "Autobiography and *Bildungsroman* in African Literature." In *The Cambridge Companion to the African Novel*, edited by F. Abiola Irele, 195–208. Cambridge: Cambridge University Press, 2009.
Anker, Elizabeth S. *Fictions of Dignity: Embodying Human Rights in World Literature*. Ithaca, NY: Cornell University Press, 2012.
Annan, Kofi. "The Meaning of International Community." Address to DPI/NGO Conference, 15 September 1999. www.un.org/press/en/1999/19990915.sgsm7133 .doc.html.

Appiah, Kwame Anthony. "The Case for Capitalizing the B in Black." *The Atlantic*, 18 June 2020. https://www.theatlantic.com/ideas/archive/2020/06/time-to-capitalize -blackand-white/613159/.

———. *Cosmopolitanism: Ethics in a World of Strangers*. New York: Norton, 2006.

———. Foreword to *Nervous Conditions*, by Tsitsi Dangarembga. New York: Seal, 2004.

———. *In My Father's House*. Oxford: Oxford University Press, 1992.

Attwell, David. "Reprisals of Modernity in Black South African 'Mission' Writing." *Journal of Southern African Studies* 25, no. 2 (June 1999): 267–85.

———. *Rewriting Modernity: Studies in Black South African Literary History*. Athens: Ohio University Press, 2005.

Ayandele, E. A. *The Missionary Impact on Modern Nigeria, 1842–1914*. London: Longmans, 1966.

Bakhtin, Mikhail. *The Dialogic Imagination*. Edited by Michael Holquist, translated by Caryl Emerson and Michael Holquist. Austin: University of Texas Press, 1981.

Bal, Mieke. "In the Absence of Post-." In *Narratology and Ideology: Negotiating Context, Form, and Theory in Postcolonial Narratives*, edited by Divya Dwivedi, Henrik Skov Nielsen, and Richard Walsh, 231–50. Columbus: Ohio State University Press, 2018.

Ballantyne, R. M. *The Coral Island*. 1825. Oxford: Oxford University Press, 1990.

Banks, Nicola, David Hulme, and Michael Edwards. "NGOs, States, and Donors Revisited: Still Too Close for Comfort?" *World Development* 66 (2015): 707–18.

Barker, Derek Alan. "Escaping the Tyranny of Magic Realism? A Discussion of the Term in Relation to the Novels of Zakes Mda." *Postcolonial Text* 4, no. 2 (2008): 1–20.

Barnard, Rita. "Fictions of the Global." *NOVEL: A Forum on Fiction* 42, no. 2 (2009): 207–15.

Barnett, Michael. *Empire of Humanity: A History of Humanitarianism*. Ithaca, NY: Cornell University Press, 2011.

Barnett, Michael, and Janice Gross Stein, eds. *Sacred Aid: Faith and Humanitarianism*. Oxford: Oxford University Press, 2012.

Barnett, Michael, and Thomas G. Weiss. *Humanitarianism Contested: Where Angels Fear to Tread*. Abingdon, UK: Routledge, 2011.

———. *Humanitarianism in Question: Politics, Power, Ethics*. Ithaca, NY: Cornell University Press, 2008.

Bebbington, Anthony J., Samuel Hickey, and Diana C. Mitlin, eds. *Can NGOs Make a Difference? The Challenge of Development Alternatives*. London: Zed, 2008.

Bellow, Saul. *Henderson the Rain King*. 1958. New York: Penguin, 1996.

Berman, Marshall. *All That Is Solid Melts into Air: The Experience of Modernity*. New York: Penguin, 1982.

Beti, Mongo. *Mission to Kala*. 1957. Translated by Peter Green. London: Heinemann, 1964.

Beyer, Cornelia. "Non-governmental Organizations as Motors of Change."
    Government and Opposition 32, no. 4 (September 2007): 513–35.
Bhabha, Homi K. *The Location of Culture.* London: Routledge, 1994.
Bhana, Hershini. "The Political Economy of Food: Hunger in Tsitsi Dangarembga's
    Nervous Conditions." *Proteus* 17, no. 1 (2000): 18–24.
Bornstein, Erica. *Disquieting Gifts: Humanitarianism in New Delhi.* Stanford, CA:
    Stanford University Press, 2012.
Brantlinger, Patrick. *Victorian Literature and Postcolonial Studies.* Edinburgh:
    Edinburgh University Press, 2009.
———. "Victorians and Africans: The Genealogy of the Myth of the Dark
    Continent." In "'Race,' Writing and Difference." Special issue, *Critical Inquiry*
    12, no. 1 (Autumn 1985): 166–203.
Brass, Jennifer N., Wesley Longhofer, Rachel S. Robinson, and Allison Schnable.
    "NGOs and International Development: A Review of Thirty-Five Years of
    Scholarship." *World Development* 112 (2018): 136–49.
Brontë, Charlotte. *Jane Eyre.* Oxford: Oxford University Press, 1999.
Brooks, Peter. "An Unreadable Report: Conrad's *Heart of Darkness.*" In *Joseph
    Conrad's* Heart of Darkness (Modern Critical Interpretations), edited by Harold
    Bloom, 105–27. New York: Chelsea House, 1986.
Bulawayo, NoViolet. *We Need New Names.* New York: Little, Brown, 2013.
Burke, Kenneth. *Counter-statement.* Berkeley: University of California Press, 1931.
Caputo, Philip. *Acts of Faith.* New York: Vintage, 2005.
———. *Horn of Africa.* New York: Dell, 1980.
———. "Putting the Sword to the Pen." *South Central Review* 34, no. 2 (Summer
    2017): 15–25.
Carusi, Annamaria. "Post, Post and Post: Or, Where Is South African Literature in
    All This?" *Ariel* 20, no. 4 (October 1989): 79–95.
Césaire, Aimé. *Discourse on Colonialism.* 1955, translated by Joan Pinkham. New
    York: Monthly Review, 1972.
Childers, Sam. *Another Man's War: The True Story of One Man's Battle to Save
    Children in the Sudan.* Nashville, TN: Thomas Nelson, 2009.
Chomsky, Noam. "Humanitarian Imperialism: The New Doctrine of the Imperial
    Right." *Monthly Review*, 1 September 2008. https://monthlyreview.org/2008/09/01
    /humanitarian-imperialism-the-new-doctrine-of-imperial-right/.
Choudry, Aziz, and Dip Kapoor. *NGOization: Complicity, Contradictions and
    Prospects.* London: Zed, 2013.
Chouliaraki, Lilie. *The Ironic Spectator: Solidarity in the Age of Post-
    humanitarianism.* Cambridge: Polity, 2013.
Clendinnen, Inga. "Preempting Postcolonial Critique: Europeans in the *Heart of
    Darkness.*" *Common Knowledge* 13, no. 1 (2007): 1–17.
Clifford, James. *The Predicament of Culture: Twentieth-Century Ethnography,
    Literature, and Art.* Cambridge, MA: Harvard University Press, 1988.
Cole, Teju. "The White-Savior Industrial Complex." *The Atlantic*, 21 March 2012.

www.theatlantic.com/international/archive/2012/03/the-white-savior-industrial
-complex/254843/.

Colson, Robert L. "Arresting Time, Resisting Arrest: Narrative Time and the African
Dictator in Ngũgĩ wa Thiong'o's *Wizard of the Crow.*" *Research in African
Literatures* 42, no. 1 (Spring 2011): 133–53.

Comaroff, Jean, and John L. Comaroff. *Of Revelation and Revolution.* Vol. 1,
Christianity, Colonialism, and Consciousness in South Africa. Chicago: University
of Chicago Press, 1991.

Comaroff, John L., and Jean Comaroff. *Of Revelation and Revolution.* Vol. 2, *The
Dialectics of Modernity on a South African Frontier.* Chicago: University of
Chicago Press, 1997.

Connolly, William E. *Capitalism and Christianity, American Style.* Durham, NC:
Duke University Press, 2008.

Conrad, Joseph. *Heart of Darkness.* 1899. New York: Modern Library, 1999.

Coundouriotis, Eleni. *The People's Right to the Novel: War Fiction in the Postcolony.*
New York: Fordham University Press, 2014.

Creamer, Heidi. "An Apple for the Teacher? Femininity, Coloniality, and Food in
Nervous Conditions." *Kunapipi* 16, no. 1 (1994): 349–60.

Curtis, Heather D. *Holy Humanitarians: American Evangelicals and Global Aid.*
Cambridge, MA: Harvard University Press, 2018.

Dangarembga, Tsitsi. *The Book of Not.* Banbury, UK: Ayebia Clarke, 2006.

———. *Nervous Conditions.* 1988. New York: Seal, 2004.

———. *This Mournable Body.* Minneapolis, MN: Graywolf, 2018.

Dawes, James. *The Novel of Human Rights.* Cambridge, MA: Harvard University
Press, 2018.

de Kock, Leon. *Civilising Barbarians: Missionary Narrative and African Textual
Response in Nineteenth-Century South Africa.* Johannesburg: Witwatersrand
University Press, 1996.

Derrida, Jacques. *Given Time: I. Counterfeit Money.* 1991. Translated by Peggy
Kamuf. Chicago: University of Chicago Press, 1992.

Desai, Gaurav. *Subject to Colonialism: African Self-Fashioning and the Colonial
Library.* Durham, NC: Duke University Press, 2001.

Desgrandchamps, Marie-Luce. "'Organising the Unpredictable': The Nigeria-Biafra
War and Its Impact on the ICRC." *International Review of the Red Cross* 94, no.
888 (Winter 2012): 1409–32.

de Waal, Alex. "Democratizing the Aid Encounter in Africa." *International Affairs*
73, no.4 (1997): 623–39.

———. *Famine Crimes: Politics and the Disaster Relief Industry in Africa.* Oxford:
James Currey, 1997.

Dunch, Ryan. "Beyond Cultural Imperialism: Cultural Theory, Christian Missions,
and Global Modernity." *History and Theory* 41 (October 2002): 301–25.

Dwivedi, Divya, Henrik Skov Nielsen, and Richard Walsh. "Introduction." In
Narratology and Ideology: Negotiating Context, Form, and Theory in Postcolonial

Narratives, edited by Dwivedi, Nielsen, and Walsh, 1–33. Columbus: Ohio State University Press, 2018.

Easterly, William. *The White Man's Burden: Why the West's Efforts to Aid the Rest Have Done So Much Ill and So Little Good*. New York: Penguin, 2006.

Edwards, Brent Hayes. *The Practice of Diaspora: Literature, Translation, and the Rise of Black Internationalism*. Cambridge, MA: Harvard University Press, 2003.

Eilersen, Gillian Stead. *Bessie Head: Thunder behind Her Ears—Her Life and Writings*. Johannesburg: Witwatersrand University Press, 1995.

Escobar, Arturo. *Encountering Development: The Making and Unmaking of the Third World*. Princeton, NJ: Princeton University Press, 1995.

Etherington, Norman, ed. *Missions and Empire*. Oxford: Oxford University Press, 2005.

Etzioni, Amitai. "The Third Sector and Domestic Missions." *Public Administration Review* 33, no. 4 (July–August 1973): 314–23.

Fanon, Frantz. *Black Skin, White Masks*. Translated by Charles Lam Markmann. New York: Grove, 1967.

———. *The Wretched of the Earth*. Translated by Constance Farrington. New York: Grove, 1963.

Farah, Nuruddin. *Gifts*. New York: Arcade, 1993.

Fassin, Didier. "Humanitarianism as a Politics of Life." Translated by Rachel Gomme. *Public Culture* 19, no. 3 (2007): 499–520.

———. *Humanitarian Reason: A Moral History of the Present*. Berkeley: University of California Press, 2012.

Feher, Michel. *Powerless by Design: The Age of the International Community*. Durham, NC: Duke University Press, 2000.

Ferguson, James. *Give a Man a Fish*. Durham, NC: Duke University Press, 2015.

———. *Global Shadows: Africa in the Neoliberal World Order*. Durham, NC: Duke University Press, 2006.

Festa, Lynn. "Humanity without Feathers." *Humanity: An International Journal of Human Rights, Humanitarianism, and Development* 1, no. 1 (Fall 2010): 3–28.

Fisher, Julie. *Nongovernments: NGOs and the Political Development of the Third World*, West Hartford, CT: Kumarian, 1998.

Foucault, Michel. *Ethics: Subjectivity and Truth*. Edited by Paul Rabinow. New York: New Press, 1997.

Freire, Paulo. *Education for Critical Consciousness*. London: Continuum, 1973.

———. *Pedagogy of the Oppressed*. 1970. Translated by Myra Bergman Ramos. New York: Seabury, 1973.

Friedman, Susan Stanford. "Periodizing Modernism: Postcolonial Modernities and the Space/Time Borders of Modernist Studies." *Modernism/Modernity* 13, no. 3 (2006): 425–43.

Ganguly, Debjani. *This Thing Called the World: The Contemporary Novel as Global Form*. Durham, NC: Duke University Press, 2016.

Gates, Henry Louis. *The Signifying Monkey: A Theory of African-American Literary Criticism*. New York: Oxford University Press, 1988.

George, Olakunle. *African Literature and Social Change: Tribe, Nation, Race*. Bloomington: Indiana University Press, 2017.

———. "The National and the Transnational: Soyinka's *The Interpreters* and *Aké: The Years of Childhood*." *NOVEL: A Forum on Fiction* 41, no. 2–3 (Spring–Summer 2008): 279–97.

———. "The 'Native' Missionary, the African Novel, and In-Between." *NOVEL: A Forum on Fiction* 36, no.1 (Autumn 2002): 5–25.

———. *Relocating Agency: Modernity and African Letters*. Albany: SUNY Press, 2003.

Gérard, Albert. *African Language Literatures: An Introduction to the Literary History of Sub-Saharan Africa*. Washington, DC: Three Continents, 1981.

Gikandi, Simon. *Maps of Englishness: Writing Identity in the Culture of Colonialism*. New York: Columbia University Press, 1996.

———. *Ngũgĩ wa Thiong'o*. Cambridge: Cambridge University Press, 2000.

———. "Poststructuralism and Postcolonial Discourse." In *The Cambridge Companion to Postcolonial Literary Studies*, edited by Neil Lazarus, 97–104. Cambridge: Cambridge University Press, 2004.

———. "Review: The Postcolonial Wizard." *Transition* 98 (2008): 156–69.

———. "The Role of Colonial Institutions." In *Encyclopedia of African Literature*, edited by Simon Gikandi, s.v. "colonialism, neocolonialism, and postcolonialism," 172. London: Routledge, 2003.

Gilroy, Paul. *The Black Atlantic: Modernity and Double Consciousness*. London: Verso, 1993.

Gĩthĩĩnji, Mwangi wa. *Ten Millionaires and Ten Million Beggars: A Study of Income Distribution and Development in Kenya*. 2000. London: Routledge, 2019.

Göbel, Walter. "The Birth of Modernism in the 'Heart of Darkness.'" In *Conrad in Germany*, edited by Walter Göbel, Hans Ulrich Seeber, and Martin Windisch, 107–21. New York: East European Monographs, 2007.

Goldberg, Elizabeth Swanson. *Beyond Terror: Gender, Narrative, Human Rights*. New Brunswick, NJ: Rutgers University Press, 2007.

Gourges, Michel. "The Priest, The Levite, and the Samaritan Revisited: A Critical Note on Luke 10:31–35." *Journal of Biblical Literature* 117, no. 4 (Winter 1998): 709–13.

Graham, Kenneth. "Conrad and Modernism." In *The Cambridge Companion to Joseph Conrad*, edited by J. H. Stape, 203–22. Cambridge: Cambridge University Press, 1996.

Greene, Graham. *A Burnt-Out Case*. New York: Viking, 1961.

———. *The Heart of the Matter*. 1948. New York: Penguin, 1999.

Gutiérrez, Gustavo. *A Theology of Liberation*. 1971. Translated by Sister Caridad Inda, John Eagleson, and Matthew J. O'Connell. Maryknoll, NY: Orbis, 1988.

Hall, Catherine. *Civilising Subjects: Metropole and Colony in the English Imagination 1830–1867*. Chicago: University of Chicago Press, 2002.

Halttunen, Karen. "Humanitarianism and the Pornography of Pain in Anglo-American Culture." *American Historical Review* 100, no. 2 (April 1995): 303–34.

Hardt, Michael and Antonio Negri. *Empire*. Cambridge, MA: Harvard University Press, 2000.

Hawkins, Hunt. "Conrad's Critique of Imperialism in *Heart of Darkness*." *PMLA* 94, no. 2 (March 1979): 286–99.

Hay, Eloise Knapp. *The Political Novels of Joseph Conrad*. Chicago: University of Chicago Press, 1963.

Head, Bessie. *A Question of Power*. London: Heinemann, 1974.

———. *When Rain Clouds Gather*. Evanston, IL: McDougal Littell, 1968.

———. *A Woman Alone: Autobiographical Writings*. Edited by Craig MacKenzie, London: Heinemann, 1990.

Henderson, Lawrence W. *Development and the Church in Angola: Jesse Chipenda the Trailblazer*. Nairobi: Acton, 2000.

Hofmeyr, Isabel. "Dreams, Documents, and 'Fetishes': African Christian Interpretations of *The Pilgrim's Progress*." In "Signs, Texts, and Objects within African Christian History." Special issue, *Journal of Religion in Africa* 32, no. 4 (November 2002): 440–56.

———. "Reading Debating/Debating Reading: The Case of the Lovedale Literary Society, or Why Mandela Quotes Shakespeare." In *Africa's Hidden Histories: Everyday Literacy and Making the Self*, edited by Karin Barber, 258–77. Bloomington: Indiana University Press, 2006.

Hogan, Patrick Colm. "Christian Pharisees and the Scandalous Ethics of Jesus: Teaching Luke's Gospel at the End of a Millennium." *College Literature* 26, no. 3 (Fall 1999): 95–114.

Houghteling, Marla Kay. "Ma Kamanda's Latrine." In *Living on the Edge: Fiction by Peace Corps Writers*, edited by John Coyne. Willimantic, CT: Curbstone, 1999.

Hughey, Matthew W. *The White Savior Film: Content, Critics, and Consumption*. Philadelphia: Temple University Press, 2014.

Hunt, Lynn. *Inventing Human Rights: A History*. New York: Norton, 2007.

Ignatieff, Michael. *The Needs of Strangers: An Essay on Privacy, Solidarity, and the Politics of Being Human*. New York: Penguin, 1984.

———. *The Warrior's Honor: Ethnic War and the Modern Conscience*. New York: Metropolitan, 1997.

Ingleby, Arthur G. *Pioneer Days in Darkest Africa*. London: Pickering and Inglis, 1935.

Irele, Abiola. "Narrative, History, and the African Imagination." *Narrative* 1, no. 2 (May 1993): 156–72.

Jabavu, Noni. *The Ochre People*. London: John Murray, 1963.

Jackson, Jeanne-Marie. *The African Novel of Ideas: Philosophy and Individualism in the Age of Global Writing*. Princeton, NJ: Princeton University Press, 2021.

Jay, Paul. "The Cultural Politics of Development in Zakes Mda's *The Heart of Redness.*" In *Global Matters: The Transnational Turn in Literary Studies*, 137–53. Ithaca, NY: Cornell University Press, 2010.

Jeal, Tim. *For God and Glory.* New York: William Morrow, 1996.

Johnston, Anna. *Missionary Writing and Empire, 1800–1860.* Cambridge: Cambridge University Press, 2003.

Jolly, Rosemary. "Rehearsals of Liberation: Contemporary Postcolonial Discourse and the New South Africa." *PMLA* 110, no. 1 (January 1995): 17–29.

Kaloudis, George. "Non-governmental Organizations: Mostly a Force for Good." *International Journal on World Peace* 34, no. 1 (March 2017): 81–112.

Kalu, Ogbu, ed. *The History of Christianity in West Africa.* London: Longman, 1980.

———. "Protestant Christianity in Igboland." In *Christianity in West Africa: The Nigerian Story*, edited by Ogbu Kalu, 308–22. Ibadan: Daystar, 1978.

Kaplan, Carola M. "Colonizers, Cannibals, and the Horror of Good Intentions in Joseph Conrad's *Heart of Darkness.*" In *Joseph Conrad*, edited by Harold Bloom, 67–80. New York: Chelsea House, 2003.

Kayser, Georgia L., Namratha Rao, Rupa Jose, and Anita Raj. "Water, Sanitation, and Hygiene: Measuring Gender Equality and Empowerment." *Bulletin of the World Health Organization* 97 (2019): 438–40.

Kemedjio, Cilas. "Of Aid and the African Renaissance." *Critical Investigations into Humanitarianism in Africa Blog (CIHA)*, 14 April 2010. http://www.cihablog.com /debating-aid-and-the-african-renaissance/.

Kennedy, David. *The Dark Sides of Virtue: Reassessing International Humanitarianism.* Princeton, NJ: Princeton University Press, 2004.

Kenyatta, Jomo. *Facing Mount Kenya.* New York: Vintage, 1965.

King, Martin Luther, Jr. *Strength to Love.* 1963. Minneapolis, MN: Fortress, 2010.

Kingsolver, Barbara. *The Poisonwood Bible.* New York: Perennial, 1998.

Kony 2012. Directed by Jason Russell. *YouTube*, uploaded by Invisible Children, Inc., 5 March 2012. www.youtube.com/watch?v=Y4MnpzG5Sqc.

"Kony 2012 and the Potential of Social Media Activism." *New York Times*, Room for Debate, 9 March 2012. www.nytimes.com/roomfordebate/2012/03/09/kony-2012 -and-the-potential-of-social-media-activism.

Krakauer, John. *Three Cups of Deceit: How Greg Mortenson, Humanitarian Hero, Lost His Way.* New York: Anchor, 2011.

Kristof, Nicholas. "Westerners on White Horses . . . ." *New York Times*, 14 July 2010. kristof.blogs.nytimes.com/2010/07/14/westerners-on-white-horses/?src=tptw.

Laclau, Ernesto. "Universalism, Particularism and the Question of Identity." In *The Identity in Question*, edited by John Rajchman, 93–108. New York: Routledge, 1995.

Lambert, John Chisholm. *The Romance of Missionary Heroism: True Stories of the Intrepid Bravery, and Stirring Adventures of Missionaries with Uncivilized Man, Wild Beasts and the Forces of Nature in All Parts of the World.* 1907. Shawnee, KS: Gideon House, 2017.

Lazarus, Neil. *Nationalism and Cultural Practice in the Postcolonial World.*
    Cambridge: Cambridge University Press, 1999.
———. "The Politics of Postcolonial Modernism." In *Postcolonial Studies and
    Beyond,* edited by Ania Loomba, Suvir Kaul, Matti Bunzl, Antoinette Burton,
    and Jed Esty, 423–38. Durham, NC: Duke University Press, 2005.
Le Carré, John. *The Constant Gardener.* New York: Scribner, 2001.
Lewis, Desiree. *Living on a Horizon: Bessie Head and the Politics of Imagining.*
    Trenton, NJ: Africa World, 2007.
Livingstone, David. *Missionary Travels and Researches in South Africa.* 1857.
    Cambridge: Cambridge University Press, 2012.
Loomba, Ania, Suvir Kaul, Matti Bunzl, and Jed Esty. *Postcolonial Studies and
    Beyond.* Durham, NC: Duke University Press, 2005.
Luthuli, Albert. *Let My People Go.* New York: McGraw-Hill, 1962.
Lyotard, Jean-François. *The Postmodern Condition: A Report on Knowledge.* 1979.
    Translated by Geoff Bennington and Brian Massumi. Minneapolis: University
    of Minnesota Press, 1984.
MacDonald, Ian P. "The Cybogre Manifesto: Time, Utopia, and Globality in
    Ngũgĩ's *Wizard of the Crow.*" *Research in African Literatures* 47, no. 1 (Spring
    2016): 57–75.
Mahoney, Daniel J. *The Idol of Our Age: How the Religion of Humanity Subverts
    Christianity.* New York: Encounter, 2018.
Majeke, Nosipho. *The Role of the Missionaries in Conquest.* Johannesburg: Society
    of Young Africa, 1953.
Makuwira, Jonathan J. *Non-governmental Development Organizations and the
    Poverty Reduction Agenda: The Moral Crusaders.* London: Routledge, 2014.
Malkki, Liisa H. *The Need to Help: The Domestic Arts of International
    Humanitarianism.* Durham, NC: Duke University Press, 2015.
Mamdani, Mahmood. *Citizen and Subject: Contemporary Africa and the Legacy of
    Late Colonialism.* Princeton, NJ: Princeton University Press, 1996.
———. *Saviors and Survivors: Darfur, Politics, and the War on Terror.* New York:
    Doubleday, 2009.
———. "What Jason Didn't Tell Gavin and His Army of Invisible Children."
    Daily Monitor, 13 March 2012. www.monitor.co.ug/artsculture/Reviews/691232
    –1365090–120px9hz/index.html.
Mandela, Nelson. *Long Walk to Freedom.* New York: Little, Brown, 1994.
Manji, Firoze, and Carl O'Coill. "The Missionary Position: NGOs and
    Development in Africa." *International Affairs* 78, no. 3 (2002): 567–83.
Maren, Michael. *The Road to Hell: The Ravaging Effects of Foreign Aid and
    International Charity.* New York: Free Press, 1997.
Marx, John. "Fiction and State Crisis." *NOVEL: A Forum on Fiction* 42, no. 3
    (2009): 524–30.
Mauss, Marcel. *The Gift: The Form and Reason for Exchange in Archaic Societies.*
    1950. Translated by W. D. Halls. London: Routledge, 1990.

Mbembe, Achille. "African Modes of Self Writing." Translated by Steven Rendall. *Public Culture* 14, no. 1 (2002): 239–73.

———. *Critique of Black Reason*. Translated by Laurent Dubois. Durham, NC: Duke University Press, 2017.

———. "On the Power of the False." *Public Culture* 14, no. 3 (2002): 629–41.

McClintock, Anne. "Introduction: Postcolonialism and the Angel of Progress." In *Imperial Leather: Race, Gender and Sexuality in the Colonial Contest*. New York: Routledge, 1995.

McClure, John A. "Do They Believe in Magic? Politics and Postmodern Literature." *Boundary* 2 36, no. 2 (2009): 129–43.

———. *Kipling and Conrad: The Colonial Fiction*. Cambridge, MA: Harvard University Press, 1981.

———. *Partial Faiths: Postsecular Fiction in the Age of Pynchon and Morrison*. Athens: University of Georgia Press, 2007.

———. "The Rhetoric of Restraint in *Heart of Darkness*." *Nineteenth-Century Fiction* 32, no. 3 (December 1977): 310–26.

McDonnell, Faith J. H., and Grace Akallo. *Girl Soldier: A Story of Hope for Northern Uganda's Children*. Grand Rapids, MI: Chosen Books, 2007.

McLaren, Joseph. "From the National to the Global: Satirical Magic Realism in Ngũgĩ's 'Wizard of the Crow.'" *Global South* 2, no. 2 (Fall 2008): 150–58.

Mda, Zakes. *The Heart of Redness*. New York: Picador, 2000.

———. "A Response to 'Duplicity and Plagiarism in Zakes Mda's The Heart of Redness' by Andrew Offenburger." *Research in African Literatures* 39, no. 3 (2008): 200–203.

Michael, Sarah. *Undermining Development: The Absence of Power among Local NGOs in Africa*. Bloomington: Indiana University Press, 2004.

Miller, J. Hillis. *Poets of Reality: Six Twentieth-Century Writers*. Cambridge, MA: Harvard University Press, 1965.

Mortenson, Greg, and David Oliver Relin. *Three Cups of Tea: One Man's Mission to Promote Peace . . . One School at a Time*. New York: Penguin, 2006.

Moyo, Dambisa. *Dead Aid: Why Aid Is Not Working and How There Is a Better Way for Africa*. New York: Farrar, Straus, Giroux, 2009.

Moyn, Samuel. *The Last Utopia: Human Rights in History*. Cambridge, MA: Belknap, 2010.

Mudimbe, V. Y. *The Invention of Africa: Gnosis, Philosophy, and the Order of Knowledge*. Bloomington: Indiana University Press, 1988.

Mugambi, J. N. K., ed. *Critiques of Christianity in African Literature*. Nairobi: East African Educational Publishers, 1992.

Ndegwa, Stephen N. *The Two Faces of Civil Society: NGOs and Politics in Africa*. West Hartford, CT: Kumarian, 1996.

Neiberg, Michael, Thomas G. Bowie, Jr., and Donald Anderson. "A Rumor of War: A Conversation with Philip Caputo at 58." *War, Literature, and the Arts* 12, no. 1 (2000): 4–17.

New Oxford Annotated Bible. Edited by Michael D. Coogan. 3rd ed. Oxford: Oxford
    University Press, 2001.
Ngaboh-Smart, Francis. "Dimensions of Giving in Nuruddin Farah's *Gifts.*"
    Research in African Literatures 27, no. 4 (1996): 144–56.
Ngũgĩ, Mũkoma Wa. *The Rise of the African Novel: Politics of Language, Identity,
    and Ownership.* Ann Arbor: University of Michigan Press, 2018.
Ngũgĩ wa Thiong'o. "Church, Culture and Politics." In *Homecoming.* Brooklyn, NY:
    Lawrence Hill Books, 1972.
———. *Decolonising the Mind: The Politics of Language in African Culture.* 1981.
    London: James Currey, 1986.
———. *Dreams in a Time of War: A Childhood Memoir.* New York: Pantheon, 2010.
———. *A Grain of Wheat.* 1967. Rev. ed., London: Heinemann, 1986.
———. *In the House of the Interpreter.* New York: Anchor, 2012.
———. "Literature and Society: The Politics of the Canon!" In *Writers in Politics:
    A Re-engagement with Issues of Literature and Society,* 3–27. 1981. Rev. and enl.
    ed. Oxford: James Currey, 1997.
———. *Moving the Centre: The Struggle for Cultural Freedoms.* Oxford: James
    Currey, 1993.
———. *Petals of Blood.* 1977. New York: Penguin, 1991.
———. *The River Between.* London: Heinemann, 1965.
———. *Something Torn and New.* New York: BasicCivitas Books, 2009.
———. *Weep Not Child.* 1964. London: Heinemann, 1987.
———. *Wizard of the Crow.* New York: Anchor, 2006.
Ngwira, Emmanual Mzomera. "'He Writes about the World That Remained Silent':
    Witnessing Authorship in Chimamanda Ngozi Adichie's *Half of a Yellow Sun.*"
    English Studies in Africa 55, no. 2 (2012): 43–53.
Nixon, Rob. "Border Country: Bessie Head's Frontline States." *Social Text* 36
    (Autumn 1993): 106–37.
———. "Preparations for Travel: Naipaul's Conradian Atavism." In *London Calling:
    V. S. Naipaul, Postcolonial Mandarin,* 88–108. Oxford: Oxford University Press,
    1992.
Njambi, Wairimũ Ngarũiya. "Rescuing African Women and Girls from Female
    Genital Practices: A Benevolent and Civilizing Mission." In *Burden or Benefit?
    Imperial Benevolence and Its Legacies,* edited by Helen Gilbert and Chris Tiffin,
    160–79. Bloomington: Indiana University Press, 2008.
Offenburger, Andrew. "Duplicity and Plagiarism in Zakes Mda's *The Heart of
    Redness.*" *Research in African Literatures* 39, no. 3 (October 2008): 164–99.
Olaniyan, Tejumola. "'Living in the Interregnum': Fela Anikulapo-Kuti and the
    Postcolonial Incredible." In *Arrest the Music! Fela and His Rebel Art and Politics,*
    1–6. Bloomington: Indiana University Press, 2004.
———. "The Paddle That Speaks English: Africa, NGOs, and the Archaeology of
    an Unease." *Research in African Literatures* 42, no. 2 (Summer 2011): 46–59.
———. "Postmodernity, Postcoloniality, African Studies." In *African Literature:*

An Anthology of Criticism and Theory, edited by Tejumola Olaniyan and Ato Quayson, 637–45. Malden, MA: Blackwell, 2007.

Olaniyan, Tejumola, and Ato Quayson, eds. *African Literature: An Anthology of Criticism and Theory*. Malden, MA: Blackwell, 2007.

O'Sullivan, Kevin. "Biafra's Legacy: NGO Humanitarianism and the Nigerian Civil War." In *Learning from the Past to Shape the Future: Lessons from the History of Humanitarian Action in Africa*, edited by Christina Bennett, Matthew Foley, and Hanna B. Krebs, 5–13. London: Overseas Development Institute, October 2016.

Oyêwùmi, Oyèrónké, ed. *African Women and Feminism: Reflecting on the Politics of Sisterhood*. Trenton, NJ: Africa World, 2003.

Paras, Andrea, and Janice Gross Stein. "Bridging the Sacred and the Profane in Humanitarian Life." In *Sacred Aid: Faith and Humanitarianism*, edited by Michael Barnett and Janice Gross Stein, 211–39. New York: Oxford University Press, 2012.

Parikh, Crystal. *Writing Human Rights: The Political Imaginaries of Writers of Color*. Minneapolis: University of Minnesota Press, 2017.

Parry, Benita. *Conrad and Imperialism: Ideological Boundaries and Visionary Frontiers*. New York: Macmillan, 1983.

——. "The Presence of the Past in Peripheral Modernities." In *Beyond the Black Atlantic: Relocating Modernization and Technology*, edited by Walter Goebel and Saskia Schaibo, 13–28. London: Routledge, 2006.

Parliament of South Africa. *Population Registration Act*, Act No. 30 of 1950. https://www.sahistory.org.za/sites/default/files/DC/leg19500707.028.020.030/leg19500707.028.020.030.pdf.

Paustian, Megan Cole. "'A Real Heaven on Their Own Earth': Religious Missions, African Writers, and the Anticolonial Imagination." *Research in African Literatures* 45, no. 2 (Summer 2014): 1–25.

Peel, J. D. Y. *Religious Encounter and the Making of the Yoruba*. Bloomington: Indiana University Press, 2000.

Perera, Sonali. *No Country: Working-Class Writing in the Age of Globalization*. New York: Columbia University Press, 2014.

Petersen, Kirsten Holt. "Charity Wounds Him Who Receives: Nuruddin Farah's Gifts." In *Emerging Perspectives on Nuruddin Farah*, edited by Derek Wright, 591–610. Trenton, NJ: Africa World, 2002.

Peterson, Bhekizizwe. *Monarchs, Missionaries and African Intellectuals: African Theatre and the Unmaking of Colonial Marginality*. Johannesburg: Wits University Press, 2000.

Pettifer, Julian, and Richard Bradley. *Missionaries*. London: BBC Books, 1990.

Phelan, James. *Experiencing Fiction: Judgments, Progressions, and the Rhetorical Theory of Narrative*. Columbus: Ohio State University Press, 2007.

Piot, Charles. *Nostalgia for the Future: West Africa after the Cold War*. Chicago: University of Chicago Press, 2010.

Porter, Andrew. *Religion versus Empire? British Protestant Missionaries and Overseas Expansion, 1700–1914*. Manchester: Manchester University Press, 2004.

Puledda, Salvatore. *On Being Human: Interpretations of Humanism from the Renaissance to the Present*. Translated by Andrew Hurley. San Diego, CA: Latitude, 1997.

Rankine, W. Henry. *A Hero of the Dark Continent: Memoir of Rev. WM. Affleck Scott*. Edinburgh: William Blackwood and Sons, 1896.

Richey, Lisa Ann, ed. *Celebrity Humanitarianism and North-South Relations: Politics, Place, and Power*. London: Routledge, 2016.

Rieff, David. *A Bed for the Night: Humanitarianism in Crisis*. New York: Simon and Schuster, 2002.

Robbins, Bruce. *The Beneficiary*. Durham, NC: Duke University Press, 2017.

———. *Feeling Global: Internationalism in Distress*. New York: New York University Press, 2003.

———. "Race, Gender, Class, Postcolonialism: Toward a New Humanistic Paradigm?" In *A Companion to Postcolonial Studies*, edited by Henry Schwarz and Sangeeta Ray, 556–73. Malden, MA: Blackwell, 2000.

Robbins, Sarah, and Ann Ellis Pullen. *Nellie Arnott's Writings on Angola, 1905–1913: Missionary Narratives Linking Africa and America*. Anderson, SC: Parlor, 2011.

Robert, Dana L. "Introduction." In *Converting Colonialism: Visions and Realities in Mission History, 1706–1914*, 1–20. Grand Rapids, MI: William B. Eerdmans, 2008.

Rose, Jacqueline. "Apathy and Accountability: South Africa's Truth and Reconciliation Commission." *Raritan* 21, no. 4 (Spring 2002): 175–95.

———. "On the Universality of Madness." *Critical Inquiry* 20, no. 3 (1994): 401–18.

Roy, Arundhati. "Help That Hinders." *Le Monde Diplomatique*, November 2004. mondediplo.com/2004/11/16roy.

Rush, Norman. *Whites*. New York: Vintage, 1984.

Sachs, Jeffrey D. *The End of Poverty: Economic Possibilities for Our Time*. New York: Penguin, 2005.

Said, Edward. *Culture and Imperialism*. 1993. New York: Vintage, 1994.

———. *Orientalism*. 1978. 25th Anniversary Edition. New York: Vintage, 1994.

Saldaña-Portillo, María Josefina. *The Revolutionary Imagination in the Americas in the Age of Development*. Durham, NC: Duke University Press, 2003.

Sanneh, Lamin. "'They Stooped to Conquer': Vernacular Translation and the Socio-cultural Factor." *Research in African Literatures* 23, no. 1 (1992): 95–100.

———. *Translating the Message: The Missionary Impact on Culture*. Maryknoll, NY: Orbis Books, 1989.

———. *West African Christianity: The Religious Impact*. London: Hurst, 1983.

Scott, David. *Refashioning Futures: Criticism after Postcoloniality*. Princeton, NJ: Princeton University Press, 1999.

Scott, James C. *Domination and the Arts of Resistance: Hidden Transcripts*. New Haven, CT: Yale University Press, 1990.

Searle, Alison. "The Role of Missions in *Things Fall Apart* and *Nervous Conditions.*" *Literature and Theology* 21, no. 1 (March 2007): 49–65.

Shivji, Issa G. *The Concept of Human Rights in Africa.* London: Codesria, 1989.

———. *Silences in NGO Discourse: The Role and Future of NGOs in Africa.* Nairobi: Fahamu, 2007.

Singer, Peter. "Famine, Affluence, and Morality." *Philosophy and Public Affairs* 1, no. 3 (Spring 1972): 229–43.

Slaughter, Joseph R. "Foreword: Rights on Paper." In *Theoretical Perspectives on Human Rights and Literature*, edited by Elizabeth Swanson Goldberg and Alexandra Schultheis Moore, xi–xiv. London: Routledge, 2012.

———. *Human Rights, Inc.: The World Novel, Narrative Form, and International Law.* New York: Fordham University Press, 2007.

Slim, Hugo. *Humanitarian Ethics: A Guide to the Morality of Aid in War and Disaster.* New York: Oxford University Press, 2015.

Smillie, Ian. *The Alms Bazaar: Altruism under Fire—Non-profit Organizations and International Development.* London: Intermediate Technology, 1995.

Sontag, Susan. *Regarding the Pain of Others.* New York: Picador, 2003.

Soper, Kate. *Humanism and Anti-humanism: Problems of Modern European Thought.* London: Hutchinson, 1986.

Soyinka, Wole. *The Burden of Memory, the Muse of Forgiveness.* New York: Oxford University Press, 1999.

Spivak, Gayatri Chakravorty. "Can the Subaltern Speak?" In *Marxism and the Interpretation of Culture*, edited by Cary Nelson and Lawrence Grossberg. Urbana: University of Illinois Press, 1988.

———. *A Critique of Postcolonial Reason.* Cambridge, MA: Harvard University Press, 1999.

———. "Religion, Politics, Theology: A Conversation with Achille Mbembe." *Boundary* 2 34, no. 2 (2007): 147–70.

Stamatov, Peter. *The Origins of Global Humanitarianism: Religion, Empires, and Advocacy.* New York: Cambridge University Press, 2013.

Stanley, Brian. *The Bible and Flag: Protestant Missions and British Imperialism in the Nineteenth and Twentieth Centuries.* Leicester, UK: Apollos, 1990.

———, ed. *Missions, Nationalism, and the End of Empire.* Grand Rapids, MI: William B. Eerdmans, 2003.

Stewart, Frances. *Planning to Meet Basic Needs.* London: Macmillan, 1985.

Streeten, Paul, Shahid Javed Burki, Mahbub ul Haq, Norman Hicks, and Frances Stewart. *First Things First: Meeting Basic Human Needs in the Developing Countries.* Published for the World Bank by Oxford University Press, 1981.

Sugnet, Charles. "*Nervous Conditions*: Dangarembga's Feminist Reinvention of Fanon." In *The Politics of (M)Othering: Womanhood, Identity, and Resistance in African Literature*, edited by Obioma Nnaemeka, 33–49. London: Routledge, 1997.

Suleiman, Lina. "The NGOs and the Grand Illusions of Development and Democracy." *Voluntas* 24 (2013): 241–61.

Táíwò, Olúfẹ́mi. *How Colonialism Preempted Modernity in Africa.* Bloomington: Indiana University Press, 2010.

Terry, Fiona. *Condemned to Repeat? The Paradox of Humanitarian Action.* Ithaca, NY: Cornell University Press, 2002.

Theroux, Paul. *Girls at Play.* 1969. In *On the Edge of the Great Rift Valley: Three Novels of Africa*, 175–357. New York: Penguin, 1996.

Tiffin, Chris, and Helen Gilbert, eds. *Burden or Benefit? Imperial Benevolence and its Legacies.* Bloomington: Indiana University Press, 2008.

Titlestad, Michael, and Mike Kissack. "'The Foot Does Not Sniff': Imagining the Post-anti-apartheid Intellectual." *Journal of Literary Studies* 19, no. 3–4 (December 2003): 255–56.

Tredell, Nicolas, ed. *Joseph Conrad: Heart of Darkness.* New York: Columbia University Press, 1998.

Twain, Mark. *King Leopold's Soliloquy.* New York: International, 1961.

Unger, Peter. *Living High and Letting Die: Our Illusion of Innocence.* New York: Oxford University Press, 1996.

"UNICEF USA: Save a Child for Only 50 Cents a Day." *YouTube*, performed by Alyssa Milano, uploaded by UNICEF, 4 September 2013. www.youtube.com/watch?v=XozrqJHA-yI.

Viswanathan, Gauri. *Outside the Fold: Conversion, Modernity, and Belief.* Princeton, NJ: Princeton University Press, 1998.

Wainaina, Binyavanga. "How to Write about Africa." *Granta* 92 (Winter 2005). granta.com/how-to-write-about-africa/.

Walkowitz, Rebecca L. "Conrad's Naturalness." In *Cosmopolitan Style: Modernism beyond the Nation.* New York: Columbia University Press, 2006.

Watt, Ian. "Conrad's *Heart of Darkness* and the Critics." In *Essays on Conrad*, 85–95. Cambridge: Cambridge University Press, 2000.

Wenzel, Jennifer. *Bulletproof: Afterlives of Anticolonial Prophecy in South Africa and Beyond.* Chicago: University of Chicago Press, 2009.

White, Andrea. "Conrad and Imperialism." In *The Cambridge Companion to Joseph Conrad*, edited by J. H. Stape, 179–202. Cambridge: Cambridge University Press, 1996.

———. *Joseph Conrad and the Adventure Tradition: Constructing and Deconstructing the Imperial Subject.* Cambridge: Cambridge University Press, 1993.

Willey, Ann Elizabeth, and Jeanette Treiber, eds. *Negotiating the Postcolonial: Emerging Perspectives on Tsitsi Dangarembga.* Trenton, NJ: Africa World, 2002.

Wiredu, Kwasi. *Cultural Universals and Particulars: An African Perspective.* Bloomington: Indiana University Press, 1996.

Woloch, Alex. *The One vs. the Many: Minor Characters and the Space of the Protagonist in the Novel.* Princeton, NJ: Princeton University Press, 2003.

Woods, Tim. "Giving and Receiving: Nuruddin Farah's *Gifts*, or, The Postcolonial Logic of Third World Aid." *Journal of Commonwealth Literature* 38, no. 1 (2003): 91–112.

Wright, Derek. "'More Than Just a Plateful of Food': Regurgitating Colonialism in Tsitsi Dangarembga's *Nervous Conditions.*" *Commonwealth* 17, no. 2 (1995): 8–18.

———. *The Novels of Nuruddin Farah.* Bayreuth: Eckhard Breitinger, 1994.

Young, Robert. *White Mythologies: Writing History and the West.* London: Routledge, 1990.

Zachernuck, Philip S. *Colonial Subjects: An African Intelligentsia and Atlantic Ideas.* Charlottesville: University Press of Virginia, 2000.

Index

Aburĩria. See *Wizard of the Crow* (Ngũgĩ)
Acaye, Jacob, 2
Achebe, Chinua, 6, 8, 18, 26, 27, 34, 63, 66–67, 98–100, 117, 171, 175–76, 213. See also *Arrow of God* (Achebe); *Education of a British-Protected Child, The* (Achebe); *No Longer at Ease* (Achebe); *Things Fall Apart* (Achebe)
Acts of Faith (Caputo), 136–37; aid as unsavory business in, 164–65; ascetic altruism, 159–61; capacity for critique in, 156–59; humanitarian technologies of self in, 155–66; idealist-entrepreneur conflict in, 160–62; inevitability of failure in, 165–66; rearticulating humanitarian Atlantic in, 207–14; reckoning on donations, 155–56; shifting among perspectives in, 156–57; significance of gender in, 162–63; style of being, 162; United Nations, 157–59
Adichie, Chimamanda Ngozi, 6, 18, 29, 134, 176, 209. See also *Half of a Yellow Sun* (Adichie)
Africa: being white in, 60, 165, 167, 209; as a category, 16–18; darkest Africa, 147; grand narrative of salvation in, 11–16; history of mission impulse in, 33–66; humanitarian Atlantic and, 16–20; image of, 62–63, 135, 171; narrating improvement of, 6–9; and narrative problem of humanitarianism, 1–6; NGOs in, 169–72; postcolonial, 16,

99, 176, 179; South Africa, 5, 17, 28, 36, 72, 104–5, 108, 118; spectacle of poverty in, 195; stories of aid to, 1–6; storytelling about, 29–32; temptation of tragedy in, 62–65; third sector novel, 20–26; writing about, 143–44. See also Africans; white savior narrative
Africa-Is-a-Country literary criticism, 17–18
African literature, language debate, 87–88
African National Congress, 95
African nationalism, 68, 70, 72, 87, 104, 119
African novelists and mission education, 83–86
African Queen, The (film), 63
Africans: emancipated African, 67–100; exclusion from humanity, 97, 103, 121; as flattened victims, 2, 102, 151; Starving African, 144, 176, 181, 185–86
age of liberal humanitarianism, 136
agency of African people, 22, 66, 69, 71–72, 86, 168, 171, 194–96, 204, 208, 212–13
aid, 1, 6, 8–9, 23, 206; aesthetics/politics of emergency aid, 175–81; aid-centric frame, 29; aid entrepreneur, 62, 160; aid package, 152, 154; aid relationship, 28, 136, 154, 168, 170, 190, 195, 204; debating through micro-NGO, 196–203; development aid, 8, 174; dilemmas of, 137–41; emergency aid, 8, 189; foreign aid, 29, 49, 148, 183; humanitarian, 22, 28, 135–37, 141, 155–56, 161, 205, 210; international, 4, 102, 140,

267

aid (*continued*)
   149, 171, 191; politics of emergency aid,
      175–81; Western aid, 29; workers, 6–7, 10,
      17, 22, 51, 120, 138–39, 154–57, 166, 168, 183
Ajayi, J. F. Ade, 72, 96
allies, ambiguity of, 83–86, 100
altruism, 5; annihilation and, 49; ascetic,
      160; authority of, 155–56; complicating,
      36; of imposition, 116; international, 2,
      122; of the poor, 196–97; and third sector
      novel, 20–26; transnational, 36, 51
Angola, 12, 61, 82
Anker, Elizabeth, 19
Annan, Kofi, 102
anticolonialist, 25, 72, 90, 113
anticolonial project, 68, 85, 96
antihumanism, 114, 237n35
anti-neocolonial, 107, 116, 119, 122
apartheid, 90, 95–96, 104–5, 111, 116, 118,
      234n10
apolitical, 8–9, 29, 172–74, 190, 200, 208
Appiah, Kwame Anthony, 19, 80, 115,
      137–38, 180
Armah, Awi Kwei, 134
arrogance, missionary mentality, 120–22
Arrow of God (Achebe), 73, 85; position of
      education in, 92
asceticism, 130, 159–61, 166, 211
assault of images without context, 179–80
Athomi, or "people of the book," 188
Atlantic, humanitarian, 16–20, 34, 98–100,
      101, 156, 168, 193, 207–8, 213–14
Attwell, David, 67–68
autobiography, 36–41, 68–69, 95
Ayandele, E. A., 72, 96

Bakhtin, Mikhail, 46–47, 119
Barnard, Rita, 19
Barnett, Michael, 10, 51, 65–66, 136, 140,
      173, 179, 187
*Bed for the Night: Humanitarianism in
      Crisis, A* (Rieff), 138
Bellow, Saul, 62
beneficiaries, 21–22, 53, 59, 111, 121, 126, 136,
      146, 195, 213; term, 167
benevolence, 27, 43–44, 67, 110, 117, 136,
      139, 144, 153, 167–68, 190, 197, 208, 214
benevolent gift: dilemmas of aid, 137–41;
      distribution problem, 137–41; domination
      problem, 137–41; material conditions,
      141–48; questions of power, 166–68;

religious missions, 141–48; technologies
      of self, 155–66
Berlin Conference, 36
Bhabha, Homi, 22, 25, 71, 82, 98, 194
Biafra-Nigeria conflict, 175–76
Biafran Baby. See *Half of a Yellow Sun*
      (Adichie): starving African child
Biafran War, 175–76; in *Half of a Yellow Sun*
      (Adichie), 184–85, 188
Bible, 37–38, 54, 58, 97, 127; accessibility of,
      93–97; as consolation prize, 72; deception
      by, 70; providing inspiration, 93; standard
      of empire and, 71; translating, 87. *See also*
      Moses, allusion to
Bible Belt, 150
biblical concepts, adoption of, 95–96
"Biggles, Mau Mau, and I" (Ngũgĩ), 89–90
biography, 36–41, 88
Black Atlantic, The (Gilroy), 168
blackness, 3, 78, 209, 219n4
Bokwe, John Knox, 67
Book of Not, The (Dangarembga), 148
Bornstein, Erica, 136
both-and, perspective, 22, 84
Botswana, 17, 104, 128–30, 135, 139
Brantlinger, Patrick, 36, 39, 64
bridge characters, 30–31, 184
Buddhism, 127, 197, 211
Bulawayo, NoViolet, 23–25, 169
Burke, Kenneth, 21
Burnt-Out Case, A (Greene), 101

call, term, 37, 125, 156
Caputo, Philip, 6, 7, 19, 62, 136, 155–56, 167.
      See also *Acts of Faith* (Caputo)
Césaire, Aimé, 113, 119, 132, 236n29
Chomsky, Noam, 7
Choudry, Aziz, 174
Christ figure, 54, 197
Christianity, 27, 39, 50, 53, 88, 94, 121, 216;
      African forms of, 91; allegiance to, 78;
      anticolonialism and, 68, 71–72, 77, 90–92,
      95–98, 107; ascetic form of, 211; Buddhism
      and, 197; Christian missions, 83–86; con-
      version to, 106; colonialism and, 69–72;
      decapitalization of, 97; as discourse, 68;
      face of, 74; freedom struggles and, 98–
      100; humanitarian Atlantic and, 98–100;
      language in (Conrad), 41–45; literacy and,
      98; pattern of Christianization, 39–40;
      shared language of struggle, 97; "shorn of

Megan Cole Paustian is Associate Professor of English at North Central College.